The mechanization of British and Household Cavalry regiments took place between the two World Wars and on into 1942. This book describes the process by which many horsed cavalrymen were re-trained to operate and fight in Armoured Fighting Vehicles (AFVs) and the experiences of some of the men and regiments involved. Extensive use has been made of regimental and War Office archives, and particularly from the Imperial War Museum's sound archives – the oral testimonies of soldiers who had experienced this huge change. A small number of veterans are, or were, still living and were interviewed by the author for this work. The reason given for the delay in cavalry mechanization – cited in some military histories and much influenced by the writings of Sir Basil Liddell Hart – was the reluctance by the cavalrymen to part with their horses and their technophobic attitude. This book tests the accuracy of this assertion, together with what was the availability of suitable and sufficient armoured fighting vehicles to replace the cavalry's horses. Of special interest is the examination of the historical papers of the tank manufacturers Vickers, held at the Cambridge University Library, regarding tank development and production. This story of mechanising the cavalry has been set against the backdrop of the social, economic and political climate of the 1920s and 1930s, and the pressure on politicians of the wider franchise and public opinion. In researching this aspect, the Britain by Mass Observation archives – held at the University of Sussex – have been most illuminating. The interwar impact on cavalry mechanization; the role of the British Army in general; disarmament; and rearmament are described – again with illustrations from oral testimonies.

Roger Salmon, the son of an interwar cavalry soldier, spent his working life (from 1962) in management and leadership in an industrial environment during an era when many technological and cultural changes were demanded. Retiring early from a successful business career to indulge his own passion for horses and riding – and to formally study Military History – he was curious about the process undertaken by the army to mechanise horsed cavalry. Little of consequence had been researched. Soon after embarking on finding and interviewing veteran cavalrymen, it became clear to Salmon that what little that had been written might not be either accurate or perhaps somewhat selective in explanation. Having achieved a First Class Honours Degree in War Studies at the University of Birmingham, Salmon was invited to research the subject of cavalry mechanization first at Birmingham and subsequently at the University of Wolverhampton, where he was awarded a PhD in 2014. Dr Salmon has published a number of articles on different aspects of military history. He lives in Essex and has three children and two granddaughters. He is a member of The Royal United Services Institute and The British Commission for Military History; a Freeman of the City of London; a Past Master of the Worshipful Company of Launderers; and a Member of the Order of St John of Jerusalem.

"EVERYTHING WORKED LIKE CLOCKWORK"

"Everything worked like clockwork"

The Mechanization of the British Cavalry between the Two World Wars

Wolverhampton Military Studies No.18

Roger E Salmon

Helion & Company Limited

Helion & Company Limited
26 Willow Road
Solihull
West Midlands
B91 1UE
England
Tel. 0121 705 3393
Fax 0121 711 4075
Email: info@helion.co.uk
Website: www.helion.co.uk
Twitter: @helionbooks
Visit our blog http://blog.helion.co.uk/

Published by Helion & Company 2016
Designed and typeset by Mach 3 Solutions Ltd (www.mach3solutions.co.uk)
Cover designed by Paul Hewitt, Battlefield Design (www.battlefield-design.co.uk)
Printed by Short Run Press, Exeter, Devon

Text © Roger E Salmon 2016
Images © as individually credited
Front cover: "Victory at Beda Fomm" – British Vickers Mk VI light tanks of the 3rd
Hussars, 7th Armoured Division celebrate their part in the momentous victory over
Italian forces in North Africa, February 1941. (Image courtesy of the artist, David
Pentland, 1997). Rear cover: Crossley Armoured Car – maximum speed 45 mph,
circa 1930. (Source: The Tank Museum Bovington – 9361-A3).

ISBN 978-1-910777-96-1

British Library Cataloguing-in-Publication Data.
A catalogue record for this book is available from the British Library.

For details of other military history titles published by Helion & Company Limited
contact the above address, or visit our website: http://www.helion.co.uk.

We always welcome receiving book proposals from prospective authors.

Dedicated to the memory of my father.

Trooper William Salmon
Hussar of The Line.

Royalties accruing from this book will be directly paid to The Chigwell Riding Trust for Special Needs, Essex. Registered Charity Number 212644

Contents

List of Illustrations

List of Tables

The Wolverhampton Military Studies Series
Series Editor's Preface

As series editor, it is my great pleasure to introduce the *Wolverhampton Military Studies Series* to you. Our intention is that in this series of books you will find military history that is new and innovative, and academically rigorous with a strong basis in fact and in analytical research, but also is the kind of military history that is for all readers, whatever their particular interests, or their level of interest in the subject. To paraphrase an old aphorism: a military history book is not less important just because it is popular, and it is not more scholarly just because it is dull. With every one of our publications we want to bring you the kind of military history that you will want to read simply because it is a good and well-written book, as well as bringing new light, new perspectives, and new factual evidence to its subject.

In devising the *Wolverhampton Military Studies Series*, we gave much thought to the series title: this is a *military* series. We take the view that history is everything except the things that have not happened yet, and even then a good book about the military aspects of the future would find its way into this series. We are not bound to any particular time period or cut-off date. Writing military history often divides quite sharply into eras, from the modern through the early modern to the mediaeval and ancient; and into regions or continents, with a division between western military history and the military history of other countries and cultures being particularly marked. Inevitably, we have had to start somewhere, and the first books of the series deal with British military topics and events of the twentieth century and later nineteenth century. But this series is open to any book that challenges received and accepted ideas about any aspect of military history, and does so in a way that encourages its readers to enjoy the discovery.

In the same way, this series is not limited to being about wars, or about grand strategy, or wider defence matters, or the sociology of armed forces as institutions, or civilian society and culture at war. None of these are specifically excluded, and in some cases they play an important part in the books that comprise our series. But there are already many books in existence, some of them of the highest scholarly standards, which cater to these particular approaches. The main theme of the *Wolverhampton Military Studies Series* is the military aspects of wars, the preparation for wars or their prevention, and their aftermath. This includes some books whose main theme is the technical details of how armed forces have worked, some books on wars and battles, and some books that re-examine the evidence about the existing stories, to show in a different light what everyone thought they already knew and understood.

As series editor, together with my fellow editorial board members, and our publisher Duncan Rogers of Helion, I have found that we have known immediately and almost by instinct the kind of books that fit within this series. They are very much the kind of well-written and challenging books that my students at the University of Wolverhampton would want to read. They are books which enhance knowledge, and offer new perspectives. Also, they are books for anyone with an interest in military history and events, from expert scholars to occasional readers. One of the great benefits of the study of military history is that it includes a large and often committed section of the wider population, who want to read the best military history that they can find; our aim for this series is to provide it.

Stephen Badsey
University of Wolverhampton

Acknowledgements

There is really no order of precedent for my appreciation, for I am equally grateful to each of the following academics, archivists, curators, librarians, regimental secretaries, friends and family, all who have provided pieces, great and small, in this "jigsaw" that eventually have formed a completed "picture". I must, however, and understandably, place at the top of this list the veteran servicemen and women who allowed me to interview them, and to confer and clarify points with them on a number of subsequent occasions. The detailed list of these officers and men and women, and their units, can be found in the bibliography. All had checked the transcripts of their interviews that were then amended if necessary. I am sad to report that some have since died and I dedicate this work to their memory and to their comrades who live on, now all aged in their 90s.

The Veterans

Kay Ash 1920–2013
William Bate 1925–2012
John Bennett 1921–2008
Thomas Bishop
Raymond Bullock
Stanley Chapman
Eric Clayton
William Cross
Robert Cruddace
William Davidson MBE 1921–2012
R L Val ffrench Blake DSO 1913–2011
Joseph Hodgeson 1921–2011
George Husband
Basil Jeffcut
Ronald Lucas 1917–2014
Charles Need 1914–2010
James Randall MID
Aiden Sprot MC
Margorie Stead 1914–2015

The Academics

Professor Stephen Badsey – The University of Wolverhampton
Dr Phylomena Badsey – The University of Wolverhampton
Professor John Buckley – The University of Wolverhampton
Dr Robert Bushaway (1952–2013) – The University of Birmingham
Mr Peter Hart – The Imperial War Museum London
Professor Robert Self – The London Metropolitan University
Professor Peter Simpkins – The University of Birmingham
Professor David Stephenson – The London School of Economics

Archivists, Curators, Librarians and Regimental Secretaries of the following

The National Archives – Kew
Imperial War Museum – Department of Sound Records – London
Stuart Wheeler and Katie Thompson – The Tank Museum – Bovington
The Cambridge University Library
The University of Birmingham Library
Lianne Smith – Liddell Hart Centre for Military Archives, King's College – London

With grateful acknowledgment of the permission of The Trustees of the Liddell Hart Centre for Military Archives to use selected quotations.

University of Sussex Library – Brighton
The University of Wolverhampton Library
Essex County Library Services – Loughton
The British Library – St. Pancras and Colindale – London
The Household Cavalry – Windsor
Royal Scots Greys – Edinburgh
The Queen's Hussars – Warwick
Angie Wallace – The Museum of The King's Royal Hussars – Winchester
Major David Innes-Lumsden Regimental Secretary – The Queen's Own Hussars Home Headquarters – London
Captain (Retd) C N Bird Assistant Regimental Secretary – Home Headquarters Light Dragoons – York
Captain Mick Holtby – The Queen's Royal Lancers – Grantham
The 9th/12th Lancers – Derby
The 15th/19th Hussars – Newcastle

Friends and family

Peter Armitage FCA
Kathryn Ash
Susan Debnam
Malcolm Clough
Charles Mathiesen
William M Salmon
John Sly
Susan Smith
David Thomas 1947–2011

And for their love and encouragement, my son and daughters – Glenn, Emily and Paula Salmon.

Definitions

MechaniZation and MechaniSation

The spelling used in this work is the traditional form using the letter "z" from the Greek *mĕkhanikos* (machine); the exceptions being direct quotes from written sources where the original spelling with an "s" has been used.

In considering the issues surrounding the mechanization of British horsed cavalry regiments, it important to know that this study makes a distinction between three key terms, *armour, mechanization* and *motorization*. Some contemporary sources do not make these terms clear. The following are the definitions used in each case with in this study:

Armour – A term applied to two kinds of armouring; on land, a wheeled vehicle (armoured car) or a tracked vehicle (tank). The term "tank" was "coined in 1915 to conceal the true purpose of early "landships which has stuck"[1] to describe a vehicle powered by an internal combustion engine and covered with protective armoured plate, armed with machine guns, cannon or both. Later designs combined the feature of a revolving turret.

Mechanization – A term usually associated with the debate between the wars on the development of armoured warfare that included the role of air power. With both land and sea applications the inference is that the mechanically propelled vehicle is covered with protective armour plate.

Motorization – This term is applied to the substitution of horses for wheeled vehicles powered by internal combustion engines for the transportation of personnel or equipment. These vehicles are not usually covered with protective armoured plate.

"Charger" – Officers alone were allowed to keep their horses, known as "chargers" or "officer's mounts". The common term, and dictionary definition, for a cavalry horse is

---

1   Fletcher, David "Tanks" in Holmes. R. (ed.) [2001] *Oxford Companion To Military History*, (Oxford University Press, Oxford) p.898.

a charger, but most cavalry horses were (and still are) not chargers as such but troop-horses or "troopers". Cavalry horses are of mixed breed, "hunter-type" usually with some "thoroughbred" blood in them for stamina, well mannered, capable of carrying weight and currently stand no less than 16.3hh., although some cavalry horses of the inter-war period may have been smaller. Officers, and trumpeters on grey horses, who accompany officers, ride chargers. "Charger Definitions" – Animal Defence Centre; personal correspondence with the author 8 May 2012; also see Tylden, Major G., [1980], *Horses and Saddlery*, (J A Allen & Company, London) pp.3,5/6,8 – passim – Tylden acknowledged the difficulty of definition p.17 and Scott Daniell, David [1959], *4th Hussar: The Story of The 4th Queen's Own Hussars 1685–1958*, (Gale and Polden, Aldershot) p.283 re Captain Scott-Cockburn's horse "Carclew… brought out of the ranks as a charger".

Introduction

For the British horsed cavalryman undergoing "motorization" or "mechanization the move from horses to vehicles, there were many changes to which he had to adapt other than the form of transportation and weapons platform. In motor vehicles, tanks, or other armoured fighting vehicles (AFVs), the cavalrymen's individual role changed. As a horseman he had a dual role of being part of a mobile arm, but was equipped and trained to fight equally well mounted or on foot.[1] In his new role in a vehicle it was different; he became part of a crew. His personal armaments were exchanged, swords and rifles for revolvers.[2] The weapons platform transferred from an individual conveyance, "grace laced with muscle and strength by gentleness confined,"[3] to a clanking, hot, claustrophobic, metal capsule that had to be shared with other men.[4] George "Yorkie" Husband of the 16th/5th Lancers[5] explained, when interviewed for this book in 2010 and having undergone mechanization, that "the training was better as a horseman than [in] a tank. Tank life [he remembered], takes a bit of getting used to, one horse and you together and then you finish up with five of you, it was a different world".[6]

Sharing, mutual dependence and teamwork brought a cultural as well as a mechanical change to cavalry regiments. Horsed troopers, unless they were in a specialist group, such as machine-gunners or signallers, were all trained for a similar role, and with their horse were solo performers. More importantly, mounted cavalry officers both lived and worked separately from the men they led.[7] A tank crew had to form a team, equal in status, except for the commander, but nonetheless mutually dependent as a driver, signaller, gunner or commander. The commander of a tank could be any rank from a lance corporal to a major, or sometimes the commanding officer of the

---

1   Personal interview with ffrench Blake (2006); by the author.
2   Personal interview with Randall (2006); by the author.
3   From a poem by Ronald Duncan collected in Way, *The Poetry of Horses,* p.59.
4   Interview with Parnell by Dr Peter Liddle; Tape 623 – The Second World War Experience Centre.
5   See Appendix A for the Regiment's full title.
6   Personal interview with Husband (2010); by the author.
7   Personal interviews with Lucas (2007); and Bennett (2007); by the author.

regiment, who would ordinarily be a lieutenant colonel.[8] Tank crews fought, cooked, ate and slept together, totally reliant on each other, for each other. As a consequence of mechanization and because of this new closeness between officers, NCOs and troopers, the style and nature of the leadership changed.[9]

How did they do it?

The Army Council, following the end of the Great War, had no intention for the British Army's Regular cavalry regiments other than to mechanize them.[10] The majority of regiments took about twelve months to convert from horses to AFVs, but much depended on the availability and continuity of the supply of equipment with which to train. Elements of the 8th Hussars regiment achieved an effective transition to vehicles in five months in 1936, and in 1942 the Royal Scots Greys took just eight months to convert the whole regiment from horses to tanks. Interviewed in 2007, Lieutenant Colonel Aiden Sprot of the Royal Scots Greys, the last British Regular cavalry regiment to become armoured, contended that one of the most singularly exceptional achievements of the British Army was that all Regular horsed cavalry regiments had become armoured by 1942:

> [It is] really rather remarkable that from that time, August 1941, we [the Royal Scots Greys] went from a completely horsed regiment to a completely mecha-nized one. It is quite a complicated thing, for someone who has never driven a motor car before to then suddenly drive a tank. And someone who had never played with a wireless before – nobody had wirelesses in those days. Only about fifty men out of 500 could drive a motor vehicle in August 1941. And it was rather remarkable that from that time, August 1941, we were fit to go into battle with Rommel in the desert in June the following year.[11]

This was a particularly notable feat given that there was hardly a man who had not previously taken his place in the regiment as a horseman.[12]

    A change of this magnitude, to be successfully achieved, would need appropriate leadership, strong motivation and an effective training programme. The principles of the original programme ordered by the War Office for the management of mecha-nized training appeared to have been similar for each cavalry regiment. Cavalry regi-ments had a higher proportion of NCOs to men, about 1 NCO to 6 or 7 troopers,

---

8   Personal interview with Sprot (2007); by the author.
9   Personal interviews with ffrench Blake (2006); and Husband (2010); by the author.
10   TNA WO 32/5959 Army Organisation: Cavalry (Code 14(D)): Scheme for reduction of Cavalry Regiments – hand written note p.3, 24 February 1921.
11   Personal interview with Sprot (2007); by the author.
12   Royal Scots Greys historical records G219 Case GB51, p.4.

than did infantry regiments.[13] This ratio was a better one for effective leadership and should have enhanced the efficiency of the training. However, the Army Council and the War Office throughout most of the inter-war period faced two other challenges: what mechanical vehicles should replace horses and how was the capital cost of the vehicles to be afforded.

Why then did take so long?

In researching and critically examining the change process employed by the British cavalry to replace horses with vehicles and train cavalrymen in their operation, the question inevitably arose, why did this take so long? If each regiment took, typically, one year to dispose of their horses and learn to use the AFVs and the whole process took about 20 years, perhaps the Army Council's budget could afford to equip only one regiment each year. That was not the case; the mechanization of the cavalry regiments was not evenly spaced in this logical fashion. Perhaps the change was poorly managed, the expertise inadequate or the men difficult to train, but when ordered to do so the regiments appeared to have moved effectively from one operational method to the other. Perhaps there were other, less obvious, reasons for the protracted mechanization of the cavalry, perhaps the change from horses to vehicles was resisted by the officers and men tasked to bring it about as has been suggested in popular historiography.

A cursory, superficial reference to popular British cavalry historiography[14] soon revealed the "Liddell Hart paradigm":[15] that the cause of the delay was the resistance to change exerted by the cavalry corps itself. Lieutenant Colonel R L "Val" ffrench Blake of the 17th/21st Lancers, interviewed for this book in 2006, wrote in 1962 that:

> There is a tendency to regard the failure to mechanize the cavalry early enough after the First World War, as being due to an influential and powerful clique based on the Cavalry Club, which steadily resisted all efforts on the part of the progressive elements to deprive the cavalry of their horses, and thwarted all efforts in the War Office and in Parliament. In fact, strong resistance was put up by some individual regiments on their own behalf, but not generally by the cavalry as a whole.[16]

---

13 French, D., *Military Identities*, p.148. Infantry regiments were multi-battalions, in the Great War era the full strength was around one thousand soldiers. A cavalry regiment is a single "battalion".
14 Phillips, "The Obsolescence of the Arme Blanche and Technological Determinism in British History" War *in History* Volume 9, No. 1, pp.37–74.
15 Harrison Place, *Military training in the British Army*, p.95.
16 ffrench Blake, *A History of The 17th/21st Lancers 1922–1959*, pp.61/62.

Liddell Hart and the "Zombie" Myth

The source of this "tendency" can be traced to the mid-1960s and the memoirs of Sir Basil Liddell Hart. Liddell Hart was a journalist from 1924, and a writer of many works of popular military history. His publications were influential, as were his contacts and networking, culminating in his becoming, in 1937, an unofficial advisor to the Secretary of State for War, Leslie-Hore Belisha (1937–1940), who considered Liddell Hart a "military expert".[17] In his memoirs, Liddell Hart proclaimed, "Wellington's reputed saying that the Battle of Waterloo was won on the playing fields of Eton is merely a legend, but it is painfully true that the early battles of World War II were lost in the Cavalry Club".[18] An assertion justified this claim with the equally sweeping statement that the cavalry had an "inbuilt technophobia and a "misplaced sentimental attachment to the horse".[19]

Evidence *has* been found to support Liddell Hart's assertion. Individual regiments, to which ffrench Blake correctly referred, did resist mechanization, but only two of them; this is explored and exposed with in this book.

Liddell Hart's influence had been considerable, widespread and persistent, and most cavalry regimental histories had done little justice to the subject of mechanization either, certainly in terms of specific details. They had tended to give credence to a reluctance to change, the idea of the sentimental attachment to the horse and concerns over the destruction of three hundred years of tradition. Hector Bolitho's comment in his history of The 3rd The King's Own Hussars was typical:

> It would be idle to assume that either the officers or the troopers, who loved their horses in a way that Englishmen can never love machines, took kindly to their task.[20]

---

17 Minney, *The Private Papers of Hore-Belisha*, p.40. See Appendix C for brief biography of Liddell Hart.
18 Liddell Hart, *Memoirs Volume I*, p.77; Liddell Hart had been critical of the involvement of the cavalry units in the Great War, he "insisted [the cavalry] caused more trouble to their own sides than to the enemy". See Phillips "Who Shall Say That the Days of Cavalry Are Over? The Revival of the Mounted Arm in Europe, 1853–1914" *War in History*, URL: <http://wih.sagepub.com/content/18/1/5> accessed 01.12.2011. Although it is beyond the scope of this book, "many of our failures and early difficulties in armoured fighting in North Africa" was caused, according to Field Marshal Lord Alanbrooke, by the "failure to provide adequate spare parts for tanks"; meeting of Churchill's "Tank Parliament" 5 May 1941; and on 28 June 1942, Alanbrooke, regarding the war in the Middle East and how it would end, wrote "the trouble is due to our tanks being under armed as compared to the Germans"; Danchev and Todman, *War Diaries*, pp.155/156 and 274.
19 Liddell Hart [1959], *The Tanks: The History of the Royal Tank Regiment and its Predecessors, Heavy Branch MGC, Tank Corps and Royal Tank Corps, 1914–1939*, (Cassells, London), p.200, in French, D., *Military Identities*, p.263.
20 Bolitho, *The Galloping Third*, p.243.

In similar vein, regarding the 4th Hussars, the author David Scott Daniell asserted "life without the horse seemed no life at all [because in many cases] the horse, his care and ministration, his grace and beauty, was the main spring of a cavalryman's life".[21] Other examples are the 8th Queen's Royal Irish Hussars Short History in which it is stated: "For the Regiment came the change over from horses to tanks. To a Regiment so basically Light Cavalry in deeds and spirit this change came as a grievous blow".[22] The 10th Royal Hussars regimental history warned: "The regiment now [1927] had on its official strength, fourteen motor lorries, three motor cycles and three motor cycle combinations, but the *danger* of complete mechanisation still seemed distant[sic]".[23] A further example is the history of the 15th/19th The King's Royal Hussars in which Bastin wrote the questionable statement that:

> While everyone knew in their heart of hearts that mechanization one day was inevitable, they hoped to enjoy a few more years with their horses. Hitler put paid to those hopes... The vehicles on which driving instruction was to be given began to arrive in the early summer... They were greeted with gloomy silence.[24]

Field Marshal Sir John French's second son Lieutenant Colonel The Honourable Edward Gerald French's 1951 book, *Goodbye To Boot And Saddle or The Tragic Passing of British Cavalry*, added authenticity to Liddell Hart's later assertions. French clearly implied in the title of his book that the cavalry objected in some way to being mechanized. French commented that the cavalry "*suffered* the gradual process of mechanization... [and] had there been a plebiscite in the cavalry... an overwhelming majority would have cast their votes in favour of disbandment [rather than mechanization]".[25]

This book will examine how much the esprit de corps of the cavalry regiments supported or hindered the change management programme of mechanization. British cavalry regiments were, however, eventually transformed into armoured units with their histories and traditions intact that would continue to inspire and motivate continuing generations of soldiers.

Some later historians have followed the Liddell Hart orthodoxy too. In 1980 Brian Bond was of the opinion that "the cavalry, by and large, was reluctant to change its mental outlook" and cited in support Major General Horace Birks of the Royal Tank Corps (RTC), who asserted that the cavalry was "frightened of losing their horses and their hunting".[26] Kenneth Macksey of the Royal Armoured Corps in 1983 concurred: "Senior cavalry officers still clung to their horses. Royal Tank Corps officers persisted in believing that not only were the cavalry "supremely ignorant" of mechanical matters,

21   Scott Daniell, *4th Hussar*, p.290.
22   Strawson and Rhoderick-Jones, *Irish Hussar*, p.95.
23   Brander, *The 10th Royal Hussars*, p.103 – emphasis added.
24   Bastin, *The History of The 15th/19th The King's Royal Hussars 1945–1980*, p.12.
25   French, E. G., *Goodbye To Boot And Saddle*, p.271.
26   Bond, *British Military Policy Between the Two World Wars*, p.175.

but also unlikely to learn".[27] This book includes the testimonies of Royal Tank Corps officers seconded to train cavalry regiments in driving, maintaining and deploying AFVs; consideration of their experiences is commented on throughout.

Further examples of the Liddell Hart paradigm include John Ellis who, in his book *Cavalry*, originally published in 1978 and republished in 2004, referred to several examples to support his assertion "that right up to the outbreak of the next European conflagration there were many [in Great Britain] who refused to believe that the age of the horse warrior was past". Ellis quite relevantly quoted the speech made by the Secretary of State for War, Duff Cooper, who said, on 10 March 1936, when ordering the mechanization of two further horsed cavalry regiments:

> All the traditions of the regiment are bound up with their horses. It is like asking a great musical performer to throw away his violin and to devote himself in future to a gramophone. It is a great sacrifice for the cavalryman.[28]

The two regiments to which Duff Cooper referred were the 3rd Hussars and the 9th Lancers and the account of their experiences has been examined.

Christy Campbell in his work on the tank pioneers in 2008 persisted with the "Liddell Hart paradigm" with his comments on the cavalry's "forbearance" in giving up their horses, and of the cavalry's "reluctance" to move to armoured fighting vehicles.[29] Shelford Bidwell and Dominick Graham too were sure of the cavalry's "instinctive [resistance to the] conversion to motorised and armoured troops".[30] They were critical of the post Great War Royal Field and Royal Horse Artillery for being obsessed with horses. Bidwell and Graham failed to mention, however, Armstrong's (later Vickers Armstrong and in conjunction with the War Office), successfully designed tractors of 1924. Instead of horses, these so-called "dragons" towed the guns. Two brigades of Field Artillery were mechanized and a report at that time commented that:

> … one of these brigades was by reputation the most "horsey" brigade in the Royal Artillery; and had been chosen [for mechanization] for that purpose, because it was desired to see how officers and men who were devoted to horses would shape with tractors… [After an initial resentment at losing their horses, the officers and men] took the same detailed interest and pride in their machines as they had done with their horses and guns, and turned themselves into a highly efficient mechanized unit.[31]

---

27   Macksey, *A History of The Royal Armoured Corps*, p.50.
28   Ellis, *Cavalry*, pp.181.182; Liddell Hart, *Memoirs Volume I*, p.277; for the context see Minney, *The Private Papers of Hore-Belisha*, pp.92–98.
29   Campbell, *Band of Brigands*, p.409.
30   Bidwell & Graham, *Fire-Power*, p.152.
31   TNA WO 32/3059 Army Organisation: Cavalry (Code 14(D)): Reconstruction of the Corps of Cavalry Point 3 in draft memorandum, marked "secret" to C I D Sub Committee

Liddell Hart's enduring influence has been considerable and it continues still.[32] Recent examples of this include the Chief of The Defence Staff, General Sir David Richards, calling for military ideas and equipment to change in response to the new nature of warfare such as "cyber-attacks". Calling it a new "horse versus tank moment General Richards compared his critics "to the cavalry officers who insisted, long after the introduction of the tank in the First World War, that it would never replace horses".[33] In a similar vein Dan Byles, the Conservative Member of Parliament for North Warwickshire, in his speech on 16 September 2010 referred to "the old guard, resistant to change who had influenced the disbandment of the Experimental Mechanised Force [in 1928]."[34] The disbandment of the Experimental Mechanised Force, or Armoured Force as it was called later, will also be discussed in this book.

Clearly, many believed Liddell Hart's assertions were accurate, but revisionist cavalry historians have challenged the accuracy of his opinions.

Timothy Harrison Place has stated:

> Until recently, historians' understanding of the British armoured arm between the wars has been governed by what might be called the "Liddell Hart paradigm"... Indeed, the Army and the high command were far less hostile to mechanization than Liddell Hart had claimed.[35]

Barton C Hacker, who in 1968 researched for his PhD the "controversy over mechanization" soon realised that Liddell Hart's ideas on cavalry mechanization were the established primary orthodoxy, but Hacker came to other conclusions summarized below.[36] In 1998, historian Brian Holden Reid pronounced that "Liddell Hart's own contribution [had] clouded the history of mechanization, which had done so much to influence the judgement of other writers".[37]

Liddell Hart's historical depiction of the events surrounding the substitution of vehicles for horses contrasted starkly with the perceptions of those soldiers directly engaged in the process. This suggests scope for scepticism about the accuracy of

---

on the Strength and Organisation of the Cavalry from the Director of Mechanization, War Office, February 1928 marked 13A; probably a submission to the Committee chaired by Lord Salisbury; Bidwell & Graham, *Fire-Power,* p.154 mentions four mechanized batteries in 1924.

32   Holden Reid, *Studies in British Military Thought,* p.15.

33   *The Sunday Times,* 17 January 2010; URL <http://timesonline.co.uk/tol/news/uk/article6991030.ece> accessed 10.05.2011.

34   See URL <http://www.theyworkforyou.com/debates/?id=2010–09–16a.1037.0&s=mechanisation+cavalry#g1084.2> accessed 10.05.2011 – regarding the "Strategic Defence and Security Review".

35   Harrison Place, *Military training in the British Army 1940–1944,* p.95.

36   Hacker, Barton C, "The Military Machine: An Analysis of the Controversy over the Mechanization of the British Army 1919–1939"; PhD, University of Chicago, 1968, p.14.

37   Holden Reid, *Studies in British Military Thought,* p.15.

Liddell Hart's and others' indictment of the cavalry and its attitudes towards mechanization. Liddell Hart complained of the "enormous number of influential people in the House [of Commons in 1933–1934] and in the counties who were pro-cavalry implying pro-*horsed* cavalry". He cited General John Edward Bernard (Jack) Seely, a former Secretary of State for War (1912–1914) and distinguished Great War Yeomanry Cavalry officer who, in parliament in 1933, "scornfully" referred to tanks as "those petrol things".[38] Liddell Hart grieved that:

> A love of the horse and of hunting seems to blunt all their reasoning faculties... such a prejudice, of social roots, was no novelty in our military history... The Cavaliers of the twentieth century jeopardised their country under the influence of a similar social convention, the preference for the horse and prejudice against the machine.[39]

It is interesting to note, but so far defies explanation, that examination of Liddell Hart's diary and the notes made during the inter-war period have revealed little, if any such sentiments.

Liddell Hart's influence persisted nonetheless and had impacted upon historian Elizabeth Kier in 1999. Kier quoted General Seely's comments, cited by Liddell Hart, as if these had come from a serving officer rather than a retired Yeomanry Cavalry officer. Kier questioned the ability of the British "gentleman officer [and his] subordinates with little or no initiative [to adapt to] the increased firepower, mobility and mass of modern warfare [that had] exploded the traditional dimensions of the battlefield".[40] In correspondence with the author, ffrench Blake challenged Kier's assertion; he responded that "the cavalry were quite accustomed to speed and movement".[41] Kier also said: "Tanks, or [quoting Seely] those petrol things, had little place in the British Army officer's vision of war".[42] To this comment ffrench Blake retorted: "If you haven't got them, you can't work with them or study [them]"[43] and in his 2003 article "The Mechanization of the British Cavalry" David French agreed that a lack of equipment restricted the cavalry's opportunity to perfect new techniques.[44] Regarding Kier's comments that:

---

38 Referred to by Kier, *Imagining War*, p.132 as an example of the anachronistic attitude that pervaded the interwar army officer corps. For "Jack" Seely's cavalry exploits see Anglesey, *A History of the British Cavalry*, Volume 5, pp.48, 73 & 199. In Volume 4 Anglesey dated Seely's appointment as Secretary of State for war as 1908, p.377, but *Hansard* dates his appointment as 1912–1914; URL: <http://hansard.millbanksystems.com/offices/secretary-of-state-for-war> accessed 22 April 2013.
39 Liddell Hart, *Memoirs Volume I*, pp.242/243.
40 Kier, *Imagining War*, p.132.
41 Personal correspondence with ffrench Blake (2009); by the author.
42 Kier, *Imagining War*, p.132.
43 Personal correspondence with ffrench Blake (2009); by the author.
44 French, D., "The Mechanization of the British Cavalry" in *War in History*, July 2003, p.299.

… the regimental officer, with his rural and gentlemanly culture, could not easily adjust to a "garage mechanics" war, [because he] did not have the skills, understanding of technology and command structure.[45]

ffrench Blake remembered, "it wasn't like this – we adjusted easily and willingly".[46]

The merits of these comments are carefully examined. Research for this work has probed whether the supply of AFVs with which the cavalry had to train was a significant factor in the change process and how enthusiastically the cavalry responded to mechanization when given the vehicles to do so. Comments such as Kier's are compared and contrasted with archival material and the testimonies of the officers and other ranks involved. Kier's analysis nonetheless has served to perpetuate the popular historiography of the cavalry promulgated by Liddell Hart.

In part, the mythology of technophobic cavalry officers resistant to change is symptomatic of a broader indictment of the British Army during the immediate post-Great War period encapsulated in the notion of "lions led by donkeys". Stephen Badsey concluded:

> By the last quarter of the twentieth century, the term "cavalrymen" in the context of the First World War had become little more than a vague expression of abuse.
>
> This perception of the cavalry general and the cavalry charge has taken on the qualities of what are sometimes called zombie myths: those that will not die no matter how many times they are destroyed … The metaphor of an uncomprehending cavalry general… has spread beyond military studies into the general vocabulary of historians and readers of history, as a touchstone for all that is reactionary, foolish and futile. It is probably too well established ever to be removed.[47]

David Keynon agreed with Badsey in his recent examination of the canon of Great War literature.[48] Gervase Phillips viewed the cavalry as the British Army's "scapegoat" arm that had been treated unfairly by military historians.[49] Phillips demonstrated that the obsolescence of horsed cavalry had been overstated and distorted by traditionalist Great War historians.[50] Cavalrymen had been portrayed as technophobic and anachronistic, and Phillips argued that this was a distortion within popular Anglophile

45   Kier, *Imagining War,* p.133.
46   Personal correspondence with ffrench Blake (2009); by the author.
47   Badsey, *Doctrine and Reform,* p.307.
48   Kenyon, *British Cavalry on The Western Front,* pp.1/2.
49   Phillips, Gervase "Scapegoat Arm: Twentieth-Century Cavalry in Anglophone Historiography" in Vandervort, Bruce (ed.) [2007] *The Journal of Military History* Volume 71, No. 1, (Society for Military History, Lexington, Virginia), pp.37–74.
50   Phillips, Gervase "The Obsolescence of the Arme Blanche and Technological Determinism in British History" [2002] *War in History* Volume 9 No. 1, (Arnold, London), pp.39–59.

cavalry historiography.[51] David French asserted that the underlying assumption that some British cavalry officers were "so stupid that even their brother officers noticed… has dominated the literature on the mechanization of the cavalry between the wars".[52]

Gilman Barndollar argued that:

> … thanks to a handful of recent revisionist British cavalry historians the traditional view of twentieth century British cavalry, dominated by the biases of Liddell Hart and Royal Tank Corps has been challenged and perhaps even overturned.[53]

This may be so, but there remains a general lack of detailed scholarship on the actual process of mechanization. Very few historians have sought specifically to explore cavalry attitudes towards mechanization, and the degree to which there was any real evidence of resistance to change that was capable of challenging or supporting the prevailing orthodoxy of Liddell Hart which had been perpetuated by others.

Alternative explanations

Some historians have attributed other reasons for the delay in mechanizing the cavalry. The Marquess of Anglesey, in the last chapter of his much acclaimed eight volume *A History of the British Cavalry* has summarized, in a "much over-simplified" form, the events leading up to mechanization.[54] He correctly stated that the background against which these events were acted out was complex:

> The period 1919–1939 was a depressing one in the history of the armed forces. It was even more depressing for the mounted branch of the army, for when these two decades, known aptly as "the lean years" came to an end, it had for some time been clear that the [horsed] cavalry as a force in war, everywhere in the world, was facing the same death-throes experienced long ago by the dodo.

Liddell Hart did acknowledge that the chance of mechanization was diminished by the Conservative Government under Baldwin that was "cutting down national expenditure in every direction; its belief that another war in Europe was most unlikely; and a widespread lack of public, and thus political, interest in modernising the Army".[55] From *The Private Papers of Hore-Belisha*, the Secretary of State for War 1937–1940, R J Minney concurred: "The mood of the people was for peace… 'Axe the services' was

---

51   Ibid., pp.37–74.
52   French, D., "The Mechanization of the British Cavalry" p.296.
53   Gilman Clough Barndollar, "British Use of Armoured cars 1919–1939" PhD, Cambridge University 2010, p.275.
54   Anglesey, *A History of the British Cavalry, Volume 8,* p.306. "Marquess" not "Marquis" is the correct spelling for the UK title.
55   Liddell Hart, *Memoirs Volume I,* p.173.

the popular and political cry, and Conservative and Labour ministries vied with each other in axeing [sic] them to the bone".[56]

Barney White-Spunner's 2006 comprehensive history of the Household Cavalry regiments particularly commented on the shortage of adequate equipment for training, as did Allan Mallinson in his unreferenced history, *Light Dragoons*.[57]

Benjamin Coombs's analysis of British tank production 1934–1945, concludes that although the production of light tanks increased in the run-up to the Second World War, this "did not quicken the mechanization of cavalry regiments, resulting in many units having insufficient time to adequately train with new equipment before the start of hostilities in 1940".[58]

David French has examined the subject, and in his article he firmly concluded that "it was the lack of sufficient funding" that retarded cavalry mechanization.[59] This book will carefully consider this point.

Anglesey also included a brief, balanced and useful account of the officers and other ranks' attitudes towards mechanization.[60] The reorganisation problems of the British cavalry are explained in context, but his account lacked the detail on how the change process was managed and the practicalities of the transition from horses to AFVs. ffrench Blake in his two books, *The 17th/21st Lancers*,[61] and later, *A History of The 17th/21st Lancers 1922–1959*,[62] covered the subject better than most others, but the process of change was not the detailed account gained from his interviews and correspondence for this book. Robert H Larson in his work included the "social conservatism in the officer corps" and "short sighted government policy" as reasons for the delay in mechanizing horsed cavalry regiments.[63]

Stephen Badsey attributed the failure to develop a "genuinely fast tank" to the delay in changing horsed cavalry to armoured fighting vehicles.[64] David French also wrote that not until the mid-1930s could "even half-satisfactory [armoured fighting] vehicles be anticipated".[65] Badsey also sets into context the dilemma facing the British Army after 1918. He correctly argued that horsed cavalry was vulnerable on a modern battlefield, but until suitable mechanical armoured vehicles became manoeuvrable over all terrain, horses would not become obsolete.[66] David French too, attributed the

56   Minney, *The Private Papers of Hore-Belisha*, p.31.
57   Mallinson, *Light Dragoons*, pp.221/222.
58   Coombs, B, *British Tank Production and the War Economy 1934–194*, p.19.
59   French, D., "The Mechanization of the British Cavalry", p.320.
60   Anglesey, *A History of the British Cavalry 1816–1919, Volume 8*, p.306–317.
61   ffrench Blake, *The 17th/21st Lancers*, pp.78–82.
62   ffrench Blake, *A History of The 17th/21st Lancers 1922–1959*, pp.60–68.
63   Larson, *The British Army and the Theory of Armored Warfare*, p.15.
64   Badsey, Stephen "Cavalry and the Development of Breakthrough Doctrine" in Griffith, Paddy [1996] *British Fighting Methods in the Great War*, pp.138–174.
65   French, D., "The Mechanization of the British Cavalry", pp.298/299.
66   Badsey, Stephen "Cavalry and the Development of Breakthrough Doctrine" in Griffith, Paddy [1996] *British Fighting Methods in the Great War*, pp.138–174.

delay in mechanizing the cavalry to the lack of suitable armoured fighting vehicles.[67] However, some genuinely fast tanks had been constructed between the wars, but how many and what happened to them? The examination of Vickers' historical documents on tank development and production tests the proficiency of these opinions.

Correlli Barnett, when questioning why the British Army in the Second World War came to rely on American tanks, laid blame for the lack of British tank development on "the incompetence of the British motor industry, and of British engineering in a wider sense". Coombs argued that tank production was a "unique industrial process" that required specialised experience that Barnett had underestimated and that commercial motor development had, in any case, stalled due to the economic depression.[68] Barnett, however, cited the later "cruiser" tank, the so-called "backbone of future armoured divisions" and singled out Nuffield Mechanization's "over-hasty, botched and piecemeal testing" for particular criticism.[69] Light is cast on Barnett's opinion that the eventual production model of the cruiser tank, the "Crusader" in 1941, was a most unreliable vehicle, by the experiences of veteran cavalry officers Lieutenant Colonels Aiden Sprot of the Royal Scots Greys and R L Valentine ffrench Blake of the 17th/21st Lancers, interviewed for this study by the author in 2006 and 2007. Sprot confirmed that, "British tanks, I am afraid were very, very bad, the Crusader and all those other ones".[70] ffrench Blake commented, "everything (the mechanization process) worked like clock-work except for the fact that our tanks were about as good as clocks for fighting in".[71]

J P Harris felt that mechanizing cavalry regiments with light tanks "was both expensive and one of dubious wisdom"[72] but little else was available for the cavalry to use. Harris was correct in as much that the light tank and its weapons were found to be inadequate when engaged against German armour in 1940. Former 15th/19th Hussars John Bennett and Ronald Lucas remembered their experiences in France in 1940. Harris also wrote, however, remaining within the Liddell Hart paradigm, that "[although] most cavalry officers were prepared to accept mechanization… they had little enthusiasm for it".[73] Harris had previously referred to the "experiment" of the 3rd Hussars, (see Chapter Four of this work) but did not mention how their enthusiasm grew for mechanization once the process was underway. It is reasonable too, to point

67   French, D., "The Mechanization of the British Cavalry" pp 296–320.
68   Coombs, B, *British Tank Production and the War Economy 1934–194,* pp.6 & 13.
69   Barnett, Correlli, "The Desert Generals Revisited" Talk given to the Annual General Meeting of the British Commission for Military History, 2005, p.7/8.
70   Personal interview with Sprot (2007); by the author.
71   Personal interview with ffrench Blake (2006); by the author. See also Danchev and Todman, *War Diaries,* 2 October 1940 "all the cruiser tanks must be pulled back at once for an overhaul"; p.112 and French, D., *Raising Churchill's Army,* "cruisers had to be abandoned… because they broke down"; pp.98/99.
72   Harris, *Men, Ideas and Tanks,* p.263.
73   Ibid., pp.258–259.

out that the Vickers Light tanks, Marks IIIs and VIBs were successful when used by the 3rd Hussars against units of the Italian 10th Army at Beda Fomm in Libya in early 1941.

The reasons for any lack of tank development and production are germane and significant to this book. Insufficient, inadequate, obsolete AFVs on which to train the cavalrymen would have made the change from horses more challenging than it otherwise might have been both in duration and process.

David French, in his 2003 article "The Mechanization of the British Cavalry" and in his 2005 book *Military Identities*, examined the social and cultural aspects within cavalry regiments, that "in some sense promoted" mechanization; the determination to preserve their own regiment, horsed or armoured, the regimental pride of still being the "best cavalry regiment" whether horsed or armoured, and the cautious welcome of mechanization given by both officers and men.[74]

French's views were explored in the experiences of the veteran cavalrymen. Particularly worth recounting are those of Sergeant Ronald Lucas of the 15th/19th Hussars and Corporal Charles Need of the 13th/18th Hussars interviewed by the author in 2007. Lucas recalled his enthusiasm for the change to AFVs:

> This is a new challenge, something completely new, I was excited about it. I think the attitude was look, this is something new the horses have gone, and this is a new life for us. The fact that you lived a life of discipline in effect, you did it. We didn't have people leave the army because they didn't like it, some liked the tanks, belting around and things, but you stuck up for your troop, your squadron and your regiment, that came first, horse or armour.[75]

Need also confirmed the strength of the regimental culture: "we were cavalrymen and proud of it, we thought that we were better than the rest – the best of the best".[76]

Hacker (mentioned above) concluded in his analysis of articles that were published during the inter-war period, that the opponents of mechanization which included, but were not exclusively cavalrymen, were not "simply stupid, irrational or blindly opposed to change"; nor were the advocates of mechanization "particularly far-sighted visionaries" as there were sound practical reasons behind both, those arguing for mechanizing the cavalry, and those that were against it.[77] Opposition to the substitution of tanks or armoured cars for horses came, Hacker speculated, from those involved with

---

74   French, D., "The Mechanization of the British Cavalry" pp.299,302 & 315 and *Military Identities*, p.263.
75   Personal interview with Lucas (2007); by the author.
76   Personal interview with Need (2007); by the author.
77   Hacker, Barton C, "The Military Machine. An Analysis of the Controversy over the Mechanization of the British Army 1919–1939 PhD, University of Chicago,1968, pp.209/210. See also French, D., "The Mechanization of the British Cavalry", regarding the rhetoric in support of the Royal Tank Corps' exclusive control of AFVs, p.311.

peace-keeping, so-called imperial policing that was the "every day concern" of the interwar army.[78] In "terrain and climate [that were ill-suited to armour] and enemy too elusive for tanks to bring to bay horsed cavalry played a significant role.[79] Veteran Royal Scots Greys Sergeant James Randall, who served both as a horsed cavalryman during the British mandate in Palestine and later as a tank commander in battle, interviewed for this book by the author in 2006, confirmed Hacker's reasoning:

> Oh yes, you could go anywhere on a horse... up into these little villages dotted about up in the hills, in fact in horse days we used to ride these patrols all over the country... Tanks wouldn't have been any good, getting up these tracks in the hills on the sort of patrols that we did, and at any rate it would have been a waste of tanks – they were for modern warfare and we were not in modern war at that time, we were still peace keepers that was all.[80]

Although Gwynn asserts the need for mobility in imperial police work, he also confirmed that armoured cars were vulnerable to obstacles, and AFVs generally, "require special and favourable conditions to enable their full potentialities to be exploited".[81]

"Don't believe what you want to believe until you know what you need to know"[82]

What was written at the time either in favour of, or against, mechanization, what might have been said, or felt, about mechanization that went unrecorded was of little consequence. The only consequence was what happen and how, and why and when it actually took place as it did.[83] To reiterate the assertion of Lieutenant Colonel Aiden Sprot of the Royal Scots Greys, one of the most remarkable achievements of the British Army was that Regular horsed cavalry regiments were all armoured by 1942.

Given the conflict of interpretation on the subject of cavalry mechanization, some crucial questions require analysis: were entire regiments of horseman trained to enable them to fight in AFVs in every case, or just a capable few? If so, when and how was this managed and was it successful? Why did it take so long to mechanize the British

---

78   Ibid., p.251.
79   Ibid., also Gilman Clough Barndollar, "British Use of Armoured cars 1919–1939"; PhD, Cambridge University, 2010; armoured cars were not ideal either because their tyres were unsuitable, but were of use in the urban areas, pp.157 &177. French argued that armoured cars "also had tactical limitations when performing internal security duties"; French, D., "The Mechanization of the British Cavalry"; p.308.
80   Personal interview with Randall (2006); by the author; French, D., "The Mechanization of the British Cavalry", p.306.
81   Gwynn, Charles W, *Imperial Policing*, pp.21, 24, 29 &116.
82   Crow's Law (so called).
83   See Ruskin, John [1886], "The Crown of Wild Olive".

Regular cavalry and to adopt and implement a policy that appeared such an obvious and logical decision, and was always the intention of the Army Council? Did a lack of esprit de corps and resistance to change retard its implementation; were cavalrymen "supremely ignorant of mechanical matters" and difficult to train? Were suitable AFVs available in sufficient numbers for training purposes or did a lack of funding retard both the development and production of AFVs for the cavalry?

These points have been investigated by researching archived records and collecting and analysing the oral testaments of some of the officers and men who took part. Only through a critical examination of these areas of controversy will it possible for the reader to consider any mythology perpetuated by popular history. In particular, this book will explore the fundamental question of whether any lack of preparedness in this field, when war broke out in 1939, can be attributed, as Liddell Hart suggested, to cavalry intransigence.

The principal purpose of this book is to fill this significant lacuna in historical understanding. In so doing it will consider the reasons for the slow and apparent late move from horses to AFVs. It will critically examine the management of change process set in the context of the crucially important social, economic and political challenges of the period.

1

A "Horsed" British Regular Cavalry Regiment between the Two World Wars

A cavalry regiment, as a matter of routine, spent three years in rotation, in a number of the of locations, or stations, in England and Scotland the "Home" stations included: Aldershot, Colchester, Edinburgh, Shorncliffe, Tidworth and York. Hounslow was frequently the station of embarkation and Shorncliffe the station for regiments returning from overseas. Nine years were spent away when a regiment was posted abroad, usually to Egypt and India, but there were exceptions, such as the 1st (King's) Dragoon Guards and the 1st (Royal) Dragoons (The Royals) that were overseas for just six years. The 12th Lancers, in armoured cars, served in Egypt from 1927 until 1934 when they were replaced by the other cavalry armoured car regiment, the 11th Hussars, whose tour of duty was extended by the outbreak of war. The 3rd Hussars served in Constantinople in 1922, followed by three years in Egypt and six in India. The 15th/19th Hussars served in Egypt and Palestine between 1924 and 1928, moved then to India until 1933, when the regiment returned home to Shorncliffe in early 1934. The Army List for any given period gave the main location for the regiment (see Appendix A), but detachments from the regiment were posted around the region of their main station to carry out police and security duties. The 15th/19th Hussars postings were an example.[1] The regiment left Tidworth on 11 January 1924 and disembarked at Port Said on 25 January. Between 1924 and 1928 the regiment's main locations were in Palestine and Egypt, at Helmieh (now in the Yemen), and Abbassia, near Cairo. Regimental detachments were stationed at Sidi Bishr near Alexandria, Mena Camp, outside Cairo and within site of the Pyramids ["mena" – a military acronym for Middle East and North Africa], Helwan, south of Cairo, and Wadi El Natrum 100 km northwest of Cairo.

The 15th/ 19th Hussars embarked on 28 October 1928 for India and travelled 1,400 miles to Risalpur via Bombay (now Mumbai), Surat, Baroda, Agra, Delhi, Ambala, Lahore and Rawalpindi; they arrived at Risalpur 14 November 1928 where

---

1 Thompson, *The 15th/19th The King's Hussars – A Pictorial History* – appendix.

C Squadron of the 15th/19th Hussars on their desert march between Helmieh to Abbassia, December 1926. (Courtesy: The Light Dragoons archives, Newcastle upon Tyne)

they took over the station from the 5th Inniskilling Dragoon Guards. Detachments of the regiment were then stationed at Kanpur, Arbi-Ksli, Peshawar, where in 1930 the unit was called out to assist the civil power during "disturbances" in the district. In 1931 a detachment in Tulandi was called out "to quell the Red Shirt troubles". Detachments were variously at Hoti Mardan, Charsadda, Swabbi, Rashkai, Lahore, Kohat, Kaganath and Jalbai.[2] The regiment embarked for Shorncliffe, England, 15 January 1934, handing over the station to the 14th/20th (King's) Hussars. George "Yorkie" Husband, who served with the 16th/5th Lancers in Secunderabad in 1937, confirmed in 2010 that he sometimes "never saw [a] barracks for two to three weeks at a time, whole squadrons patrolled and troops split up to patrol different areas".[3]

British horsed cavalry regiments of the period were similar, but not identical, in structure and organisation. There was a "recommended" establishment for both "peace" and "war",[4] but this varied with circumstance, such as home or overseas postings, recruitment levels, whether a regiment had just returned home when large numbers of time-expired men might be demobilised,[5] or when the regiment was about to be

2   Thompson, *The 15th/19th The King's Hussars – A Pictorial History* – appendix.
3   Personal interview with Husband (2010); by the author.
4   TNA WO 32/11369 Army Organisation: Cavalry (Code 14(D)): Reports of committee on war and peace time establishment – Appendices.
5   Personal interviews with Lucas (2007); and Bennett (2007); by the author.

posted abroad and was most likely to be brought up to full establishment. Every effort was to be made to ensure regiments serving overseas were fully manned. Regiments serving abroad were loosely "linked" with regiments at home to train new recruits and provide drafts to serve abroad.[6] At home the regiment's peace time establishment was 560, and 574 war time establishment – men of all ranks; regiments serving in the colonies had an establishment of 575 men of all ranks and in India 596 men of all ranks.[7]

A Lieutenant Colonel commanded the regiment. The Army Lists indicated, that in most cases, but not all, officers, up to and including Lieutenant Colonel, were promoted from within their own regiment. It was likely, therefore, that the Lieutenant Colonel commenced his career as a subaltern in the regiment.[8] The second in command of the regiment was a Major; he was likely to succeed the Lieutenant Colonel in due course, perhaps after three to four years in post.[9] The executive was supported by a Head Quarters Squadron that included: the Adjutant (usually a Captain, who was responsible for the day to day administration of the regiment), signals officer (usually a subaltern), a Quartermaster, responsible for clothing and equipment, the Regimental Sergeant Major and the Band Master (both Warrant Officers Class I), and the Farrier Quartermaster-Sergeant (Warrant Officer Class II). Other roles and ranks included: Warrant Officers responsible for instruction such as rough-riders and musketry: Sergeants, Corporals and Privates (known as Troopers after 1924) were responsible for policing the regiment (provost), tailoring, cooking, saddler, transport, and the officers' mess. The Headquarters Squadron establishment totalled around 160 of all ranks.[10]

The operational or fighting soldiers, totalled around four hundred men of all ranks, and were divided between three Squadrons, known as "Sabre" or "Lance" Squadrons. Each squadron was commanded by a Major with a Captain as his second in command, and these officers were supported by a small squadron headquarters of perhaps twenty men of all ranks.[11] The squadron was divided into four troops, each troop commanded by a subaltern with a sergeant as second in command. One troop in each regiment had a sergeant in command of a troop. In three of the troops the soldiers were armed with a sword (1908 pattern) or lance (final pattern), or both, and a rifle, the Short Magazine Lee Enfield Mark III (S.M.L.E.). Officers and non-commissioned officers

---

6   TNA WO 32/5959 Army Organisation: Cavalry (Code 14(D)): Scheme for reduction of Cavalry Regiments.
7   TNA WO 32/11369 Army Organisation: Cavalry (Code 14(D)): Reports of committee on war and peace time establishment – Appendices; Evans, *The Story of The Fifth Royal Inniskilling Dragoon Guards*, p.172–598; men of all ranks.
8   The Army Lists.
9   The Army Lists.
10 TNA WO 32/11369 Army Organisation: Cavalry (Code 14(D)): Reports of committee on war and peace time establishment – Appendices.
11 Ibid.

(NCOs) carried revolvers (the Webley Mk VI).[12] On active service the officers would probably carry the same 1908 pattern sword as the troopers, but in a brown leather covered wooden scabbard, rather than the more elaborate officer's 1912 pattern sword in a metal scabbard.[13] Each of the troops was divided into three sections of eight men each led by a corporal;[14] one man in four, the Number Three, was designated as the "horse-holder enabling the other three men to fight dismounted when such action was required. When fighting dismounted the Troop Sergeant was responsible for the horse-holders and the led horses.[15] It was found to be a very difficult task for one man to hold on to four horses whilst under fire, especially artillery fire, and the timing was critical to bring up the horses for remounting the rest of the troop after dismounted action had taken place.[16] The fourth troop was the "machine-gun" or "Hotchkiss" Troop and was divided into four sections.[17] This troop was armed with Vickers or Hotchkiss machine-guns, sometimes both. Machine-guns were carried on led pack-horses.[18] At home the regiments had around 360 horses, 515 in the colonies and a little over 600 in India.[19]

The British Army, post 1918, was designed in the main for home security, and to defend and protect the British Empire, including new responsibilities in Africa, the Pacific and those Middle-Eastern lands mandated to Great Britain following the San Remo Conference in April 1920. There was also a commitment to the Anglo-French army of occupation in the Rhineland as well as home-service in Ireland.[20] By 1922 the British Empire spanned one quarter of the globe and one quarter of the world's population.[21] In some countries within the Empire a growth of self-determination and anti-Imperialism caused a huge strain on British military resources.[22] War, certainly another European war, was not contemplated during the 1920s. Had a war happened, horsed cavalry would have performed as it had done so during the previous wars of the

12   Ibid. Chappell, *British Cavalry Equipment 1800–1941*, pp.37–39.
13   Robinson, *Swords of the British Army*, p.100.
14   Kenyon, *Horseman in No Man's Land*, p.21.
15   Personal interview with ffrench Blake (2006); by the author.
16   TNA WO 95/1466 4th Division War Diaries; 19th Hussars; B Squadron, 26 August 1914.
17   Evans, *The Story of The Fifth Royal Inniskilling Dragoon Guards*, p.162.
18   TNA WO 32/11366 Army Organisation: Cavalry (Code 14(D)): Abolition of certain weapons to improve efficiency; Oatts, *I Serve – Regimental History of 3rd Carabiniers (Prince of Wales's Dragoon Guards)*, p.247.
19   TNA WO 32/11369 Army Organisation: Cavalry (Code 14(D)): Reports of committee on war and peace time establishment – Appendices.
20   Bond, *British Military Policy Between the Two World Wars*, pp.15, 17, 32.
21   Anglesey, A History of the British cavalry 1816–1919, Volume 8, *The Western Front 1915–1918 Epilogue, 1919–1939*, p.310.
22   Bond, *British Military Policy Between the Two World Wars*, pp.10/11.

twentieth century, and would do again in future conflicts as an armoured corps. This was succinctly summarized in 1935[23] as:

Long distance reconnaissance
To seize and hold ground
Flank and rear guards
To follow-up a break into an enemy position
To raid back areas
The pursuit of a broken enemy

Imperial policing (this term was coined in the 1930s to reflect the changing methods used to control the Empire), employed some mechanized forces in the form of armoured cars and aircraft.[24] In some areas however, horses were invaluable. In Ireland, after the Easter uprising of 1916, military action by the self-styled Irish Republican Army (IRA) increased. British Army numbers in Ireland rose to almost 40,000 troops by 1921. As well as lorries, the British troops were equipped with aircraft and 100 armoured cars.[25] Armoured cars, not being cross-country vehicles, were vulnerable to road obstructions, such as tree felling and bridge blowing, that were frequent tactics of the IRA, but tactics that failed to halt the progress of horse cavalry. The cavalry squadrons were dispersed over a wide area of Ireland and were engaged in wide sweeps of the countryside looking for arms and armed men. Five cavalry regiments were engaged in this work, sometimes working dismounted when "on steep hills and rocky ground" and sometimes at night; the cavalry was supported by infantrymen and armoured cars.[26] Oatts, the historian of the 3rd Hussars, argued that this demonstrated that horsed cavalry had "not yet become obsolete, but was still indispensable in mobile operations however useless it might be considered in trench warfare", a view supported by Lord Carnock, the historian of the 15th Hussars.[27]

The horse cavalry arm of the British Army was particularly efficient in dealing with public disturbances, using methods now adopted by mounted police.[28] Peter Neyroud CBE QPM, The Institute of Criminology, University of Cambridge, a trained public order commander, confirmed that

---

23 "3rd Hussars Experiment in Mechanization April-September 1935" in TNA WO32/2847 Army Organisation: Cavalry (Code 14(D)): Introduction of a Mobile Division 1934–1936 20/Cav/831.
24 Holmes, *The Oxford Companion to Military History*, p.433.
25 James, *Warrior Race – A History of The British at War*, p.577.
26 Oatts, *I Serve – Regimental History of 3rd Carabiniers (Prince of Wales's Dragoon Guards)*, p.244; Carnock, *The History of the 15th The King's Hussars 1914–1922* pp.212–220.
27 Ibid.
28 Oatts, *I Serve – Regimental History of 3rd Carabiniers (Prince of Wales's Dragoon Guards)*, p.244.

There is a credible case to be made in favour of horses as a key component of a strategy to manage disorder. Police horses can be deployed to divert crowds, disperse crowds and ultimately to break up crowds by force. They are much more effective than a cordon of police officers for most urban crowds because most urban crowds are not comfortable with horses and are very, very wary of a mounted section. Used effectively, they do add greatly to the flexibility of public order policing. They also add the capability to get police away from a hostile mob, which I imagine was a major consideration in India.

Neyroud is correct, and mounted officers are still used extensively in India for law and order duties, "controlling huge crowds during rallies, processions, festivals etc". The Delhi police, for example, has 60 mounted officers distributed across 7 districts, during 2008 the mounted force undertook 12,384 hours of duty, each horse undertaking 5 to 6 hours per shift.[29]

In this regard, British cavalry horsemanship changed its emphasis after the Great War, by keeping the horse "on-contact" all the time. This style of riding, a more "collected" dressage type of movement, was highly suitable for close contact pressure on a crowd: it was argued that the horse, "still the best cross country conveyance available at the time... did not properly demonstrate its capability" in later experiments comparing the horse to other forms of transport,[30] where speed and stamina were required. Lieutenant Colonel ffrench Blake confirmed that the horses were no longer trained for endurance, nor tested in that respect, but to look impressive.[31]

Ronald Lucas remembered "shop window riding" through York, where the troopers checked their own riding positions by observing their reflections in the shop windows; mirrors are used in riding schools for the same purpose. Lucas's comment demonstrated that the men had been trained to get their mounts "on contact" or "collected".[32] This technique enabled better control of the animal in walk, trot and canter, and was essential for crowd control. A somewhat different technique is employed for the gallop, a "pace" essential for the latter stages of a mounted charge of an earlier era.[33] The catalyst for the change in riding technique might have occurred in the early 1920s when Colonel Sykes, the Riding Master at Sandhurst, retired. Oatts commented that

29   The Metropolitan Police estimate "a trained officer on a trained horse can be as effective as a dozen foot officers" in situations such as demonstrations and riots; Directorate of Public Affairs, Metropolitan Police reference 205 86 (undated but approx. 2000). Peter Neyroud CBE QPM, The Institute of Criminology, University of Cambridge; personal correspondence [2013]; with the author. URL: <http://www.delhipolice.nic.in/home/mounted/mounted.aspx> accessed 13.02.2013.
30   Oatts, *I Serve – Regimental History of 3rd Carabiniers (Prince of Wales's Dragoon Guards)* pp.245/246.
31   Personal interview with ffrench Blake (2006); by the author.
32   Personal interview with Lucas (2007); by the author.
33   Richardson, *Riding,* pp.46–51.

the riding style seemed to change, to keep the horse "collected" at all times and to "never bring a horse home in a lather".[34]

Imperial policing went on in many areas of the British Empire; India, Egypt, Kurdistan, Iraq, and the North West Frontier in circumstances quite different from Ireland.[35] Such an example was in May 1919, in what was more a warlike situation than policing. The King's Dragoon Guards marched overnight at short notice to seize and hold wells on the Indian side of the Afghan border, illegally occupied by the Afghan Army. The Dragoons achieved their objective by setting up machine-gun positions, and mounted patrols. Combining with infantry and the RAF, and somewhat reminiscent of Allenby's tactics in Palestine, they drove the Afghan forces back down the pass. The force was counter-attacked; two squadrons of the regiment charged in order to give the infantry time to withdraw safely.[36] The "Third Afghan War" ended in August 1919, but agitation for Indian independence and troublesome tribesmen necessitated the continued deployment of large numbers of troops on the frontier.[37]

In Mesopotamia, between December 1919 and May 1921, the 7th Dragoon Guards, with elements of the 8th Hussars, were "chasing rebel bands in the desert between the Tigris and the Euphrates" as part of 5,000 British troops deployed to put down "this forgotten Arab rebellion".[38] The 8th Hussars had been engaged "to help in quelling grave disturbances in that country"; later they moved their horses, first by river barge, and then overland, to march "one hundred miles to Medali, near the Persian (Iran) border [to deal] with various native insurrections".[39]

Policing India and protecting the North West Frontier both against Afghan insurgents, and a possible Soviet Russian invasion, took a quarter of a million troops, sixty-thousand of whom were British troops. Units were drawn from both the Indian and British armies including five British cavalry regiments.

Queen's Bays were in action in Malabar in 1921–1922, and 15th/19th Hussars on the North West Frontier in 1930–1931. In Risalpur, India, the 5th/6th Dragoon Guards had to train for a mobile column to be prepared, "at a moment's notice to deal with a tribal raid"; this had to be practised.[40] In Palestine, 1936–1939, Royal Scots Greys, the 4th/7th Dragoon Guards and the 11th Hussars were engaged; by this time the 11th Hussars were "mounted" in armoured cars.[41] Mounted troops on horses were last deployed in England during the Liverpool Race Riots of August 1919; mounted

34   Oatts, *I Serve – Regimental History of 3rd Carabiniers (Prince of Wales's Dragoon Guards)*, p.245.
35   James, *Warrior Race – A History of The British at War*, p.576.
36   URL: <http://www.qdg.org.uk/pages/Afghanistan-1919–121.php>
37   Anglesey, A History of the British cavalry 1816–1919, Volume 8, p.307.
38   Brereton, *A History of the 4th/7th Royal Dragoon Guards and their predecessors 1685–1980*, p.346; Joslin Litherland, Simpkin, *British Battles and Medals*, pp.220, 238–240.
39   Strawson, Pierson, and Rhoderick-Jones, *Irish Hussar* p.95.
40   Evans, *The Story of The Fifth Royal Inniskilling Dragoon Guards*, p.173.
41   Joslin Litherland, Simpkin, *British Battles and Medals*, pp.220, 238–240.

police later took over this type of work.[42] For the 4th Hussars in India for nine years (1921–1930):

> Life was very pleasant… untroubled by anything more strenuous in the way of duty than the occasional quelling of Hindoo-Moslem riots… [sic] There were two long marches on change of station: two hundred and fifty miles from Muttra to Lucknow in February, 1924, made in twenty-six days, and three hundred miles from Lucknow to Meerut in twenty days in October, 1927.[43]

In 1927, in a memorandum to the Secretary of State for War, the Military members of the Army Council reminded him that since the end of the Great War, the British Army had already been involved with seven emergencies: "the Third Afghan War, the Rebellion in Mesopotamia, Chanak, Ireland, Egypt, China, and not least the General Strike".[44]

Part of the British Army's role during the early period between the wars was reminiscent in many ways to the role of the late Victorian British Army. It was not surprising, therefore, that the British Army reverted to the tried and tested so-called "Cardwell system" to garrison and police the Empire with a non-conscript army.[45] The Cardwell System was re-introduced to infantry battalions at the end of the Great War, but it did not apply directly to regular cavalry regiments (the Household Cavalry only served abroad during war-time), but in essence it appeared to have operated, as cavalry regiments were unofficially linked, such as the 15th Hussars and the 19th Hussars described below. Prior to 1932, the British cavalry was formed as a Corps of Dragoons, Corps of Lancers and Corps of Hussars. On enlistment, men agreed, and were obliged, to serve within their own corps. A Hussar enlisted as a "Hussar of The Line"; although he joined a particular Hussar regiment, he might be required to serve in any other of the Hussar regiments. The 15th Hussars were an example, engaged in Ireland in 1919, where "the Irish Republican Army was very active at the time". The 15th Hussars had to:

> … find armed guards, and pickets, escorts and patrols, and there was hardly a man in the Regiment at the time who knew how to ride, or use his arms…

42   Anglesey, A History of the British cavalry 1816–1919, Volume 8, p.311–322.
43   Scott Daniell, *4th Hussar*, p.28.
44   TNA WO 32/2846 Army Organisation: Cavalry (Code 14(D)): Reduction of expenditure on Cavalry 1927; *Memorandum on the Reorganization of The Cavalry* (Secret), 30 June 1927.
45   Spiers discusses the Cardwell System in Chandler, David (Ed) [1994], *The Oxford Illustrated History Of The British Army* pp.189–193; also Cornish, in Holmes, Richard [2003], *The Oxford Companion to Military History* pp.175 & 176; also, in respect of the cavalry, Anglesey, *A History of the British Cavalry 1816–1919*, Volume 3: *1872–1898*, pp.30–39.

As soon as men became slightly trained they had to be despatched to the 19th Hussars in India, where men were wanted as badly as in Ireland.[46]

The author's father was one of these men who served in five different Hussar regiments between 1919 and 1926 (the 13th – enlistment and training, the 15th – The Rhine and Ireland, the 19th and the 4th – India, and the 8th – home and demobilization), although most of his service was in only two of these regiments and the majority in just one, the 4th (Queen's Own) Hussars.[47] In 1924, the rank of "Private" was changed to the rank of "Trooper"[48] and from 1932, the separate Corps was abolished and a single Corps formed, known as "Cavalry of the Line".[49] From then on a cavalryman of any rank was required to serve in any cavalry regiment anywhere in the world.

46 Carnock, *The History of the 15th The King's Hussars 1914–1922*, p.217.
47 Army form B.200 (Trial) Statement of the Services of No. 537071 Salmon. W; (Army Personnel Centre, Glasgow).
48 Army Order 222/1923; Army form B.200 (Trial) Statement of the Services of No. 537071 Salmon. W; (Army Personnel Centre, Glasgow); Oats, *I Serve – Regimental History of 3rd Carabiniers (Prince of Wales's Dragoon Guards)*, p.244.
49 TNA WO/32 3059 Army Organisation: Cavalry (Code 14(D)): Reconstruction of the Corps of Cavalry Brereton , *A History of the 4th/7th Royal Dragoon Guards and their predecessors 1685–1980*, p.354.

2

The Backdrop to Military Policy Decisions 1918–1929

Zara Steiner's assertion in *The Lights That Failed* was that "the 1920s should be treated as a decade that followed an earlier war … rather than, as was common, the precursor of the war that followed".[1] This being so, it might be considered reasonable, that with no direct military threat to Great Britain, which is reasonable enough in itself, the government gave a low priority to defence spending generally and the army in particular during the 1920s. Were there, however, other influences on their policy decisions? A policy of arms reduction, the perception of public opinion, particularly the absence of an identifiable aggressor, and economics (mechanization was considered unaffordable),[2] are central to understanding why cavalry mechanization took so long. These factors affected both the process and the delay in re-equipping horsed cavalry regiments with AFVs. Conversely, however, it was economic pressure that drove the decision to mechanize the first two horsed cavalry regiments in the latter part of the 1920s, but perversely stopped any further cavalry mechanization for another eight years.[3]

Economic management at any level is the application of choice, because there is never enough money to satisfy all needs. Government funds were limited, choices had to be made and therefore economic policy decisions were based on a priority assessment. Re-equipping the army in general and horsed cavalry in particular was considered neither a priority nor politically acceptable, except at times by the Treasury if large savings could be made by doing so.[4] It is too counterfactual to question whether,

---

1   Steiner, *The Lights That Failed*, Preface v.
2   TNA WO 32/2846 Register 16/General/5558 minute 14 – Milne to Sir Laming Worthington-Evans 3 November 1927.
3   TNA WO 32/2842 Army Organisation: Cavalry (Code 14(D)): Cavalry – Report by the "Salisbury Committee"; TNA WO 32/2845 Army Organisation: Cavalry (Code 14(D)):Future organisation of the Cavalry: Cavalry Committee: Final report 1926–1927; 20/Cavalry/612 7(a), 6 June 1928; Sub-committee of Imperial Defence 1927–1928.
4   TNA WO 32/2842 Army Organisation: Cavalry (Code 14(D)): Cavalry Committee: Final report 1926–1927; 20/Cavalry/612 no.6, 17 November 1927; also TNA WO

had favourable economic conditions prevailed, the government would have mechanized the cavalry sooner, but to have done so the government would have had to ignore the foregoing factors, especially that of public opinion.

The post Great War economic pressures, priorities and politics.

Successive British Governments reduced military spending during the 1920s; this suited both the need to reduce government expenditure overall or to divert it to social projects that reflected the needs and views of the majority of the electorate. In Great Britain between the two world wars, as the later Britain by Mass Observation (BMO) survey indicated, economic decisions had far more impact on voters' views than did the decisions on defence expenditure. Donald Winch stressed the importance of economic factors in defining the policy environment for both voters and governments after 1918; "it was one of the most confused, frustrating, and unsuccessful periods in the history of economic policy-making in Britain".[5] "The war had wrecked international finance and trade,"[6] but post 1918 reconstruction and pent-up demand drove an "economic boom… factories were deluged with orders".[7] Around April 1920 this "boom" collapsed.[8] It was sudden and had the potential to do more economic damage to Great Britain than had the Great War itself.

The total cost of the Great War to Great Britain was £2,579,000,000, and in the last three years of the war accounted for almost 60 percent of government expenditure. Professor Robert Self had calculated from Treasury records that Britain's Great War debt totalled £7,500,000,000.[9] In addition to this debt, argued Self, was the loss of the revenue earning potential of 723,000 war dead,[10] and the loss of over 7,000,000 gross tonnage of shipping. The influenza pandemic of 1918–1919 further increased the loss of talent and productive labour from industry and commerce.[11] Added to this were the costs of looking after, and the inevitable loss of the revenue earning capability, of 1,600,000 wounded service personnel.[12] Churchill, as the Secretary of State for War, presenting his Estimates in February 1920, set aside £300,000 to bury the war

32/2845 Army Organisation: Cavalry (Code 14(D)): Future organisation of the Cavalry: Sub-committee of Imperial Defence 1927–1928; 20/Cav/612 minute 19, 8 June 1928.

5   Winch, *Economics and Policy*, p.73.

6   Steiner, *The Lights That Failed*, p.182.

7   Lewis, *Economic Survey*, p.18; see also Howson, *Domestic Money Management In Britain*, pp.9–30.

8   Middlemass,(ed.), *Thomas Jones – Whitehall Dairies Volume I*, p.96.

9   Self, *Britain, America and the War Debt Controversy*.

10   Wasserstein, *Barbarism and Civilization*, p.128 cites this figure from "more recent research"; Stevenson, *Cataclysm*, p.442.

11   Wasserstein, *Barbarism and Civilization*, p.128.

12   Self, R., "The Perception and Posture in Anglo-American Relations: The War Debt Controversy in the 'Official Mind' 1919–1940", [2007], *The International History Review XXIX (No.2)*: 237– 472, p.287.

dead, provide for the wounded and pay for war medals. £20,000,000 was estimated for the repatriation of soldiers, shipping costs, payments to French and Belgian railways and refurbishing civilian buildings occupied by the military during the war.[13] The Ministry of Pensions report of October 1922, stated that there were 3,000,000 people receiving benefit that included 900,000 disabled ex-servicemen[14] of which 240,000 were major amputees, 60,000 had shell shock and 10,000 were blinded.[15] Seven to eight percent of the national budget was allocated to war pensions.[16] During the Great War, in order to help cover its needs, the Treasury had sold-off large quantities of overseas assets and investments which later weakened the inter-war balance of payments because of the reduced dividends; Wasserstein has suggested that this dividend income from overseas, on which the Treasury "had previously relied on heavily reduced by 15 percent".[17]

January 1 1920 the *Daily Mail* reported the close of year Stock Market as "very cheerful" and the continuance of "boom-like" conditions among Textile shares "was most noteworthy".[18] Part of the cause of the "boom" and later "bust was due to the government, in 1920, lifting the economic controls it had imposed during The Great War on shipbuilding, railways, munitions and food. "Hoards of War surplus" and the factories that had produced war materials were sold off.[19] This helped to satisfy the accumulated demand that had built up between 1914 and 1918. Steiner's analysis concluded: "The removal of wartime controls fuelled the inflationary spiral; the pound, off [the] gold [standard] and no longer pegged to the dollar, began to fall below its pre-war dollar-exchange rate".[20] By the end of 1919 the pound sterling had devalued from $4.67 to $3.81.[21] Deflationary policies were adopted; the objective was to return to the pre-war Gold Standard, which eventually happened on 28 April 1925.[22] In April 1920 the Bank rate was raised to 7 percent in an attempt to control the boom, the first time this technique had been used.[23] The economy then collapsed; this brought with it rapidly falling prices and rising unemployment.[24] "With the slump, men were standing idle in millions, industrial unrest was high, and the future was

13   *The Times*, 24.02.1920, p.9.
14   *The Times*, 31.10.1922, p.9; Wasserstein, *Barbarism and Civilization*, p.128.
15   Stevenson, *Cataclysm*, p.448.
16   Wasserstein, *Barbarism and Civilization*, p.128.
17   Ibid., p.129.
18   *Daily Mail*, 01.01.1920, Stock Market Report.
19   Mowat, *Britain between the Wars*. p.29, some controls did continue until 1921.
20   Steiner, *The Lights That Failed*, p.186.
21   Wasserstein, *Barbarism and Civilization*, p.129; see Howson, *Domestic Money Management In Britain*, re the government "unpegged" sterling from the gold standard, April 1919, p.11.
22   Wasserstein, *Barbarism and Civilization*, p.133.
23   Howson, *Domestic Money Management In Britain*, pp.9 and 22.
24   Mowat, *Britain between the Wars*, p.26.

black and uncertain".[25] Unemployment during the ensuing decade never fell below ten percent.[26] (See Table 2 for the fall in GNP from 1919 until a modest rise in 1922; also the increase in unemployment from 3.9 to 16.9 percent, over 2,000,000 people).

The "Great War debt" added to Great Britain's economic problems and dominated the international scene too both economically and politically. Great Britain's war debts "mainly to the United States were immense".[27] Self-argued that the war debt "was one of the most complex and controversial problems blighting international relations [with its complicated] web of financial obligations".[28] The British Government, concerned about post war reconstruction, sought a mutual writing-off of these debts. The United States did not agree.[29] Government expenditure was therefore further inflated by these war debt repayments. The prevailing economic orthodoxy was one of a "balanced budget".[30] "Peacetime government expenditure should not exceed revenue,"[31] was the product of what is sometimes referred to as "Gladstonian Liberalism, low taxation and limited government expenditure that continued until the late 1930s when the security considerations forced a change.[32]

Faced with these ever-increasing economic challenges, on 16 August 1921, the Liberal Prime Minister, David Lloyd George, set up a high-powered committee of businessmen, The Committee of National Expenditure, under the chairmanship of Sir Eric Geddes. The committee was tasked to find cuts in public expenditure of £100,000,000 pounds *in addition* to the £75,000,000 of cuts *already* planned by the Treasury. In its subsequent report the committee actually proposed a reduction in expenditure of £87,000,000. Between 1921 and 1925 around 23 percent was reduced from government spending.[33] These cuts in expenditure, referred to later as "the Geddes Axe", "hit the army the hardest of all the services".[34] Liddell Hart called these cuts "reckless";[35] they resulted in the sixteen most junior cavalry regiments, by date of formation, eventually amalgamating to eight (described in Chapter Three). Some Members of Parliament, it was reported, mounted a stout defence for the cavalry's

25   Lewis, *Economic Survey*, p.19.
26   Hobsbawm, *The Age of Extremes*, p.89; some statistics cite 9.7 percent as the lowest – see Table 2.
27   Wasserstein, *Barbarism and Civilization*, pp.129/130.
28   Self, The Perception and Posture in Anglo-American Relations, p284; Kennedy, *The Rise and Fall of The Great Powers*, p.358.
29   Wasserstein, *Barbarism and Civilization*, p.131.
30   . Steiner, *The Lights That Failed*, p.187; Overy, *The Morbid Age*, p.57.
31   Peden, *British Rearmament and the Treasury*, p.62.
32   URL: <http://www.politics.guardian.co.uk> accessed 26.06.2011; Templewood, *Nine Troubled Years*, p.19. Personal discussions with Professor Self 2009/10 by the author.
33   Hood, Emmerson and Dixon, *Public Spending in Hard Times;* Wasserstein, *Barbarism and Civilization*, p.130; Aldcroft, *The British Economy Volume1*, pp.25/26; Middlemass, (ed.), *Thomas Jones – Whitehall Diaries Volume I*, p.124.
34   Anglesey, *A History of the British Cavalry, Volume 8*, p.312.
35   Liddell Hart, *Memoirs Volume I*, p.50.

retention and so did Field Marshal Douglas The Baron Haig of Bemersyde, although *The Times'* opinion was the government's mind seemed quite made up from the start.[36] Haig, who spoke in Canterbury in October 1921, stressed that horsed cavalry was not a "dead-arm".[37] He supported his argument with examples from the Great War and in so doing was later condemned by some historians as a horse-loving technophobe. Liddell Hart in 1965 unfairly cites Haig's speech as a "foreshadow" of the resistance to come to mechanization.[38] Haig was reported to have said that the time had not yet come when cavalry was indispensable:

> [I am] certainly not among those who hold that the place of flesh and blood of man and horse could ever be wholly taken by petrol and machinery... cavalry was still and essential arm, even in a European war, and more especially to an Imperial Army such as ours.[39]

At that time Haig was correct; the vehicles available in 1921 could not have wholly replaced the role required of horsed cavalry.

Table 1 UK Government Spending per Fiscal Year (£ millions)[40]

	1920	1925	1930
Health care	25	38	46
Education	110	135	154
Defence	694	120	119
Welfare	156	208	251
Protection	34	33	37
Transport	75	128	161
General Govt.	19	18	12
Other Spending	620	275	278
Interest	375	383	413
Balance	-123	-122	-114
Total Spending	1,985	1,225	1,356
Public Net Debt	+7,810	+7,585	+7,457

36   *The Times*, 03.09.1921.
37   See Appendix C – biographies.
38   Liddell Hart, *Memoirs Volume I*, p.100.
39   *The Times*, 11.10.1921.
40   URL: <http://www.ukpublicspending.co.uk/spending_brief.php> accessed 25.05.2011.

Later, in 1922, David Lloyd George's coalition government began to come apart.[41] Public opinion polls were not used until the 1930s so it is impossible to accurately assess the mood of the voters in earlier elections, but in 1922 there were difficulties within the coalition, the country and in Ireland, and a period of relative political instability ensued. The General Election of 15 November 1922 returned a Conservative government and another election just a year later, on 6 December 1923, returned the minority Labour Government of James Ramsey MacDonald. The Labour Government saw "solving the European problem" as the objective; to reverse the decline in trade with Germany, Austria and Russia was considered the key to stimulating exports and reducing unemployment.[42] MacDonald was believed to have influenced the political framework that enabled the Versailles Treaty (1919) to be amended by the so-called "Dawes plan" in July 1924. This led eventually to "a massive infusion of American capital into Europe,"[43] a reduction in tension, particularly between Germany and France, and an "outbreak in common sense" resulting in a number of treaties, notably the Locarno Treaty in 1925.[44]

The Labour Government only held office for eight months. A Conservative Government, under Stanley Baldwin with Winston Churchill as Chancellor of the Exchequer, was formed on 6 November 1924 and served until June 1929.[45] Economic orthodox thinking prevailed and influenced the decision for Great Britain to return to the Gold Standard at the pre-Great War rate of $4.86 to the £ sterling on 28 April 1925.[46] The economist John Maynard Keynes opposed the decision and Churchill later admitted "that the decision was the biggest blunder of his life… [Churchill however] was hardly in a position to withstand the overwhelming official backing for a return to gold at pre-war parity".[47] The return to the gold standard seriously over-valued sterling and over-priced British export goods. This hampered any fragile recovery in the export industries already burdened by excessive borrowing during the earlier, brief, post-war boom.[48] The gold standard was not again suspended until 1931.[49]

41   Middlemass, (ed.), *Thomas Jones – Whitehall Dairies Volume I*, pp.188–217; Thorpe, *A History of The Labour Party – Second Edition*, p.47.
42   Hinton, *Protests and Visions*, p.77.
43   Steiner, *The Lights That Failed*, pp.244–250; Overy, *The Morbid Age*, p.xxi.
44   Kennedy, *The Rise and Fall of The Great Powers*, p.358.
45   Graves & Hodge, *The Long Weekend*, pp.157/8.
46   Wasserstein, *Barbarism and Civilization*, p.133.
47   Steiner, *The Lights That Failed*, pp.439 & 187, "there was no mention of any alternative"; see Howson, *Domestic Money Management In Britain*, p.13, re the Cunliffe Commission "took for granted [the]eventual return to gold at pre-war parand"; p.14, a similar view was held by the Bank of England; also Winch, *Economics and Policy*, pp.82/83.
48   Aldcroft, *The British Economy Volume 1*, p.4; Wasserstein, *Barbarism and Civilization*, p.133; Kennedy, *The Rise and Fall of The Great Powers*, p.363; Graves & Hodge, *The Long Weekend*, p.158.
49   Peden, *British Rearmament and the Treasury*, p.62.

British trade failed to return to the pre-1914 levels... major industries (cotton, shipbuilding, coal, iron and steel) suffered heavily in the 1920s... resulting in long term unemployment in particular regions of the country.[50]

New industries, however, such as the electrical, distributive and retail, began to grow.[51] The following Table 2 shows an economic summary of the decade.

Table 2 UK economic summary 1918–1929

Year	Unemployment Total Number Registered Unemployment (000; Average for 12 Months) %[1]	Imports £m[2]	Direct Exports £m[3]	Re-Exports £m[4]	Balance of Payments £m –/+ (imports less exports)	GNP[5] £m
1918	0.8					
1919	n/a					4652
1920	691 3.9	1,933	1,334	223	-376	4346
1921	2038 16.9	1,086	703	107	-276	3953
1922	1543 14.3	1,003	720	104	-179	4094
1923	1275 11.7	1,096	767	119	-210	4236
1924	1130 10.3	1,277	801	140	-286	4367
1925	1226 11.3	1,321	773	154	-394	4602
1926	1385 12.5	1,241	653	125	-463	4413
1927	1088 9.7	1,218	709	123	-386	4719
1928	1217 10.8	1,916	724	120	-1072	4795
1929	1216 10.4	1,221	729	110	-382	4910

Notes
1   Cook and Stevenson, *The Longman Handbook of Modern British History*, p.270; 1920 and 1921; Laybourn, *Britain on the Breadline*, p.9.
2   Steiner, *The Lights That Failed*, from Appendix A, Table A-5a.
3   Ibid.
4   Ibid.
5   Houston, *Domestic Monetary Management in Britain*, p.157.

Unemployment remained over 1,000,000 throughout the 1920s, and apart from 1927, over 10 percent of the workforce. The early boom and then the slump can be seen from the import and export figures with the short period of boom around 1928 drawing in imports, but increasing the balance of payments deficit. The key figure of Gross National Product (GNP) demonstrates the slump, but then a sustained growth, with the exception of 1926 – the year of the General Strike – until the end of the decade.

50   Overy, *The Morbid Age*, p.xxi.
51   Briggs, *A Social History of England*, p.276.

World peace would prevail

The question of mechanizing the army was marginal in the minds of both the public and politicians during the 1920s. In any case, why should such a measure have even been contemplated? After 1918, Germany and the Central Powers were defeated and Russia was weakened by revolution. The expectation of the British public was that world peace would prevail.[52] Prime Minister Lloyd George's argument was that, "in the present circumstances (1919–1920) the Government could take some risks in defence, but *none* in social and economic affairs".[53]

On 15 August 1919 the Government undertook what now would be regarded as a "risk assessment" the so-called Ten Year Rule. The conclusion was that Britain was unlikely to take part in a major war for the next ten years. The flaw, in what became a policy rather than an on-going risk assessment, was that it continued for too long and was not abandoned until 1932,[54] but it dominated defence expenditure planning for much of the period. Brian Bond and N H Gibbs argued the effect of the Ten Year Rule, and the dominance of the Treasury in defence expenditure, an influence that continued into the next decade.[55] Later scholars, that included John Ferris, concluded that the Treasury and the Ten Year Rule, a term not coined until after 1932, had little impact on the armed services until after 1924, but did so afterwards.[56] Coombs pointed out that The Army Estimates came under Treasury control from 1922 and the other two services from 1928.[57] Relevant to cavalry mechanization, as will become apparent, was the closure of the tank design centre in Woolwich in 1923 that impacted later on tank development and production.[58]

Domestic Policy – The influence of Public Opinion and of a wider enfranchisement.

Of great concern to the British Government in the immediate post-war period was the prospect of civil unrest in which troops would be needed to aid the civil powers. A Bolshevik administration was taking control in Russia and in Great Britain

---

52   See later reference to *Britain by Mass Observation* – this majority view prevails almost until the outbreak of The Second World War.
53   Quoted in Gibbs, *History of the Second World War Volume 1*, p.5.
54   Bond, *British Military Policy between the Two World Wars*, p.25; Gibbs, *History of the Second World War Volume 1,* Chapter III, pp.69–87.
55   Bond, *British Military Policy between the Two World Wars*, p.39; see also Peden, *British Rearmament and the Treasury.*
56   Ferris, "Treasury Control, the Ten Year Rule and British Service Policies, 1919–1924" *The Historical Journal* Vol.30, No. 4, December 1987, pp.859–883; Ferris, *Men Money and Diplomacy* chap 2; Bell, "Winston Churchill and the Ten Year Rule" *The Journal of Military History* Vol.74, No. 4 October 2010, pp.1097–1128.
57   Coombs, *British Tank Production*, p.9.
58   Macksey, *A History of The Royal Armoured Corps,* p.47.

the government was aware of both the grievances of working-class people and of their expectations of a "big and rapid improvement in their social and industrial conditions".[59] A clear demonstration of the government's concern was the Emergency Powers Act (1920), invoked by the government in 1921 and 1926, when "the military authorities were told to be prepared to meet an outbreak of civil war".[60] George Orwell wrote in 1937 that:

> Throughout the whole nation there was a running wave of revolutionary feeling … By 1918 everyone under forty was in a bad temper with his elders, and the mood of anti-militarism that followed naturally upon the fighting was extended to a general revolt against orthodoxy and authority.[61]

During 1919 major strikes were threatened that were intended to paralyse the transport network, especially in London, and to cut off the electricity supply.[62] The miners insisted the Military Service Act (1916), which brought in conscription, should be repealed and threatened industrial action if it was not.[63] By January 1920 "the industrial situation" had put Field Marshal Sir Henry H Wilson, Chief of the Imperial General Staff (CIGS) "in a state of dreadful nerves on the subject"; there was talk of "Red revolution and blood and war at home and abroad".[64] At a conference on 2 February 1920 the country's so called "defenceless condition" was discussed; this issue had been previously voiced by Winston Churchill (Secretary of State for War), and the CIGS. The prospect of revolution was taken very seriously and the police force was considered inadequate to deal with large industrial strikes or sabotage.[65] Concerns extended for some time; on 4 April 1921 the Cabinet, at which the CIGS was present, discussed the so-called "Triple Alliance" of the miners', railway and dockworkers' trades unions and a possible forthcoming strike. It was suggested that more armed forces were needed. Consideration was given to repatriating troops from Malta or Silesia and whether Yeomanry troops should be used.[66] On 8 April a draft Royal Proclamation to call-up army reserves was discussed.[67] Thomas Jones, the assistant to the Cabinet Secretary Maurice Hankey, noted with what seriousness the government considered both the strength of public opinion and possible actions.[68] Had mass civil

59   Middlemass, (ed.), *Thomas Jones – Whitehall Dairies Volume I*, pp.73–74; Thomas Jones to the Prime Minister, 8 February 1919.
60   Liddell Hart, *Memoirs Volume I*, p.58.
61   Orwell, *The Road to Wigan Pier*, p.121.
62   Middlemass, (ed.) [1969], *Thomas Jones – Whitehall Dairies Volume I*; Sir Maurice Hankey to Thomas Jones 10 February 1919, p.75.
63   Ibid.,Thomas Jones of Sir Maurice Hankey, 26 March 1919, pp.81–82.
64   Ibid.,Sir Maurice Hankey to Thomas Jones, 17 January 1920, pp.97–98.
65   Ibid.,From Thomas Jones notes, 2 February 1920, pp.99–104.
66   Ibid.,From Thomas Jones notes,4 April 1921, pp.132–136.
67   Ibid., From Thomas Jones notes, 8 April 1921, p.144.
68   Ibid., pp.144–152.

unrest occurred, horse mounted cavalry would have been invaluable in assisting the police in trying to restore order. There was no revolution.

The majority of Great Britain's electorate, which now included enfranchised women of qualifying status, was clearly more concerned about the basic necessities for life than international relations and policing the Empire, and the politicians responded accordingly.[69] The Representation of the People Act, 6 February 1918, ensured, as Asa Briggs expressed, a "genuinely democratic franchise,"[70] but not quite at that time; only those women of thirty years and over who were householders and those who were wives of householders, occupiers of property with an annual rent of £5, or graduates of British universities were allowed to vote.[71] It was not until May 1928 that the voting age for women at 21 was aligned with men that the "genuinely democratic franchise" was secured. Briggs also wrote the women's vote "did not transform politics,"[72] but this too must be challenged; 6,000,000 women became eligible to vote and did make a difference to the thoughts and policies of the government.[73] Paula Bartley has argued that enfranchised women looked to "revolutionise government thinking". Bartley also pointed out in 1998 that, during the first ten years of women's enfranchisement, twenty-one pieces of legislation concerning women passed through the House of Commons, unprecedented before or since.[74] Women's influence in society stepped forward in another way too in 1919, with the passing of the Sex Disqualification Act. This Act opened the way for women to participate fully in professions such as the law and accountancy, including a British woman League of Nations delegate.[75]

The Great War dead were overwhelmingly men; the significant proportion of the bereaved was women, all of whom *eventually* became eligible to vote after 1928. These women shared the common emotion of grief. Clearly politicians did not ignore the new voting power of women. What cannot be argued with certainty, however, is that the majority of women, who were united by grief, were antimilitarists or supported pacifist or pacificist[76] ideas and demanded a reduction, or elimination of armaments.

69 Gibbs, *History of the Second World War Volume 1*, p.81. Gibbs devotes Chapter II to "The Operation of The Ten Year Rule", p.35.
70 Briggs, *A Social History of England*, p.263.
71 "Votes for WomenURL: <http://www.spartacus> accessed 18.08.2008; soldiers and sailors over 19 years of age were also placed on the Electoral Register.
72 Briggs, *A Social History of England*, p.263.
73 Lynch, *Beyond Appeasement*, p.98; "Votes for WomenURL: <http://www.spartacus> accessed 18.08.2008; The Equal Franchise Act, July 1929, 4,750,000 women became eligible to vote.
74 Bartley, *Votes for Women*, p.104.
75 Bartley, *Votes for Women*, pp.106/107.
76 Ceadel analysed those actually involved in the peace movement, not just those that "merely prefer peace to war". The popular peace movement embraced the pacifists, those who believed that war is always wrong whatever the circumstances, and the pacificists, those who accepted that war is sometimes necessary although an irrational and inhumane way to

Sharing a common emotion of bereavement, however, it is reasonable for the historian to consider the question, if not, why not? It is equally reasonable to contemplate that this is what politicians concluded, reliant as they were on a proportion of the women's votes to gain or maintain their election. Following the extension of the franchise in 1928, "women's groups soon played up their new found political power"; eighteen women's groups formed the British Peace Crusade claiming to represent 2,000,000 women. They made a deputation to the government.[77] It was "Women's groups [that] took the lead in articulating the views of peace movements on disarmament".[78] In order to remain in power any government would have been unwise to have ignored the new lobbying and voting power of women, many of whom did take an anti-war stance in whatever guise or expression best suited them.

Foreign Policy, The League of Nations and the growth of pacifism

Rebuilding international trade was essential; the maintenance of international peace was therefore the prevailing objective of Great Britain, and many other countries too. The League of Nations, its drive for "collective security disarmament and non-military solutions to inter-national disputes, was fully supported.[79] James Hinton's view was that, for a time, British foreign policy was, in part, subordinate to the League of Nations' policy, and that with a "small army and vast Empire... support for the League was the cheapest way of maintaining the Empire".[80] The Versailles (1919) and Locarno (1925) Treaties, overseen by the League, were just part of the web of inter-national undertakings that bound countries together in non-aggression, mutual defence pacts that ensured the sanctity of national boundaries.

Widespread faith in the League of Nations, its collective security and its pacificist views were not misplaced. Now almost ridiculed, the League of Nations was not a disaster, although it was eventually a disappointment. Cecelia Lynch questioned if the League of Nations "failed so miserably" why did states "bother to create a new global organisation in the form of the United Nations".[81] Much of the idea and structure for the League of Nations originated from British Liberal and socialist thinkers.[82] It was axiomatic therefore, that the British Government would give its full support and

---

solve disputes. Both saw the prevention of war as the political priority. Both doctrines were called "pacifism" although "pacificism" was the most popular.

77 Women's Peace Crusade Deputation, 6 February 1930 – Cab 21/341, cited in Lynch, *Beyond Appeasement*, p.98.
78 Lynch, *Beyond Appeasement*, p.97.
79 See Appendix E – US President Wilson's proposal generally supported by the British Government.
80 Hinton, *Protests and Visions*, p.77.
81 Ibid., p.8.
82 Wasserstein, *Barbarism and Civilization*, p.125.

although it was criticised as Euro-centric,[83] twenty-four countries became founder members of the League of Nations as well. The driving force was passion; the belief that the pressure of "public opinion could restrain Governments from going to war".[84] David Stevenson has written that the British Government needed the League of Nations to satisfy a "public clamour" for such an organisation. This was not surprising; 3,000,000 British people were mourning the loss of a close relative due to the Great War; the public feeling was "never again views much supported by the press and the main political parties.[85]

The League of Nations was supported by the League of Nations Union (LNU) formed in the United Kingdom in 1918, "The heart of the new pacifist establishment".[86] There had been a League of Nations Society from 1915 that merged with the LNU in 1918. By 1926 half the Members of the House of Commons were members of the LNU. Robert Cecil, a dominant member of the LNU, was also a member of Baldwin's Government.[87] The LNU's objective, until 1936, was general disarmament made possible by creating the right conditions for international security. A Royal Charter was granted to the LNU in 1925, when the membership was 950,000, (but not all "paid-up" subscriptions). Ceadel has compared this with the influential Committee for Nuclear Disarmament (CND) that had, in 1986, only 110,000 members.[88]

The League of Nations produced; an "optimistic structure" for settling disputes peacefully, administering the former enemy colonies, and a faith that the application of economic sanctions would bring into line transgressor states.[89] It was the communications hub for monitoring the Versailles Treaty. Article One of the League's inaugurating Covenant reaffirmed national boundaries and the demilitarised zone of the Rhineland detailed in the Versailles Treaty. Under its auspices the Geneva Protocol of 1924, supported by a network of other treaties, sought to "outlaw aggressive war" replaced by compulsory arbitration.[90]

The political left, including the trade union movement, supported the League of Nations and advanced anti-war, pro-disarmament views. Most British troops had, by October 1919, been withdrawn from a disastrous intervention in the Russian civil war, although elements of British forces remained until 1920.[91] An early indication to the government of the strength of public opinion came in August 1920, with a

---

83   Kennedy, *The Rise and Fall of The Great Powers*, p.357.
84   Stevenson, *Cataclysm*, p.418.
85   Ibid., pp.418/419 and p.443.
86   Ceadel, *Pacifism in Britain*, p.75.
87   See Appendix C – biographies.
88   Hinton, *Pacifism in Britain*, p.80; Overy, *The Morbid Age*, puts the LNU membership at over 1,000,000 and 388,255 "paid-up" in 1933; a considerable number of people, p.229.
89   Marks, *The Illusion of Peace*, p.25.
90   Gibbs, *History of the Second World War Volume 1*, pp.39–42.
91   See, for a discussion of this débâcle – Hudson, *Intervention in Russia* and Knightley, *The First Casualty*, pp.163–184.

possibility of more British military intervention, this time to assist Polish forces confronting the Soviet Army's move into Poland. This "triggered a massive upsurge of anti-war sentiment… it seemed that a new wave of revolutionary-pacifism might erupt".[92] London Dockers refused to load the *Jolly George* ship with munitions bound for Poland. The Trades Union Congress (TUC), representing a total membership of 8,000,000,[93] and the Labour Party, asserted that industrial workers would be organized to resist the war. A strike call went out and action committees were formed throughout the country waiting for events to unfold.[94] A "Hands off Russia" committee was formed by the far left, but was also supported by the Quakers and the Union of Democratic Control (UDC).[95] The UDC was funded partly from Quaker business interests as a peace pressure group; its membership later totalled 300,000 people.[96] An estimated 6000 people demonstrated in London against military intervention in Poland. The Home Office considered this an *anti-war* demonstration rather than *pro-Soviet support*; a view shared, perhaps surprisingly, by British communists.[97]

The key issue here was the people's *belief* that the government would intervene militarily between the Soviets and Poland and it was this that led on to a government acknowledgement of the strength of the anti-war feeling amongst a significant proportion of the population.

Cavalry and tanks – argument and attitude

The first Labour Government (1924) was almost a pacifist government. It included thirteen members of the UDC,[98] nine of whom were in the cabinet. The Chancellor of the Exchequer, Philip Snowden, was one; [99] he had been a hard-line pacifist during the Great War.[100] The Prime Minister, James Ramsay MacDonald, was among the UDC's founding committee members.[101] It was clear that, if not for economic and security reasons, then certainly for ideological ones, investment in military development was well down on a list of priorities. Lord Thomson, Minister for Air in the MacDonald Government:

---

92 Hinton, *Pacifism in Britain*, p.79.
93 Middlemass,(ed.)*Thomas Jones – Whitehall Dairies Volume I*, p.96; URL: <http://www.hull.ac.uk/arc/downloads/DDCcatalogue.pdf> *Records of The Union of Democratic Control (1914–1966)* Hull University Archives – DDC; accessed 20.06.2012.
94 Hinton, *Pacifism in Britain*, p.79.
95 Ibid., p.82.
96 Diary entry, 19 January 1920; Middlemass, (ed.) *Thomas Jones – Whitehall Dairies Volume I*, p.263.
97 Hinton, *Pacifism in Britain*, pp.82/83.
98 URL: <http://www.hull.ac.uk/arc/downloads/DDCcatalogue.pdf> *Records of the Union of Democratic Control (1914–1966)* Hull University Archives – DDC; accessed 20.06.2012.
99 See Appendix C – biographies.
100 Hinton, *Pacifism in Britain*, p.79.
101 See Appendix C – biographies.

… [had shown] a keen appreciation of the possibilities [of mechanization] but in pressing the proposal he had to contend with the reluctance of some of his chief colleagues in the cabinet to take decisions that might sound discordant with their pacific principles and look like a measure of rearmament. The substitution of tanks for horses would have such an appearance, even though most conservative soldiers might not think so.[102]

Such was the strength of opinion that tanks were offensive weapons that, within the Versailles Treaty, the French insisted Germany was to have no tanks or other "aggressive" weapons within their limited armed forces.[103] As no war was foreseen for the next ten years, and with the growing "never again" mentality among the people, it is doubtful whether the electorate gave much thought to the subject of tanks and mechanization, other than the few people immediately affected, such as the Tank Corps[104] and the armaments manufacturers. Tanks did their job in the unique circumstances of the Western Front, but, it was thought, were unlikely ever to be needed again. In 1921, however, there was little doubt in the minds of the Army Council that horsed cavalry would be mechanized; the General Staff "hoped" horsed cavalrymen would transfer to an expanded Tank Corps that was thought must happen "in the near future".[105] The only questions that needed answers were when and into what mode of organization and vehicles were the cavalry to be moved.

Tank development was reported from time to time in 1920s newspapers, but not on the front pages. Not long before that the public had been wooed by some dramatic reports of the derring-do of Allied tanks and their crews in the "all-arms" actions of the later stages of the Great War. On 1 July 1918, *The Times* reported the success of French light tanks on the north side of Villers Cotterets successfully attacking German positions. The five-and-a-half ton tanks were "handy enough to work over steep and difficult ground".[106] Readers were excited again a few days later by the headline "Infantry, airman and tanks together" to capture Hamel and Vaire Wood. Through the smoke and uproar created by aerial bombing and artillery rolled the tanks, it reported. The tanks, it later contended, "contributed largely" to the victory. There were areas of ground, however, that made the use of tanks impossible and infantry had to be relied upon with "bomb and bayonet".[107]

102   Liddell Hart, *Memoirs Volume I*, p.175.
103   Richardson, *The Evolution of British Disarmament Policy*, p.4.
104   The Tank Corps was formed on 27 July 1917 and had developed (from March 1916) from the Heavy Section, later (November 1916) the Heavy Branch, Machine Gun Corps. The "Royal" prefix was added from 18 October 1923.
105   TNA WO 32/5959 Army Organisation: Cavalry (Code 14(D)): Scheme for reduction of Cavalry Regiments – hand written note p.3, 24 February 1921.
106   *The Times*, "The success of Light Tanks.8.
107   *The Times*, 04.07.1918, p.6.

The cavalry had its own share of press adulation too: "since the period of open warfare [began]the attack fell on the enemy like a flash of lightning,"[108] read *The Times* in a report on the actions of infantry with cavalry and tanks between the Aisne and Marne Rivers.

> The cavalry came into their own… fighting on horseback for about the first time since the very early days of the war… debouching from the forest and seen by airmen at 2 p.m. … far beyond our original front.[109]

A report of another action south east of Marcelcave on 12 August 1918 regarding horsed cavalry may later have influenced the tactical arguments in the minds of the public, military intellectuals, and theorists, and especially the government. It informed its readers that the cavalry was held up by German machine-guns. Light tanks made an attack and the machine-gunners ran with the cavalry charging in pursuit "swords drawn, between them taking seven hundred prisoners".[110] Further reports followed, and although far from disparaging the cavalry, it explained that machine-guns and ground broken by old trenches and wire hampered the cavalry's progress.[111]

Such a report certainly appeared to have influenced J F C Fuller, former Tank Corps Chief of Staff, later Staff College Chief Instructor, assistant to the CIGS, military theorist and journalist, who viewed cavalry as "excessively vulnerable in the face of modern firepower".[112] Fuller later thought that tanks could replace not only horsed cavalry, but infantry and artillery once it had abandoned "horse traction" and adopted "cross-country mechanical traction… [artillery] would in effect become big-gunned tanks".[113] The debate on the vulnerability of horsed cavalry to "modern" weapons had waged on since the early 1850s, but the cavalry had adapted, developed doctrine and had survived.[114] Its survival was partly, if not entirely, due to the horse remaining the only capable cross country conveyance for mobile troops that was speedier than soldiers on foot. Each time the cavalry was engaged in a conflict the debate on its future had re-emerged. The cavalry was "a well tried arm"[115] and the successful charges made by J P D French's cavalry division at Klip Drift during the Second Boer

---

108 Ibid., 20.07.1918, p.7.
109 Ibid., 20.07.1918, p.7. There had been mounted actions since 1914, see for details Kenyon, *Horsemen in No Man's Land*.
110 *The Times*, 12.08.1918, p.12.
111 *The Times*, 13 and 14.08.1918 p.7.
112 See Appendix C – biographies; Harris, *Men, ideas and tanks*, p.206; Ellis, *Cavalry*, pp.176/177.
113 Harris, *Men, ideas and tanks*, p.206; Holden Reid, *Studies in British Military Thought*, p.17.
114 Badsey, *Doctrine and Reform*, pp.2 &16; also Kenyon, *Horseman in No Man's Land*, for detailed case studies.
115 LHCMA, Broad 1–3; Lt. Gen. Charles Broad's reply to Mr R Alastair Rickard's letter, University of Ontario, May 21 1970. See Appendix C – biographies.

War (1899–1902),[116] and that of the 4th and 12th Australian Light Horse Regiments at Beersheba (Third Battle of Gaza 1917),[117] were strong counter-arguments to the abolitionists of horsed cavalry.[118]

The tanks were stealing the glory in 1918, however, as a report of 12 August typifies:

> The crews drove their tanks into the thick of battle, shrinking before no obstacle, and attacking hostile centres of resistance and batteries under terrible fire of the machine-guns and special guns which the enemy concentrated upon them. Each section of tanks overcame 15 to 20 German machine-guns.[119]

Three years later, in an amendment debate in parliament, the disbandment of four British cavalry regiments was proposed in the interests of economy. The Secretary of State for War, Sir Lamming Worthington-Evans,[120] was reported to have said that the lessons of war had shown the cavalry vulnerable to machine-guns and air attack; in future wars there would be times when cavalry could not be used. It was not his intention to "reduce the mobility of the army, but to replace four cavalry regiments with tanks and armed motor-cars".[121] Confirming the disbandment of four cavalry regiments on 5 August 1921, another report informed readers, "the cavalry could be spared more easily and more safely than any other arm of the Services".[122] But in what vehicles did Worthington-Evans really think he could maintain the mobility of the army?

Previously, in March 1919, following the Armistice of November 1918, Fuller had produced a "statement" showing the current state of the Tank Corps, tank training, development and production. His concerns for the future included the premature demobilization of Armies of Occupation through public pressure; Fuller thought it was going to be difficult to raise a "reliable Voluntary Army" to replace the conscript army being demobilised. If this happened, garrisoning the Empire and maintaining civil order within it would become difficult. Fuller worried about the spread of Bolshevism that might also embrace Great Britain and argued "a force weak in man-power must

116 Badsey, *Doctrine and Reform*, pp.101–103.
117 Ibid., p.286; Ellis, *Cavalry*, pp.176/177.
118 LHCMA, Broad 1–3; Lt. Gen. Charles Broad's reply to Mr R Alastair Rickard's letter, University of Ontario, May 21 1970 in which he agrees with this assessment.
119 *The Times*, 29.07.1918, p.7.
120 From 13 February 1921 until 19 October 1922 and again from 6 November 1924 until 4 June 1929.
121 *The Times*, 12.04.1921, p.15; see Phillips, Gervase "Who Shall Say That the Days of Cavalry Are Over? The Revival of the Mounted Arm in Europe, 1853–1914" in *War in History*, URL: <http://wih.sagepub.com/content/18/1/5> accessed 01.12.2011 for similar assertions made in the mid nineteenth century that "the days of cavalry were passed" due to the development of new weapons.
122 *The Times*, 05.08.1921, p.8.

be strong in machine powerand the best machine power available at that time was the Medium D tank.[123]

In 1919 tanks were considered too slow and their "radius of action too limited" to be useful in a guerrilla type war waged by a local dissident force. One Medium D tank had been built, but more were needed to rectify "teething problems and it took four months, it was thought, to retrain an infantryman to be an efficient tank driver or gunner.[124] Fuller urged a "speedy decision" on what further tank requirements would be necessary; he foresaw "guerilla [sic] warfare and police work" as the future role of the army for which it was not properly equipped.[125] Churchill, the Secretary of State for War (10 January 1919–13 February 1921), called for proposals for the "formation of a Tank Expeditionary Force" and Fuller submitted these to the Army Council in mid-April 1919. Fuller foresaw the role of the tank "in a guerrilla war... would be that of a moving blockhouse line which would clear an extensive area of country".[126] His report assumed the Medium D tanks to be available by April 1920.[127] Fuller wanted a meeting arranged with the tank manufacturers to speed-up the production process with overtime or double-shifting; "an immediate arrangement should be made with Vickers Fuller insisted.[128] The Deputy CIGS Major General Sir Charles H "Tim" Harrington's comment encapsulated the difficulties faced by the post Great War Army Council: "Colonel Fuller's schemes of "thinking ahead" are always interesting but he is not faced with the problem with which we are faced viz to get the best value out of a very limited sum of money".[129] The Master General of The Ordnance, Lieutenant General Sir W T Furse concurred: "We have more than enough we can do to keep afloat and abreast of immediate needs in almost every corner of the globe".[130]

The British Army's tank establishment was effectively 531 vehicles in France, including 89 expected to be repaired and serviceable by 1 June 1919, and 414 in Great Britain and Ireland, including 95 "new types for which no spares [were] in existence" and 30 Medium "C" tanks also for which there were no spare parts.[131] Regarding mechanizing the cavalry, however, the tanks currently in service were built for the unique circumstances of the Great War (Mark Vs and Mark V*s, Mark VIIIs and IXs and Medium A, B and Cs) and were unsuitable for a war of rapid movement,[132] therefore, and by extension, unsuitable for replacing horses for cavalry work.

---

123 TNA WO 32/5685 Army Organisation: Tanks (Code 14 (G)): Proposals concerning formation of tank expeditionary force and use of tanks in Russia – 1919; S.D.7 Minute 4 – DDSD to DSD, 31 March 1919.
124 Ibid., Minute 1, 25 March 1919.
125 Ibid., Minute 4, 31 March 1919.
126 Ibid., referred to in Minute 9 and marked 9A, 14 April 1919.
127 Ibid.
128 Ibid., Minute 4, 31 March 1919.
129 Ibid., Minute 13, 6 May 1919.
130 Ibid., Minute 14, 8 May 1919.
131 Ibid., referred to in Minute 9, 14 April 1919; marked 9A Appendix A.
132 Ibid., marked 5A, 14 April 1919 and marked 9A Appendix A.

In terms of the future, Fuller considered the position of tank design as "satisfactory the emphasis being "towards high speed, extensive radius of action and greatly improved wearing capabilities". Regarding "Experimental production one Medium D was completed, but was still not satisfactory. Variations on this Mark (the Medium D* and D**) were being produced and were hoped to be ready for trials in July or August 1919 but, commented Fuller:

> The firms with whom contracts are placed are concentrating on commercial programmes and take little or no interest in war work [and the contracts placed] pre-armistice are now not considered satisfactory by the Contracts Departments... [There was] a dispute between Messrs Vickers and the Contracts department of the W.M.D.... At present all production has ceased... The only bright spot is the work which is being carried out by Woolwich Arsenal on the experimental light cross country Machines.[133]

The challenges of early tank developments

Lieutenant Colonel Philip Johnson did develop a "Light Infantry" tank by 1921 at the Royal Ordnance Factory, in the Royal Arsenal at Woolwich, referred to by Fuller in his "Plan 1919" report.[134] This model weighed eight tons with a top speed of 30 miles per hour (mph) and was "mechanically successful". No more were produced and Johnson's tank design centre was shut down in 1923.[135] Vickers was working on its own light tank design and had, by 1921, produced the light "tropical" tanks Nos.1 to 3.[136] It was possibly the development of these models that Winston Churchill had in mind in his speech to parliament in February 1920 when, as Secretary of State for War, he announced the proposed strength of the peacetime army. Churchill waxed lyrical about "the most surprising development in tanks that have taken place since the war". Technical changes had been made he explained; tanks could now reach speeds up to twenty mph over ditches and hedges across country "a good deal faster than any fox hound". He also reassured members of parliament that the new tank engines had "a refrigerating effect" making them suitable for use in India and other hot climates.[137] Churchill pointed out, however, that much of the tank development

---

133 Ibid., Minute – 9 marked 5A, p.2. WMD presumably relates to the Ministry of Munitions, created in 1915, and responsible, with concurrent powers with the War Office, for procurement of munitions of war.
134 Harris, *Men, ideas and tanks,* pp.165–172.
135 Macksey, *A History of The Royal Armoured Corps,* p.47; Fletcher, *Mechanised Force* p.5; Beale, *Death by Design,* pp.146/7 – after which the Director of Artillery was placed in charge of "mechanization".
136 Vickers historical document 895, *Tanks and Armoured Cars built by Vickers 1919–1942,* Cambridge University Library Manuscripts Department.
137 Gilman Clough Barndollar, "British Use of Armoured cars 1919–1939"; PhD, Cambridge

was experimental, but there had also been developments in anti-tank warfare too, such as rifle propelled grenades that were "capable of inflicting mortal injury on the new machines".[138]

Confusion might have been planted in the minds of members of the public keen on what economies might derive from these tank experiments because of an earlier criticism from Lord Weir.[139] In January 1920, the *Daily Mail*, which boasted a 1,000,000 circulation, reported that Great Britain, the inventor of the tank, had not maintained her lead. Opinions of "experienced officers" were asserted who were of the view that fast tanks could largely replace cavalry *and* infantry "and enable substantial economies to be effected in those arms".[140] If this was to happen, the report stressed, the tank must be perfected, and "the present Tank Staff... retained... and not starved of funds as at present appears to be the danger".[141] The paper's Military Correspondent[142] supported this argument. In his article under the headline "Threat to Tank Corps the Military Correspondent drew the public's attention to the suggestion that tanks might be attached to infantry battalions; such a suggestion was "condemned" by Tank Corps officers and was compared in the article to the failure of the use of machine-guns in the early part of the Great War when these weapons were originally attached to infantry battalions.[143]

Newspaper comments such as those in the *Daily Mail* in January 1920, however sincerely held these views might have been, were unlikely to improve inter-arms cooperation and endear the relatively new Tank Corps to the older service arms of infantry, cavalry and artillery, especially when they were each competing for a share of scarce financial resources; competition between them that continued into the next decade.[144] Much to the chagrin of the Tank Corps officers no doubt, and probably something of a relief to the other service arms, it was announced later the same month that the Tank Corps would remain intact, but greatly reduced in size.[145]

University, 2010; the interior of the India pattern armoured car was lined with "Raybestos a combination of asbestos and closely-woven copper wire that reduced radiated heat and it also contained "bullet splash" – shards of armour plate that splintered-off inside the vehicle when it was hit with bullets on the outside, p.266.
138 *The Times*, 24.02.1920, p.10.
139 See Appendix C – biographies.
140 *Daily Mail*, 02.01.1920, p.6.
141 Ibid.
142 It would be interesting to know who the newspaper's Military Correspondent was; unfortunately the *Daily Mail* has "no record of staff members from this time"; Reference Librarian, Associated Newspapers; personal correspondence with the author, February 2012.
143 Griffith, *Battle Tactics of the Western Front*, pp.121/122; Griffith compared the "focus of naked empire-building and institutional infighting" over the formation of the Machine Gun Corps with the later arguments over the development of the Tank Corps.
144 Liddell Hart, *Memoirs Volume I*, p.125.
145 *Daily Mail*, 02.01.1920, p.6.

On Saturday 10 January 1920, the public might have thought that any funding problem had been quickly solved. Tank developments were forging ahead by leaps and bounds according to the newspaper reports. Readers attracted by the headline in the *Daily Mail* "Tanks that can swim" would have been astounded to read of the "extraordinary revolution in mechanical warfare already accomplished".[146] It seems that "strange monsters" looking like tanks, but with "uncanny silence and swiftness of motion" unlike the tanks seen in France, had been spotted travelling at 20 mph in the Bournemouth area. With sprung tracks and powered by discarded 250 horse power Rolls Royce aero engines, these vehicles had been tested for over one thousand miles with just £10 worth of repairs becoming necessary. In a slight to the mounted service, it reported that the speed attained, 16 to 17 mph across country, was "faster than the best mounted of hunting men, and it can run rings around any cavalry". One new version of this new Mark tank, superior to the Mark V*, was "one pattern [that] will cross rivers with ease" and one that will "cross the Channel" moving at 20 mph on land and fitted with a propeller for water. The report forecasted that Jules Verne's vision of 50 years ago "now stands on the point of realisation by British brains and British engineering skill".[147] Liddell Hart also reported an experiment of a tank with a watertight hull held in the Christchurch area in May 1919. This prototype tank, a development of the Medium D tank by Lieutenant Colonel Philip Johnson, "attained a speed of 28 mph… [and] repeatedly swam across the river, climbing out unaided on reaching the far bank. But its reliability was not equal to its speed and performance".[148] It appeared to the newspaper correspondent that two basic types of fast tanks were planned that could accomplish what infantry and cavalry "of the old type could never do": a fast type relying on speed for protection, and a slower model, heavily armoured and armed, that only "mountains and precipices" could stop. "Trenches will be useless it asserted. The report ominously and futuristically stated that this tank will be an "Ideal police weapon for dealing with mobs". There would be no bloodshed, rioters would be anaesthetised by ejected gas; the tank itself, guided by wireless from an aircraft, would be sealed against gas attack and would be submersible too.[149] Civil disturbance, even revolution, it will be remembered, was anticipated and the report of such a weapon, released to the general public, might have been viewed as a deterrent.

The origin of the light tank, as a concept, lay in Major (later Lieutenant General Sir) Giffard le Quesne Martel's "partially armoured one-man vehicle which could be used to assist infantry".[150] Martel built the first one himself; further models were built by the company owned by Messrs. Carden and Loyd. The so-called "Carden-Loyd" AFVs were trialled from 1925; twenty different marks were developed over the next

---

146 Ibid., 02.01.1920, p.6; & 10.01.1920, p.7.
147 *Daily Mail,* 02.01.1920, p.6.
148 Liddell Hart, *Memoirs Volume I,* p.94.
149 *Daily Mail,* 02.01.1920, p.6.
150 Vickers historical document 618, Cambridge University Library Manuscripts Department.

six years. Vickers acquired the Carden-Loyd Company in 1928 following which the "Carden-Loyd-Vickers" light tanks were developed from then on.[151] Vickers produced 2.5 ton, two-man turreted light tanks from 1929; these were armed with one Vickers .303 machine gun and protected with areas of 14mm (maximum thickness) armour, many of these tanks were exported.[152]

Tank development was a conundrum: what type, what role, and who should have them, and for Vickers Armstrong, the only tank manufacturer for much of the inter-war period, what was the commercial viability of tank development and production. Vickers origins can be traced from an engineering works on Tyneside established in 1847 by W G (later Lord) Armstrong to develop his ideas on hydraulic engines. Armstrong merged with Sir Joseph Whitworth's company in 1897. Vickers of Sheffield was developing high quality steel castings; both Vickers and Armstrong-Whitworth grew by acquisition and merged in 1927 to form Vickers-Armstrong Limited. Sir Noel Birch, Master General of the Ordnance from 1923 until 1927, retired that year from the army to become a director of Vickers.[153] On 1 January 1928, under the chairmanship of Major General Sydney Capel Peck,[154] The Mechanised [sic] Warfare Board was created by the War Office

> ... to act in an advisory capacity on technical problems in connection with mechanical transport... and to secure liaison with the mechanical engineering industry so that the army may be in close touch with engineering and commercial production.[155]

The War Office Selection Board had been told that Peck was "indispensable to mechanization".[156] On 28 January 1928 Giffard le Quesne Martel, in conversation

---

151 Vickers historical document 895, *Tanks and Armoured Cars built by Vickers 1919–1942*, Cambridge University Library Manuscripts Department. The spelling of "Carden-*Loyd*" or "*Lloyd*" varied throughout the Vickers' papers, Loyd is sometimes spelt with the double "l"; Foss, and McKenzie, *The Vickers Tanks*, used the single "l" spelling, this author has done likewise. Also, Vickers historical document 618, Cambridge University Library Manuscripts Department.

152 Macksey, *A History of The Royal Armoured Corps*, p.52.

153 Foss and McKenzie, *The Vickers Tanks*, p.9. See Appendix C – biographies.

154 Major General S C Peck CB DSO pac (sc) was the first to be appointed to this position that reported to the Master General to the Ordnance; the Assistant Director of Mechanization was "tank pioneer" Colonel F A Pile DSO MC psc.

155 Macksey, *A History of The Royal Armoured Corps*, p.52.

156 LHCMA – LH11/1928/1 Diary Notes – talk with David Campbell, Government House Aldershot, 14 June 1928. General Sir David Graham Muschet "Soarer" Campbell (28 January 1869–12 March 1936) – General Officer Commanding-in Chief of the Aldershot Command 1927–1931. Campbell was commissioned into the 9th Lancers on 15 March 1889 and took command of the regiment on the same date in 1912. A Boer War and Great War veteran, he was a renowned equestrian sportsman. "Soarer" that became his nick-name, was the name of the horse Campbell rode to victory in the Grand National on 27 March 1896.

with Liddell Hart at the Army and Navy Club in London speculated that Major General Peck, the Director of Mechanization, should have got the position at Vickers, but Birch, his superior, "cut him out, securing the job for himself. Vickers will have a shock when they find out how little he [Birch] knows about the subject [mechanization]".[157]

What about the Tank Corps?

In the meantime the Tank Corps had to manage with vehicles that had already been produced[158] and no suitable vehicles yet existed with which to mechanize or armour the British Army's Regular horsed cavalry regiments.

The Tank Corps itself was short of men in 1919, "bled white through demobilization eight battalions remained, only three of which were "at war strength". The training school had "become practically inoperative" and recruitment into the Corps was at a "standstill".[159] The Army Council's expectation that cavalry regiments would soon move en-masse to the Tank Corps would have solved this recruitment problem. It was, however, impossible for this to take place as the current AFVs were unable to match the speed and mobility of horsed cavalry and the army would have been denied their use as effective imperial policemen.

In 1923 the Tank Corps received the prefix accolade of "Royal but at the same time had remaining just 36 Medium C tanks.[160] The change of title was recommended by the War Office Tank Corps Committee during April 1922 and accepted by the Army Council on 27 July 1922; it was part of a raft of recommendations to attract more officers to the Corps.[161] Other recommendations included, notably: "There should be a separate tank Corps [sic] with a permanent list of officers"; this too was accepted.[162] Also accepted was the recommendation for newly commissioned officers to come from both the Royal Military Academy Woolwich, where students underwent engineering and technical training for the Royal Artillery and Royal Corps of Engineers, and from the Royal Military College Sandhurst, where officer cadets underwent general military and leadership training for both cavalry and infantry units; applicants from Kingston and Duntroon, the Canadian and Australian military academies, would

---

157 LHCMA – LH11/1928/3.
158 Liddell Hart, *Memoirs Volume I*, pp.94/95.
159 TNA WO 32/5685 Army Organisation: Tanks (Code 14 (G)): Proposals concerning formation of tank expeditionary force and use of tanks in Russia – 1919; referred to in S.D.7 Minute 9 DDSD to DSD and marked 5A.
160 Macksey, *A History of The Royal Armoured Corps*, p.45.
161 TNA WO 32/5072 Conditions of Service (Officers): Appointment, Gazetting and issue of Commissions (Code 59 (E)): Report of Peyton Committee on Formation of Permanent List of Officers for Tank Corps: establishment to be adopted and conditions on transfer and promotion; Register No.100/Tank Corps/151 p.6, 27 July 1922.
162 Ibid., Report of Peyton Committee on Formation of Permanent List of Officers for Tank Corps: establishment to be adopted and conditions on transfer and promotion.

Medium Tank Mark C. (Source: The Tank Museum, Bovington – 0891-B2)

also be accepted into the Corps. It was advised that this balance of officer recruits best suited the "varied requirements of the [Tank] Corps".[163] A further recommendation was the accelerated promotion for officers who transferred from other arms, the exceptions were the Royal Army Service Corps and the Royal Army Ordnance Corps that were each short of officers and could not spare any for transfer.[164] Captains from cavalry and infantry regiments, either or both through interest or opportunity, were attracted by this offer and the prospect of accelerated promotion.

What did the cavalry need in order to mechanize and economise?

Pressure continued, however, for the government to increase expenditure on social reform and with it the pressure to reduce expenditure on the armed services.[165] In 1928 when, in the interests of further economy, the decision was taken to mechanize two horsed cavalry regiments with armoured cars, the Director of Mechanization, Major General Peck, gave thought to the cavalry's future requirements. "Up until this time armoured cars had been designed to function on roads only but now some cross-country capability was required "if they [the cavalry] were to be able to perform

---

163 Ibid., 28 April 1922.
164 Ibid., memo, October 1922.
165 *The Times*, 24.02.1920, p.10.

The Martel Tankette prototype 1925. (Source: The Tank Museum, Bovington – 1396 – E4)

their reconnaissance duties satisfactorily".[166] He thought the following characteristics necessary:

i.   High road speed – "a speed across country depends entirely on that country and is therefore difficult to define. The speeds of a race-horse and a cart horse are the same when in a bog".
ii.   Fairly heavy armour.
iii. Must be able to cross a divisional bridge.
iv.   Should be a commercial chassis if possible.
v.   If possible, "have a certain cross country capacity".[167]

In his memorandum to the sub-committee of the Committee of Imperial Defence, he pointed out that the science of cross-country traction was "practically a new one, and moreover, is one of the most difficult that engineers have had to tackle". Some

166 TNA WO 32/3059 Army Organisation: Cavalry (Code 14(D)): Reconstruction of the Corps of Cavalry Point 3 in draft memorandum, marked "secret" to C I D Sub Committee on the Strength and Organisation of the Cavalry from the Director of Mechanization, War Office, February 1928 marked 13A; probably a submission to the Committee chaired by Lord Salisbury.
167 Ibid.

of the best-known motorcar companies were, he wrote somewhat pessimistically, "frequently having to withdraw their models after a few months production" in spite of the fact that they had undergone sometimes "a year or two in [the] experimental stage". There were "frightening aspects" to be considered when applied to the design of cross-country traction and "it is always necessary to have "something in hand [sic] both as regards speed and strength". Machines needed to be "fool-proof... good starters... gas-proof... quiet... inconspicuous and capable of being loaded and carried on standard size railway trucks. Puncture-proof tyres were under experiment and intended for use on cavalry vehicles. With these considerations and those of vehicle accommodation and maintenance training, and the continuity of investment required to provide them, "our progress in mechanization must be rather a gradual evolution". Continuing on "hand to mouth each financial year" as had been the case would not ensure success.[168]

The Director's specification for the cross-country capability of cavalry vehicles was supported later the same year in a report on the French Army's manoeuvres on the Rhine. Although these manoeuvres were held in dry weather, the report stressed that French horsed cavalry units were actually "held up" by their mechanized cavalry units who were "seriously hampered by the scarcity and quality of the roads".[169] The French Army too was still to develop an armoured vehicle with a suitable cross-country capability.

Peck's forecast that continuing on "hand to mouth each financial year" would not ensure success proved correct. Sufficient vehicles, armoured and unarmoured, were not available until well into the Second World War and British made tanks, with the possible exception of the Matilda tank, remained unfit for purpose until almost the end of the Second World War. In February 1943 Martel wrote, in a secret and confidential note from the War Office, to Major General P C S "Hobo" Hobart, who had commanded and trained the 11th Armoured Division and was then training the 79th Armoured Division:

> We have well trained armoured troops and a sound technique... on the other hand the equipment side is frightful. So long as we can get American tanks it will be alright... But it is rather dreadful that we have, at present, no British tank that is any use.[170]

---

168 Ibid.
169 TNA WO 32/3579 OVERSEAS: Europe (Code 0 (V)): Report on manoeuvres of French Army and participation of British Cavalry 1928–1928, 10 September 1928, Appendix C.
170 LHCMA – LH15/11/16–65; from Martel to Hobart, WO Room 15, 4 February 1943. See Appendix C – biographies.

Enter, and exit, the Sixteen Tonner

This situation had severely restricted the progress of cavalry mechanization. Badsey's suggestion that cavalry mechanization was delayed by the failure to develop a genuinely fast tank was certainly true of the 1920s, but *might not* have been so for the 1930s had it not been for the further reduction in the defence estimates.[171]

Without suitable equipment the task of armouring horsed cavalry in either armoured cars or tanks was just impossible, regardless of what feelings existed for or against the idea. Published literature of the types of tanks produced by Vickers or the Royal Ordnance Factory at Woolwich during the interwar period can, without careful examination, confuse the historian. There were Marks and Models a plenty, but few were much more than prototypes. Charles Broad in 1925 had worked on one tank known as the "Independent" and wrote in 1970 that it was "a quite reasonable modern tank… sufficient speed… sufficiently bullet proof, and had a good radius of action, [but]… no more were built on account of expense".[172]

Between 1928 and 1939, eighteen different models are listed as having been produced by Vickers or their subsidiaries.[173] Peter Beale accurately asserted that "a large amount of effort was spent in projects that resulted in nothing useful".[174] By 1928, however, Vickers had constructed the A6 Mk III tank, also known as the "Sixteen-Tonner". The Sixteen-Tonner was thought to be "the best Medium tank in the world at that time"[175] at a cost of £16,000 each.[176] Interestingly, on 27 September 1928 at the Cavalry Club, in a conversation over lunch with Liddell Hart, Brigadier (later General Sir) Frederick A "Tim" Pile, the Assistant Director of Mechanization, said the Sixteen-Tonner would cost £28,000, but the War Office would pay no more than £15,000, and then only order ten.[177] This was no great incentive for a commercial company to press on with the development of this AFV. The model suffered from some track problems, but its trials were generally satisfactory and it was considered "a fighting vehicle of great potential".[178] The Sixteen-Tonner had a range of 100 miles

---

171 Badsey, Stephen "Cavalry and the Development of Breakthrough Doctrine" in Griffith. Paddy [1996] *British Fighting Methods in the Great War*, (Frank Cass, London), pp.138–174; p.164.

172 LHCMA – Broad 1–3; Lt. Gen. Charles Broad's reply to Mr R Alastair Rickard's letter, University of Ontario, May 21 1970.

173 Macksey, *A History of The Royal Armoured Corps*, p.50.

174 Beale, *Death by Design*, p.67.

175 Harris, *Men, ideas and tanks* p.238.

176 Liddell Hart, *Memoirs Volume I,* pp.176 & 209. This aligns with Liddell Hart's notes LHCMA – LH11/1930/8, "Talks with Colonel F A Pile", 15 October 1930 the tank was costed at £12,000 and the engine another £3,000.

177 LHCMA – LH11/1928/1, Diary Notes, "Lunch with Pile at the Cavalry Club"; Beale, *Death by Design*, p.49.

178 Macksey, *A History of The Royal Armoured Corps*, p.52.

and top speed of 30 mph, and according to Pile, 15 mph uphill.[179] It was armed with a 3 pounder gun and a machine-gun in its main turret, and two machine-guns in each of its forward-mounted subsidiary turrets.[180] Commenting on 29 January 1929, Brigadier George M Lindsay, the Inspector of the Royal Tank Corps (1925–1929), said "the new 16 ton tank is far better mechanically and in fire-power than was ever thought at first". The plan was, Lindsay had expected, for eleven more to be built to add to the three already available, but Lindsay now thought that only one more would be built "out of Peck's own surplus from the experimental vote".[181] In fact only six Sixteen-Tonners were ever built and so there was little opportunity to correct the teething problems and develop the model any further.[182]

Abandonment of any future Sixteen-Tonner developments for the British Army was rooted in another round of defence expenditure cuts later in 1931.[183] Writing in 1995, Harris suggested the failure to allow this model of tank to go into production was a pivotal moment in both tank and doctrinal development. The RTC, he suggested, "would have continued to use a single type of medium tank both for the close support of attacking infantry and for more mobile roles".[184] Harris made no suggestion, however, that this tank could have been used for cavalry regiments, but he is critical of cavalry regiments being mechanized later into *light* tanks.[185] Peden pointed out that the cavalry were equipped with light tanks because of "the absence of any satisfactory alternative".[186]

With hindsight, had the Sixteen-Tonner been developed, powered by a diesel engine, it might well have been the vehicle suitable to armour horsed cavalry regiments and the RTC. The suitability of the Mark III Sixteen–tonner can be seen by comparing its specification to that of the much later M4 Sherman tank [Table 3]. The A6 E2 prototype of the Mark III Sixteen–Tonner was powered by the Ricardo C1 less flammable diesel engine;[187] the other marks had flammable petrol engines

179 LHCMA – LH11/1928/1, Diary Notes, "Lunch with Pile at the Cavalry Club" 15 October 1930.
180 Harris, *Men, ideas and tanks*, p.238.
181 LHCMA – LH/1929/4, "Talk with Brigadier G M Lindsay" 29 January 1929.
182 Vickers historical document 895, *Inter War Period*, pp.10/11, Cambridge University Library Manuscripts Department; Harris, *Men, ideas and tanks*, p.238 – six prototypes were built at a unit cost of £16,000 each; Macksey, *A History of The Royal Armoured Corps*, p.52 – three were built and Fletcher, *Mechanised Force*, pp.15 &16 – six were built – 1 by The Royal Ordnance Factory, p.18.
183 LHCMA – Broad 1–3; Lt. Gen. Charles Broad's reply to Mr R Alastair Rickard's letter, University of Ontario, May 21 1970; Harris, *Men, ideas and tanks* p.238; Vickers historical document 895, *Inter War Period*, pp.10/11; Macksey, Kenneth [1983], *A History of The Royal Armoured Corps*, p.54.
184 Harris, *Men, ideas and tanks*, p.278.
185 Ibid., p.263, emphasis added.
186 Peden, *Arms, Economics and British Strategy*, p.124.
187 LHCMA – LH11/1930/8, "Talks with Colonel F A Pile", 15 October 1930 Pile was keen to try this new engine.

as did the Sherman tank used in the European theatre. Considered vulnerable to fire and explosion when hit by enemy fire, Sherman tanks were allegedly referred to by British soldiers as "Ronsons" a popular cigarette lighter, or "Tommy cookers" by German soldiers.[188] The numerous and successful Russian T-34 tank of the Second World War had a diesel engine, probably developed from the Russian T29 model with 22mm of armour; the Sixteen-Tonner had been influential on its design.[189] It was later established, however, that the vulnerability of the Sherman tank to fire and explosion was *not* due to its petrol engine, as has often been thought, but to the position of the ammunition storage magazine.[190]

The American M4 Sherman tank used by some British Royal Armoured Corps regiments from 1942 was, nonetheless, both popular with the crews and generally successful as an all-round battle tank. It is important to note, however, that during the inter-war period an all-round battle tank was *not* what was being considered for armoured or mechanized cavalry units expected to carry out the "light cavalry" roles of reconnaissance, screening, pursuit etc. During the Second World War, the lighter, faster (up to 35 mph) American Stuart tanks, known to the British as Honey tanks, as well as armoured cars and scout cars, were also used by Royal Armoured Corps regiments, especially for reconnaissance work.[191]

The Light tank

It was a light tank, however, that the War Office had in mind for cavalry regiments, or for cavalry work, whosoever should undertake that role. To fully replace a horse, it was thought a tank also needed to be amphibious. The need for a cheaper tank was the catalyst for the regeneration of light tank development at Vickers armament manufacturers in 1931 that followed the abandonment of the medium (Sixteen-Tonner) tank programme.[192] What a light tank was, was yet to be clearly specified; there can be some confusion, however, as in the archived records the term "light tank" was often used to describe the "infantry armoured machine-gun carrier".[193] It is not always clear what was being developed and Liddell Hart noted in 1929 that "the progress of mechanization also suffers from the technical expert's pursuit of an ideal machine

188 Personal discussion with Buckley [2013]; by the author.
189 LHCMA – LH15/11/1–11, 3; General Wavell's Report on Red Army Manoeuvres 1936, Copy 18 –Secret, pp.8,19 & 27.
190 Personal discussion with Buckley [2013]; by the author.
191 Personal interviews with Sprot and Randall (both of the Royal Scots Greys) [2007]; by the author.
192 Vickers Archives 1870–1970 number 895, *Inter War Period*, pp.10/13 and Vickers historic document 618, *Tanks 1934–1939*, Cambridge University Library Manuscripts Department.
193 LHCMA – LH 11/1928/20, p.62.

that will meet every improbable condition, instead of being content with a cheap and practical one".[194]

The General Staff's view, assessed David Fletcher, was that a "cavalry tank" must be "a high-speed machine, capable of working in mobile exploitation and scouting roles normally allotted to [horsed] cavalry".[195] Beale's later view was that the lead time for developing any new tank was three to six years assuming that there was a clear statement "of what tanks were supposed to do". Without such a statement the major problem for tank designers, asserted Beale, was the lack of a detailed AFV specification that led on to "doubt, change, multiple designs and wasted resources".[196] Crucially, and in regard to mechanizing the cavalry, it "created difficulties" in setting up and delivering training for British Army tank crews.[197]

Table 3 Specification comparison A6 Mark III and M4 British Sherman 1

AFV	A6 Mark III – "Sixteen-Tonner"[1]	M4 (British Sherman 1)[2]
Weight	39,200 lbs	66,500 lbs
Speed	max 30 mph cross country 19 mph	max 24–29 mph cross country 15–20 mph
Armour	max 14 mm	min 12 mm max 75 mm – turret
Armament	1 × 3 pounder gun + 5 .303 Vickers machine guns	1 × 75 mm M3 gun 2 × .30 cal + 1 × .5 cal. machine guns
Road Radius	Road – 100 miles	road – 100–150 miles
Fording Depth	Not known	3 feet
Trench Crossing	Not known	7 feet 5 inches

1   Harris, *Men, ideas and tanks*, p.238 & Fletcher, *Mechanised Force* pp.15 & 16: URL:<http://www.wwiivehicles.com/unitedkingdom/tanks-medium/mk-iii.asp> accessed 02.04.2011.
2   Chamberlain and Ellis, *British and American Tanks of World War II*, p.115.

194 LHCMA – LH11/1929/12, "Memo of the Experimental Force and Re-organization of the Home Army".
195 Fletcher, *Mechanised Force,* pp.3/4.
196 Beale, *Death by Design*, p.207.
197 Ibid.

The A6 Mark III "Sixteen-tonner, circa 1929.
(Source: The Tank Museum, Bovington – 1631-E4)

The M4 A1 Sherman II. (Source: The Tank Museum, Bovington – 1631-E4)

In summary

By the late 1920s a tank suitable for armouring horsed cavalry had been built, but economic restraint placed priorities elsewhere; with no perceived threat to national security, these tanks were never developed or produced other than in prototype form.[198] Liddell Hart commented in 1965 that in any case, in pressing for the substitution of tanks for horses, some members of the Labour Cabinet would be going against "that party's pacific ideals and anti-military tradition…[but] in the economic circumstances of the time no big change [in mechanized development] was practicable save by such compensating economies".[199] In 1928 he had noted that "the main trouble in the way of mechanisation [sic] is the capital cost… that had frightened off "His Worthiness" [Sir Laming Worthing-Evans, Secretary of State for War]".[200] To bring the tank battalions up to strength and completing the mechanization of the artillery was estimated to cost £5,000,000 to £6,000,000, and equipping an armoured brigade would cost £1,500,000.[201] He made no estimate of the cost of mechanizing the cavalry.

It would have been a bold decision for the Army Council to risk any of its anticipated, but reduced, budgets on such tank experiments. Both as a policy and as a perception no war was foreseen in the next ten years and horsed cavalry was adequate, even more suitable as an aid to the civil powers; "armoured forces… added little capability to armies deployed for colonial peace keeping".[202] Had more money been allocated to the army, such experiments might have been risked, but as Lindsay despaired in 1929, "we have reached the "saturation point" of mechanised [sic] progress within the present money restrictions – unless and until a reduction of infantry takes place".[203]

Therefore, recalling Steiner's assertion at the opening of the Chapter that "the 1920s should be treated as a decade that followed an earlier war… rather than, as was common, the precursor of the war that followed,"[204] a reminder is useful of why the government spent less and less of defence generally and the army in particular.

---

198 Fletcher, *Mechanised Force,* p.2 states a £30,000 budget for development – the cost of a tank was £12,250. By 1922 the construction budget was £220,000 for 42 tanks; p.7; Harris, *Men, ideas and tanks,* p.274 reported that between 1927 and 1936 the annual allocation of funds to tank development varied from £22,500 to £93,750 – to develop a Medium tank could cost as much as £29,000.
199 Liddell Hart, *Memoirs Volume I,* pp.174–176.
200 LHCMA – LH11/1928/2, "Talk with Colonel CNF Broad Director of Staff duties, Army and Navy Club2 February 1928.
201 Ibid.
202 Millet, Allan R "Patterns of Military Innovation" in Millet, A R and Williamson M, [1996] (eds.), *Military Innovation in the Interwar Period,* (Cambridge University Press, Cambridge), p.340 cited in Gilman Clough Barndollar, "British Use of Armoured cars 1919-1939" PhD, Cambridge University, 2010, p.8.
203 LHCMA – LH11/1929/4, "Talk with Brigadier GM Lindsay Inspector of the Royal Tank Corps", 29 January 1929.
204 Steiner, *The Lights That Failed,* Preface v.

The back drop to the military policy decisions of the 1920s can be summarised as optimism, economics, and social and political pressures. The successive British Government's optimism was manifest in the 10 Year Rule; this gave little incentive to the army to mechanize the cavalry or the engineering industry to produce a suitable vehicle in which this could be achieved. There was a political determination; some might argue an economic need, to "balance the budget". The priority was therefore on social expenditure. The enlargement of the franchise, particularly the inclusion of women, fear of social unrest, unemployment and the growth of pacifism forced politicians to take "public opinion" more seriously than had been done hither to. Cecelia Lynch has argued that during the interwar period, there was an "excessive preoccupation with the mood of the electorate".[205] The electorate's mood of that period has to be open only to speculation; there were no opinion surveys and politicians, in order to seek or retain power, reflected in their policies their own perception of what was public opinion. They needed to do so of course; as well as being democratic, the political class was mindful of the changes the Great War had brought about. Monarchies had fallen, dynasties ended, and a Bolshevik government was ensconced in Russia. Until the mid-nineteen thirties the mainstream political parties, in terms of defence spending, had similar policies and would otherwise have stood little chance of success at an election.

These factors together with the engineering challenges involved restricted the development of a suitable AFV with which to mechanize horsed cavalry. On the one hand there was no apparent urgency, if indeed such a vehicle would ever be required for a future war, on the other hand there was sustained pressure on the army, and especially on the cavalry, to economise; mechanization was one route that was expected to achieve a significant reduction in defence costs.

205 Lynch, *Beyond Appeasement*, p.4.

3

Mechanization – The First Phase 1918–1929

1921–1922 – Disbandment and Amalgamation

The Army General Staff in its intension for horsed cavalrymen to transfer to an expanded Tank Corps "in the near future,"[1] wanted cavalry regiments to transfer intact; that is to say, as whole regiments, thus retaining their regimental identities, traditions etcetera, and thereby helping to maintain morale during the period of change:[2]

> It is suggested that an endeavour should be made to retain the entity of the regiments by eventually transferring their names and numbers to new tank units, of which seven are proposed for 1922. It offers a means of disposing of large numbers of officers it would otherwise be difficult to absorb. It will also preserve the regimental traditions, plate, funds etc.[3]

This was not done in 1921, but it was implemented seventeen years later when The Royal Armoured Corps (RAC) was formed composed of Battalions of the Royal Tank Corps and the mechanized cavalry regiments of the Cavalry Corps. In a minute to the Treasury in 1938, the War Office pointed out their concerns on "esprit de corps… [that would] need careful handling".[4] The subsequent report from the Sergison-Brooke Committee acknowledged that cavalry regiments had long traditions and "must retain their separate identity"; witnesses to the committee "stressed the importance of the

---

1   TNA WO 32/5959 Army Organisation: Cavalry (Code 14(D)): Scheme for reduction of Cavalry Regiments – hand written note p.3, 24 February 1921.
2   Ibid.
3   TNA WO 32/5959 Army Organisation: Cavalry (Code 14(D)): Scheme for reduction of Cavalry Regiments.
4   TNA WO 32/16406 Committee on Organisation of Mechanised Cavalry and Royal Tank Corps: formation – 20/Cav./1039 Confidential Report A4535 no.9(c), April 1938.

regimental spirit".[5] In April 1939 the Royal Armoured Corps was created on that basis and continues still with the names and traditions of the cavalry regiments still intact, although with further, later amalgamations.[6] This sequence of events demonstrated both the wisdom and the continuity of thinking of successive General Staffs; it also testifies more to a commitment to mechanize the cavalry than to any resistance to do so.

The decision to reduce the size of the cavalry arm by disbanding, initially, four regiments was regarded as "hasty" and entirely for financial reasons when the demands on the army as imperial policeman had expanded: the General Staff of 1921 objected strongly.[7] There was no mention at this juncture, as there was the following year, of the Geddes Committee report; what can be inferred, therefore, was that the demand to reduce costs originally came from the Treasury via the Secretary of State, Sir Laming Worthington Evans, "consequent on the development of mechanical warfare".[8]

The War Office needed to overcome a number of problems to expedite the Treasury's demands, such as what to do with redundant soldiers. Cavalry soldiers, other than commissioned officers, could transfer to other units within their own corps of Dragoons, Lancers or Hussars to replace time-expired men and to save on recruitment costs, but redundant officers were a different matter. Also, there was the need to maintain an equal number of regiments at home to relieve those serving abroad. Any reduction therefore, would mean the disbandment of an *even number*, two, four, six etc., and not an odd number of regiments. How these regiments were to be chosen was another dilemma, for each regiment had history, patronage, regimental artefacts and silver. After debate and deliberation "juniority," that is to say the least old regiments in the Army List, was the criterion decided upon: those regiments formed or re-raised after the Peninsular War (1807–1814).[9] It was also felt that not all the regiments should be English ones and Irish regiments should share the burden too. The following regiments were selected: the 5th Royal Irish Lancers, the 19th (Queen Alexandra's Own Royal) Hussars, the 20th Hussars and the 21st (Empress of India's) Lancers. The result of this decision added a further complication; the 19th Hussars and the 21st Lancers enjoyed royal patronage, and additionally, Queen Alexandra was Colonel–in–Chief of the 19th Hussars. This problem, however, was overcome quite easily with King George V's approval who "recognised the force of the arguments,"[10] and this was later published in Army Order 319 1921 "Reduction in Establishments".

5   Ibid.
6   URL: <http://www.army.mod.uk/armoured/1614.aspx > accessed 30.06.2012; The Reconnaissance Corps was absorbed into the RAC in 1944.
7   TNA WO 32/5959 Army Organisation: Cavalry (Code 14(D)): Scheme for reduction of Cavalry Regiments.
8   Ibid., draft of the subsequent Army Order and Royal Assent, July 1921.
9   TNA WO 32/5959 Army Organisation: Cavalry (Code 14(D)): Scheme for reduction of Cavalry Regiments.
10   Ibid., letter to Sir Laming Worthington Evans from Buckingham Palace, 11 March 1921.

The question of royal patronage is interesting in so much as the argument for adding the prefix "Royal" to the Tank Corps in 1923 might have been thought to have made disbanding such a unit more difficult; clearly this was not the case.

Protests over the disbandments rained down upon the Secretary of State, especially letters from past senior officers, notably from General Sir Dighton Probyn VC on 11 March, Field Marshal French on 15 March and Field Marshal Allenby on 23 March 1921. The regiments were nonetheless expected to be disbanded by 31 March 1922.[11] By July 1921 pressure was further exerted upon the War Office to reduce the cavalry by five more regiments, making nine in all, an *odd* number that did not lend itself to the home/overseas balance of regiments.[12] A number of alternative schemes were considered. These included reducing the regiments of the Household Cavalry as they did not feature in overseas postings during peace time, together with, in some way, taking the opportunity to "restore to life the four regiments recently disbanded".[13] Commanding officers of several cavalry regiments were consulted as were the Commandants of the three cavalry brigades. Here it is interesting to read the following comment, unsigned, but thought to be written by Major General Ivo Lucius Beresford Vesey, Deputy Director of Organisations at the War Office:

> I am still of the opinion that the cavalry made a mistake in not accepting conversion to tanks, and I doubt the wisdom of accepting the views of existing Commanding Officers, who are naturally "crusted" horse soldiers, on a question in which opinion is likely to change very, very rapidly in the near future. We would not allow similar objections on the part of mechanicalising batteries, or we would never make any progress.[14]

No record has been found of any offer to, or rejection by, the cavalry to convert to tanks, although clearly some discussion must have taken place to induce this comment. Such proof would add credence to the criticism that the cavalry resisted mechanization especially that levelled by Liddell Hart but, as has already been said, tanks appropriate for cavalry work did not exist at that time.

Eventually, the Secretary of State proposed a scheme on 27 March 1922 that would meet "the least opposition" and be acceptable to both the King[15] and the Cabinet. Army Order 133 1922 was therefore issued announcing the amalgamation of the 1st and 2nd Life Guards to form The Life Guards (1st and 2nd);[16] and, by taking two

---

11   Ibid., Proposals for reorganisation of Cavalry of the line: Amalgamation of various regiments.
12   Ibid.
13   Ibid.
14   Ibid.
15   The Royal Approval was granted 4 April 1922.
16   White-Spunner, *Horse Guards*, pp.489/490. TNA WO 32/2843 Army Organisation: Cavalry (Code 14(D)): Regiment of Household Cavalry: Reorganisation 1927, 20/

squadrons from the senior regiment and one from the junior regiment, the amalgamations of regiments of the Cavalry of the Line that became known as "the fraction cavalry" or "the vulgar fractions":[17]

The 3rd/6th Dragoon Guards
The 4th/7th Dragoon Guards
The 5th/6th Dragoons
The 13th/18th Hussars
The 14th/20th Hussars
The 15th/19th Hussars
The 16th/5th Lancers
The 17th/21st Lancers

1927 – Further pressure to reduce the cost of the cavalry

The Prime Minister Stanley Baldwin and the Standing Committee on Expenditure had, in February 1927, received from the Secretary of State for War, Sir Laming Worthington-Evans, some form of explanation on his "general mechanisation [sic] proposals". What was expected from him was, once again, a "substantial and immediate reduction of expenditure in respect of the cavalry".[18] In a report signed by the military members of the Army Council on 30 June 1927 and marked "secret"[19] (which appears to have been sent by Worthington-Evans to Baldwin), it had been pointed out "that an efficient mechanical substitute for the horse does not at present exist". Worthington-Evans informed the Prime Minister that some "promising types" of vehicles were on trial, but that "it would be courting disaster to send them on active service in place of cavalry in their present form".[20] Baldwin and the Committee expected horsed cavalry "to be abolished in the near future" and found it difficult "to justify the heavy expenditure involved in recruiting and training men for the Cavalry and in providing generally for the special requirements of that arm".[21] Baldwin noted Sir Laming had "urged the Committee to refrain from pressing these considerations at the moment in view of the fact that comprehensive experimental tests of your mechanisation [sic] schemes were about to be undertaken".[22]

Cav/599 minutes 1–31, March – July 1927 and 13B; In the interests of economy there was a further consolidation of the Household Cavalry Regiments in 1927–1928.
17 French, D., The Mechanization of the British Cavalry, p.304.
18 WO 32/2846 Reduction of Expenditure on Cavalry; Baldwin to Sir Laming Worthington-Evans, 20 July 1927.
19 Ibid., War Office Marked Secret, 30 June 1927.
20 Ibid., Sir Laming Worthington-Evans to Baldwin, 1 July 1927.
21 Ibid., Baldwin to Sir Laming Worthington-Evans, 20 July 1927.
22 Ibid.

The former cavalry subaltern Winston Churchill, still Chancellor of the Exchequer,[23] insisted, more for reasons of economy than military doctrine, that cavalry regiments be mechanized or disbanded.[24] This was a pivotal point for cavalry mechanization; the government's determination to reduce defence spending in 1927 was the catalyst for the first move towards armouring the cavalry. This decision was probably a political one, a compromise with the Treasury, or perhaps was seen by the War Minister as a small sacrifice to keep the Treasury off his back until a suitable AFV was ready. Whatever the politics of the matter, this was a significant moment in the history of the British Regular cavalry.

Churchill put pressure on the War Minister with other suggestions too; these included a further amalgamation of cavalry regiments, except the Household Cavalry and the Royal Scots Greys, to whom he gave the sobriquet the "Household Cavalry of Scotland".[25] Churchill also suggested a reduction of six regiments[26] and the deployment of yeomanry regiments to supplement regular cavalry in the event of war, particularly in the role of "divisional cavalry". Yeomanry regiments, suggested Churchill, with "additional instructors [and] an obligation to serve abroad in the event of a national emergency [would provide] at a comparatively small cost… an ample margin and a pool to draw on".[27]

The Chief of the Imperial General Staff, Field Marshal George Milne acknowledged, without indicating any reluctance to comply, the principle that "cavalry must give way to a mechanised arm… it may be five years, it may be ten".[28] Milne argued in the intervening period:

> The Army in war must have some fast moving troops which will be able to protect it, and to perform the close reconnoitring duties which aeroplanes cannot do. Both these functions must be performed for the present by cavalry until we can afford mechanisation [sic]. You have cut them down, to what you consider, and what you have accepted, as the closest margin of safety.[29]

23 See Appendix C – biographies. For an illuminating debate on Winston Churchill as Chancellor of the Exchequer and his propagation and reliance on the Ten year Rule see Bell, Christopher M. "Winston Churchill and the Ten Year Rule," *The Journal of Military History* Volume 74, No 4, October 2012, pp.1097–1128.
24 Anglesey, A History of the British Cavalry, Volume 8, p.337.
25 WO 32/2846 Register 16/General/5558 Minute 13A; Churchill to Sir Laming Worthington-Evans, 27 October 1927.
26 Ibid., Minute 14A.
27 Ibid., Minute 13A; Churchill to Sir Laming Worthington-Evans, 27 October 1927.
28 Ibid., Minute 14; Milne to Sir Laming Worthington-Evans, 3 November 1927.
29 Ibid.

As David French clearly identified, the General Staff were willing to mechanize the cavalry, but were short of funds to do so.[30] It was a risk too far to reduce horsed cavalry still further.

The Final Report of the Army Council's Cavalry Committee had been presented earlier, on 4 January 1927.[31] Chaired by Lieutenant General Sir Archibald Montgomery-Massingberd, a former Royal Horse Artillery officer, the committee considered mobility and what measures could be taken to reduce the weight carried by a cavalry horse, and the type of weapon to be used, especially the so-called *arme-blanche* weapons of sword and lance. The committee was keen to mechanize as much of the cavalry division as was possible at that time, although this report expressed uncertainty on when or whether this was possible. An earlier Interim report, 23 November 1926, envisaged a two year period necessary to develop a "reliable cross-country armoured car".[32] Two years later, 3 December 1928, Montgomery-Massingberd wrote of recent AFV developments to General Sir Philip W Chetwode, the Commander-in-Chief of the Army of India: "It looks to me as if the Cavalry will want the Light Tanks and the Infantry the Machine Gun Carriers [sic]".[33] He thought there to be not much difference between the two; the tanks had more armour and machine-guns would normally be fired from them, whereas machine-guns would usually be removed from the carriers and fired mounted on a tripod. The trial had taken place of a "Carden-Loyd Tank… with a sort of armoured roof… [it] did 49 mph, for which a track is undreamable [sic]".[34] The track life was now 2000 miles and Carden-Loyds were trying to raise this to 4,000 miles he reported. In a later letter to Chetwode, 18 January 1929, Montgomery-Massingberd wrote in anticipation of a Carden-Loyd track "which would even stand the rocks of India".[35] In his previous letter he wrote that at a weight of 25 cwt the "cross-country capacity of these [Carden-Loyd armoured fighting] vehicles is quite good".[36] But this may not have been entirely accurate; in September 1928 Frederick "Tim" Pile, the Deputy Director of Mechanization, had told Liddell Hart that the Carden-Loyds had "trouble with steering and [with the] axle and tracks coming off". There was to be a revised model, but with a top-speed of 20 mph.[37] Montgomery-Massingberd hoped too for ten to fifteen Austin Seven cars per cavalry regiment and to "get their Machine Gun Squadrons in Light Tanks we

30   French, D., "The Mechanization of the British Cavalry", p.298.
31   TNA WO 32/2842 Army Organisation: Cavalry (Code 14(D)): Cavalry Committee: Final report 1926–1927.
32   TNA WO/32 3059 Army Organisation: Cavalry (Code 14(D)): Reconstruction of the Corps of Cavalry; Précis For Army Council No. 1279 Cavalry Establishments and Organization (Interim Report of the Cavalry Committee) marked 6A, pp.5 & 7; February 1927, (the Interim Report is dated 23 November 1926).
33   LHCMA – MM158/1a 10/1–10/10, The Montgomery-Massingberd Papers.
34   Ibid.
35   LHCMA – MM158/2a 10/1–10/10, The Montgomery-Massingberd Papers.
36   Ibid.,1a 10/1–10/10, The Montgomery-Massingberd Papers.
37   LHCMA – LH11/1928/1, "lunch with Pile at the Cavalry Club", September 27 1928.

ought to be able to have a very different Cavalry formation, [but] it is not going to be easy to handle a semi-mechanized Cavalry Division in the future".[38]

In the meantime, in early 1927, there was much to be considered. In order to be completely mechanized the headquarters of cavalry divisions (three brigades each of three regiments) also needed cross-country vehicles for their dismounted troops and stores.[39] However, if the rest of the cavalry had to remain horsed, read the report, so must the artillery needed to accompany it; the 13 pounder quick-firing field guns used by Royal Horse Artillery were considered no longer good enough for "modern warfare". The more suitable 18 pounder models, however, were too heavy for the horse teams pulling them to keep pace with cavalry over a long distance. The report recommended therefore, that when the cavalry was mechanized, so would be the horse artillery, adding further to the cost of any cavalry mechanization project.[40] To improve the speed and endurance of the horsed units, the report continued, a reduction in the weight carried by the horses was recommended by removing from them to the first-line transport (motor lorries) some of the kit, such as great-coats, extra ammunition and rations. The horse artillery first-line transport should be mechanized too and, except for a few mounted troops for reconnaissance and orderly duties, the engineers should be carried in mechanized cross-country vehicles and should carry bridging equipment.[41] Similarly the Signals Section was to be mechanized (in small cars) and to include soldiers riding motor-cycles.[42] The field ambulance also was to be completely mechanized and the first-line transport of the Veterinary and Provost Sections. Other recommendations included recruiting lighter weight troopers [43] "of a tall, slight, wiry type [of man]," by reducing to the infantry standard the chest measurement criteria for troopers (a 1 inch reduction in chest measurement could equate to a reduction of 7–10 lbs. in a man's weight it was suggested). The maximum weight of cavalry recruits to be reduced, therefore, from 10 stones and 7lbs to a maximum of 10 stones for men aged 20 years and over, and less for men of 18 and 19 years old.[44] Regarding cavalry weapons, read the report, the experience in Palestine and Mesopotamia (during Allenby's Great War campaign),[45] indicated there was, in addition to the rifle, a need to retain one type of *arme blanche* weapon, but not both.[46] To this report were added

38 LHCMA – MM158/1a 10/1–10/10, The Montgomery-Massingberd Papers.
39 TNA WO 32/2842 Army Organisation: Cavalry (Code 14(D)): Cavalry Committee: Final Report 1926–1927, p.8; Final Report of the Cavalry Committee, Appointed on 20/Cavalry/582, Reported on 20/Cavalry/595; marked 4A, p.3.
40 Ibid., p.4.
41 Ibid., p.5.
42 Ibid., P.6.
43 Ibid., p.8.
44 Ibid., pp.9 &10.
45 For example see Wavell, *Allenby*, pp.221 & 281 and Badsey, *Doctrine and Reform*, pp.283–288.
46 TNA WO 32/2842 Army Organisation: Cavalry (Code 14(D)): Cavalry Committee: Final Report 1926–1927, p.10.

some modifications of detail; in particular two regiments of armoured cars are "to be found from two of the existing Cav. Regts. [sic]".[47]

Milne, the CIGS, presented the report to the Parliamentary Under Secretary at the War Office, Colonel Rt. Hon. The Earl of Onslow, in July 1927. Milne's concerns were finance; to convert the two horsed regiments to armoured cars was estimated to cost £384,000, unless cars were used from an existing unit. The motor vehicles required for the other recommendations were estimated to cost £242,000 and another £34,000 for the changes to the Royal Horse Artillery. There would, however, be some savings in the cost of horses.[48] In a scrawled note dated 14 August 1927, the Secretary of State for War, Sir Lamming Worthington Evans, gave his approval "in principle" for the detailed work for implementation to begin.[49] No further progress took place, however, pending the report by Lord Salisbury's Sub-Committee, yet to be appointed. On making the decision how and when to communicate these changes to the Cavalry arm, the Adjutant General, General Sir Walter P Braithwaite, wrote:

> … [he felt] that the good cavalryman will welcome this, and he is the man we want to carry with us. The man who goes into the cavalry for a few years to have a good time, may talk large on the subject, and possibly get silly questions asked in Parliament, but I think we can ignore him and his hypothetical member that he may get to represent his views in Parliament.[50]

No announcement was made at that time because neither the Secretary of State nor the Army Council was in complete control of its own destiny. Worthington Evans, concerned, penned Minute 35 to Milne telling him Churchill would not be satisfied with the estimated expenditure reductions then offered by the Council. He would not sanction any announcement regarding mechanization, "so long as there is a risk that something more drastic may become necessary".[51] The Cabinet, still anxious about the cost of the cavalry, agreed on 16 November 1927, to appoint a Sub-Committee of the Committee of Imperial Defence to be chaired by Lord Salisbury, The Lord Privy Seal, and to include the Chancellor of the Exchequer, "to enquire and report what strength of Cavalry of the Line should be maintained".[52] The following June (1928) the Cabinet had before it the Sub-Committee's report together with its recommendation from the Committee of Imperial Defence. The Sub-Committee could not propose *any* reorganization of the cavalry that would save money; the progressive mechanization of the

---

47   Ibid., 20/Cavalry/595 Minute 19, point 6.
48   Ibid., Minute 20, 5 August 1927.
49   Ibid., Minute 22, 14 August 1927.
50   Ibid., Minute 3, 21 September 1927.
51   Ibid., Minute 35, 21 October 1927.
52   Ibid., 20/Cavalry/612 no.6, 17 November 1927; also 20/Cav/612 minute 19, 8 June 1928; TNA WO 32/2845 Army Organisation: Cavalry (Code 14(D)): Future organisation of the Cavalry: Sub-committee of Imperial Defence 1927–1928.

cavalry's machine-gun equipment and transport, and the conversion of two cavalry regiments into armoured car units, however, "should be approved". It was desirable, the report recommended, that "as increased mechanization becomes possible, of making the fullest use of the traditions of the Cavalry and of the spirit and special qualities of its personnel in its mechanized substitute". The capital cost of mechanization was noted in the report and any progress in that direction had to have "regard to financial considerations".[53] Churchill, supported by the Secretary of State for Air, Lord Thomson, was "content" with the mechanization of two cavalry regiments for the current financial year, but urged "that further measures should be taken as rapidly as possible to furnish the British cavalry with equipment suitable to modern war"; he would not be associated with a report that suggested mechanization should not take place "as rapidly as we can possibly afford".[54] No disagreement to this sentiment by other Cabinet members was recorded.

Churchill, as the Chancellor of the Exchequer, had the power to ensure mechanization *could* be afforded by allocating the necessary funds or allowing the savings in one area to be reinvested in AFV development. David French agreed: "Churchill's policy meant that he [Worthington-Evans] did not have enough money to buy enough of them [AFVs]".[55] It was perverse of Churchill to expect both mechanization, and at the same time, demand cuts in the Army Estimates. Winton was critical of the Treasury's stultifying effect on modernizing the British Army:

> Every entry [was] scrutinized and compared with the previous year … each increase had to be explicitly justified. This meant that savings in one area could not be automatically credited to additional expenses in any other area.[56]

Winton's last point that savings in one area of expenditure could not be automatically moved to another was crucial to the army's whole mechanization conundrum. Barndollar acknowledged too that the Army Estimates covered the running cost of the army, but not the "substantial outlays in research and development and even more money to manufacture [AFVs]".[57] Savings made by the army in reducing or mechanizing horsed cavalry could not then, automatically, be spent on further developing AFVs from which further savings could have accrued. It was a short-sighted,

53   Ibid., 7(a), 6 June 1928; TNA WO 32/2845 Army Organisation: Cavalry (Code 14(D)): Future organisation of the Cavalry: Sub-committee of Imperial Defence 1927–1928.
54   TNA WO 32/2842 Army Organisation: Cavalry (Code 14(D)): Cavalry Committee: Final report 1926–1927; 20/Cavalry/612 7(b), 6 June 1928; TNA WO 32/2845 Army Organisation: Cavalry (Code 14(D)): Future organisation of the Cavalry: Sub-committee of Imperial Defence 1927–1928.
55   French, D., "The Mechanization of the British Cavalry", p.311.
56   Winton, *To Change An Army*, p.25.
57   Gilman Clough Barndollar, "British Use of Armoured cars 1919–1939,"PhD, Cambridge University, 2010, p.23.

hand-to-mouth policy, but as with successive Chancellors, and Neville Chamberlain in particular, Churchill had other priorities that took precedent over mechanizing the cavalry. Without sufficient financial resources to develop suitable cross-country vehicles, however, the army was unable to make much progress.

In October 1928 two "schemes" were considered to begin the process of mechanizing the cavalry. The "Scheme A" proposal was to amalgamate two existing cavalry regiments and call for volunteers from the cavalry to form an armoured unit; later to repeat the exercise with two other cavalry regiments by some form of rotation and remounting on horses the first unit. The more logical "Scheme B" was implemented; to select two line cavalry regiments to be permanently converted to AFVs, one regiment in England and one in Egypt. The advantages of "Scheme B" were the officers and men's probable preference for conversion rather than amalgamation; efficiency would be enhanced and morale maintained by keeping the regimental identity, and continuity would be more effective than a rotation of roles as proposed with "Scheme A".[58]

The 12th Lancers

In 1928 the 11th Hussars and the 12th Lancers commenced their move from horses to armoured cars, but it took until April 1930 for the last of their horses to depart.[59] These two regiments were chosen because they were the two most junior cavalry regiments that had not been subjected to the disbandments and amalgamations of 1922. The veterans interviewed in 1977 from the 12th Lancers, seeming typical of their peers, chose to join a cavalry regiment because of their keenness for horses.[60] The 12th Lancers was a very efficient regiment, well led by officers who "knew a lot about horses, they were very able people and one needed to work hard to keep up with their standards".[61] The regiment's role in war was chiefly reconnaissance, but by dismounting, three-quarters of a troop could carry out an infantry role working with other arms and getting around the flank of an enemy to pin them down.[62] In peacetime the regiment's role was internal security, particularly in India and Egypt. The 12th Lancers was in Egypt in 1927; their horses had adapted to desert conditions,

---

58 TNA WO 32/2844 Army Organisation: Cavalry (Code 14(D)): Armoured Car Regiment: Organisation 1927–1928 – "Secret – Two schemes for the creation of cavalry armoured car units have been examined", 15 October 1927, marked 3B.

59 *XII Lancers Journal*, May 1930.

60 Colonel Kenneth Edward Savill, IWM Sound Collection, recorded 1977, access number 933, reel 1; Brigadier Rupert Harding-Newman, IWM Sound Collection, recorded 1977, access number 834, reel 3; Sir Andrew Marshall Horsburgh-Porter, IWM Sound Collection, access number 905, recorded 1977, reel 1; Colonel George Jardine Kidston-Montgomerie; IWM Sound Collection, recorded 1977, access number 892, reel 1.

61 Savill, reel 1.

62 The remainder of the troop was deployed as "horse-holders", one man per Section of four men.

moving well over both hard and soft sand, and the climate was good for their health.[63] The regiment had hoped to stay horsed and become a horsed machine-gun regiment.[64] The news came in "1926 or 1927" that the regiment would become an armoured car regiment, remembered Sir Andrew M Horsburgh-Porter. Interviewed in 1977 having retired as a colonel after the Second World War, he was a subaltern at that time, and said he knew about the conversion to armoured cars when he joined the regiment in Egypt in 1927.[65] George J Kidston-Montgomerie, also interviewed in 1977 having retired as a colonel in 1949, was a second lieutenant with the 12th Lancers in 1929; he remembered rumours were circulating, but the final decision to implement mechanization was in 1928 and this is confirmed by the Army Council records.[66] Kenneth Savill, interviewed too in 1977 and having retired from the 1st (King's) Dragoon Guards as a colonel in 1939, was also a second lieutenant with the 12th Lancers at that time. Savill remembered that when the officers and men were told they were shocked at the prospect of losing the horses:

> [But] we got over it after about a fortnight or three weeks, when we talked to others, like the Tank Corps, and decided it wasn't at all a bad thing. It was a shock to start with and rather awful, you joined the army to be on a horse, to be a cavalry soldier. We were allowed to keep two chargers each for quite a few years.[67]

63   Savill, reel 1; Kidston-Montgomerie, reel 1; personal interview with Randall (2006); by the author; personal interview with Husband (2010); by the author, regarding the effectiveness of horses in Palestine and the North West Frontier of India due to the terrain. The horses' range was 30 miles maximum and, like the armoured cars, they needed water en route. In some areas of the world the horse is still the most appropriate form of conveyance. Special Forces personnel due for deployment in Afghanistan in 2010 undertook horse riding lessons with the Household Cavalry at their Barracks in Windsor; this information gleaned by the author whilst on site researching the Household Cavalry archives, Windsor; also Stanton, *Horse Soldiers*, p.148, regarding United States Special Forces mounted on horses in Afghanistan to access, "where no truck or tank had ever been". Gilman Clough Barndollar, "British Use of Armoured cars 1919–1939,"PhD, Cambridge University, 2010, pointed out that cavalry was particularly useful "for reasons of culture, [it seems there was] a real dread of [mounted] cavalry" among the local people on the North West Frontier, pp.216/7.
64   Savill, reel 1; Kidston-Montgomerie, reel 1.
65   Horsburgh-Porter; comments on both reels 1 & 2.
66   Kidston-Montgomerie, reel 1; TNA WO 32/2844 Army Organisation: Cavalry (Code 14(D)): Armoured Car Regiment: Organisation 1927–1928 20/Cavalry/619 War Office letter to Army Commands and Cavalry and Tank Records, 4 April 1928 marked 19A.
67   Savill, reel 1; Officers alone were allowed to keep their horses, known as "chargers" or "officers' mounts".

The general reaction was one of shock, but the officers were pleased to stay within the comradeship of the regiment.[68] Concern had been expressed that by disbanding cavalry regiments, or by requiring officers and men to serve in cavalry regiments without horses, the army would be disadvantaged. Without horsed cavalry, it was suggested, the army would fail to attract the type of men, be they officers or other rank soldiers that were "by birth and upbringing, and by their habits in boyhood, natural leaders with a keen eye for the country".[69] This much feared exodus from the 11th Hussars and the 12th Lancers of officers disenchanted by the loss of their horses did not materialise; examination of the Army Lists from 1928 to 1931 show that very little change occurred. The commanding officer of the 11th Hussars, Lieutenant Colonel F H Sutton MC, was replaced and went onto half-pay, but this might have happened anyway. The only officer to move to a Regular horsed cavalry regiment was Lieutenant P R R Dunne in 1930; he moved from the 11th Hussars to the Royal Horse Guards. Captain C H Tremayne moved to the Nottinghamshire Yeomanry as a Reserve Officer. This regiment had converted to artillery in 1920, but was probably still horsed.[70] Two other officers left the regiment, Major J C Humfrey and Captain H A Jaffray; they no longer appeared on the Army List, together with Captain E Smith a year later.[71] The 12th Lancers were even less affected by officer turnover: Captain S R F Spicer transferred to the Royal Wiltshire Yeomanry, a horsed regiment, to serve as Adjutant. Captains R G Goldsmith and H Alsop disappeared from the Army List. Lieutenant W S McCleery transferred to the North Somerset Yeomanry, a horsed regiment, as temporary Captain and Adjutant. Posting a regular captain to serve as an adjutant to a yeomanry regiment was normal practice.[72] Examination of the Army Lists shows that there was usually some officer turnover from year to year.[73] Asked if any officer had left the regiment, Kenneth Savill affirmed: "No, none; they all went on with it, some of the older ones, I think, found it a bit difficult to assimilate the inside of a motor car".[74] Colonel Savill also said that the other ranks were rather pleased with the prospect:

> On the whole, because they didn't have to groom the horses anymore – from 6 am until 5 pm; grooming, feeding, cleaning – they thought they [armoured cars] would just need a bit a greasing and put petrol in, but they found they needed

68   Ibid.
69   Anon, "The Mounted Trooper in 1918 and 1930,"in *The Cavalry Journal*, October 1930, (London, Royal United Services Institution) quoted in Anglesey, *A History of the British Cavalry* Volume 8, p.336; Macksey, *A History of The Royal Armoured Corps*, p.48.
70   Mileham, *The Yeomanry Regiments*, p.104.
71   *The Army Lists*, January to March 1928, 1929, 1930 and 1931.
72   Badsey, *Doctrine and Reform*, p.76.
73   *The Army Lists*, January to March 1928, 1929, 1930 and 1931.
74   Savill, reel 1, Horsburgh-Porter, comments on both reels 1 & 2.

to do a bit more than that when the time came, but I think they rather looked forward to the change.[75]

A team of instructors, both officers and NCOs, from the 3rd Armoured Car Company of the Royal Tank Corps, facilitated the management of change.[76] Colonel Savill later said that:

They were very nice people, 3rd Armoured Car Company, very helpful. They came over every day from Abbassia to train us. They brought some armoured cars over and put them in a shed.[77]

Lieutenant R D W "Robby" Uniacke (later killed in battle during the Second World War), one of the RTC instructors was considered a most effective organiser. The other officers in the team were subalterns "Pip" Roberts (later considered by many the best armour commander of the Second World War: G P B "Pip" Roberts CB DSO MC was a Captain in 1939 and by 1943 a Major General), and Lieutenant G L Prendaghast, (who served with the Long Range Desert Group during the Second World War).

Later, the 12th Lancers took over all the 3rd Armoured Car Company's vehicles. The 3rd Armoured Car Company was sorry to lose their armoured cars as they were destined for heavy tanks.[78] "But there was no resentment,"said Savill.[79] George Lindsay confirmed this and reported that there was "good comradeship" between the RTC and the 12th Lancers.[80] After getting their armoured cars the 12th Lancers were:

Bent on mechanization and they were very keen indeed, the men very, very keen and so were the officers and we had to get on with it quickly – Colonel

75   Savill, reel 1.
76   TNA WO 32/2842 Army Organisation: Cavalry (Code 14(D)): Cavalry Committee: Final report 1926–1927; "Armoured Car Regiments – Secret,"1 December 1927, marked 9a.
77   Savill, reel 1; Harding –Newman, reel 1; Kidston-Montgomerie, reel 1 & Horsburgh-Porter, reel 1.
78   The 3rd Armoured Car Company was later equipped with six Mark IIA tanks, adapted for service in Egypt. The tanks were "sun protected by an ineffective covering of asbestos sheeting. The temperature became too hot for these tanks to be used after 10.30 each morning"; Harding Newman, reel 3. TNA WO 32/2842 Army Organisation: Cavalry (Code 14(D)): Cavalry Committee: Final report 1926–1927; "Armoured Car Regiments – Secret,"1 December 1927, marked 9a; the original plan was equip 3rd Armoured Car Company with "tankettes". Also LHCMA – LH15/12/3, Reports for the CIGS on the Royal Tank Corps for1927 and 1928.
79   Savill, reel 2.
80   LHCMA – LH15/12/21 (Private file) 341; Lindsay to Hotblack, 24 December 1929.

Charrington (the 12th Lancers commanding officer) was a great inspiration in this – and he took to it like a duck to water.[81]

Unlike the 11th Hussars, which underwent the mechanization process in one year, it took three years to mechanize the 12th Lancers. The regiment mechanized by squadron: B Squadron was the first, from the summer of 1927 (some months before the decision was confirmed by the Army Council),[82] whilst the other two squadrons, A and C, remained horsed.[83] Horsburgh-Porter explained why B Squadron was chosen to lead the change process. The regiment was in an operational role in Egypt and could spare only one squadron at a time for retraining. The machine-gun section was "rather the elite of the regiment, specialists, more intelligent chaps,"and B Squadron contained the machine-gun section. The mounted men from B Squadron went to A and C Squadrons. They were replaced in B Squadron by other men, presumably thought to be more suitable, from A and C Squadrons, and together with the machine-gun section retrained for mechanization.

The 12th Lancers continued to exercise as a complete regiment as Savill explained:

> Joint training was novel. The colonel arranged exercises we could do together –
> the armoured cars couldn't always go where the horses went, but armoured cars
> could go further and faster – horses seven mph over a twenty mile radius, the
> armoured car would go fifty miles.[84]

In 1928 six officers were sent from the 12th Lancers for training to the Royal Tank Corps depot at Bovington.[85] Training was for the Rolls Royce armoured car and the machine gun. This course was especially arranged for the cavalry officers from both the 11th Hussars and the 12th Lancers. The course took the students through "mechanics" demonstrated by a cut down bench model of a Rolls Royce car so that the workings of the engine, electrics and brakes could be carefully examined. The students were also taught to drive the car around Bovington. This proved poor preparation for driving in Egypt where the sand could overturn an armoured car, buckling the steering arms and snapping a half-shaft. Machine-gun training was at Lulworth, firing the .303

---

81   Horsburgh-Porter, reel 1; Lieutenant Colonel H V S Charrington MC had taken command of the 12th Lancers in September 1927. Lieutenant Colonel J W Hornby MC took over command on 6 September 1931; *Army Lists* 1928–1931.

82   TNA WO 32/2844 Army Organisation: Cavalry (Code 14(D)): Armoured Car Regiment: Organisation 1927–1928 20/Cavalry/619 War Office letter to Army Commands and Cavalry and Tank Records, 4 April 1928 marked 19A.

83   Kidston-Montgomerie, reel 1.

84   Savill reel 1; Horsburgh-Porter, reel 1.

85   Savill reel 2; Horsburgh-Porter, reels 1 & 2; Kidston-Montgomerie, reel 1.

weapon from the car's turret.[86] The veterans interviewed in 1977 praised the welcome, enthusiasm and support of the Royal Tank Corps instructors.

1928 also brought training in wireless and all three squadrons of the 12th Lancers took part. Five wireless sets were provided; one was for each squadron and two for Regimental headquarters. These sets were operated by Lieutenant Hepper and his men from the Royal Corps of Signals. One wireless set was for forward communications with the squadrons and the other wireless set was for communications with Brigade headquarters.[87] At the same time the 11th Hussars had similar wireless sets issued in England. These sets were powerful enough for the two regiments to communicate with each other between England and Egypt. When horsed, the regiments had used flags for signalling, effective for up to a mile, but the increased range afforded by the armoured cars forced a change in technology, although flags still had to be used for some time.[88]

As a horsed cavalry regiment, the three "sabre squadrons" of the 12th Lancers were organised into four troops each of thirty men and horses. As an armoured car regiment, a squadron operated five troops, each having three armoured cars with a crew of five men, saving up to forty horsemen from the establishment of each squadron. Each car and its machine-gun were the responsibility of its crew. Crew roles were intended to be interchangeable. The regiment's role and tactics for armoured cars evolved from the horsed cavalry tactics manual as there were no training manuals for armoured car regiments.[89] Savill's view was that armoured cars were not more effective than horsed cavalry, but could cover a larger area. The RTC had only used armoured cars on the roads, but Colonel Hornby, who had succeeded Colonel Charrington as commanding officer in September 1931, was determined to get into the desert.[90] Techniques were developed for getting a stuck car out of the desert sand: bamboo racks and sand mats, together with a new design of tyre, wider and at a lower air pressure that better traversed soft sand.[91] "We soon learned being an armoured car regiment was a jolly good life".[92]

Sir Andrew Horsburgh-Porter (12th Lancers) was pressed during his interview in 1977, to comment on the attitudes of officers and men to the 12th Lancers becoming mechanized. Of particular importance was whether Colonel Charrington's inspirational leadership was typical of other senior officers, he replied:

> Yes – I think so – the great thing was to get on with it quickly – and the 11th Hussar officers were the same – no doubt the 11th and 12th were hand over

86   Savill, reel 2.
87   Ibid.
88   Savill, reel 2; Horsburgh-Porter, reel 1.
89   Kidston-Montgomerie, reel 1.
90   Horsburgh-Porter, reel 1; Lieutenant Colonel J W Hornby MC, *Army List* 1932.
91   Savill, reel 2.
92   Savill, reel 1.

The Troop leader of a section of Lanchester Mk.II Armoured Cars of the 12th Lancers signaling by flag to the other vehicles during manoeuvres, circa 1938.
(Source: The Tank Museum, Bovington – 3405-F5)

fist the best trained regiments when war broke out and supplied a great many commanders to other mechanized units.[93] The junior officers' opinions don't really count at all – all they wanted to do was stay on a horse, but they soon came round… Those who joined cavalry regiments – we liked playing polo, hunting or racing – we liked the horse…. Old "unmechanizable" sergeants and warrant officers who had spent their whole time with horses, they were very upset, naturally, and most of them, [but actually] very few of them, got transfers into other regiments.[94]

93   Sir Andrew Horsburgh-Porter was probably recalling the 11th Hussar officers such as Major General J F B Combe CB DSO who commanded "Combe Force" at the Battle of Beda Fomm in 1941, also Colonel D McMorrough-Kavanagh KCVO, who commanded the 2nd Light Armoured Brigade in the Battle for France in 1940, and Brigadier D S Schreiber, who commanded an Indian Army Tank Brigade during the Second World War; The Army List; also Upton, The Cherry Pickers.
94   Horsburgh-Porter, reel 2.

Kidston-Montgomerie agreed: the senior NCOs in particular, "old horsemen, the "rough-riders" were very sad" at losing the horses. Although most stayed, some NCOs did transfer to horsed regiments. He stated that those who stayed might not have liked mechanization, but "they did it and got used to it; most of the corporals came through as good instructors". Horsburgh-Porter confirmed that once the work load of the other ranks in the mechanized B Squadron was compared with their own as horsemen in A and C squadrons, this had a "very good psychological effect – roll on the time when we get our cars [they said]".[95]

The 11th Hussars

As with the 12th Lancers, the 11th Hussars interviewees recorded in 1977 joined the regiment because they were keen horsemen.[96] A high standard was expected of the officers and, until he had proved himself, it could be an unfriendly place for a newly arrived subaltern.[97] The regiment was at Aldershot and their role was reconnaissance.[98] The regiment already had motorised regimental transport; lorries to carry the fodder, horse shoes and spare equipment,[99] but interviewees had no remembrance of any talk of mechanization before the actual announcement. This was made on 10 March 1928 to the officers in the mess one lunch time by Major General Thomas Tait Pitman, the Colonel of the 11th Hussars.[100] He inspired the officers by talking of the regiment's proud traditions and hoped that no officer would choose to leave the regiment.[101] At the same time, recalled Peter Wiggin, then a second lieutenant (interviewed in 1977 having retired a colonel in 1942), the commanding officer "Lieutenant Colonel Sutton said: "We all go or we all stay," so we all stayed".[102] Viscount [Dudley] Allenby, interviewed by the Imperial War Museum in 1977, was a lieutenant and the Adjutant of the 11th Hussars from 1927 until 1930. Allenby joined the regiment in 1923 and said during the interview that "virtually every officer was told no one was to hand in their commission, and no one did; the spirit was good".[103] The NCOs were told three days later on 13 March.

95   Ibid.
96   Lieutenant Colonel D Forster IWM Sound Collection, access number 919, recorded 1977, reel 1. Colonel Peter Milner Wiggin, IWM Sound Collection, access number 918, recorded 1977, reel 1. Viscount Dudley Jaffray Hynman Allenby, IWM Sound Collection, access number 878, recorded 1977.
97   Wiggin, reel 1.
98   Allenby, reel 1.
99   Wiggin, reel 1.
100 Ibid; Forster, reel 1; Allenby, reel 1. This is confirmed in the regimental journal – *XI Hussar Journal* Vol. XII, Aldershot, April 1928, No.1, p.21.
101 Forster, reel 1; Allenby reel 1.
102 Wiggin, reel 1.
103 Allenby, reel 1.

The War Office envisaged five phases to the management of change from horses to armoured cars involving the 21 officers and 415 men of the regiment each of whom had at least twelve months of service remaining:-

1. Horses, except officers' chargers and fifty riding horses, together with the saddlery no longer required, to be withdrawn between 20 and 30 April 1928.
2. 13 of the 21 Regimental Officers and 20 warrant officers (WO) and non-commissioned officers (NCOs) to go to Wool for driving and maintenance training and to Lulworth for gunnery training – May to July 1928, the remainder to administer the regiment and train the men in driving and machine-gun work.
3. During manoeuvres in August and September two parties of officers and NCOs that have been trained by the RTC to be attached to the RTC's armoured car companies; parties of other ranks from the 11th Hussars to go for driving and maintenance and gunnery training at the RTC schools.
4. A return to the RTC schools for the first 13 officers and 20 WOs and NCOs for the second phase of training from September to December, to become fully qualified instructors in gunnery and driving and maintenance. At the end of this course they were to return to the regiment as instructors. During the same period at the regiment, driving and machine-gun training [was] to continue. During December the arrival of the first allotment of armoured cars was planned.
5. Those officers who had remained with the regiment were now to go for their training at Wool and Lulworth until March 1929 when they would return to the regiment for the training season after which they would complete their training at the RTC schools – September to December 1929.[104]

The last mounted parade of the 11th Hussars occurred in mid-April 1928 as planned, and then everything moved rapidly. Most of the horses went as remounts to other horsed regiments, others were sold.[105] The officers were upset at the prospect of losing the horses, but like the 12th Lancers, officers were allowed to keep two "chargers" and Wiggin remembered fifty horses remaining for the men to appear mounted in the Royal Tournament. Douglas Forster, then a subaltern (interviewed in 1977, having retired a lieutenant colonel after the Second World War) remembered:

> Practically everyone decided to stop on and see what happened. We were allowed to keep two chargers and a soldier-servant as a groom – we could hunt or use them as polo ponies – of course they all went in the end. It was an order and that

104 TNA WO 32/2844 Army Organisation: Cavalry (Code 14(D)): Armoured Car Regiment: Organisation 1927–1928 20/Cavalry/619 War Office letter to all Commands, 4 1928.
105 Wiggin, reel 1; Allenby, reel 1 – This is confirmed in the regimental journal – *XI Hussar Journal* Vol. XII, Aldershot, April 1928, No.1, p.41.

was that. After one had got over the initial shock, one realised that we, and 12th Lancers, had the advantage; it appeared then that the cavalry was going to be mechanized over a period and we would be the first in. It was up to us to do it well and others would look to our experience.[106]

Wiggin confirmed this:

The reaction was one of horror, we thought it would never happen to us, but as it would happen eventually to every cavalry regiment and we were getting in on the ground floor, we could see the advantage of being first.[107]

Viscount Allenby spoke of the 11th Hussars' resolve:

[There was] utter determination to make a success of it – by then even the junior regimental officer knew the role of [horsed] cavalry was coming to an end sooner or later – and it was some years later – it [mechanization] was a test and a challenge and useful for other regiments later on that it could be done and wasn't dreadful.[108]

Allenby also said that although losing the horses was disappointing, mechanization was seen as a bit on an adventure. As for the reactions of the other ranks to the news, neither Forster nor Wiggin could remember anyone wanting to leave the regiment. Although not welcomed, except for not needing to do all the work associated with horse care, mechanization soon became accepted.[109] "They were 11th Hussars and had to get down to it".[110] Some men were posted away, however, such as the farriers.[111]

The 11th Hussar officers attended the course at Bovington almost en masse, including the senior officers, and had to rent a country house nearby for accommodation. The initial course at Bovington also included 10 NCOs from the 11th Hussars. A sergeant and 6 other ranks attended a technical store-keeping course at the Royal Army Ordnance Corps (RAOC) depot at Aldershot.[112] Like the 12th Lancers, the 11th Hussars much praised the enthusiasm and efficiency of the Royal Tank Corps instructors who taught the officers mechanics and how to instruct others.[113] Although Wiggin remembered that:

106 Forster, reel 1.
107 Wiggin, reel 1.
108 Allenby, reel 1.
109 Forster, reel 1.
110 Wiggin, reel 1.
111 Ibid.
112 *XI Hussar Journal* Vol. XII, Aldershot, October 1928, No.2, p.53.
113 Allenby, reel 1; Forster, reel 1.

There was some antipathy in those days, originally [between cavalry and Royal Tank Corps] because of different interests. I want to make this quite clear that this disappeared a long time ago now'.[114]

"Mechanics" at that time, appears to refer to planned, preventative vehicle maintenance such as changing the engine oil, lubricating wheel bearings, cleaning engine spark plugs, etc., together with basic repairs, such as replacing a broken wheel or water pump. Although some soldiers in the Royal Tank Corps might have thought cavalry soldiers incapable of doing these things and resented their involvement with armoured fighting vehicles, Wiggin went on to say that:

They [the Royal Tank Corps] seemed happy for us to take over reconnaissance. The Tank Corps had no long distance reconnaissance vehicle and was more interested in being in large numbers and closely involved in battle – the cavalry's role was to see and not be seen – get as much information as you could in that way. Relationships were good with the Tank Corps; they were very kind to us.

The cavalry NCOs emerged as more "mechanically-minded" than some of the officers and later became effective regimental instructors. Much time was spent driving as most of the officers had little previous driving experience, although some owned cars, "and could change a wheel".[115] The armoured cars were heavy, clumsy and "the brakes were not very good".[116]

Back at Aldershot the regiment was issued with a few, (probably Rolls Royce) armoured cars. The regiment also had Morris saloon cars in which to train soldiers to drive. The newly trained officers taught the NCOs to drive, none had ever driven a motor vehicle before and there was a plethora of accidents and some "hair-raising moments up Guildford High Street".[117] By September 1929 the 11th Hussars had been equipped with 22 Rolls Royce armoured cars and 6 Lanchester armoured cars.[118] This was half the army's total establishment of armoured cars, other than the armoured cars in India, the army establishment was only 56 and the 12th Lancers had the other half.[119] Gunnery was taught and eventually, the wireless. Wiggin said that gunnery

114 Wiggin, reel 2.
115 Wiggin, reel 2.
116 Forster, reel 2; Wiggin, reel 2.
117 Forster, reel 2.
118 *XI Hussar Journal* Vol. XIII, Aldershot, March 1929, No.1 p.10 and *XI Hussar Journal* Vol. XIII, Aldershot, October 1929, No.2 p.54.
119 TNA WO 32/2844 Army Organisation: Cavalry (Code 14(D)): Armoured Car Regiment: Organisation 1927–1928; "Armoured Car Regiments – Secret,"1 December 1927, marked 9a; 3rd Battalion RTC 12 cars, 12th Armoured Car Company 12 cars, 3rd Armoured Car Company (Egypt) 16 cars, 5th Armoured Car Company (Shanghai) 16 cars.

from the car was "very dicey in those days… it was very dicey if you hit the target at all". He also added that wireless "was very slow in coming".[120]

The full complement of armoured cars took a long time to arrive and lorries were used instead of armoured cars for driver training,[121] but discipline was maintained by keeping to previous horsed cavalry practice: routine vehicle maintenance replaced "stables" and the old armoured cars with which the regiment had been issued took a lot of work. Traditions died hard; some officers continued to wear spurs (as they were required to do until a change in dress regulations),[122] but spurs were totally impractical (and useless of course) for driving and soon went. "We took to wearing overalls, not very willingly".[123]

Out on exercise with the infantry, the 11th Hussars used motorcycle despatch riders for communication. Tactics, however, were mostly theoretical:

> There was a tactical school, but it was mostly discussions because we were the first, I don't think anybody knew much – it was just one's own common sense really, after all we had been trained with the horses [on reconnaissance]. The cars were so slow then, I think we thought we could have been better on a horse because if you went forward you had to get your information back – there was only the motorcycle… I certainly didn't feel any safer in an armoured car than on a horse. The tactical use of an armoured car was, up to a point, the same as a horse, but you could cover more distance, but I had never fought on a horse.[124]

Wiggin explained, the Lanchester armoured car was particularly "very heavy, unwieldy and slow," and the men of the 11th Hussars did not like them; Wiggin implied the men's preference for the Rolls Royce model.[125] The maximum speed of each armoured car was similar at 45 mph. The Rolls Royce, however, weighed 4.5 tons, with armour of 12 mm thickness and almost certainly accelerated at a greater rate than the Lanchester that weighed 7 tons, with 9 mm of armour.[126] Wiggin also stated:

> The armoured car wasn't meant to be an offensive weapon – it was like the cavalry – we had to fight to get our information, not to have a pitched battle… Reconnaissance with armoured cars was more restricted than on horses that

---

120 Forster, reel 2; Wiggin, reel 2; the armoured car was armed with the .303 Vickers machine-gun.
121 Wiggin, reel 2.
122 TNA WO 32/3302 Regimental Dress and badges: Other Arms (Code 43(K)): Wearing of spurs in mechanised and converted units 1937–1938.
123 Wiggin, reel 2.
124 Forster, reel 2.
125 Wiggin, reel 2.
126 URL: <http://en.wikipedia.org/wiki/Lanchester_6x4_Armoured_Car> accessed 06.04.2011.

Crossley Armoured Car – maximum speed 45 mph, circa 1930.
(Source: The Tank Museum Bovington – 9361-A3)

A Lanchester 6x4 Armoured Car, 1938 The 12th Lancers; note the Warrant Officer is still wearing spurs and two of the men appear to be wearing the cavalry style "tent" hat rather than the "tank" beret. (Source: Source: The Tank Museum, Bovington – 9361-A2)

The Rolls Royce Armoured Car, circa 1930.
(Source: The Tank Museum, Bovington – 0796-G4)

could go across country – Salisbury Plain and the desert were OK – otherwise [the armoured cars were] restricted by roads, villages and bridges, but if you were fired upon, unlike the horse, you couldn't get off the road, jumping a fence, but at least you were protected by a few inches of armour that you weren't on a horse. [We did not know] half the time, what we were doing. We started writing the armoured car manuals plus training directives, probably for the whole British Army.[127]

Each crew was allocated its own vehicle, in the way that a horseman had been allocated his own horse, to take pride in and to care for. Gradually "trades" began to emerge: gunner, wireless operator, driver, car commander, but this seems not to have been fully in place until after 1932. In the beginning the "heavy maintenance" was carried out by mechanical engineers in Aldershot, (probably the Royal Army Ordnance Corps), but later the 11th Hussars had their own regimental fitters.[128] "It was difficult to start with… [but later] we got rather good at it and could repair our own cars".[129] In the years that followed some officers and NCOs went on advanced engineering courses at the College of Military Science in Woolwich.[130] Wiggin

127 Wiggin, reel 2.
128 Forster, reel 2.
129 Wiggin, reel 2.
130 Allenby, reel, 1; Wiggin, reel 2.

remembered too that these were younger men and although not selected because of it, they were keen on mechanics as younger men were at that time.[131] The 11th Hussars was "a family" and was determined to do a good job of something that they originally did not want to do. Ralph Younger remembered that: "Both 11th Hussars and 12th Lancers were outstandingly good regiments and took mechanization in their stride, as they had to do".[132]

In summary

In the 1920s politicians and public alike looked forward to a world of peace. This expectation was reinforced by a growing web of inter-national treaties that confirmed non-aggression or mutual defence pacts. The League of Nations successfully worked to resolve many disputes by non-military methods. In Great Britain successive governments told the armed services no war was to be planned for, for the ensuing ten years. A peace movement, growing in numbers and influence, coupled with the electorates' gradual drift to support anti-war left of centre views (see Appendix D), made increased defence spending politically unacceptable. Service budgets were consequently reduced and pressure was exerted upon the army in particular to further reduce its expenditure. The army's role was one of peace keeping both in Great Britain and the Empire; horsed cavalry was particularly useful for this purpose.

Development in cross-country AFV engineering was in its infancy and needed a considerable financial investment to progress. When a successful prototype tank was made, with little need for it, the government chose not to fund its refinement and production. The only vehicles with which to mechanize horsed cavalry regiments were the army's 56 armoured cars. The officers and men of the regiments chosen to be mechanized were initially shocked and upset at the prospect of losing their horses, but they quickly saw the opportunity of leading the way to what both the General Staff and cavalrymen had expected to be the future for their arm of the service; in any case there was little choice, it was an order that had to be followed. Morale remained high; almost all the officers, warrant officers, NCOs and men stayed with their regiments and successfully managed the change from horses to AFVs. When eventually engaged in battle the 11th Hussars and the 12th Lancers proved to be two of the British Army's most effective armoured regiments during the Second World War.[133]

---

131 Ibid.
132 Major General Ralph Younger, IWM Sound Collection, access number 913, recorded 1977, reel 1. Larson, *The British Army and the Theory of Armored Warfare* correctly claimed that the experience of the 11th Hussars and 12th Lancers showed that "the cavalry were willing, if not eager to convert themselves into mechanised soldiers," quoted in Gilman Clough Barndollar, "British Use of Armoured cars 1919–1939," PhD, Cambridge University, 2010, p.341; French, D., "The Mechanization of the British Cavalry," p.299.
133 Larson, *The British Army and the Theory of Armored Warfare*, pp.339–340.

4

Mechanization Phase Two 1930–1936

The Experiment – the dragons porté and the 3rd Hussars

Malcolm Smith argued in 1984, that for historians, the problem we have in considering the Thirties is the Second World War; "such a crucial phase in British history, refracts [our] perspectives on the Thirties".[1]

The pressures and influences that drove government policies in the 1920s continued into the next decade, perhaps even with greater intensity, certainly during the first half of the 1930s. The security situation was, for much of the period, the least of the worries of many of the electorate in Great Britain. The political situation, moving on from the late 1920s and into the early 1930s, appeared if not unstable, then uncertain. First a minority Labour Government was in power followed quickly by a Conservative dominated National coalition Government led by the same Labour Prime Minister whose "sole, original raison d'être" was financial recovery.[2] The earlier politicians' fear of civil unrest or even revolution appears to have reduced, but there was anxiety amongst the cabinet and security service regarding communist infiltration and subversion within the armed services. The so-called "Invergordon mutiny" was viewed by some as an industrial strike, but not by others in whom it evoked recollections that the downfall of both the Tsar and the Kaiser was aided and abetted by naval mutinies.[3] "Invergordon produced an extensive purge of naval personnel. Almost a thousand were discharged".[4] There were attempts to subvert soldiers in British barracks; Ronald Lucas of the 15th/19th Hussars acknowledged, with a knowing smile, "yes, we knew about that",[5] and this led, in 1934, to the

---

1   Smith, *British Air Strategy*, p.306.
2   Ibid., p.307.
3   Andrew, *The Defence of the Realm*, p.163.
4   Ibid., p.164.
5   Personal interview with Lucas (2012); by the author.

passing of the Incitement to Disaffection Act; however, few prosecutions have occurred under this Act.[6]

Army operations

As for army operations, there was no longer a military commitment in Turkey; in Ireland eight infantry battalions of British troops were needed, but only in Northern Ireland, and by December 1920 British troops had withdrawn from the Rhineland. India was another matter. In 1930 Gandhi began a civil disobedience campaign. Harold Pyman remembered in 1971, that when he was posted there as a RTC subaltern in 1934 the sub-continent of India "was in a state of political eruption and remained so for years… this usually resulted in some part of the Army being called out to assist the civil power in restoring order".[7] There were incursions on India's North-West frontier to be dealt with too. The 15th/19th Hussars were stationed in Peshwar, the 4th/7th Dragoon Guards in Kohat, the 4th Hussars in Karachi, the 3rd Hussars in Lucknow and the 9th Lancers in the Mehow District. These horsed cavalry regiments, supported by RTC armoured car companies, were part of the large deployment of British troops on the sub-continent. There was a cavalry brigade in Egypt; in 1929 this was made up of The Royals, the 10th Hussars and the 12th Lancers. British troops continued to be deployed in Bermuda, Ceylon, Cyprus, Hong Kong, Shanghai, and West Africa. (see Appendix B for detailed deployment)

The Great Depression

Europe's economic regeneration of the second half of the 1920s was heavily reliant on both the moral and financial support of the United States. US money gave confidence to European investors and American financial support had provided a permissive basis through the Dawes Plan (1924) for the Locarno Treaty (1925) to be agreed.[8] Susan Howson argued US investment "virtually kept the German economy going".[9] The United States economy, the world's largest, boomed and American loans to European countries started to reduce during 1928 diverted away to a more attractive US stock market.[10] The US Central Bank, the Federal Reserve, known as "the Fed", worried that over investment had taken place and the US economy would "over-heat". To try to restrict the money supply, and apply a gentle brake, the Federal Reserve raised the so-called discount rate,

6   Ibid., pp.164–166; URL: <http://www.parliament.the-stationery-office.co.uk/pa/ld200203/ldselect/ldrelof/95/9508.htm> accessed 25.04.2013.
7   Pyman, *Call to Arms*, p.20.
8   Steiner, *The Lights That Failed*, p.101.
9   Howson, Domestic Money Management In Britain, p.64.
10   Lewis, *Economic Survey 1919–1939*, p.57; Howson, *Domestic Money Management In Britain*, p.65.

or inter-bank lending rate.[11] The effect of this was not as envisaged. Investors were bold and risk averse when confidence was high, but with large sums of accumulated wealth at stake, were somewhat nervous people. By autumn 1929 the Feds gradual tightening of the money supply had caused an increasing unease among the members of the New York Wall Street Stock Exchange. This unease suddenly tipped over to a panic. In a few hours on 24 October 1929 (so called "black Thursday" or Friday in Europe due to the time difference), millions of dollars evaporated from the value of government stocks and corporate shares. The US economy began to collapse causing an economic tsunami that eventually engulfed most of the world, but especially Europe.[12] Austria, Hungary, and Germany, that had been so reliant on American funds,[13] were the first European countries to be hit. In May 1931 *Credit Anstalt*, a Viennese bank, collapsed and created a crisis of confidence in the European banking system beginning with the German *Reichsbank*.[14] It was this banking crisis by the summer of 1931 "that actually plunged Europe into the depths of an unprecedented structural crisis that fundamentally altered the financial and economic landscape for the rest of the decade";[15] the "depression" had begun. In September 1931 "Great Britain was forced to leave the gold standard, allowing the pound to float freely, its value determined by market forces".[16]

The 1930s was later called the "Devil's Decade", the "Morbid age", "the Hungry Thirties", "the economic blizzard", and other such dismal titles. For many in Great Britain it was a very difficult time. World trade had already contracted by the time the crash occurred in Great Britain. The older industries that had led the pre-Great War export trade were under pressure from foreign markets.[17] The "ailing giants" of British industry were textiles, coal mining, the iron and steel industries and ship building;

11   Remarks by Governor Ben S. Bernanke at the H. Parker Willis Lecture in Economic Policy, Washington and Lee University, Lexington, Virginia, March 2, 2004; citing 1963, Milton Friedman and Anna J. Schwartz, [1963] – *A Monetary History of the United States, 1867–1960*. Princeton, N.J.: Princeton University Press for NBER; URL: <http://www.federalreserve.gov/boarddocs/speeches/2004/200403022/default.htm> accessed 29.06.2011; Steiner, *The Lights That Failed*, p.803.
12   Ibid.; Stevenson and Cook, *The Slump*, p.1.
13   Steiner, *The Lights That Failed*, p.803.
14   Stevenson, and Cook, *The Slump*, p.2; Lewis, *Economic Survey*, p.63; Howson, *Domestic Money Management In Britain*, p.75.
15   Steiner, *The Lights That Failed*, p.804.
16   Remarks by Governor Ben S. Bernanke At the H. Parker Willis Lecture in Economic Policy, Washington and Lee University, Lexington, Virginia March 2, 2004, citing Milton Friedman and Anna J. Schwartz, [1963] – *A Monetary History of the United States, 1867–1960*; Choudhri, Ehsan, and Levis Kochin (1980). "The Exchange Rate and the International Transmission of Business Cycle Disturbances: Some Evidence from the Great Depression", *Journal of Money, Credit, and Banking*, 12, pp.565–74; Eichengreen, Barry, and Jeffrey Sachs (1985). "Exchange Rates and Economic Recovery in the 1930s", *Journal of Economic History*, 45, pp.925–46, URL: <http://www.federalreserve.gov/boarddocs/speeches/2004/200403022/default.htm> accessed 29.06.2011.
17   Howson, *Domestic Money Management In Britain*, p.66.

the areas of the country where these had traditionally predominated suffered badly. Concern over these domestic issues returned to Westminster the minority Labour Government of James Ramsay MacDonald, but the Wall Street Crash ended any hopes of an economic recovery.[18] Some of the fiscal measures insisted upon by the Conservatives as a condition of their support, such as the 10 percent cut in unemployment benefit "across the board", were an anathema to socialist members of the Labour Government and the government resigned.[19] From 24 August 1931, Ramsay MacDonald continued as Prime Minister at the head of a National Government that included members of the three main political parties, the majority of whom were Conservatives. A general election in October 1931 gave the National Government a mandate with a majority of 497 seats.[20]

Economic orthodoxy prevailed;[21] the government's reaction was predictable, regardless of political affiliation.[22] The large deficit in the National Budget was addressed by increased taxes and reduced government expenditure. With the need to reduce public expenditure and a hopeful outcome for the disarmament talks going on in Geneva, the government took the line of least resistance and continued to reduce the defence estimates. The army in 1931 was reduced in size from 325,000 to 207,537 men.

Geneva Disarmament Conference, the Church and the Peace Movement

The Geneva Disarmament conference expected an attendance of 2,400 delegates, representing 1,700,000,000 of the world's population, experts and secretaries together with 500 journalists. A further encouragement of success was the participation of Turkey and the United States as they were not members of the League of Nations. A reduction to the $4,000,000,000 dollars spent on armaments by the sixty-one nations represented was hoped for that would help solve the economic problems experienced by most of them.[23]

Support for the Geneva talks in particular and the peace-movement in general was popular, even fashionable, and the Non-Conformist churches began to align themselves with it. In October 1929 the "Christ for Peace" campaign was launched and called on all churches to condemn modern warfare. Also in 1929, Dr Leyton Richards, a well-known Birmingham pacifist clergyman, published *The Christians Alternative to War*; a measure of the growing popularity of the peace-movement was its four reprints

---

18   Stevenson, and Cook, *The Slump*, p.1.
19   Ibid., pp.2 & 61; Steiner, *The Lights That Failed*, p.808; "The ravages of the depression did much to discredit not only the capitalist system but also liberal democratic practices".
20   Stevenson, and Cook, *The Slump*, p.2; Pugh, *The Making of Modern British Politics*, p.259.
21   Steiner, *The Lights That Failed*, pp.802 & 806; Self, *Neville Chamberlain*, p.188.
22   Winch, *Economics and Policy*, p.209.
23   *The Times*, 02.02 1932; report of the Conference President Sir Arthur Henderson's comments.

in thirteen months.[24] The Church of England did not support the campaign at first, but in 1930 the Lambeth Conference of bishops of the Anglican Communion past the unequivocal resolution, "War as a method of settling international disputes is incompatible with the teaching of our Lord Jesus Christ".[25] At the same time Mahatma Gandhi's encouragement of non-violent action inspired many, and peace activists met Gandhi on his visit to Britain in 1931; he stayed at Kingsley Hall hosted by Christian pacifist Miss Muriel Lester. The Church of England's peace standard-bearer soon emerged as the charismatic broadcaster and author Reverend Dick Sheppard, Canon of St Paul's Cathedral.[26] Dick Sheppard had been a Chaplain in the Great War, albeit briefly, but was not a pacifist until 1927, the year his book *The Impatience of a Parson* was published. Ceadel argued that Sheppard was looking for a cause to "revitalize" the Church of England; "the memory of unseemly Christian enthusiasm for the Great War had urgently to be purged if purity and prestige of organized religion were to be restored".[27] Through his radio broadcasts Sheppard became very influential.[28] Four interviewees, speaking in 2008 and 2009, remembered Dick Sheppard quite vividly: Margorie Stead attended a Sheppard meeting, Stanley Chapman listened to him on the radio, William Bate was "well aware of his efforts", and Kay Ash, an avid newspaper reader, clearly recalled Sheppard's popularity.[29]

At the beginning of the conference the dream of disarmament and peace throughout the world was within reach. A rally of all Great Britain's churches and religious organisations was held in the Royal Albert Hall presided over by the Archbishop of Canterbury. Congregational, Wesleyan, Roman and Anglo-Catholics, men, women and children sang and joined in prayer that the Geneva conference would be successful in eliminating bombers, submarines and all aggressive weapons.[30]

Within government, security concerns appeared on the horizon with unrest between Japan and China. In 1932 the British Government appraised the nation's defence capability and abandoned the "10 year rule", but, Smith argues, "no assumption took place while Geneva [Disarmament Conference] was in session".[31] This delayed rearmament, but demonstrated the government's cognisance of both the economic situation and public opinion hopeful for success at Geneva.

24   Ceadel, *Pacifism in Britain*, pp.67/70; Britain by Mass Observation papers (1940) (Box 1 file A), University of Sussex.
25   Ceadel, *Pacifism in Britain*, p.68.
26   See Appendix C – biographies; also – Scott, *Dick Sheppard*, p.232; "Friends", *Dick Sheppard By His Friends*, pp.39, 66 and 81–100.
27   Ceadel, *Pacifism in Britain*, p.59.
28   "Friends", *Dick Sheppard By His Friends*, p.116.
29   Personal interviews with Ash, Bate, Chapman and Stead (2008/9); by the author.
30   *The Times* 14.02.1932 p.14; *Daily Mail* 05.02.1932 p.16 – The Church Assembly Resolution report; 09.02.1932 p.10 – bombing of Shanghi report.
31   Smith, *British Air Strategy*, p.124.

Geneva, banning bombers tanks and heavy guns

The amazingly popular cinema had screened on the "newsreel" in 1931 pictures of the Japanese invasion of Manchuria. This was an example of what future war would be like. William Bate confirmed newsreels "were staple parts of the programme", and particularly remembered seeing the bombing of Shanghai.[32] Stanley Chapman remembered newsreels of the Japanese bombing of Nanking, and later the war in Abyssinia; he said these stoked up fears of what aerial bombing could do.[33] Bate and Chapman confirmed Hinton's assertion that the newsreel footage of the bombing of Shanghai caused much anxiety.[34] The Shanghai bombing "magnified worries of the peace groups and validated claims underlying the call for their [bombers] abolition".[35] In a speech on 10 November 1932, Stanley Baldwin coined the phrase, "the bomber will always get through", and "he [Baldwin] was right", confirmed veteran cavalryman Robert Cruddace, (in correspondence in 2007 and who was serving in India in 1932).[36] Winston Churchill, the Member of Parliament for Epping and a backbencher at that time, who later worried about the danger of the "thermite (incendiary) bombs",[37] recalled that Baldwin's speech "produced so great an impression" and put an "official seal" on these fears.[38]

Financial constraints meant that "full security could not be achieved by rearmament" alone, especially when threats from Japan were increased by concerns over Italy and Germany.[39] A coherent policy was produced in which diplomacy, in the form of appeasement,[40] was intended to play a dominant role; what was not dominant was any role for the army.

The proximity of Germany and the growth of its air-force "concentrated attention and resources on this particular threat".[41] Hugh Trenchard (1st Viscount and Marshal of the RAF), Chief of the Air Staff, and his later cohorts of senior airmen, had "claimed that the bomber offered a wholly new method of waging war", victory would come from destroying the enemy's industry and supplies.[42] What was required was a "first-strike capability" air-arm to deter aggression on Great Britain's particularly vulnerable industrial areas and densely populated conurbations and, perversely,

32   Personal correspondence with Bate (2008); by the author.
33   Personal interview with Chapman (2008); by the author.
34   Hinton, *Protests and Visions*, p.92.
35   Lynch, *Beyond Appeasement*, p.107.
36   Personal correspondence with Cruddace (2008); by the author.
37   Liddell Hart, *Memoirs Volume I*, p.305.
38   Churchill, *The Second World War*, p.133.
39   Smith, *British Air Strategy*, pp.308 & 309.
40   Ibid.
41   Ibid.
42   Ibid., p.310.

to add weight to its negotiating position for disarmament.[43] The cabinet discussed how this would relate to its disarmament policies.[44]

Bialer has asserted that the danger of air attack and concern over public opinion motivated the government to "search for an international air disarmament agreement".[45] Smith has placed this in context as the option most favoured by the cabinet, but as part of a three pronged policy: the development of a deterrent bomber force, a ban on bombing by international agreement and, as the cabinet eventually adopted in late 1937 and 1938 when it realised the combination of the first two had failed, protection by fighter aircraft and radar.[46]

Major Clement Attlee,[47] the Member of Parliament for Labour, Limehouse, and shortly to be deputy leader of his party, called on the British Government to give "a clear and decided lead at the [Geneva] Disarmament Conference" to rid the world of the "menace of the air weapon".[48]

The Times end-of-session leading article explained to readers "probably the largest international conference of Governments ever held naturally had a few problems to overcome such as defining terms".[49] Great Britain's support for the United States proposal of a "Ban on Tanks and Heavy Guns" was a headline in *The Times* of 11 April 1932. The obstacle to achieving arms reduction was the threat to a nation's security; if aggressive weapons were banned, this would open the way to an overall reduction in military hardware. The "solution was to remove [the] fear [of invasion... the] mechanization of attack".[50] The proposal was to scrap all existing weapons and abolish their future manufacture. The British Government "found themselves in substantial agreement" with this proposal.[51]

At Vickers

The Vickers engineering company, the only British commercial tank manufacturer at that time,[52] it might be thought was alarmed at the prospect of disarmament, but demonstrated only a little concern by the "tank banning" proposal, and the company was not deterred from their commercial pursuits abroad for sale of tanks. There was some rationalisation of production, however, in as much that what little tank and Carden-Loyd "carrier" production there was that "had sunk to a mere trickle", took place at the

---

43   Ibid., pp.44–46,62 & 310–311 & 314.
44   Steiner, *The Triumph of the Dark*, p.87.
45   Bialer, *The Shadow Of The Bomber*, pp.3,9, 17 & 18.
46   Smith, *British Air Strategy*, pp.311 & 317.
47   See Appendix C – biographies.
48   *Manchester Guardian*, 12.11. 1932.
49   *The Times*, 25.02.1932, p.13.
50   Ibid., 12.04.1932; *The Daily Mail*, 21.04 1932, p.3.
51   *The Times*, 12.04.1932.
52   Peden, *Arms, Economics and British Strategy*, p.124.

Elswick Works in Newcastle upon Tyne and all AFV manufacture ceased at Erith in Kent (the design and demonstration centre at Chertsey, Surrey remained operational until 1953).[53] Vickers development designer Sir John Carden suggested the company ceased making "any further new [tank] models for at least two years".[54] Carden encouraged the need to "keep ahead of everyone" and implied possible competition coming from the War Office to manufacture AFVs at Woolwich Arsenal. It is important to note that by Vickers' own admission, until 1929 Vickers "had no designs [of tanks] whatever of marketable value"; sometimes the design work had been rushed in order to get the Elswick Works into production and defray the development costs.[55] By 1932, however, Carden thought Vickers' range of tanks "very excellent and complete" and "well in advance of anything anyone else is likely to produce for several years", but he did question what would now be called Vickers' marketing policy.[56] Suggesting an improvement or variation to an existing development model (probably the Sixteen-Tonner or perhaps the new turreted light tank undergoing tests in India), and clearly not anticipating a world-wide tank ban, Carden wrote: "If we make the machine bullet proof, this tank will be the most advanced in the world of its kind and if the War Office won't buy it the foreigner will".[57] He was correct; between 1930 and 1938 Vickers Six-Ton tanks, the downgraded version of the Sixteen-Tonner, were purchased by Bolivia, Bulgaria, China, Finland, Greece, Poland, Russia and Thailand.[58] As mentioned earlier, Russia further developed this AFV to produce the T-26 model of tank and later, with the Christy suspension from the USA, the most produced Second World War T-34 tank.[59]

The cost of producing bulletproof plate escalated in Britain in the 1930s partly due to the increased price of imported nickel "which has risen due to this country [Great Britain] going off the Gold Standard".[60] There was concern expressed too about competition from Skoda and Madsen who "both had guns which are superior to ours [Vickers]".[61] Sir Noel Birch, former Master General of the Ordnance and Great War artillery general, a director of Vickers, on 27 April 1932 wrote regarding, among other matters, trade with Latvia, Rumania and Poland, and "machine-gun tests" from Greece:

53   Foss, and McKenzie, *The Vickers Tanks*, p.72.
54   Vickers Papers; historic document 744, letter dated 08.01.1932 from Sir Noel Birch's file in Sir Frank Yapp's cabinet, Cambridge University Library Manuscripts Department. See Appendix C – biographies.
55   Ibid., 8 January 1932, "Report on Suggested Future Development on Tank Work".
56   Ibid.
57   Ibid., 25 January 1932, letter from Sir John Carden to Sir Noel Birch.
58   Coombs, *British Tank Production*, p.16.
59   Foss, and McKenzie, *The Vickers Tanks*, p.75; Liddell Hart, *Memoirs Volume I,* p.390; Harris, *Men, Ideas and Tanks*, p.277.
60   Vickers Papers; historic document 744, 11 January 1932, letter to Sir Noel Birch from E R Micklem, Elwick Works, Newcastle upon Tyne. See Coombs, *British Tank Production*, p.14 for details on the development of armour plate especially in the mid 1930s.
61   Ibid., 14 January 1932, letter from Sir Noel Birch to Colonel Neilson and Lord Falmouth.

The Disarmament Conference at Geneva is now settling whether tanks should be retained in service or not. I am not particularly anxious about this because Lord Hailsham [Viscount Hailsham, Secretary of State for War and Leader of the House of Lords] is in the Chair, but still it is a factor that must be taken into account.[62]

Later, on 7 November 1932, the Chairman of Vickers, General Herbert A Lawrence, was obviously concerned about his order-book and wrote to Sir Maurice Hankey,[63] the Secretary of the Committee for Imperial Defence. Lawrence asked Hankey for greater support from the British Government as Vickers was providing "practically every requisite for the three [British] fighting services" that required the maintenance of "large research and experimental establishments"; he wanted more orders, fewer restrictions on overseas arms sales, an extension of the "Export Credit Scheme" and further assistance generally.[64] A restriction on the sale of the "small tank" to Poland had already been lifted.[65]

Coombs commented that "it is commendable that Vickers maintained any form of new tank development at all... given the financial stringency and negligible demand from the War Office".[66]

Back at Geneva

Great Britain's support at Geneva for the tank-banning proposal did not enjoy universal support at Westminster, which probably alleviated Birch's anxiety at Vickers. Under the headline "Armoured Cars and Tanks", Lord Stanhope was reported to have argued that banning all AFVs would restrict mechanization and its consequent reduction in manpower. Light tanks and armoured cars, it was pointed out, were useful for imperial policing. The British counter proposal should be to ban tanks that possessed the "knock-out blow", those over 25 tons.[67] Such a counter proposal would have caused no difficulty as the British Army had no tanks of that size; the few Vickers Medium Mark II tanks in service weighed about 14 tons.[68]

The *Daily Mail* published an article by Winston Churchill on 26 May 1932 in which Churchill wrote of the hopes of millions of well-meaning people still attached to the disarmament conference, but, he asserted, it was easy to talk of peace and then leave the details until later or to be sorted out by technical experts. Dividing weapons into categories "Offensive (Naughty) and Defensive (Virtuous)... [was the] silliest plan of all... Every weapon of war can be used for both. The most offensive weapon of all is

62 Ibid., see Appendix C – biographies.
63 See Appendix C – biographies.
64 Vickers Papers; historic document 772.
65 Vickers Papers; historic document 744, 21 September 1932, memo initialled "EB".
66 Coombs, *British Tank Production*, p.16.
67 *The Times*, 01.06.1932, p.13.
68 Fletcher, *Mechanised Force*, p.12.

surprise", and he asked: "How can this ever be banned"?[69] Liddell Hart saw a need to "transcend all such bickerings"; he had studied the problem and:

> … came to see the root of it lying in the kind of weapons which inherently favoured the offensive. If an international agreement could be attained for their universal abolition, there could be a real chance of nullifying the prospects of successful aggression.[70]

Liddell Hart wrote of this difficult argument with which he had to come to terms as he had spent the past ten years preaching the concept of war as "lightning [attacks] with highly mobile mechanised forces", and he published the essence of his argument in the *Daily Telegraph*.[71]

It is impossible to know how the many British newspaper readers and voters were influenced by Churchill's argument or by Liddell Hart's, but the British counter-proposal at Geneva to ban only "big" tanks was supported by just three countries; thirteen other countries favoured the proposal to "declare all tanks illegal". *The Times* continued to report from the Geneva Conference together with the reactions of the British parliament, especially on what benefits disarmament might bring to the taxpayer.[72] One Member of Parliament expressed his clear understanding of the role of the navy and air force in Britain's defences: "But it was impossible [for him] to say that was true of the Army", and this question [the role of the army] "ought to be thought through more seriously now than at any time since the [Great] war".[73] Concern was expressed, however, that in anticipation of the success of the disarmament conference the reduction in the defence Estimates were most severe.[74] The actual defence expenditure estimate for 1932 was reduced to £103,199,000, described by Peden as the "nadir" of the interwar years defence spending.[75]

The end of Geneva and the slippery slope to war

The League of Nations in 1932 had appointed a commission under Lord Lytton to review the Japanese declaration of a separate state for part of a disputed area of

69   *Daily Mail*, 26.05.1932, p.12; see Liddell Hart, *Memoirs Volume I*, p.207, re Churchill's attack on the proposal as "a silly expedient", in the House of Commons debate, 13 May 1932 and Liddell Hart's response in his *Daily Telegraph* article, 17 May 1932.
70   Liddell Hart, *Memoirs Volume I*, p.186; for his paper on this copied to Sir Sam Hoare and Lord Robert Cecil see pp.187–190.
71   Ibid., pp.194/195.
72   *The Times*; examples include Mr G Hall (Aberdare, Labour), 08.02.1932 p.8 and Mr D Adam (Poplar South, Labour), 09.03.1932, p.6.
73   Ibid., an example is Mr Amery (Birmingham, Sparkbrook, Unionist), 09.03.1932, p.6.
74   Ibid., an example is Mr A Chamberlain (Birmingham, Unionist), 08.02.1932, p.8.
75   Peden, *British Rearmament and the Treasury*, p.3.

Manchuria. The League accepted Lord Lytton's report in which he said the state the Japanese had created was "against the popular will of the inhabitants".[76] This declaration, which came in March 1933, was the reason the Japanese gave to leave the disarmament conference in Geneva, and to leave the League of Nations.[77] On 30 January 1933, Adolf Hitler became Chancellor of Germany. Earlier, at the peace conference, the German delegation had argued for more concessions as a tactic "to forestall" Hitler's further political advance. The gap between Germany's demands for military equality and France's insistence on security could not be bridged argued Marks "for the Hitlerian tide was at the flood".[78] Neither had German expectations been fulfilled at the separate economic conference on war reparations at Lausanne in the summer of 1932. This further inflamed German resentment and exacerbated the political situation.[79] These events in Manchuria, involving the Japanese, and the political situation in Germany, destabilised the conference to the extent that it staggered on through 1934,[80] because "too much effort and public attention had been focused on the talks to abandon the scheduled summer session".[81] It ended with unfulfilled expectations.

So what to do now for Great Britain?

The British Government was then in a dilemma: an international agreement to ban bombing had failed, and Baldwin in Cabinet argued that if an agreement to limit air-forces could not be achieved "public opinion *might* be willing to agree to anything which could prevent a foreign air-force from getting any closer than they are today".[82] Regarding British air strength, Baldwin announced on 8 March 1934, "[Britain] shall no longer be in a position inferior to any country within striking distance of our shores".[83] In response, first "deterrent" and then "air defence" became the government's rearmament priorities.

What is crucial to this account is that at that time there was no thought by politicians of sending another British Expeditionary Force (as in 1914) to fight in a land war on the continent of Europe in which AFVs would be required. There had been such thoughts earlier by the General Staff, but the plans for an expeditionary force

76   Gibbs, N. H. [1976], *History of the Second World War Grand Strategy* Volume 1 *Rearmament Policy,* (HMSO, London) p.75 The report of the Lytton's Commission to the British Government – URL: <http://hansard.millbanksystems.com/lords/1932/nov/02/manchuria-report-of-the-lytton-commission>
77   Marks, Sally, *The Illusion of Peace*, p.136.
78   Ibid., p.128.
79   Ibid., p.135.
80   'The Bureau of the Disarmament Conference continued to meet periodically until February 1935' – Steiner, Zara [2011], *The Triumph of the Dark*, p.55.
81   Ibid.
82   Bialer, *The Shadow Of The Bomber*, pp.49/50; emphasis added.
83   Ibid.

had been scrapped.[84] The Royal Air Force was the priority and that left the army, and tanks, well down the order for funding. Smith has concluded that the government had little alternative given the economic, diplomatic and geographic parameters.[85]

Running a side-lined army

"It was a most unpleasant position for me" wrote Sir Archibald Montgomery-Massingberd in 1946, who had been the CIGS from February 1933 until April 1936, "for war loomed on the horizon... for three successive years... I knew the Army was totally unready for war".[86] Montgomery-Massingberd had in mind: Japan 1933, with the invasion of Manchuria, Italy 1935, when Abyssinia was invaded and Germany 1936, on their reoccupation of the Rhineland, and:

> During my time at Aldershot [Commanding 1st Division], and as time went on so did the demand for mechanization. But there was a break on it and a very severe one – the want of money. During all the years between the wars, and especially between 1922 and 1932, the Army was starved and little or no money was made available for mechanization or the supply of tanks, guns and vehicles, when by trial these had proved satisfactory.[87]

Sir Archibald Montgomery-Massingberd has been much criticised, even blamed, for his tardiness to mechanize the army more than was achieved during his tenure of office.[88] Harris wrote that Montgomery-Massingberd "became a *bête-noire*" for the newspaper journalist and later historian Basil Liddell Hart.[89] Liddell Hart's criticism seemed centred upon the CIGS's attitude to the RTC of which Liddell Hart was a great advocate. Liddell Hart argued that the CIGS took a "definite line... that the RTC should not be expanded at the expense of the older arms", and stressed Montgomery-Massingberd's continued determination to "placate" the cavalry whose anxiety to keep their horses defied logic.[90]

Harris criticised subsequent historians' assessments of Montgomery-Massingberd as "sometimes... unbalanced and unfair".[91] Coombs agreed.[92] Norman Dixon's influential book *On The Psychology of Military Incompetence* is an example. Dixon employed similar derogatory rhetoric to Liddell Hart and linked Montgomery-Massingberd

---

84   LHCMA – MM159/1jjj.
85   Smith, *British Air Strategy*, p.317.
86   LHCMA – 10/11–10/13 159/1ggg, The Montgomery-Massingberd Papers.
87   Ibid., 159/1ww, The Montgomery-Massingberd Papers.
88   Harris, *Men, Ideas and Tanks*, p.242.
89   Ibid.
90   Liddell Hart, *Memoirs Volume I*, p.265.
91   Harris, *Men, Ideas and Tanks*, p.242.
92   Coombs, *British Tank Production*, p.10.

to General Sir Philip Chetwode for criticism of their "romantic behaviour" towards horsed cavalry.[93] Dixon condemned Chetwode, as Commander-in–Chief India, for not promoting cavalry mechanization on the sub-continent. This accusation ignores the fact that mechanization *was* taking place in other parts of the Indian Army such as the artillery, signals and engineers (as it was in other parts of the army in Great Britain as far this could be afforded), it was not in fact completed until 1937.[94] In 1925 the Indian Army had 2,350 "mechanical vehicles" and by 1936 had 4,700.[95] The accusation was also incorrect because examination of the correspondence between Chetwode and Montgomery-Massingberd demonstrated clearly that both were keen to press-on with mechanization, but were frustrated by lack of funds.[96] Montgomery-Massingberd wrote to Chetwode in December 1928:

> The question, as you know, is one of money, and one can't carry out much in the way of experiments unless one has some machines to do it with. What we want most at present is Light Tanks or Machine Gun carriers, people are not however clear which is best [sic].[97]

Montgomery-Massingberd was chairman of the 1926–1927 Cavalry Committee that recommended the "first phase" of mechanization: the conversion of two cavalry regiments to armoured cars discussed earlier. As CIGS he directed the implementation of "the second phase" discussed later. The Field Marshal was also condemned for disbanding the Armoured Force in 1928. Montgomery-Massingberd as Commander in Chief of Southern Command acknowledged the so called Armoured Force was "doing good work as an experimental organization" under Brigadier Collins, but Montgomery-Massingberd was concerned, and in his unpublished memoirs he explained why:

> It [Armoured Force] was definitely affecting adversely the morale and training of the Cavalry and Infantry. In my opinion this organisation should not have been based on the medium Tank [sic]. What should have been done was to gradually mechanize the Cavalry Division and Infantry Divisions and not to introduce

---

93 Dixon, *On The Psychology of Military Incompetence*, pp.116–117. Dixon incorrectly ascribes Montgomery-Massingberd's term of office as CIGS as 1926 until 1933, whereas he served only for three years as CIGS 1933–1936 and was Adjutant General from 1931–1933, p.164.
94 LHCMA – LH10/1937/206, *The Times*, 5 March 1937.
95 LHCMA – LH11/1936/93.
96 LHCMA – MM158/1a – 3 .12.1928 , MM158/2a – 18.01.1929; also "Handing Over Notes" (April 1936), MM158/t; The Montgomery-Massingberd Papers 10/1–10/10; Winton, *To Change An Army*, pp.29 & 31, assesses Chetwode as a "progressive" officer who commanded a Corps that included a tank battalion in 1925 and deployed them in a wide flanking movement.
97 Ibid., The Montgomery-Massingberd Papers 10/1–10/10.

Mr Philip Chetwode (on the right), a Subaltern in the 19th Hussars – on cavalry manoeuvres, September 1890 (The other officer is Captain Young). (Source: From the *Journals of Hilda Zigomala* Number 1; The Norfolk Records Office, Norwich Ref; MC 2738/1)

Field Marshal Sir Philip Chetwode, 1st Baron Chetwode.

an entirely new formation based on the medium Tank. Nor was it sound to pit the new formation, with its modern armaments, against the older formations in order to prove its superiority. What was wanted was to use the newest weapons to improve the mobility and firepower of the old formations by the introduction into them, as a result of trial and error, of modern inventions. What I wanted, in brief, was evolution not revolution.[98]

Academics and journalists have questioned this decision but, for those of us who have experienced assuming the leadership of an underperforming organization, starved of investment, as Montgomery–Massingberd had, this decision was entirely supportable. To make any sort of progress in managing change the maintenance of morale was vital, and during the period in which Montgomery-Massingberd made his decision, there were concerns about subversion in the military, and recruitment problems. Holding his unit together as a cohesive force was paramount; also there was little equipment with which to develop the Armoured Force had he chosen to do so. Montogmery–Massingberd was an experienced and competent commander who cared for his people, and they seemed to have cared for him; John Kennedy, who served under Montgomery-Massingberd during the Great War and later in two other appointments, in a letter to Lady Montgomery-Massingberd wrote "we all thought he would be a great CIGS, and he was, and we all loved him… He was a wonderful judge of character".[99] Winton, who was largely critical of Montgomery-Massingberd, nonetheless argued that Montgomery-Massingberd was following his own vision of a future war; he foresaw a British Army equipped with AFVs in greater numbers than any other army it was likely to encounter. Rather than further develop one part of an armoured unit, he wanted to mechanize the whole army, but was frustrated due to "financial stringency".[100]

As CIGS, Montgomery-Massingberd had to allocate appropriately his meagre budget between the needs of the current operations, and equipping and training the army to fulfil what he envisaged was its future role. In this he had the foresight, not shared at that time by his political masters, to anticipate the need for a continental expeditionary force.[101] As Harris has written, "If Montgomery-Massingberd is judged on the decisions he made as CIGS he appears, on balance, an enlightened officer".[102]

98   LHCMA – MM 159/zz, Montgomery-Massingberd's unpublished memoirs, [1946]; The Montgomery-Massingberd Papers.
99   LHCMA – 159/3a and 159/3c 10/11–10/13, 20 February 1958 and 11 March 1958; The Montgomery-Massingberd Papers 10/1–10/10.
100 Winton, *To Change An Army*, pp.89–99; Winton's book is a biography of General John Burnett-Stuart who did not enjoy a good relationship with Montgomery-Massingberd; pp.91 & 186/187.
101 Kennedy, *The Business of War*, pp.1, 2 and 7; "Statement by the Chief of the General Staff" (DRC7), 9 January 1934, PRO CAB 16/109, cited in Harris, *Men, Ideas and Tanks*, p.243.
102 Harris, *Men, Ideas and Tanks*, p.244.

Therefore rather than retarding the modernization of the Army that included mechanizing the cavalry, Montgomery-Massingberd actually tried to further it.

Charles Broad wrote in 1970 that Montgomery-Massingberd in 1933 had "begun to realise that there was something in the tank idea" and envisaged the cavalry taking over the tank role; this had upset the Tank Corps officers.[103] On 15 October 1934 Montgomery-Massingberd informed the senior Army Council members of his thoughts on a "Mobile Division". These included a change from having an independent tank brigade and a cavalry division to the creation of a Mobile Division that include the tank brigade and one mechanized cavalry brigade "together with an adequate proportion of reconnaissance and supporting troops".[104] After implementation of these changes the remaining horsed cavalry would include a brigade of three regiments "for use as GHQ [General Headquarters] troops or for operations requiring horsed cavalry outside Europe". The CIGS hoped that India and Australia would make up any shortfall of horsed cavalry should these be required for hostilities "outside Europe". He was expecting the horsed cavalry based in Egypt to be mechanized "eventually", and later expanded this forecast to "as soon as we mechanize one regiment at home"; this was to best enable rotation and training.[105]

The Experiment

"Mechanization" in this instant was envisaged as equipping the cavalry regiments with four and two-seater cars for officers, two-seater cars for the scout troop and light trucks to transport the men. The proposal was to experiment in April 1935 with units of the 2nd Cavalry Brigade at Tidworth, one regiment, not specified at this stage, to be equipped with twenty light trucks (the 3rd Hussars, the 4th Hussars and the 9th Lancers made up this brigade at that time). Additionally, the 12th Lancers (already mechanized with armoured cars) was intended to form one squadron with Mark II and Mark IIA light tanks that would be transferred to the 2nd Cavalry Brigade from the tank brigade as Mark V tanks arrived to replace them. No evidence has been found that this actually happened; the 12th Lancers continued as an armoured car regiment throughout the forthcoming Second World War. Extra funding to the existing Estimates was needed to buy 15 more vehicles for the experiment.[106]

Future drafting difficulties were envisaged with men being sent abroad, especially to India, unless troopers of mechanized regiments continued to learn to ride.[107] Other concerns expressed by the Quarter-Master-General Sir Felix Ready, included

---

103 LHCMA – Broad 1–3; Lt. Gen. Charles Broad's reply to Mr R Alastair Rickard's letter, University of Ontario, May 21 1970 p.4.
104 TNA WO 32/2847 Army Organisation: Cavalry (Code 14(D)): Introduction of a Mobile Division 1934–1936 20/Cav/831, Minute 1.
105 Ibid., Minutes 1 and 3.
106 Ibid., Minute 1.
107 Ibid., Minute 2.

Field Marshal Sir Archibald
Montgomery-Massingberd.

the cost of vehicles and their accommodation that would include converting
existing buildings (probably the stables)
into garages, albeit temporary, during
the "experiment"; some cost savings
were expected, however, with the rede-
ployment of the displaced horses.[108]
Experience so far was, suggested the
CIGS, who responded on 7 November,
that it was "very difficult to train men
of a mechanized unit to ride" and only
officers' horses would be retained in the
regiment. He did not expand on what
experience there was of training men to
ride who were from mechanized units,
but Colonel ffrench Blake's regiment, the 17th/21st Lancers enjoyed "horsing" Harold
('Pete') Pyman, and his family, when Pyman was posted with a team of instructors
from the 9th Light Tank Company, Royal Tank Corps, in January 1938 to train the
cavalrymen for mechanization.[109] The CIGS was also against the cross-posting of men
from mechanized to horsed regiments, presumably for the same reason, and expected
the five British cavalry regiments based in India to remain horsed for "a few years".[110]
This would necessitate keeping a similar number of horsed regiments at home to facil-
itate regimental rotation and training recruits to replace time-expired men serving in
India, usually between 85 and 115 men annually.[111] Egypt would be garrisoned only
by mechanized cavalry regiments.

The consultation and discussions completed, the War Office, on 8 December 1934,
notified the various Army Districts and commanders that in 1935 experiments would
begin:

108 Ibid., Minute 4 & 5.
109 Personal interview with ffrench Blake [2006]; by the author; Pyman, *Call to Arms*,
     pp.27–29.
110 TNA WO 32/2847 Army Organisation: Cavalry (Code 14(D)): Introduction of a Mobile
     Division 1934–1936 20/Cav/831, Minute 3.
111 Ibid., Minute 4.

in the 2nd Cavalry Brigade with a mechanized cavalry regiment ... the 3rd King's Own Hussars have been specially selected for these experiments and, in recognition of the regiment's action in volunteering for this important duty, the Army Council wishes it made clear that the claims of the 3rd King's Own Hussars to remain horsed will not be prejudiced by this experimental mechanization should it be eventually decided to mechanize part of the cavalry.[112]

The regiment's equipment was listed and included eight light cars, three "general service" trucks and ten "personnel" trucks, with an additional fifteen light cars for the scout troop, headquarters and four sections. Machine-gun tripods and rifle grenade dischargers completed the list of equipment; all animals and their equipment, surplus to requirements during the experiment, were to be withdrawn.[113] The task of mobile troops was outlined as follows:

a) Reconnaissance and protection.
b) In battle to delay the enemy: to safeguard the flank; to form a mobile reserve, or to cover withdrawal.
c) Special missions and raids.[114]

It was pointed out that in its existing form the cavalry division, made up of armoured cars, two horsed cavalry brigades, mechanized artillery and supporting troops, was unsuited to its task because the horse mounted troops had neither the speed nor range to keep up with tanks with which they had to cooperate. A new formation, a Mobile Division, was the answer. Made up of three brigades, the Mobile Division included armoured cars, mechanized cavalry and tanks, with mechanized artillery and mechanized supporting troops. The Mechanized Cavalry Brigade consisted of an armoured regiment of light tanks, similar to a light tank battalion of the Royal Tank Corps. This new Mobile Division was planned to replace the existing Tank Brigade and the Cavalry Division. It was envisaged that these changes would make the new Mobile Division "capable of [a] wide range of action and would have increased striking power".[115]

The organization envisaged for the mechanized cavalry regiment differed little from that of a horsed cavalry regiment: a Head Quarters Squadron "possibly including; signal troop, administration troop, mortar troop", and a scout troop consisting of "six sections each of three light cars"; three "Mechanized Squadrons – each of three troops

---

112 Ibid., 1C War Office letter to various military commands, schools and overseas establishments, 8 December 1934.
113 TNA WO32/2847 Army Organisation: Cavalry (Code 14(D)): Introduction of a Mobile Division 1934–1936 20/Cav/831; 1C War Office letter to various military commands, schools and overseas establishments, 8 December 1934.
114 Ibid.
115 Ibid.

B Squadron the 3rd Hussars – Wiltshire 1935. (Source: Original photograph by the *Daily Sketch*, this image from *The 3rd Hussars Regimental Journal*)

of three sections".[116] The "section" organization was a little different to a horsed cavalry regiment in which a section was eight men, but usually two men were horse-holders (the "Number 3s" of each half-section of four men) allowing the other six men to fight dismounted.[117] This method, introduced in the 1870s, was practiced, with some difficulty, during the Great War.[118] Ronald Lucas, who joined the 15th/19th Hussars in November 1935, said he carried out dismounted sword drill, but "never ever" trained for dismounted action with his rifle.[119] In the Mechanized Regiment what was envisaged was a rifle section or a machine-gun section, of all eight men made up of a commander, six troopers and one driver. Tactics to be adopted were all outlined in the letter: "In general the tactics of mechanized cavalry follow the principles laid down in *Cavalry Training Volume II*". The principles of dismounted action tactics were

116 Ibid.
117 Personal interview with William Cross [2012]; by the author; *Cavalry Training (Horsed) 1937*, pp.70 & 71; there were other methods of "horse-holding": "With Coupled Horses" and "With Linked Horses", this enabled more than three-quarters of the men to come into action dismounted, but this has no relevance to a comparison with a mechanized troop.
118 War Diary of B Squadron, the 19th Hussars TNA WO 95/1466 – see especially, 26 August 1914, "one man cannot apparently hold 4 horses that are fit under heavy fire at close range". The technique remained in the Cavalry Training (Horsed) manual at least until 1937, pp.163/163.
119 Personal interview with Lucas [2012]; by the author.

also unchanged; in *Cavalry Training Volume II*, speed and mobility was stressed and advised: "A cavalry leader will, before deciding to act dismounted, consider whether he could not achieve his object by remaining mounted".[120] The motorized squadron was expected to remain mounted therefore, as with horsed cavalry, "as long as ground fire will allow".[121]

A hesitant and fumbling approach?

Liddell Hart said the decision to mount part of the cavalry division in light trucks, the men then to fight dismounted as infantry, was "an imitation of the French Army's recent steps towards converting its horsed cavalry into motorised troops, called *dragons porté*".[122] He was critical of the "hesitant and fumbling way the Army Council took to what turned out to be the decisive step towards mechanising [sic] the cavalry in preference to expanding the Royal Tank Corps".[123] By "expanding the Royal Tank Corps" it is inferred that Liddell Hart meant with tanks, but only enough tanks existed at that time to equip the RTC's existing four battalions. It was evidence, he wrote in 1965, "of a disbelief in the value of armoured forces".[124] However, there were other army mechanization priorities in 1934 with which Liddell Hart, as a newspaper military correspondent, would have been aware: the replacement of horse limbers (the detachable front part of a gun-carriage, usually a two wheeled wooden box, for transporting artillery shells) with trucks and the motorization of the infantry for which an increase of funds was allocated. The Estimates of 1936/1937 therefore, provided less money for tanks and other tracked vehicles than was provided the previous year.[125]

Some evidence has been found, however, to support Liddell Hart's assertion that disbelief existed in the value of armoured forces. Prior to 1936 the Master General of The Ordnance (MGO), the Great War tank pioneer Sir Hugh Ellis, was reported to have harboured doubts of the value of tanks in a future war. Sir Noel Birch of Vickers met with Lieutenant General Ellis at the War Office on the afternoon of 30 October 1936; Birch's notes of the meeting include the following:

> The MGO said that he has again changed his mind about tanks and now thinks that instead of being useless owing to anti-tank guns, rifles, mines etc. they will

---

120 *Cavalry Training (Horsed) 1937*, p.161.
121 TNA WO 32/2847 Army Organisation: Cavalry (Code 14(D)): Introduction of a Mobile Division 1934–1936 20/Cav/831; 1C War Office letter to various military commands, schools and overseas establishments, 8 December 1934; see Badsey, *Doctrine and Reform;* throughout, for the debate on horsed cavalry tactics and mounted versus dismounted action.
122 Liddell Hart, *Memoirs Volume I*, p.261.
123 Ibid., p.262.
124 Ibid., p.263.
125 Ibid., p.276.

be of some use to the Army but that they will occupy a secondary position to what they have done in the past.[126]

Birch did not record when or why Ellis said he had changed his mind about tanks. Ellis clearly had been dubious about the deployment of AFVs in a modern war. Light tanks in the Spanish war "had not come up to scratch" and Ellis's supporters had said "we told you so [which] exasperated even more the tank enthusiasts".[127] Perhaps the recent news of the success of the Soviet T-26 tanks in Spain had encouraged his change of mind.[128] Ellis was MGO from 1934 until his retirement in 1938. With his Great War experience as the Tank Corps' first commander Ellis was the most senior general officer with AFV battle experience and therefore influential regarding their use. Ellis was "frequently the last word on all matters relating to Tanks … [but] the trouble with Sir Hugh Ellis [was] as a matter of fact [he] did not believe in tanks, or at any rate, not enough".[129] It may have been on Ellis's instigation that the cavalry, the 3rd Hussars, had to experiment with vehicles other than tanks. Ellis's later change of mind in 1936, together with the gradual availability of the light tanks, could have been the catalyst for the switch from trucks to tanks with which most horsed cavalry regiments eventually were equipped. Liddell Hart recorded in his notes on the Tank Corps dinner, 23 November 1936, that Hugh Ellis "used to be generally popular [with the RTC, but now] is held largely responsible for the failure of tank supply that recently aroused the Cabinet's anxiety".[130]

The 3rd Hussars

By 1935 when the 3rd Hussars "experiment" in mechanization commenced at Tidworth, this regiment had already built up two years motor vehicle experience; confidence was growing in its ability to take on increasing amounts of repair work.[131] Although there was understandable anxiety to change, it was decided: "the only course was to give the [mechanization] experiment a real and whole-hearted trial".[132] It is important to note that in spite of some anxiety and some scepticism, very little officer turnover occurred in the 3rd Hussars during this period of change.[133] The 3rd

---

126 Vickers historic document 744, "Sir Noel Birch's Interview with The Master General of The Ordnance at the War Office on the Afternoon of 30th October 1936".
127 Ibid.
128 Beevor, *The Battle for Spain*, pp.195–196; Lannon, *The Spanish Civil War*, p.46.
129 LHCMA – the Lindsay papers 139–141, quoted from a copy of a contemporary subscription news sheet, "The Week", 8 December 1937 sent to Lindsay by Admiral Sir Alexander Ramsay.
130 LHCMA – LH11/1936/110, "Notes on the Tank Corps dinner", 23 November 1936.
131 *3rd King's Own Hussars Magazine* Vol.1 No.3 Jan.1935, p.8.
132 Bolitho, *The Galloping Third*, p.242.
133 *Army Lists* January to March 1934, 1935, 1936 and 1937; Lieutenants Whitaker and Crewdon disappeared from the List between 1934 and 1935, Captain C D Phillips

Hussars had returned from India in November 1932 after eleven years abroad, and went from Southampton to York.[134] New recruits, untrained and mostly unskilled, replaced two hundred "time expired" NCOs and men,[135] and one hundred NCOs and men who remained in India and had been posted to other units.[136] In 1934, whilst still at York, the 3rd Hussars took over from the RAOC the responsibilities for mechanical transport. They received four six wheeled 30 cwt. lorries, one 15 cwt. tender, six motorcycles and later, six Austin cars. The motorcycles and cars went to the communications troop, the other vehicles to regimental transport. Some men with mechanical transport experience were posted into the regiment, although from which unit is not recorded.[137] What was recorded is the authorisation for the appointment of two troopers to "Driver Mechanic", these men to be "mustered as tradesmen".[138] This appeared to have been part of an authorisation for all "Regimental Cavalry of the Line" to do likewise, presumably to deal with the motorized regimental transport that was to come or had already arrived.[139]

The 3rd Hussars regimental magazine noted in January 1934 that the motorized transport was new and therefore difficult to evaluate, but it was acknowledged to be certainly quicker than using horses. There were, however, insufficient vehicles. Signals Troop learning to ride their Triumph motorcycles and to drive the Austin cars experienced "quite a lot of fun and thrills", and with seven weeks training their driving improved "tremendously".[140] In December 1934 the news came that the 3rd Hussars:

> … had been selected as an experimental mechanized cavalry regiment and that experiments were to be carried out with a variety of mechanical vehicles during

was listed as an "unemployed Captain on half pay" in 1936. In 1937 Majors Sandford and C F Clarke and Lieutenant Hutton-Wilson disappeared from the List. Captain C A Peel transferred to the 4th Hussars as a captain; this regiment was in the process of mechanizing. Captain Forestier-Walker transferred to the already mechanized 11th Hussars as a Major and Lieutenant Colonel Grubb MC was promoted full Colonel and became an instructor at the Senior Officers School, Sheerness.

134 The 3rd The King's Own Hussars Historical Records 01.04.1932–31.03.1933, p.2 File 1716 Regimental Archives Warwick; Bolitho, *The Galloping Third*, p.242.
135 French, D., *Military Identities*, p.36 and p.172; this also happened to other regiments later on, examples being the 13th/18th and 15th/19th Hussars – personal interviews with Lucas (2007); and Need (2007); by the author.
136 Bolitho, *The Galloping Third*, p.242.
137 Regimental Transport Notes in the *3rd The King's Own Hussars Magazine* Vol.1 No.1, January 1934, pp.7 and 8, Regimental Archives Warwick.
138 The 3rd The King's Own Hussars Historical Records 01.04.1933–31.03.1934, p.2. File 1716.
139 Ibid.
140 Regimental Transport Notes in the *3rd The King's Own Hussars Magazine* Vol.1 No.1, January 1934, pp.7–8.

the next two years. For these experiments A Squadron was selected to mechanize, whilst B remained a horsed squadron and C took in recruits.[141]

There was no reference or record found in the regimental archives that the 3rd Hussars had *volunteered* for this experiment as was stated in the War Office letter of 8 December quoted above. Hector Bolitho wrote:

> Brigadier-General Kelly, the Colonel of the regiment, invited Colonel Grubb and the second-in-command to dine with him at the Station Hotel York [November 1934]. He explained that the Inspector of Cavalry had been asked by the Chief of the Imperial General staff "to select a cavalry regiment to carry out an experiment in mechanization to replace horsed cavalry", and the 3rd Hussars had been *chosen* for the task.[142]

In December 1934 a draft of thirty-two "other ranks" was posted from the 3rd Hussars to the 10th Hussars in Lucknow, India.[143] It is not known from which squadron they came or how they were selected. These men could have been considered unsuitable for mechanized training, might have been the most experienced horsemen to go to India, or who had the longest time yet to serve. It was, however, probably just a routine draft to replace time-expired men serving in India and therefore of no significance to the mechanization experiment.

The reorganisation of the regiment began on 5 January 1935 with the formation of the nucleus of the mechanized squadron. Within two weeks of this 25 NCOs and men were sent to the Royal Army Service Corps Driving School at Feltham. They were trained in driving and maintenance and on their return to the regiment engaged as instructors.[144] On 9 February 1935, 127 horses left the Regiment: 38 horses to the 15th/19th Hussars, 21 to the 4th/7th Dragoon Guards, 20 to the 9th Lancers, 8 to the 16th/5th Lancers, 8 to the Military Mounted Police, 17 were destroyed, 8 sold and 7 troop-horses were reclassified as "chargers". The remainder of the Regiment's horses were posted to B Squadron. By 1 March just forty-two chargers and 93 troop horses remained.[145]

The regiment was supported throughout by its past officers:

> The consensus of opinion [of the former officers] is one of the greatest regret at the loss of the horses, but at the same time they are unanimous in wishing the

---

141 The 3rd The King's Own Hussars Historical Records 01.04.1934–31.03.1935, File 1716, p.2.
142 Bolitho, *The Galloping Third*, p.242, emphasis added.
143 The 3rd The King's Own Hussars Historical Records 01.04.1934–31.03.1935, p.2, File 1716 Regimental Archives Warwick.
144 Ibid.
145 Ibid.

Regiment to move with the times, and they consider that the eventual mechanization of the Cavalry is inevitable in some form or other.[146]

The experiment generated interest from Dominion regiments in Canada, Australia, South Africa and New Zealand and this will have contributed to the motivation of all ranks of the 3rd Hussars to ensure its success.[147] The support of the former officers, past custodians of the regiment's traditions and history, was such an important factor too, giving a sort of "permission" as it were, for the regiment to move forward. Had these former officers objected and not taken a pragmatic view, the effect on morale, especially of the officers and senior NCOs, could have presented a major management problem. Significant to this study is that no evidence has been found of criticism, equivocation or resistance to mechanization from these former horsed cavalry officers.

In the autumn of 1935, following the training season, the officer commanding 3rd Hussars, Lieutenant Colonel Grubb, submitted his report in which he assured his superiors that: "Every effort has been made throughout to keep the tactics of Mech. Cav. [sic] to the principles laid down in Cav. Training Vol. II with motor vehicles substituted for the horses".[148] These principles included both mounted and dismounted action (mentioned earlier): the approach march, deployment and the mounted attack, the methods of advancing under fire and the use of the ground (for cover and concealment).[149] Grubb was sure mechanized cavalry could successfully carry out their assigned role, and "probably be found to be able to do more than horsed cavalry"; further training would have to advance, however, and include cooperation with light tanks and mobile artillery next year "if the experiment is to be carried further". Grubb advised that such a formation be led by one commander.

Significant at this stage of AFV development, was Grubb's comment that "wheeled vehicles are more mobile than track or semi-track vehicles", therefore more suitable for mechanized cavalry. Clearly Grubb was dissatisfied with the performance of the tracked vehicles so far developed. Grubb found motorcycles the most mobile. The "section", as currently organized with a NCO and seven men, gave insufficient "power of dispersion", and was certainly a significant change from horsed cavalry. One man on a horse was a mobile unit, whereas the entire mechanized section of eight men

---

146 TNA WO 32/2847 Army Organisation: Cavalry (Code 14(D)): Introduction of a Mobile Division 1934–1936, 20/Cav/831; "3rd. Hussars Experiment in Mechanization, April–September, 1935".

147 See Mayo, "The Human Problems of an Industrial Civilization" in Thompson, Kenneth (ed.) [2003] *The Early Sociology of Management and Organizations*, especially Chapter V p.95; Gillespie, *Manufacturing Knowledge – A history of the Hawthorne experiment*; the Introduction is a useful summary.

148 TNA WO 32/2847 Army Organisation: Cavalry (Code 14(D)): Introduction of a Mobile Division 1934–1936 20/Cav/831; "3rd. Hussars Experiment in Mechanization, April–September, 1935".

149 *Cavalry Training (Horsed) 1937*, pp.104–204.

A Squadron The 3rd The King's Own Hussars 1936. The vehicles are Morris-Commercial Dragoon (or Dragon) Porté vehicles "for the dismounted cavalry role". (Source: *3rd The King's Own Hussars Magazine* Vol.1 No.4, 1936 p.4)

became one unit because it relied for its mobility on one truck. If the truck broke down the section became immobile, whereas it was unlikely all eight horses in a section would go lame or be wounded at the same time. Grubb wanted more motorcycles for scouting, sending messages and keeping in touch with other units. Also, he recommended four troops to a squadron rather than three to more effectively take advantage of the higher speed of the advance; four troops per squadron "leap-frogging" could be better employed than three, he argued.[150]

The weapons with which the regiment had been issued were insufficient to stop enemy AFVs – armoured cars and light tanks – that might be encountered by mechanized cavalry in their reconnaissance or screening roles. An anti-tank gun was necessary, and Grubb believed the French Army were using suitably armed armoured cars and light tanks for this purpose, sent ahead of their horsed cavalry. Grubb was doubtful of the suitability of the current British Army armoured cars, but was sure something of this nature was essential, four to eight vehicles for each cavalry regiment whether horsed or mechanized.[151] Wheeled vehicles, whether cars or motorcycles, had limited scope in "enclosed country", such as woodland, compared to horsed cavalry, and the men had to be prepared to go forward on foot to reconnoitre the enemy.

150 TNA WO 32/2847 Army Organisation: Cavalry (Code 14(D)): Introduction of a Mobile Division 1934–1936 20/Cav/831; "3rd. Hussars Experiment in Mechanization, April-September, 1935".
151 TNA WO 32/2847 Army Organisation: Cavalry (Code 14(D)): Introduction of a Mobile Division 1934–1936 20/Cav/831; "3rd. Hussars Experiment in Mechanization, April-September, 1935".

Grubb compared this to "the German Jager [sic] battalions in 1914". He had doubts about the Bren light machine-gun mounted on a tripod for covering fire compared to the performance of the Vickers machine-gun, and suggested the mortar troop (yet to be formed) be replaced with a troop armed with Vickers machine-guns.[152] The men transported by motor vehicle after long marches were markedly "fresher" than horseman had been after a similar experience. He suggested consideration be given to breaking up the separate large scout troop and incorporating smaller scout troops with the squadrons enabling closer cooperation. The mortar and signals troops had not been formed at that time so their progress could not be reported upon.[153]

Driver training had been rushed in order to fulfil the expectations of the experiment, the men's aptitude had not been properly assessed, consequently accidents occurred and vehicles were damaged. Grubb pressed for both a need to "sort out the most adaptable recruits" to train as drivers, and a driving school organised similarly to riding schools. He had concerns that only half of the present recruits "would make efficient drivers". Grubb was, however, pleased with the Morris trucks with which the regiment had been issued as "Section vehicles", but some design modifications would be required in future such as strengthening the front axle and heightening the position of the radiator to overcome particular obstacles. Regarding the cars, Grubb preferred the armoured Hillman Minx over the unarmoured Austin Seven.[154]

Grubb's was a long and comprehensive report covering many aspects of the experiment so far and clearly he felt positive with the outcome. Grubb's remarks and recommendations were generally supported by the Commanding Officer of the 2nd Cavalry Brigade, Colonel, acting Brigadier, F B Hurndall, and by J Blackiston Houston, the Inspector of Cavalry.[155] It was acknowledged by General Burnett-Stuart, General Officer Commanding Southern Command, who preferred the term "motorized" to "mechanized" that the experiment had been carried out with "great thoroughness and keenness by all ranks who took part… and warrants further trial and experiment on a larger scale".[156] The various comments attached to Grubb's report, as it was forwarded up the echelons of command, indicated some differences between the various senior officers of the concept or role of mechanized (or motorized) cavalry, and consequently in the detail of what were the most suitable weapons and equipment. Burnett-Stuart

---

152 Ibid.
153 Ibid.
154 Ibid.
155 TNA WO 32/2847 Army Organisation: Cavalry (Code 14(D)): Introduction of a Mobile Division 1934–1936 20/Cav/831; *3rd. Hussars Experiment in Mechanization, April–September, 1935;* minute attached to forwarded report, 8 November 1935.
156 Ibid.,12A memorandum from General Officer Commanding-in-Chief, Southern Command General Burnett-Stuart to the Under Secretary of State, The War Office, 28 October 1935.

The Hillman 10 HP Armoured
Car "did not get beyond the
experimental stage", but may
have been the vehicle preferred
by Lieutenant Colonel Grubb.
(Source: The Tank Museum,
Bovington – 9361-A4)

Austin Seven Two-seater in Service Dress. This was basically the 1934/35 civilian model
with only minor modifications. Nearly 900 of this version was delivered to the British Army.
It superseded the earlier type which had military pattern bodywork and was popularly known
as "the pram". (Source: The Tank Museum, Bovington – 6376 – B1). This vehicle was not
armour-plated.

was, nonetheless, hopeful that a "motorized" cavalry regiment "will find it easier to get recruits [than did horsed cavalry]".[157]

The "Go ahead" to more mechanization (or motorization)

Further cavalry mechanization was ordered by the Army Council in a letter to all commands on 18 December 1935. It referred to the 3rd Hussars experiment and confirmed the Army Council's belief in the need to replace the [horsed] cavalry division with a mechanized mobile division, but making a change to the mobile division's structure to that proposed the year before. Consequently:

> … as and when funds permit, two mechanized cavalry brigades will be formed in the United Kingdom, each of two motor cavalry regiments and one cavalry light tank regiment, and the cavalry brigade in Egypt will also be converted into a mechanized formation with one cavalry armoured car regiment, one cavalry motor regiment and one cavalry light tank regiment.[158]

The following regiments intended for conversion were:

To motor cavalry –	The 10th Royal Hussars – after returning from India
	The 8th King's Own Royal Irish Hussars – Egypt
	The 4th Queen's Own Hussars
	The 3rd King's Own Hussars
	The 1st King's Dragoon Guards
To light tank cavalry –	The 9th Queen's Royal Lancers
	The 7th Queen's Own Hussars – Egypt
	The Queen's Bays (2nd Dragoon Guards) – to be brought home early from India

The selection of these particular regiments was not entirely in line with the Army Council's policy of the "juniarity" of those regiments unaffected by the previous amalgamations.

The cavalry armoured car regiments, the 11th Hussars and the 12th Lancers, mechanized in the late 1920s were unchanged. Three of the regiments, the 3rd Hussars, the 8th Hussars and the 9th Lancers were already "partially mechanized", no dates were set, however, for the conversion of the rest.[159] The reason for this was the lack of suitable vehicles for equipping them for their assigned role. In Egypt, the plan was for

---

157 Ibid.
158 Ibid., 20/General/5512 (S.D.2.), 18 December 1935.
159 Ibid.

the cavalry to take over tanks from the RTC battalions as and when the new "I", or "infantry" tanks became available.[160]

On 27 January 1936, the 3rd Hussars were instructed to extend the experiment, and the regiment was reorganised as an "Experimental Motor Cavalry Regiment".[161] Thirty horses were retained "in order to keep equitation alive in the Regiment". The horses, less the 30 to remain, were distributed to the Queen's Bays, the 5th Royal Inniskilling Dragoon Guards, the 15th/19th Hussars, the 16th/5th Lancers and the Remount Depot at Melton Mowbray.[162] Further personnel postings took place from the 3rd Hussars; again there are no details of whom, and why these particular men were chosen. In March thirty-four other ranks went to India to the 13th/18th Hussars, still a horsed cavalry regiment, and eighteen other ranks to the "partially mechanized" 8th Hussars in Egypt (next Chapter). A further 28 men came into the 3rd Hussars from the 3rd Carabiniers (Prince of Wales's Dragoon Guards) who were still a horsed regiment[163] in addition to the 132 new recruits who had joined the regiment since June 1935.

Many were called, but how were they chosen?

As has been said, concern was recorded in 1935 that only 50 percent of the recruits enlisting in the 3rd Hussars at that time would actually make efficient drivers.[164] The veteran cavalrymen interviewed as part of this study underwent no selection or mechanical aptitude tests whatsoever and, as was stated in the previous chapter, officers posted from Sandhurst to the 11th Hussars and the 12th Lancers were not chosen for any mechanical aptitude either. The volunteer system of army recruitment between the wars did not incorporate any selection testing, other than a medical assessment, and neither were the authorities empowered to direct a recruit to join a particular branch of the service. Having joined his chosen Corps (Cavalry, Artillery, Infantry etc.), the Army Act (1871 – Regulation of The Forces Act – part of the "Cardwell

160 Ibid., 14 October 1935.
161 TNA WO 32/2847, 06.01.1935 – "Cavalry Re-Organization"; note of the decision to extend the trials of the 3rd Hussars as a cavalry motor unit and to organise and equip the 9th Queen's Royal Lancers "with token equipment, as a cavalry light tank regiment" signed, C P Heywood Major General Director of Staff Duties; The 3rd The King's Own Hussars Historical Records 01.04.1935–31.03.1936 p.2 File 1716.
162 The 3rd The King's Own Hussars Historical Records, 01.04.1935–31.03.1936 p.3 File 1716.
163 The regiment was renamed in 1928 and was previously the 3rd/6th Dragoon Guards. The regiment was posted to India in 1936 and was mechanized between 1938 and 1939.
164 TNA WO 32/2847 "Cavalry Re-Organization". How and why particular men were posted in or out of these regiments is unfortunately unknown. Such records that may exist for men serving during this period are governed by the rules of disclosure and are only available to surviving next of kin through the Army Personnel Centre, Historical Disclosures Department.

reforms") prevented a soldier's transfer to an alternative one.[165] Until 1927 the Cavalry Corps itself was divided into Dragoons, Hussars and Lancers "of the Line" and a transfer between these three was forbidden without the soldier's agreement.[166]

Asked how the men were selected for particular tasks in 1942, Lieutenant Colonel Sprot of the Royal Scots Greys said in 2007 that some of the older men:

> … who obviously couldn't handle mechanics were posted. They were just too old, been a cavalryman all their life, never even been inside a motorcar probably. Everyone was happily posted who couldn't fathom mechanics.[167]

The inference from Colonel Sprot's remarks is that only a few men were posted as unsuitable for mechanical training. Sergeant William Cross, interviewed for this account in 2010, remembered that up to half the men in the Royal Scots Greys were posted out, although he was away training in Cairo during part of the Greys transition from horses to tanks, and his remembrances might not be entirely accurate.[168] Ronald Lucas of the 15th/19th Hussars, interviewed for this account in 2007, did not know how or why he was chosen to train as an instructor; there was certainly no selection test.[169] Perhaps Sergeant Lucas's civilian engineering experience had been entered on his army records. Later, after the commencement of the Second World War, when it was clear more armoured units were needed, men from infantry regiments underwent aptitude tests to segregate those suitable for armoured and mechanical training from those men to stay as infantry.[170] After 1942, and therefore beyond the scope of this study, the Army's Adjutant General Sir Ronald Adam, established the Directorate of Personnel Selection to "devise and implement intelligence and aptitude tests for recruits and serving soldiers whose units were converted to other arms".[171] It is counter-factual, but nonetheless interesting, to speculate on what a positive difference systematic psychometric testing would have made to the cavalry's transition from horses to tanks had it been in place at that time.

165 French, D., *Raising Churchill's Army*, p.66.
166 TNA,WO32/3059, Register No 27/Cavalry/1247, minute 2, "Reconstitution of Corps of Cavalry".
167 Personal interview with Sprot (2007); by the author; also Sprot, *Swifter Than Eagles*, pp.7–11.
168 Personal interview with Cross (2010); by the author.
169 Personal interview with Lucas (2007); by the author.
170 Personal correspondence and discussion with Davidson (2009); & email correspondence with Bullock (2008); by the author.
171 French, D., *Raising Churchill's Army*, pp.66–68. See Roger Broad's *The Radical General: Sir Ronald Adam and Britain's New Model Army 1941–1946*, [2013].

Trooper Ronald Lucas,
The 15th/19th Hussars,
Tidworth 1935. (Source:
Author's collection, 2011)

The Late Mr Ronald Lucas, wearing on his blazer his
Regimental Crest and "Dunkirk Veteran's" lapel badge in
2010. (Source: Author's collection, 2011)

Winning them over

In spite of the justified apprehension over the change from horses to horsepower, the comments in the 1936 copy of the 3rd Hussars regimental magazine were noteworthy and illustrate how the soldiers' opinion changed from disbelief to belief in, and commitment to, the successful outcome of the so-called "experiment". Earlier the 3rd Hussars found it a "distasteful proposition for horse lovers" to have to dispose of many young horses that had been trained by the regiment since their return from India, "amongst which are some of the best show jumpers in England"; they were "comforted" by the knowledge that an experiment to replace horses with motorcars and motorbikes was "doomed to failure" and the horses would soon be returned to the 3rd Hussars.[172] With the determination and leadership to perform as ordered the experiment in mechanization did not fail, however, and their enthusiasm for it grew into passion:

> When we got going, we got keener and keener on the task. Moreover, the more we delved into it the more we believed in it, until finally we became convinced that the days of cavalry mounted on horses, are very nearly over. None of us who have fought in war can be anything but overjoyed to think that no 3rd Hussar will ever see his "long-nosed pal" – his best pal suffering in war – suffering in silence, from privation, weariness or mutilation.[173]

This comment might have been propaganda to encourage the reluctant, but more probably was a genuine reflection of the feelings of the majority of the officers and other ranks. The article acknowledged the sadness felt at the prospect of losing the horses and the "inexplicable comradeship" between horse and rider, but accepted that the superior speed of motor vehicles over horses was more in line with contemporary thought and actions.[174] It must be considered too that at that time motor vehicles were a novelty and learning to drive was a worthwhile skill to acquire for a later civilian life. By August 1936 all except two horses had left: Mary the drum horse was bought by the regiment "for sentimental reasons" and placed in retirement.[175] The remaining cavalry tradesmen, saddlers and farriers were cross-posted to the 4th/7th Dragoon Guards, the Queen's Bays, the 3rd Carabiniers, the 4th Hussars and the 13th/18th Hussars. The last troop horse to leave the 3rd Hussars remained with the Queen's Bays who took over the station when the 3rd Hussars left for Aldershot in October 1937.[176]

The Feed-back

Harris has argued that Lieutenant Colonel Grubb, the 3rd Hussars Commanding Officer, was given a narrow objective: to see if motorised cavalry soldiers armed with rifles and machine-guns could perform similar functions to those of horsed cavalry, such as reconnaissance, screening and pursuit.[177] Every effort was made by Grubb to make the tactics of his mechanized cavalry squadron conform to the principles laid down in the *Cavalry Training Manual*, with motor vehicles substituted for horses.

172 *3rd The King's Own Hussars Magazine* Vol.1 No.4, 1936, p.3.
173 Ibid.
174 Ibid.
175 The 3rd The King's Own Hussars Historical Records 01.04.1936–31.03.1937, p.2 File 1716 and the 3rd King's Own Hussars Historical Records 01.04.1937–31.03.1938, p.2 File 1716.
176 Ibid.
177 Harris, *Men, Ideas and Tanks,* pp.262–3.

These tactics included "The duties of cavalry" of which reconnaissance was the "major and usually an indispensable part of it".[178]

The demands on the cavalry were to be "inquisitive and aggressive" and to search widely and continuously.[179] The cavalry training manual draws attention to the susceptibility of cavalry to observation from the air and the need to move widely dispersed;[180] which was of relevance and concern to Lieutenant Colonel Grubb, and commented upon in his report.[181] What the 3rd Hussars motorised cavalry unit was free from was any concern of the "economy of horse flesh".[182] A motor vehicle had a greater range and road speed than a horse. The Commander-in-Chief, Southern Command, Major General John Burnett Stuart, on 28 October 1936 in a letter to the Under-Secretary of State for War Sir Herbert Creedy, expressed concern that the eight-seater wheeled vehicle that was being used by the 3rd Hussars was "entirely unsuitable" and what was needed was a "handy cross-country tracked vehicle with crews of not more than four".[183] Percy Hobart had foreseen the unsatisfactory nature of these vehicles; he supported mechanizing the cavalry, which appeared "to have great potentialities", but not in vulnerable, rubber-tyre unarmoured vehicles.[184] A debate ensued over the type of vehicle that was most suitable for motorized or dismounted cavalry; the conclusion was that the wheeled "scout" vehicle gave insufficient protection to the troopers, and that it would be better to wait to equip the cavalry with light tanks that were expected to be available from 1938.[185]

The 3rd Hussars change and progress

By January 1936, the regimental mechanical transport unit of the 3rd Hussars was becoming redundant, as there was "really no Regimental Transport" for them to maintain.[186] The vehicles now forming part of the mechanized squadron had formed the Regimental Transport for the 3rd Hussars conveying forage, horseshoes, spare ammunition and other equipment when the regiment was horsed. Eventually each squadron was to have its own lorries. The original mechanical transport personnel, with a "splendid office and stores, workshop and competent staff", became the regimental

178 *Cavalry Training (Horsed)* (1937) edition, p.118.
179 *Cavalry Training (Horsed)* (1937) edition, p.118.
180 Ibid., p.120 and p.132.
181 TNA WO 32/2847 Army Organisation: Cavalry (Code 14(D)): Introduction of a Mobile Division 1934–1936 20/Cav/831; *"3rd. Hussars Experiment in Mechanization, April–September, 1935".*
182 *Cavalry Training (Horsed)* (1937) edition, p.121.
183 TNA WO 32/2847, "Cavalry Re-Organization".
184 LHCMA – LH15/11/1–11, 36; Hobart to the Director of Staff Duties, 22 March 1935.
185 Ibid. Minutes of a meeting on 13 November 1936 attended by the Army Director of Staff Duties, the Director of Motor Transport and the Inspector of Cavalry.
186 *3rd The King's Own Hussars Magazine* Vol.1 No.4, January 1936, p.13.

The mechanized B Squadron the 3rd Hussars Cambridgeshire 1937. (Original photograph attributed to the *The Times*; this image is from *The 3rd Hussars Regimental Journal*)

"Technical Branch… [as] advisors and experts" to the mechanized squadron.[187] The Technical Branch had grown in competence and experience and was able to carry out the heavy vehicle repairs previously carried out by the RAOC workshops.[188]

In March 1937 the order was received to convert the regiment from motor cavalry to light tanks, but the regiment was told that there was a temporary shortage of tanks with which to equip them. During the 1937 training season the Regiment used "tokens" instead of tanks. 15 cwt. "box vans" and Austin cars had to suffice as token tanks: "If there is one word in the English vocabulary which every 3rd Hussar would like abolished, it is the word "Token"", reported the Regimental Journal in April 1938.[189] The 3rd Hussars reorganised as a Light Tank Regiment without tanks, with three troops per squadron and five "tanks" and two "carriers" per troop. The cars and vans used as token tanks were painted a different colour to "avoid confusion".[190] In an exercise or drill, some of the cars would perform their normal role as signals or scouting vehicles and the vans as supply vehicles. Other cars and vans, painted a different colour, would perform as token tanks.

By September 1938, only A Squadron and HQ Squadron had been equipped with tanks.[191] It is not recorded from where these tanks came or of what type they were; they might have been either the Vickers Light tank Mark V, a two-man tank, or the Mark VIB three-man tank. B Squadron was photographed mounted on horses in Wiltshire in 1935 (page 135) and one troop of the same squadron was photographed mounted in tanks in Cambridgeshire in 1937 (page 136). The latter photograph causes some

187 Ibid.
188 Ibid.
189 Ibid., Vol.II No.1, April 1938, p.6.
190 Ibid., Vol.1 No.4, January 1936, p.13.
191 Third King's Own Hussars Historical Records 01.04.1936–31.03.1937, p.3 File 1716, Regimental Archives Warwick; Bolitho, *The Galloping Third*.

confusion as the Regimental Journal states that although B Squadron expected tanks to arrive by spring 1938, the type had not been specified;[192] therefore B Squadron did not have tanks in 1937, at least not on a permanent basis, and probably neither did A Squadron. It is speculated that the photograph was "posed" for propaganda purposes to demonstrate progress in re-armament.

Whilst waiting for the tanks to arrive in 1938, B Squadron lost many of their experienced men posted away and new recruits enlisted. A Squadron too suffered from a turnover of troopers, a large number of its "best men", mechanically trained, were posted to the 8th Hussars, by then a mechanized regiment, and were replaced by 40 new recruits.[193] New recruits joining the regiment were, after 7 April 1938, sent away for training for six months to the RTC depot at Bovington. On 22 August 1939 the 3rd Hussars moved to Houghton Down, Stockbridge, and by then were equipped with 24 of the "new type" of light tank (the Vickers Mark VIB),[194] ninety-two wheeled vehicles and six dragons.[195]

In less than five years the 3rd Hussars had transformed themselves from an old fashioned mounted regiment into one of the most modern and efficient armoured units.[196]

The significance

Although the 3rd Hussars' experiment was a successful demonstration of how the change from horses to AFVs could be managed, the veterans interviewed for this study by the author had no knowledge whatsoever of the 3rd Hussars' experiment and what influence, if any, this had had on the mechanization process of their own regiments. Nonetheless, and unbeknown to these veterans, the experiment might have been a considerable influence on the training programme and management of other cavalry regiments undergoing this huge process of change. It had taken five years to completely mechanize this regiment, but not through any lack of industry on its part. The 3rd Hussars supplied many trained men to other cavalry regiments whose experience must have helped when, under the pressure of war, cavalry regiments later managed to mechanize in less than 12 months.

By the start of the Second World War the 3rd Hussars had been equipped with 52 Mark VIB tanks. The regiment served in Norway, North Africa, Crete, Italy and Java, and were re-equipped, from 1942, with Crusader, Grant and Sherman tanks. By the end of the war the regiment has lost 26 officers and 157 other ranks.[197]

192 *3rd The King's Own Hussars Journal* Vol. II No.1, April 1938, p.9.
193 Ibid., p.7.
194 Bolitho, *The Galloping Third*, p.247.
195 3rd King's Own Hussars Historical Records 01.04.1938–31.03.1939, p.2 File 1716.
196 Bolitho, *The Galloping Third*, p.245.
197 3rd King's Own Hussars Historical Records; WARHM: 1202 (Box 2) QOH-DOC-10, "Report on action fought by 3H Regimental Group in area NE of TEL EL AQQAQUIR

In summary

Great Britain entered the 1930s with growing concerns about the world's financial and trading situation and not about security. To a large extent, economic recovery and then economic resilience remained the priorities throughout the decade to sustain the country should a long war materialize – the so-called "fourth arm of defence".[198] Public opinion was largely anti-war, invigorated by Great War remembrance and commemoration, and a growing fear of aerial bombing. The depression, in the wake of the Wall Street Crash, retarded what weak economic development had begun earlier necessitating further cuts to defence expenditure and a reappraisal of priorities and costs; the outcome favoured the air-arm. For a time the Government was uncertain, the military was unpopular, recruitment a challenge (students from some leading universities resolved not to fight "for King and Country", perhaps influenced by the so-called "Joad resolution" of the Oxford Union), and there was some real and some perceived unrest within the armed services. International peaceful co-existence was encouraging to begin with in Europe, but not in the Far East. At the Disarmament Conference there was strong support for banning tanks, heavy weapons, and as part of an integrated policy, Britain was looking to ban aerial bombing too. Politically, economically and defensively this would be much welcomed by the British Government. It presented an opportunity either to divert part of the defence budget to social projects, which suited the electorate, or to reduce expenditure altogether, which suited a government keen to balance the budget. This can be seen in the following Table 4.

2 Nov 1942"; Regimental Archives Warwick. After suffering "grievous" losses in destroying over 15 enemy field-guns, 88mm and 74mm and 50mm anti-tank guns the regiment had (at the time of that report); A Squadron 5 Crusader tanks, B Squadron 7 Sherman, 5 Grant and 1 Crusader tank, C Squadron 3 Grant and 1 Crusader and HQ Squadron 3 Grant and 1 Crusader tank. By then the Vickers Mark VIB tanks were considered obsolete; Bolitho, *The Galloping Third*, pp.246, 247 & 270.
198 Smith, *British Air Strategy*, pp.183, 184 and 189; Self, *Neville Chamberlain*, pp.267–269.

Table 4 UK Government Spending per Fiscal Year (£ millions) 1931–1939[199]

	1931	1932	1933	1934	1935	1936	1937	1938	1939
Health Care	58	64	74	75	78	84	89	96	104
Education	164	163	153	152	158	168	177	185	193
Defence	117	113	111	116	122	146	195	206	266
Welfare	260	271	289	291	292	304	311	318	326
Protection	41	41	39	40	41	44	46	50	57
Transport	168	169	145	151	148	152	160	154	173
General Govt.	11	12	12	12	13	13	13	14	14
Other Spending	283	284	275	276	287	302	323	343	314
Interest	406	405	403	349	335	334	336	345	352
Balance	-124	-126	-130	-142	-124	-120	-124	-123	-73
Total Spending	1,384	1,397	1,372	1,320	1,348	1,429	1,526	1,589	1,725
Public Net Debt	7,401	7,422	7,632	7,810	7,788	7,784	7,785	8,014	8,150

Overall public expenditure reduced in 1933 and again in 1934, and for the next two years did not exceed the 1932 level. Defence expenditure continuously reduced until 1933 and did not start to recover significantly until 1936. This was of course a year after the realisation that in any practical sense the disarmament conference had failed, and after the 3rd Hussars experiment had begun at Tidworth. The development of medium tanks ceased, and those AFVs that were made by Vickers were largely for the export market; the British Army therefore, remained short of AFVs with which to mechanize the cavalry.

Tensions grew, firstly with Japan followed by Italy and Germany. The British Government reviewed the nation's defence capability and the financially restrictive 10 Year Rule was abandoned in 1932. Considering it less abhorrent to the electorate and following an integrated strategy, the government prioritised the Royal Air Force for development. The Army General Staff correctly forecast an expeditionary force would be needed should a war occur on the European continent, but this was not an opinion supported by the government. Restricted by funds to purchase equipment, the army nonetheless continued a programme of modernization. Gradually mechanizing horsed cavalry regiments was included in this programme, but with what vehicles with which to equip the cavalry was unclear, as the future of tanks, what type and their role in war, was for a time uncertain.

The 3rd Hussars was chosen to experiment with motor vehicles and did so with enthusiasm and success, although the vehicles initially employed were later considered unsuitable. This was a major change for a horsed cavalry regiment, but as with the 11th Hussars and the 12th Lancers (mechanized earlier with armoured cars); the

199 URL: <http://www.ukpublicspending.co.uk/spending_brief.php> accessed 04.07.2011.

change process was well led and successfully managed. Officers stuck to their task, NCOs became able instructors, and most of the men trained to become competent drivers and mechanics. Although initially unhappy with parting with their horses, and assured of their return if the experiment failed, neither officers nor other ranks demonstrated any resistance or hesitation to fully embrace the assignment as ordered. In December 1935 further horsed cavalry regiments were designated for conversion to motor-lorries or light tanks as soon as these vehicles became available.

5

Mechanization – The Third Phase 1936–1939:
The Mobile Force in Egypt and the Mobile Division at Home

Peace, Fear and the Voting mix

Sir Archibald Montgomery-Massingberd in 1946, as already has been recounted, wrote of the unpleasant position of knowing, in the mid-1930s, that the British Army was totally unready for war, an opinion supported by the First Lord of The Admiralty Sir Samuel Hoare, later Viscount Templewood.[1] The Japanese invasion of Manchuria was principally the concern of the Royal Navy; the German reoccupation of the Rhineland, in terms of any military action, seemed to have concerned no one much, as Templewood confirmed: "Hitler's challenge… had been ignored", except perhaps by Winston Churchill.[2] Abyssinia, however, was the concern of the Army, and mechanizing the horsed cavalry regiments in Egypt became a priority. In December 1935 Montgomery-Massingberd ordered further horsed cavalry regiments to be designated for conversion to motor-lorries or light tanks as soon as these vehicles became available.

Montgomery-Massingberd was faced with a problem that he alone could not solve: a largely pacificist electorate that was given due regard by government ministers, together with an almost global economic depression that had engulfed Great Britain in its wake. The country was recovering slowly, but only in a swathe from the West Midlands down to London and across South-East England; the rest of the country remained in a parlous state. The poor, unable to pay tax, needed state assistance and had more to concern them than international security; those enjoying increased affluence were reluctant to put this at risk.[3] The Treasury had to perform a fine balancing act

---

1   LHCMA – 10/11–10/13 159/1ggg, The Montgomery-Massingberd Papers, King's College London; Templewood, *Nine Troubled Years*, pp.138/139 re the lack of British military strength.
2   Ibid., p.201; Gilbert, *Churchill A Life*, p.552.
3   For illumination see, for example, Stevenson and Cook, *The Slump* and Hobsbawm, *Industry and Empire*, Section II "Between the Wars".

and the net result for Montgomery-Massingberd and the army was little investment in modernization.

It was not so much the "social mix" of the population that was significant, but the "voting mix" that had changed since the political class took Great Britain to war in 1914. The changes in the Representation of People Acts in 1918 and especially in 1928, enfranchised the whole adult population, regardless of income, gender, education and social status. To get elected and stay in power, politicians had to reflect the views of their voters. Public opinion became a crucial factor in policy making, but opinion surveys of public attitudes were not used until Harrison and Madge began the Britain by Mass Observation surveys in the late 1930s. Public opinion could only be assessed by behaviour and the media's agenda. Study of the 1930s invokes some sympathy for Baldwin's plight to get the British people behind a policy of rearmament.[4] Templewood's comment is crucial to appreciating the whole appeasement and rearmament issues; although the National Government had "an overwhelming majority", before the 1935 General Election, it had no mandate as such for rearmament only economic recovery. Prior to 1936 rearmament would have met formidable opposition.[5]

Of the 2,146,062 women's signatures presented in a petition at the Geneva Disarmament Conference in 1932, 1,000,000 were British women[6] who had become voters, and had different views from men on peace and war. Later surveys showed that women's views were above all "to keep the peace" and "[to] stop the men from going to war again". An observer in Ilford noted one woman respondent's retort that she "was all for peace – war was silly and futile"; she hated Hitler and Mussolini "for bringing us close to it". In all surveys following the Czechoslovakian crisis of 1938, it was the women who indicated a pro-Neville Chamberlain and appeasement opinion; 59 percent of those women surveyed supported Chamberlain with only 4 percent against, and there were 30 percent "don't knows". It should be noted that 46 percent of men surveyed supported Chamberlain too, with 20 percent against and 16 percent "vague".[7]

Faith in the League and the policy of "collective security" continued, indicated for example, in the Fulham (West) by-election result of 1938. This previously "safe" Conservative Party seat was won by the Labour Party candidate Dr Edith Summerskill. Her election leaflet was headlined "Peace before Party – Vote for Summerskill Peace and Security Through The League". As well as political activists, four Non-Conformist church ministers signed this leaflet.[8] The Labour Party, argued Summerskill, "wanted to build up an international police force" and participate

4   Barnett, Corelli "The Illogical Promise" in Panichas, George A. (ed.) [1968] *The Promise of Greatness: The War of 1914–1918*, (Cassell, London) p.571.
5   Templewood, *Nine Troubled Years*, pp.134 & 194.
6   *The Times*, 08.02.1932, p.11.
7   Ibid.
8   Britain by Mass Observation papers (1938); "Fulham".

in collective security.[9] The League of Nations had faced "an ominous test" when Mussolini attacked Abyssinia,[10] but there was still much to commend the League and the optimism of much of public opinion could be justified by the League's success.

In later analyses of inter-war attitudes regarding the League of Nations, Cecelia Lynch has stressed that Manchuria (1932), Adolf Hitler (1933), Abyssinia (1935), the Rhineland (1936), Spain (1936–1939) and the Sudetenland (1938) showed "the futility of relying on international polity to stop aggression... the idealism [of the 1920s] unravelled in the 1930s".[11] Sally Marks argued that the establishment of the League of Nations "constituted one of the dangerously misleading illusions of peace".[12] This may have been so, but only with the benefit of hindsight.

It was this so called "illusion", the belief that peace between nations could and might prevail, that so much influenced the defence expenditure decisions pertinent the story of cavalry mechanization. It was in this environmental mixture of fear, hope and determination that the popular peace movement, with support from the pacifist political "left", had grown, gathered momentum, and had influenced government policy.[13] Much of the general population continued to believe that another war *was* avoidable,[14] but nonetheless the fear of being bombed grew as a major issue of public concern, and was especially worse for mothers with young children.[15] The National Government was "particularly sensitive" to public pressure, and the bomber affected the "man [and woman] in the street" who was a voter.[16]

The civil war in Spain confirmed the public's fears. Colonel ffrench Blake remembered seeing Zeppelins over London during the Great War and said "they seemed no threat and were easily shot down", but "no one realised about bombing till Guernica".[17] Kay Ash remembered:

> Spain, about the bombing, what I can remember is people, terrified, on the street, running for cover. That's what stayed with me, that's what you imagined would happen here when the bombing came, yes, they [the British] were so sure it was [coming]".[18]

9   Ibid., D 2/A.
10   Brittain, *Testament of Experience*, p.136.
11   Lynch, *Beyond Appeasement*, p.95.
12   Marks, *The Illusion of Peace*, p.15.
13   Barnett, Corelli "The Illogical Promise" in Panichas, George A. (ed.) [1968] *The Promise of Greatness: The War of 1914–1918*, (Cassell, London) pp.566/567.
14   Hinton, *Protests and Visions*, p.90; also Templewood, *Nine Troubled Years*, p.236, re "public opinion, still apathetic", also p.239 "the hope of peace had not been finally abandoned".
15   Harrison & Madge, *Britain by Mass Observation*, pp.49–51.
16   Bialer, *The Shadow Of The Bomber* p.7; see Kyba, J P., "British Attitudes Towards Disarmament and Rearmament 1932–1935", PhD, London School of Economics, 1966, for an analysis of public opinion.
17   Personal correspondence with ffrench Blake (2008); by the author.
18   Personal interview with Ash (2008); by the author.

Colonel Sprot said, because of Spain, concern over "war and bombing moved from possibility – then gradually to a probability".[19]

In the mid-1930s the political "left" produced some anti-arms trade films: "Hell United" showed the destructive power of modern weapons and the so-called "double – dealing" of the arms trade. This short film called upon the audience to write to their Member of Parliament and to support demonstrations and strikes against any further arms expansion. The film was almost certainly produced to support the successful campaign for the establishment of a Royal Commission (see Chapter Seven) on the production and sale of arms. This opened in 1934 and must have dampened any investment in arms manufacture until it was concluded.

A pivotal time – public opinion and rearmament

The Times, in late 1935, supported rearmament and claimed to represent public opinion. Its Leader suggested the Opposition was promulgating the argument that the British Government was tricking "the people to vote for vast armaments", accusing the Government of "making the running in an armaments race". The Leader pointed out how much government arms expenditure had fallen over the previous eight years, and if the Opposition was committed to collective security the deficiencies in armaments "must be made good". The Leader supported the Prime Minister in his recent speech in Wolverhampton and his assertion that a modern navy and an industry ready to expand quickly, should there be an emergency, was entirely "consistent with membership of the League".[20] Two days later the Leader reinforced the point that in making good defence deficiencies, "there is no trace of any abandonment of the effort towards disarmament… The overwhelming majority of the British public now approve constructive rearmament" a February 1936 Leader confidently stated. Progressive and determined League policy had to have the resources "at its back".[21] Montgomery-Massingberd's view, written in 1946, was that between 1933 and 1935 "the seriousness of the military situation seemed gradually to dawn on the British public", but he offers no evidence to support that opinion.[22]

By July 1936 *The Times* reported "good progress in rearmament" and commented upon the extra funds that were forthcoming. The RAF was just ahead of the navy at £11,700,000 with the army at £6,600,000. The Leader still supported collective security: "strong British Forces [were] a stabilizing force in a disturbed world". Readers were assured that Britain threatens no one, but with weak armed forces Britain may encourage aggression.[23] From late July until October 1936 the newspaper berated

19   Personal correspondence with Sprot (2008); by the author.
20   *The Times,* 30.10.1935, p.15; the Leader states that "effective expenditure on defence fell from £103,446,000 in 1925/6 to £85,756,000 in 1932/3".
21   Ibid., 04.03.1936, p.13.
22   LHCMA – MM 159/1iii.
23   *The Times,* 10.07 1936, p.17.

Labour and condemned pacifism whilst congratulating the government on the rearmament progress. The 21 July Leader claimed Labour was "prey to a number of obsessions" from the "limitless pacifism of Lansbury" to the collective security view that seemed to mean "that other nations will fight our battles". A change of government, it proclaimed, having commented on recent by-election results, would bring no change of policy because "essentially [there was] complete unity, and behind such a policy [of rearmament] there was overwhelming public support".[24] Templewood asserted that following the 1935 General Election, Baldwin's hands were free for a definite programme of rearmament".[25]

Recent historians have identified this period 1935–36 as pivotal in the change in public opinion. Steiner wrote that the 1935 general election victory was due to the Conservative manifesto pledge "to uphold the Covenant and maintain and increase the efficiency of the League".[26] Ceadel argued that from 1936 the popular peace movement declined rapidly from its zenith of the Peace Ballot. He called 1936 "the major watershed of the decade" for momentous events: the re-militarization of the Rhineland, the Italian defeat of Abyssinia, and the civil war in Spain.[27] Lynch's view was that the peace movement was "deeply divided" over the British rearmament programme, principally "the legitimacy of the need for new weapons, the principles behind acquiring them, and the stated potential purposes of the programme".[28] The failure of economic sanctions applied via the League of Nations to persuade Italy to withdraw her troops from Abyssinia caused further fractures in the peace movement; that "division" in the peace movement "allowed the government a freer hand in determining its perceptions of British interests".[29] Lynch concluded that "popular and academic discourse" had blamed arms limitations and appeasement on "individual leaders, economic or security requirements, or structural constraints – factors that do not involve social agency". She cited Walter Lippmann, an influential journalist, who in 1943 blamed the Second World War on the peace movements in both Great Britain and the United States for their failure to "keep pace with the growth of German and Japanese armaments".[30] Lynch expressed difficulty, however, in tracing the peace movements "activities to strategic and military decision making".[31] This is understandable; many strategic and

24   Ibid., 27.07 and 29.07.1936.
25   Templewood, *Nine Troubled Years*, p.194.
26   Steiner, *The Triumph of the Dark*, p.120.
27   Ceadel, Martin "The Peace Movement between the wars: problems of definition" in Naylor, Richard & Young, Nigel (eds.) [1987] *Campaigns for Peace, The British Peace Movement in the Twentieth Century* (Manchester University Press, Manchester), p.88.
28   Lynch, *Beyond Appeasement*, p.109.
29   Ibid., p.112.
30   Lippman, Walter [1943], *US Foreign Policy: Shield of the Republic*, (Little, Brown, Boston), cited in Lynch, Cecelia [1999], *Beyond Appeasement*, pp.3–5.
31   Lynch, *Beyond Appeasement*, p.5.

military decisions would have been taken by a combination of politicians and soldiers with different agendas and influences.

Correlli Barnett argued that despite the absence of opinion polls, statesmen had to take account of the "eruption of mass opinion" following, what he called, the "un-caging of the little man" – the extension of the franchise in 1918 and again in 1928. Public opinion had become a significant force within society.[32] As mass communication widened and became more sophisticated, this brought a greater intimacy between the leaders and the led, asserted Barnett. "The emergence of mass electorates… may have set limits on what elected leaders could do", argued Steiner.[33] Field Marshal Alan Brooke, after a particularly trying day, recorded in his diary on 9 July 1941 the profound comment that "[politicians] are always terrified of public opinion as long as the enemy is sufficiently far".[34]

Financial risks considered greater than security risks

The 1930s were a difficult time in which to govern. There were fiscal constraints. Not only was the pay of military service personnel cut, Civil Service salaries were cut by 6 percent and teachers' salaries by 11 percent.[35] Means-testing was applied to state benefits[36] and regarding unemployment benefit, the attempt by the Government in 1936 to standardise benefits across the country, caused a cut in benefit to the majority of people in the hardest hit areas.[37] Although the "Ten Year Rule" was abandoned and rearmament began, the financial risks the nation faced were considered more dangerous than the security risks.[38] A White Paper dated 4 March 1935 "announced the official policy of rearmament, but it went into practice only slowly… [in financial terms], its first effects being on the 1936 budget".[39] Clearly this was anticipated and what followed was the third tranche of cavalry mechanization; the formation of the Mobile Division in England and the mechanization of the Cavalry Brigade in Egypt.

The Cavalry Brigade in Egypt – the 8th Hussars

The formation of a mechanized cavalry brigade in Egypt was a response to a possible threat from Italy. The Cavalry Brigade was made up of the 7th Hussars, eventually

---

32 Barnett, Corelli, "The Illogical Promise" in Panichas, George A. (ed.) [1968] *The Promise of Greatness: The War of 1914–1918*, (Cassell, London) p.560–71.
33 Steiner, *The Triumph of the Dark*, p.3.
34 Danchev and Todman, (eds.) [2001], *War Diaries*, p.170.
35 Stevenson and Cook, *The Slump*, p.17.
36 Evans, *On The Breadline*, p.29; Stevenson and Cook, *The Slump*, p.2.
37 <http://filestore.nationalarchives.gov.uk/pdfs/small/cab23–84–c44–36.pdf>
38 Howson, *Domestic Money Management In Britain*, p.120.
39 Ibid., p.120.

mounted in light tanks, the 8th Hussars in machine-gun mounted trucks, and the already mechanized 11th Hussars.

The prime source of the record of the activities of the 8th Hussars was the Regimental Diary. This unique document provided an almost daily account of the life of the regiment from 1923 until the outbreak of war in August 1939. The Regimental Journal expands and illuminates the diary entries in reports of several of the notable and amusing occurrences. Included in the story of the 8th Hussars are the regiment's earlier experiences of both mechanization, or motorization, and the effect on the cavalry of the cuts in military expenditure across the period.

As with other cavalry regiments, the 8th Hussars was not without some previous experience of motor vehicles: Captain D W Daly, Lieutenant J D Paton and Second Lieutenant S E R O'Neill, officers from the regiment, were sent from Germany to Aldershot on 5 March 1928 to attend a six-wheeled-lorry driving and maintenance course. The "motorization" of the "first-line" transport came after a reduction in horsed transport wagons in 1927, of six wagons and eight horses, and the reduction of one squadron. This was the case for each of the twelve cavalry regiments serving at home and on the Rhine Station where the 8th Hussars were at that time.[40]

> All but two of the Hotchies [sic] guns were to be withdrawn [and the] machine gun squadron to be mechanised in due course, and to comprise: Headquarters, 4 Troops of 2 machine guns (Vickers) each – making 8 machine guns in all, an increase of 4 over the present Peace Establishment.[41]

The number of signallers was reduced from 18 to 12 and "the total strength of the Regiment to be reduced by the following: – 3 Officers, 93 Other Ranks and 113 animals".[42] Some men were prematurely transferred to the Army Reserve and one officer was reassigned as Adjutant to the Staffordshire Yeomanry. What happened to the other men no longer allowed on the establishment is not specifically recorded, although throughout the regimental diary are recorded numerous transfers and drafts in and out of the 8th Hussars, to and from other cavalry regiments of the line.[43]

The mechanization of the Machine Gun Squadron might not have taken place as soon as it could have done, perhaps even deliberately, as *The Journal of The VIII King's Royal Irish Hussars* reported in January 1928, recording events following their return to barracks at Wiesbaden after the annual machine-gun course of April 1927 at Sonnenberg Ranges:

---

40 19 March 1927, instruction from the War Office recorded in QRH 285, *Regimental Diary 1923–1939 8th KRI Hussars*.
41 Ibid.
42 Ibid.
43 Ibid., 19 and 20 March 1927.

During this period of training we had a slight touch of "shell shock", owing to a rumour arriving that Whitehall had decided to mechanize the world, including the Machine Gun Squadron. Ford cars, Crossley tenders, hay carts [sic] and other mysteriously-driven vehicles were to be issued instead of our equine friends: but somehow or other, our Quartermaster neglected to indent for them. Mechanization may be alright, but two miles or so of bad ground with guns, tripods etc., would be all wrong, for such distances would have to be covered, on some occasions, when mechanical vehicles would become bogged down or ditched.[44]

Later in the same journal appeared the following poem that summed-up someone's contemporary thoughts on mechanization. Although the regiment was only to be partially mechanized with lorries, the poem makes clear that the assumption was, in 1927, that tanks *would* soon replace cavalry horses:

The days of the cavalry soldier are over,
If certain great brains have their way.
In future they'll issue us petrol for clover
When mechanization holds sway.

Then what will they do for a livery stable
When horses are taken away?
And how will some elderly gentry be able
To shake up their livers each day?

And who will provide all the horses for training?
Will umpires ride cycles, or run?
To some, I've no doubt, "twill appear entertaining,
But umpires won't think it much fun.

Can tanks, doing escort, compete by their crashing
With horses that gladden the eye?
Will tractors, in races, excite us by smashing
The fences the horse used to fly?

When tanks take the place of the obsolete "hairy"
D'you think that the horse show will last?
Will prizes you won with your jumpers be merely
The sign of a decadent past?

---

44 "Machine Gun Squadron Notes", *The Journal of The VIII King's Royal Irish Hussars* Volume 1. January, 1928 No.1, p.17.

Will the hunting field, too, be by tankettes invaded?
Will hounds be let out of a box?
Will we on machines, from our horses degraded,
Soon chase an electrical fox?[45]

The Machine Gun Squadron was partially mechanized by the summer of 1928 for manoeuvres with the French Cavalry, one troop in six-wheeled lorries loaned to them by the Royal Army Service Corps (RASC), and the other troop mounted with pack-horses. At the end of September the Machine-Gun Squadron "parted with our petrol mounts... and awaited their successors".[46] Some new-comers to the now mechanized squadron enjoyed not having to care for horses, but some regretted it.

The first-line transport for the manoeuvres was:

> ... improvised out of existing station transport, and consisted of four-horsed L.G.S. (Light General Service) wagons, five 30-cwt. Vulcan lorries and four 3-ton Albion lorries. There were also six 3-ton Albion lorries for supplies, working in two echelons.[47]

The road journey by lorry was very slow, with an average speed of four miles per hour, "due to break-downs and certain of the lorries being unable to get up the steep hills".[48] By May 1929 the Machine Gun Squadron was entirely mechanized with six-wheeled lorries and enjoyed not having to "box the horses, forage and saddles" when the squadron departed for its annual machine-gun course; they expected the sabre squadrons, still horsed, to be "secretly green with envy".[49] The performance of the wheeled vehicles must have improved considerably; on the course held at Bitche, "the lorries put up some quite astonishing performances and lived up to their reputation of being able to go almost anywhere".[50]

On 4 October 1929 the regiment left Germany for Aldershot, England; the advance party under the second-in-command Major Pope MC had already left on 24 September. All their horses were "evacuated", in six parties, via Antwerp and not taken over by another regiment, as all British troops left Germany at around that time. The last party of horses arrived at Aldershot on 11 October.[51] During 1930 part of the Machine-Gun Squadron was supplied with new guns and Carden-Loyd machine-gun carriers that came with the reputation:

---

45   *The Journal of The VIII King's Royal Irish Hussars* Volume 1. January, 1928 No.1, p.33.
46   Ibid., January, 1929 No.2, p.11.
47   Ibid., p.3.
48   Ibid.
49   Ibid., January, 1930 No.3, p.8.
50   Ibid., p.9.
51   QRH 285, *Regimental Diary 1923–1939 8th KRI Hussars.*

... that they could do almost anything, even turn round and snap at you ... [however], on the first day out one absolutely refused to start, and another gave up the ghost well out in the Long Valley and was ignominiously towed home.[52]

Not enough Carden-Loyd carriers appear to have been issued for the entire squadron; in a demonstration at Miles Hill for the Imperial Press Congress on 10 June 1930, "the Squadron turned out two troops, one mounted and the other mechanized".[53] Driver training continued and on 29 December 1930 "4 Tprs. [Troopers] Passed Trade Test for Trade of Driver I.C. Class III at Feltham".[54] The Carden-Loyd machine-gun troop, together with a sabre squadron, took part in a demonstration for Staff College students at Jubilee Hill in July 1931 and another, under Major E A Staniland, for the OTC (Officer Training Corps) at Miles Hill. Part of the Machine Gun Squadron was still mounted on horses and provided some of the Divisional Cavalry Regiment for the concentration of the 1st Division on exercise in August 1931.[55] The Divisional Cavalry Regiment was made up of units from several cavalry regiments, because of an acute shortage of trained men:

> Owing to the shortage of trained men in the Regiments, the Inspector General of Cavalry cancelled his usual Inspection of individual Units and instead took the 1st Cavalry Brigade on a Tactical Scheme on this day.[56]

The following day, 15 August 1931, this letter was published in Regimental Orders:-

> Sir,
> I am commanded by the Army Council to inform you that the present state of the national finances has necessitated the adoption of widespread measures of economy throughout the country.
>   In these measures the Army and all the Services of the Crown have been called upon to bear their share. The Army Council are confident that All Ranks will be ready to make the sacrifices demanded of them in order to contribute to the restoration of national prosperity.
>   I am Sir,
>   Your obedient servant,
>   (SD) H. J. Creedy[57]

---

52   *The Journal of The VIII King's Royal Irish Hussars* Volume 1. January, 1929 No.4, p.13.
53   Ibid., p.14.
54   QRH 285; recorded 30 December 1930 in the *Regimental Diary 1923–1939 8th KRI Hussars.*
55   Ibid.
56   Ibid.
57   Ibid.

The Service pay-cuts, recruitment and mechanization

These diary records demonstrate how the national and international economic situation impinged on the everyday life of a cavalry regiment, and particularly on the ordinary trooper who received the least remuneration. Whatever reaction there was to the pay cuts was not recorded. In the previous chapter the so-called mutiny of the Atlantic Fleet at Invergordon of September 1931 was cited as the reaction of naval ratings to their pay-cuts, but it appears that soldiers received the news without any demonstration of dissent.

Army recruitment in the 1930s was of concern and a cut in pay will not have helped this matter. It has been considered whether this factor affected mechanization or was affected by it. In England the popular pacifist culture and anti-war sentiment was reaching its zenith in the run-up to the League of Nations World Disarmament Conference, particularly as the Great War commemoration had emphasised the "lost generation".[58] The Army found recruitment challenging and although unemployment was on the increase a military service career was not as popular as it once might have been. Recruitment problems continued for some time throughout the 1930s. In February 1935 the Regular Army was 3,300 below recruiting establishment.[59] The Times reported the First Lord of The Admiralty Sir Sam Hoare's concerned speech at Margate in early October 1936. Hoare said: "Perverted pacifism and partisan obstruction have had their effects on the recruiting figure of the army". There was a need, he continued, "to destroy the pernicious prejudices that undoubtedly do exist, and persuade young men to adopt an inspiring and invigorating career".[60] On 31 October The Times again reported concerns about army recruitment.[61] There was certainly anxiety about the recruitment of officers in the Royal Tank Corps for example; in 1935 it was estimated that in order to fulfil the mobilization requirement by 1939, 550 officers would be needed for two "contingents", 96 of whom could come from India and 150 from the Supplementary Reserve, but leaving 300 more officers who had to be found from somewhere. An armoured car company was proposed with the objective of training future officers.[62]

---

58   A term used later, possibly originally by Ernest Hemingway, but also associated with Vera Brittain in Bishop and Bostridge (eds) [2004], *Letters From A Lost Generation*, (Abacus, London), that described those who had served, and more particular those who had died in the Great War.

59   LHCMA – LH15/12/9, 5; War Office Memorandum, Army estimates, 14 February 1935, p.4.

60   *The Times*, 02.10.1936.

61   Ibid., 31.10.1936.

62   TNA WO 32/2859 ARMY ORGANIZATION: Territorial Army (Code 14(K)): Officer's producing Units for Royal Tank Corps: Formation of 1935–1938; Reg No. 20/Gen/5496 minute 8 – the 22 (London) Armoured Car Company (Westminster Dragoons) Territorial Army was formed from an existing County of London Yeomanry regiment; also The Lindsay papers, LHCMA – LH15/12/1–2, A2b14.

Gary Evans has analysed the British *General Army Reports* that indicated to him "the cavalry was consistently able to recruit to establishment until mechanisation [sic] commenced";[63] and he dates this from 1935.[64] But the 8th Hussars' diary does not support this assertion regarding having sufficient "trained men". Evans and Gilman Barndollar agree that "the army [as a whole] struggled to recruit to full establishment".[65] Regarding the recruitment of officers, Evans wrote that 1936 and 1937 "saw the mechanisation [sic] of the cavalry enlarged"; this he insisted "had no effect upon the recruitment of officers to the cavalry. The level of officer recruitment in the Royal Tank Corps (RTC), however, reduced".[66] The "Percentage Strength of Annual Establishment – Officers" indicated an overall decline of some eight percent from 1932 to 1937; a decline of 25 percent in the RTC, but the cavalry arm was consistently above 100 percent of its officer establishment.[67] Evans asserted: "The cavalry never failed to recruit its officer cadre whether mechanised or mounted; mechanisation [sic] was never an issue for *officer* recruitment".[68] The reason for this may have been because most cavalry regiments had been in existence for two to three hundred years and had long traditions of family patronage, the Tank Corps had not. Sons, grandsons and great-grandsons would join "The Regiment" whether mechanized or not. A browse of the Army Lists shows many examples, including interviewees for this account, Val ffrench Blake of the 17th/21st Lancers and Aiden Sprot of the Royal Scots Greys, whose fathers had served in their respective regiments.[69]

Because the RTC "continued to recruit strongly to the ranks", Evans speculated that recruits were more attracted to the RTC than to horsed cavalry regiments. The medical requirements were, however, less stringent for the RTC than for the cavalry and infantry, "[but] the insinuation would appear to be that some of the lower ranks of the cavalry were more against mechanisation [sic] than the officers".[70] Evans was correct that there is insufficient information to support this and therefore this is open only to speculation. Furthermore, veterans interviewed for this account confirmed the confusion of some recruits thinking the cavalry *was* already mechanized and that the officers and other ranks got on with the job of mechanization and did not seek postings to those regiments that remained horsed. "Talk of mechanization was always there, a couple of regiments were already mechanized",[71] recalled Corporal Charles

---

63   Evans, Gary, "The British Cavalry 1920–1940", PhD, University of Kent, 2011, p.145.
64   Ibid.
65   Ibid; Gilman Clough Barndollar, "British Use of Armoured cars 1919–1939", PhD, Cambridge University, 2010, p.29.
66   Evans, Gary, "The British Cavalry 1920–1940", PhD, University of Kent, 2011, p.163.
67   Ibid., Chart 2.
68   Ibid., emphasis added.
69   ffrench Blake's father was actually a 21st Lancer; he was killed in action in the Great War – the 17th and the 21st Lancers were amalgamated in 1922 – see Chapter Three.
70   Evans, Gary, "The British Cavalry 1920–1940", PhD, University of Kent, 2011, p.165.
71   The 11th Hussars and the 12th Lancers.

Need of the 13th/18th Hussars when interviewed in 2007. Some recruits, remembered Need, had joined the cavalry believing it to be already mechanized, such as Benny Hunter, a tractor driver from Hull and Percy Britain, a bus driver who later became a motorcyclist in the signals unit.[72]

However, in August 1936, the 4th Queen's Own Hussars too were short of men. The Commanding Officer Lieutenant Colonel Scott-Cockburn speculated:

> … recruitment for the Army is very bad at the present… this is partly due to the fact that unemployment is so good, partly due to the ease with which the dole is obtained, and partly due to the fact that young fellows do not know what the Army can do for them. Every regiment in the British Army is under strength.[73]

David French has examined the social and cultural aspects of mechanization within cavalry regiments: the regimental pride of still being the "best cavalry regiment" whether horsed or armoured, and the "cautious" willingness to accept mechanization by both officers and men.[74] This cautious acceptance of mechanization was supported by veteran cavalryman Sergeant Ronald Lucas of the 15th/19th Hussars, who saw mechanization positively, as an exciting new challenge. Like it or not, however, Lucas's first loyalty was to his regiment, whatever equipment it was ordered to use.[75] Need, of the 13th/18th Hussars, confirmed how proud cavalrymen were to be part of that service arm.[76]

It is doubtful therefore, that mechanization had any bearing on recruitment. If the RTC attracted more men than the cavalry to the ranks, the physical requirements might have been a factor; so too might have been a reluctance to learn to ride a horse and the foresight to learn a skill more in tune with the needs of civilian life. All the veteran cavalrymen interviewed for this account, however, initially joined their regiments either because of a connection with family and friends, or due a keenness to work with horses. Once they became soldiers other factors, such as esprit de corps, became more important to them.

Whatever the reasons were, the British Army, including some cavalry regiments, were short of men. A significant indication of this is recorded in the Regimental Diary of the 8th Hussars at the bottom of the page for December 1931 that only one recruit had attested for the that month; and by June 1937 recruitment was still a challenge for the 8th Hussars. A discussion group of young officers and NCOs was held in the

72   Personal interview with Need (2007); by the author.
73   Speech given by Lieutenant Colonel J Scott-Cockburn, 24 August 1936, reported in *IV Hussars' Journal*, 1936, pp.34 & 35.
74   French, D., *Military Identities*, p.263.
75   Personal interview with Lucas (2007); by the author.
76   Personal interview with Need (2007); by the author.

regimental library to consider "How to improve recruiting". Regrettably no record of their conclusions has been found.[77]

Mechanization continued for the 8th Hussars

Mechanization of a sort, however, had continued for the 8th Hussars; "all Horses of Signal Troop were transferred to Sabre Squadrons, Signallers being trained as Austin Scouts and vice versa".[78] On 4 October 1932 the regiment moved to Hounslow, and probably as a result of economies, "lost several motors" along with the Carden-Loyd machine-gun carriers, with the machine-gunners being re-mounted on horseback.

By January 1933:

> The Regiment now consists of Regimental Headquarters, comprising: 1 Administrative Troop, 1 Band Troop, 1 Machine Gun Troop (on pack [horses]), 1 Signal and Austin Scout Troop, also 3 Sabre Squadrons of 3 Troops each.[79]

On 19 December 1933 the 8th Hussars, after a break of eleven years, returned to Egypt, but not until autumn 1935 did the "stop-go" policy in mechanization end for them. The Regimental Diary recorded en bloc October, November and December 1935 that marked "the rapid development of the Regiment as a mechanised force":[80]

> Initial preparations for the change-over were commenced about the 9th September when a party proceeded to Helmieh [outside Cairo] to undergo training with the 11th Hussars, and the majority of the remainder received tuition on the Vickers machine gun.[81]

This entry indicates that regiment must have had orders to begin conversion before this was officially notified to all other Army Commands. In accordance with the Army Council's orders, however, the 8th Hussars held their last mounted parade in Egypt on 11 November 1935 and began the change process from horses to petrol-driven vehicles.[82] The 11th Hussars, also stationed in Egypt, trained the 8th Hussars in driving and maintenance during 1936.

All the regiment's horses were transferred to the 1st Royal Dragoons that had recently arrived in Egypt from India. On 25 November, the whole of C Squadron was sent for training at Helmieh and the regiment was anticipating equipping with

77   28 June 1937; QRH 285, *Regimental Diary 1923–1939 8th KRI Hussars.*
78   Ibid., 1 December 1931.
79   *The Journal of The VIII King's Royal Irish Hussars* Volume 11. January, 1933 No.2, p.1.
80   QRH 285, October, November and December, 1935, *Regimental Diary 1923–1939 8th KRI Hussars.*
81   Ibid.
82   Ibid.

The 8th King's Royal Irish Hussars crossing Chertsey Bridge on their march to Hounslow, 4 October 1932. (Source: *The Journal of The VIII King's Royal Irish Hussars* Volume 11. January, 1933 No.2)

modified 15 cwt. and 30 cwt., Ford V8 vehicles and "V.B. (Vickers-Berthier) light automatic [machine-guns] in favour to the Vickers machine gun, and all personnel were instructed in its use".[83] By 18 December C Squadron was equipped to "proceed by road to Mersa Matruh... as part of the newly formed Mobile Force".[84]

The "Mobile Force" was the seed-corn of the 7th Armoured Division, later to achieve lasting fame as the "Desert Rats". The Mobile Force comprised the 7th Hussars "in an assortment of light tanks, Marks III and VIB", the 11th Hussars in their old armoured cars, and the 1st Royal Tank Regiment that had "left England in March with all the light tanks available there and with new [replacement] tracks [that] did not fit".[85] The Mobile Force also included the 3rd Regiment Royal Horse Artillery equipped with "dragons" towing 3.7 inch howitzers, and the 8th Hussars in their machine-gun mounted Ford trucks. The brigade was completed by Corps troops from the No.5 Company Royal Army Service Corps (RASC) and the 2nd/3rd Field Ambulance, Royal Army Medical Corps. The force was supported by the RAF with Lysanders of

83   Ibid.
84   Ibid.
85   Fitzroy, *Men of Valour*, p.18.

No.208 Army Cooperation Squadron, Gloster Gladiator fighters of No.80 Fighter Squadron, and Hawker Hart light bombers of No.45 Bomber Squadron.[86]

Back in Abbassia, the Regimental Headquarters and A Squadron of the 8th Hussars were trained in driving and maintenance by their own regimental instructors who had, in turn, been trained by the 11th Hussars. "The barrack square was converted into an improvised garage for this purpose".[87] The regiment was augmented in January 1936 by a sergeant and seventeen other ranks from the Royal Corps of Signals from England. Later this troop was designated "H Troop Cavalry Division Signals".[88] The same month brought some of the first casualties resulting from mechanization; Lance Sergeant Winkers and Trooper Dawson died when their Ford 30 cwt. vehicle overturned whilst on a reconnaissance mission with C Squadron.[89]

By 17 January 1936, a year after the regiment began the change process from horses to vehicles, A Squadron too was able to proceed by road to Mersa Matruh and Regimental Headquarters followed on 22 January.[90] This was a striking example of successful change management that mirrored in many respects that of the 3rd Hussars "experiment" in England. This could not have been achieved without good leadership, strong motivation, and the collective will of the troopers of the 8th Hussars to succeed in what they were ordered to do. In less than five months officers and troopers who had previously been horsemen joined the Mobile Force as a mechanized, or perhaps, motorized regiment. The training continued. On 29 January a sergeant and fifteen other ranks commenced a driving and maintenance course with the RASC and a Light Aid Detachment (LAD) joined the regiment to support them.[91] Although not recorded as such, the LAD detachment could have been from either the RASC or the RAOC. During February and March the regiment took part in "schemes", "exercises" and "battle-drills" for visiting general officers that included the CIGS, Sir Archibald Montgomery-Massingberd, and the Inspector General of Cavalry.[92] In June 1936:

> The following remarks by the GOC-in-C in connection with the Annual Part II Inspection of the Regt. are republished for information:

86 Ibid.
87 QRH 285, October, November and December, 1935, *Regimental Diary 1923–1939 8th KRI Hussars.*
88 Ibid., January 27, 1936.
89 Ibid., 11 January, 1936.
90 Ibid., 17 and 27 January, 1936.
91 A Light Aid Detachment (LAD) was made-up of a small team of specialist soldiers; engineers, fitters, armourers and electricians, in 1936 probably from the RAOC, attached to support a mechanized unit with maintenance and repairs beyond the capability of the AFV driver/mechanics. Later, after 1 October 1942, a LAD was usually formed from the Royal Corps of Electrical and Mechanical Engineers (REME).
92 QRH 285, February and March 1936, *Regimental Diary 1923–1939 8th KRI Hussars.*

I think the whole hearted way in which this Regt. adapted itself to mechanization which must have been a wrench to many, reflects the greatest credit to All
Ranks.[93]

The entire regiment left Cairo by road on 26 June 1936, ordered to proceed to Palestine
"to assist in quelling disturbances between Arabs and Jews".[94] The 8th Hussars
camped on the outskirts of Jerusalem. Throughout July patrols were regularly sent
out and after some fire-fights in which six "enemy" were killed, "armed bands" were
rounded-up in the Nablus area. Reconnaissance around Jericho was undertaken by
RHQ and B Squadrons and escort troops sent out to protect working parties repairing
damaged telegraph wires. C Squadron moved to patrol the Gaza area, and troops
from B Squadron, later reinforced with A Squadron, moved to Beersheba to search
for arms and ammunition and to protect work on the constantly sabotaged railway
line. There were a number of exchanges of gun-fire and bombing incidents in the
area, and throughout July, August and September, this work of patrolling and protection continued with a number of armed men apprehended. On 11 October, news was
received that "The Arab Committee" had ordered the rebellion to cease "uncondition-
ally", "offensive action [by British forces] ceased except to meet unprovoked assault".[95]
The regiment returned to Cairo on 14 and 15 November 1936 and ended the regiment's first action as a mechanized unit.

   Recorded in the Regimental Diary were other activities pertinent to the development of mechanization within the unit; NCOs attended three-month driving and
maintenance courses at Bovington in England at the end of 1936, and in January 1937
a draft of one captain, 88 troopers and 4 [band] boys from the 3rd Hussars replaced
time-expired men who went home to the Army Reserve. By 1937 the 3rd Hussars had
been "mechanized" [see previous chapter] – their "best men" from A Squadron were
posted to the 8th Hussars. This draft of 3rd Hussars included Charles Newman, who
had joined the regiment on what he described as a "cold December day in 1935".[96]
During his first year in the 3rd Hussars he had been taught to drive "all the regimental
vehicles, tanks, lorries, staff cars and motor cycles", had qualified as a marksman with
a Bren machine-gun and was recommended for training as an instructor. Newman
had not, however, been through riding school.[97] In November 1936 he was, without
prior warning, placed on a "draft of 90 men to be posted to the 8th King's Royal Irish
Hussars stationed in Abbassia, Egypt".[98] They sailed on 28 December 1936. When

93   Ibid., June 1936.
94   Ibid.
95   Ibid., November 1936.
96   "From Cairo to Berlin With The Desert Rats"; the memoirs of 555950 S.Q.M.S. C F A
     Newman in *The Chronicle – The Journal of The Queen's Royal Hussars Historical Society*, pp.26
     & 43 Volume 1 Number 3, November 2002.
97   Ibid.
98   Ibid., p.26.

the men arrived, after fourteen days at sea and a similar number of hours by train, they were distributed among the three squadrons of the 8th Hussars; Newman was placed in A Squadron. He recalled:

> The Regiment was in the process of mechanisation [sic] and was currently equipped with Ford pick-up cars and open backed lorries… the backs of the vehicles were fitted with machine-guns, with seats for the gunners and racks for ammunition, water etc. These had been specially designed for desert warfare and for controlling riots in the Egyptian cities; there was always something going on in Cairo… Hard going it was too.[99]

Newman remembered that in 1937 the regiment had "several old tanks for training in driving and gunnery, and a lot of time was spent on these".[100]

In April 1937 Lieutenant D R W G Charlton was sent to the Royal Tank Corps Central School for a course on driving and maintenance and several NCOs took part in instructors' courses elsewhere. Later in April all available officers were lectured on "Imperial Defence in relation to the re-armament programme" and in June, on "Supply of Forces in the Field" and the "Latest Developments in Radio transmission and Wireless Transmission [sic]". On 28 June 1937, 8th Hussar Major J P Robinson was appointed to the British Military Mission attached to the Egyptian Army as an "instructor of Motor Cavalry". This was an indication of the competency achieved by both the regiment and by Major Robinson.[101] By the end of 1937, Charles Newman, who had completed several courses, considered himself "a fully-fledged tank crew member. As a driver or gunner I could live with the best", but Newman struggled with wireless communication. In time, there were more tanks on which to train, "a couple of Armoured Cars" and Bren carriers, but new tanks were still not available.[102] In the following March 1938, some NCOs attended a "2. Pdr. A/T [anti-tank] Gun Course" and the regiment as a whole took part in "Command Manoeuvres". These were, according to the commanding officer, "a real test of stamina [in which] a high standard in driving and tactical work was well maintained" and, compared to the previous year, "the most marked improvement in the handling of vehicles over difficult country and in keeping formation". The Brigade Commander expressed similar compliments relating to the performance of the 8th Hussars.[103] In November 1938, Major General P C S (Percy) Hobart, GOC Mobile Division, lectured officers on the "Working of [the] Mobile Division".[104] The Mobile Force had become the Mobile

---

99   Ibid., p.36.
100 Ibid.
101 December 1935–June 1937; QRH 285, *Regimental Diary 1923–1939 8th KRI Hussars.*
102 Newman, "From Cairo to Berlin With The Desert Rats", p.39 Volume 1 Number 3, November 2002.
103 22 March 1937; QRH 285, *Regimental Diary 1923–1939 8th KRI Hussars.*
104 Ibid., November 1938.

Division in October 1937 "when sufficient equipment has materialized, [with a role] provisionally defined as reconnaissance before the main forces made contact".[105] Although the Mobile Division became the 1st Armoured Division in April 1939,[106] it can be argued that it was in effect the genesis of later British Army armoured divisions that included the 2nd, particularly the 7th Armoured Division, and to some extent, because of Hobart's command and influence, the 11th Armoured Division.

Under Hobart's supervision, the commanding officer, adjutant and two other officers of the 8th Hussars took part in Brigade war games and a subsequent conference. On 12 November all officers, together with 60 warrant officers and NCOs, attended Hobart's lecture on tactics. Research has not determined the content of these tactical lectures, but in his lectures at the Staff College at Quetta in 1926, Hobart had used examples of cavalry successes, especially from the American Civil War, to illustrate his points.[107] Many of the 8th Hussar officers the next day saw a demonstration given by 1st Battalion RTC in "the use of smoke projected from Light Tanks".[108] Live firing exercises took place later that month.

Cavalry officers had been allowed to keep two horses for sport and exercise at government expense after their regiment was mechanized, but in January 1939 this entitlement was reduced to one horse. Although noting this order, the 8th Hussars diary makes no reference to the disposal of the redundant animals, perhaps they had already gone.[109] During 24 and 25 January 1939, the 7th and 8th Hussars exercised together as mechanized units on "opposing sides".

On the outbreak of war the Light Armoured Brigade (later re-named the 7th Armoured Brigade) of the Mobile Division was formed by the 8th Hussars, still mounted in obsolete Mark III tanks and their Ford "pick-up" trucks, the 7th Hussars in light tanks, and the 11th Hussars in Rolls Royce and their newly acquired Morris armoured cars. The Brigade was commanded by Brigadier H E Russell and the Division by Major General P C S Hobart. In November 1939 the 8th Hussars returned to Helmieh "to be brought up to full tank strength, [but] had to wait until the end of April [1940] before this was accomplished". A and B Squadrons were equipped with Vickers Mark VIB tanks, but C Squadron continued with Mark III light tanks, C Squadron was eventually "fitted out with old Vickers Mk VI tanks" later in 1940.[110] Charles Newman, by then a sergeant and a tank commander, was put in charge of one of these:

> The main armament was one heavy machine-gun in the turret and a light machine-gun in support. As I recall it, I had a crew of three and the speed was

105 Harris, *Men, Ideas and Tanks*, pp.252 & 257.
106 French, D., *Raising Churchill's Army*, p.42.
107 LHCMA – LH15/11/1–11; Lecture VIII Staff College, Quetta, 1926.
108 November 1938; QRH 285, *Regimental Diary 1923–1939 8th KRI Hussars*.
109 Fitzroy, *Men of Valour*, p.19.
110 Ibid., p.25.

The 8th Hussars Desert Training in Vickers Mark VIB Light Tanks, Egypt 1940.
(Source: Newman, "From Cairo to Berlin With The Desert Rats,"
p.22 Volume 1 Number 4, May 2004)

supposed to be 35mph, but it had long fallen far below that. Fifteen of these comprised a Squadron and in support of the tanks came the "thin-skins"; lorries and runabouts, staff cars, water cart, wireless vans etc. Each of the lorries had a specific load to carry. There was much to be carried in desert warfare: petrol, a variety of ammunition to fit all requirements, water, reserve food rations, a fitter's lorry equipped with all the necessary tools and a second one carrying spares for tanks and vehicles.[111]

---

111 Newman, "From Cairo to Berlin With The Desert Rats,"p.22 Volume 1 Number 4, May 2004.

The 7th Hussars mechanize

The 7th Hussars, as part of the cavalry brigade, were in Egypt in 1936 where the soldiers began the change process from horses to vehicles. The regiment had been stationed in Aldershot from 1931 until 1934 when the 7th Hussars moved to Hounslow as a precursor to sailing to Egypt on 18 September 1935. The 7th Hussars, like the 8th already had some experience of motor vehicles before January 1936 when the news was received that the regiment was to convert to a "Light Tank Regiment". From 1927, with the issue of fourteen six-wheeled lorries, their horses had been relieved of carrying the heavy equipment such as machine-guns and tripods.[112] These vehicles were unable to keep pace with the mounted squadrons and were mechanically unreliable.[113] At Aldershot between 1931 and 1934 however:

> The formation of a scout troop of an NCO and 9 men on RHQ (formed as part of Regimental Headquarters) was an innovation. These are mobilized in Austin 7s (cars) and are organized as two sections of three cars each.[114]

These vehicles "in the hands of a dashing Hussar subaltern" seemed to have been enjoyed with a high road speed and some cross-country capability; it prepared the way for the conversion to a fully mechanized regiment.[115]

All the horses had gone by July 1936, to the Remount Depot at Abbassia; five horses only remained: the officers' chargers and "private horses".[116] The regiment's 530 NCOs and men were given the opportunity to transfer out to other horsed cavalry regiments; quite what would have happened had they elected to do so was not recorded. Only sixteen decided to take-up this offer, which indicated the high morale and esprit de corps of the unit, and that these cavalrymen were not "wedded" to their horses.[117]

On 4 April the GOC British troops in Egypt had asked the Under Secretary of State (USS) in London whether a date had been set for the regiment to be converted and from where the light tanks would be sourced, if not from the 1st Light Tank Battalion of the RTC.[118] The reply of 30 April was inconclusive, but the USS requested the commencement of preliminary training in driving and maintenance of

112 Brereton, *The 7th Queen's Own Hussars*, p.164/165.
113 Ibid.
114 The 7th Hussars Unit Historical Records 1910–1939, Section 1718, 01.04.1932–31.03.1933 Regimental Archives Warwick.
115 Brereton, *The 7th Queen's Own Hussars*, p.164/165.
116 IWM; Younger, reel 1; The 7th Hussars Unit Historical Records 1910–1939, Section 1718, 01.04.1936–31.03.1937. Brereton, *The 7th Queen's Own Hussars*, p.169, the horses remained for training young officers.
117 Brereton, *The 7th Queen's Own Hussars*, p.164/165.
118 TNA WO 32/2847 Army Organisation: Cavalry (Code 14(D)): Introduction of a Mobile Division 1934–1936 20/General/5512 (S.D.2.) marked 20A, 4 April 1936.

light tanks.[119] By 25 May 1936 the GOC Egypt confirmed that the 7th Hussars had commenced this training.[120] Driving and maintenance courses began the same month and continued throughout the year:

> Results were good, the majority of the Regiment being trained. Squadrons were trained independently in their new duties, B Squadron being the earliest trained, co-operated with the Canal Brigade and the Cairo Brigade in the their exercises.[121]

It was established that light tanks would not be issued to the 7th Hussars until some-time in 1937.[122] The Unit Historical Records verified that in April and May 1937 "field firing schemes were carried out for the first time in tanks".[123] Major General Ralph Younger, recorded in 1977, who had been a subaltern with the 7th Hussars in 1936, was vague about the officers' and men's reaction to mechanization. Operational necessity over-ruled sentiment, but, remembered Younger, some "reactionary people", "horsy" junior officers who were unlikely to progress beyond the rank of major, said they would leave the regiment:

> Some thought it [mechanization] was bound to happen sometime. The preva-lent mood was one of acceptance with regret. [Of] the "other ranks", under ten percent regretted mechanization; some were surprisingly adaptable – the farriers for instance.[124]

Younger was on leave in May 1936 when the process began to armour the 7th Hussars and when he came back in July "mechanization was in full swing. It was a bit of a bombshell because it changed a way of life".[125] Younger recalled that training was limited because of the shortage of spare parts for the tanks, especially tracks that broke in the desert; the regimental records confirmed this.[126] Those chosen for instructor training were trained by a team from the 6th Royal Tank Regiment under Major G

---

119 Ibid., marked 21A, 30 April 1936.
120 Ibid., marked 22A, 16 May 1936.
121 The 7th Hussars Unit Historical Records 1910–1939, Section 1718 01.04.1936–31.03.1937.
122 TNA WO 32/2847 Army Organisation: Cavalry (Code 14(D)): Introduction of a Mobile Division 1934–1936 20/General/5512 (S.D.2.) marked 1A to all Commands, unsigned and undated, but referred to on 30 September 1936 by E K Squires DSD to Army Council members – marked (DF(a).
123 The 7th Hussars Unit Historical Records 1910–1939, Section 1718, 01.04.1937–31.03.1938.
124 Younger, reel 1; *The Army Lists* show no turnover of officers occurred between 1936 and 1937.
125 Younger, reel 2.
126 Ibid; The 7th Hussars Unit Historical Records 1910–1939, 01.04.1938–31.03.1939.

J N Culverwell: "Mostly senior NCOs and very nice people they were too, high class chaps".[127] Machine-gun and driving and maintenance training had recommenced in April and May 1937 and in August new "tradesmen" appeared on the muster roll: "Driver mechanics were trained, also [a] Technical Storeman and Driver Operators".[128] Major General Younger speculated that: "It took probably until Christmas 1937 to get enough of our own [7th Hussars qualified instructors]", and he thought that instructors were probably selected because of their "education, intelligence and they already instructed in something else".[129]

During the next year the strength of the regiment was 20 officers and 544 other ranks. Some horses must either have returned, or the "all but 5" that had left the regiment for Abbassia had not included officers' mounts because the establishment numbered "40 horses". These horses would have been the two chargers each officer was allowed to keep until the beginning of 1939. In February 1938 a draft of 188 troopers from the 9th Lancers joined the 7th Hussars. These 9th Lancers had already undergone mechanization training in Great Britain which enabled the rotation of mechanized regiments and the replacement of time-expired men in Egypt.

Mechanization and the Army at home

The Army at home in the United Kingdom struggled on to modernize, criticised by the media, underfunded by the Government, and unsure of the role it would be called upon to play should a war occur. Assigned by the Army Council as a "Light Tank regiment" in December 1935, the Queen's Bays (2nd Dragoon Guards) at Aldershot in October 1937 still needed vehicles. "A few light tanks" as training vehicles were supposed to have been issued to the regiment during the winter of 1936/37.[130] This was outlined in a draft letter of October 1936 announcing a further change in the organisation of the Home Mobile Division. Motor cavalry regiments would now form part of the brigades making up the division. In future, each brigade would consist of two cavalry light tank regiments and one mechanized infantry rifle battalion. The first of these brigades was to be formed at Tidworth with its rifle battalion to be selected later. The cavalry light tank regiments chosen were the 9th Queen's Royal Lancers and the Queen's Bays.[131]

127 Ibid; *The Army List* 1937.
128 The 7th Hussars Unit Historical Records 1910–1939, Section 1718, 01.04.1937–31.03.1938.
129 Younger, reel 2.
130 TNA WO 32/2847 Army Organisation: Cavalry (Code 14(D)): Introduction of a Mobile Division 1934–1936 20/General/5512 (S.D.2.) draft marked 1A to all Commands, unsigned and undated, but referred to on 30 September 1936 by E K Squires DSD to Army Council members – marked (DF(a).
131 Ibid.

Although these proposals, put forward by the CIGS, had been approved by the Secretary of State, the problem of implementation was again one of finance for vehicles. These proposals required £500,000 more money than had been approved by the Treasury, and its further authority was necessary to procure the increased numbers of vehicles and equipment.[132] Although not specified, these included "more suitable types of vehicles" than trucks for cavalry regiments, other than those destined for light tank regiments. Notwithstanding Grubb's original and optimistic report on the "experiment" carried out by the 3rd Hussars, their trucks, unsurprisingly, had been found inadequate, but would still have to be used for training until a "hoped for… something better" was developed and procured.[133]

Charles Newman (mentioned earlier), in training with the 3rd Hussars in 1935 and 1936, and before being posted to the 8th Hussars, experienced his first funeral parade that had resulted from using unsatisfactory trucks:

> One of our own group was killed on driving instruction. We were taking instruction on an open-backed 15 cwt. truck. Several of us were riding in the back of the truck and the other actually taking instruction. He drove too fast over a humpback bridge. We were all thrown up and all landed back in safety except one, who was thrown higher and landed on his head in the road. So we had our first experience of death in the services.[134]

E K Squires, Director of Staff Duties (DSD) for the Army Council, clearly concerned about the vehicles, and the credibility of the Army Council in providing them, urged agreement to tell regiments of this intention and soon:

> We cannot allow them [the army units] to believe that it is our intention never to provide anything more suitable than the vehicles which they are now going to receive. The regiments concerned have long been waiting for the word "go"; we are most anxious and so are they that they should get rid of their horses at once, and devote their energies to training themselves in their re-organized form.[135]

Following his assertion, the Director of Finance of the Army Council (DFA) acquiesced.[136] The tone of the DSD's minute was certainly one of frustration, perhaps even anger, not at what he was expecting the cavalry to do, but with the unsatisfactory or

---

132 Ibid., 5255G/34 minute 2 DFA to DSD, 1 October 1936.
133 Ibid., 5255G/34 minute 3 DSD to DFA, 2 October 1936.
134 Newman, "From Cairo to Berlin With The Desert Rats", p.26 Volume 1 Number 3, November 2002.
135 TNA WO 32/2847 Army Organisation: Cavalry (Code 14(D)): Introduction of a Mobile Division 1934–1936 20/General/5512 (S.D.2.) 5255G/34 minute 3 DSD to DFA, 2 October 1936.
136 Ibid., 5255G/34 minute 4 DFA to DSD, 2 October 1936.

The 15th/19th Hussars in Bren-gun carriers withdrawing from Louvain 14 May 1940; the Regiment suffered appalling losses – 176 officers and men killed, wounded or captured. (Source: HHQ Light Dragoons)

"token" equipment he had to ask them to use with the hope that "something better" soon would be produced for them. This was not the "hesitant and fumbling" attitude of the Army Council that was criticised by Liddell Hart, but one of an organization making an intensive effort to achieve the best possible results with very limited resources.[137] Asked in 2007 if he or his comrades were resentful about the equipment with which they were expected to train, and later to use in battle, veteran cavalrymen Ronald Lucas and John Bennett of the 15th/19th Hussars both said they were not. The country was in a poor state and could not afford anything better, Lucas recalled, but neither of these former soldiers had realized, until engagement with the enemy on the Louvain Ridge in Belgium in 1940, how poorly the Vickers Mark VIB tanks would perform against the German tanks and anti-tank guns.[138]

137 Liddell Hart, *Memoirs Volume I,* p.262.
138 Personal interviews with Bennett and Lucas (2007); by the author.

The 15th/19th Hussars returned from Dunkirk having lost two of its three squadrons. By July 1940, when the regiment was restored to the order of battle, the replacement troopers that filled the ranks had, almost certainly, never been cavalry horseman.[139]

On 5 October 1936, DSD Squire's letter was despatched to all commands, the content of which had been eventually approved in draft by his Army Council colleagues, and in particular the Director of Finance.[140] A further, more specific letter was sent on 12 October 1936 with details of when and what vehicles the regiments could expect to receive.[141] The Queen's Bays were to receive 15 cwt. trucks, motor cycles, 6 Mark II Light tanks and "20 Utility tractors… issued for the purpose of giving training in driving tracked vehicles and not as tactical vehicles". The 4th and the 10th Hussars were to be similarly equipped, but without any Light tanks. It was ordered that all riding horses were to be "handed-over" by 31 March 1937. Temporary garaging arrangements were required for the incoming vehicles as the "conversion of barracks cannot yet be made". Regimental instructors were to be trained at the RTC Schools of Driving and Maintenance and Gunnery at Bovington. Until the instructors were trained, Commands were expected to make local training arrangements with whatever resources were on hand.[142]

The 4th Queen's Own Hussars

Motor vehicles were first anticipated by the 4th Hussars some years earlier, for the coming winter of 1928/1929 when the regiment was stationed in Meerut, 43 miles north-east of Delhi, India. Morris six-wheeler lorries were expected and some NCOs and men were being prepared "to forsake their swords for the steering wheel".[143] Before Christmas 1928 the lorries had arrived, driven by road over 400 miles from Rawalpindi to the Brigade Camp at Gurgaon, 15 miles southwest of Delhi, where the regiment was engaged in exercises. The driving party was led by Lieutenant J E Armstrong with twenty-four men from the regiment "who had attended a course of driving instruction at the M.T. depot".[144] The regiment was pleased with their lorries:

> These proved extremely mobile across all sorts of country and saved pack horses a great deal of work in the transportation of Machine Guns, the addition of two

---

139 Ibid., pp.230–236 & p.238.
140 TNA WO 32/2847 Army Organisation: Cavalry (Code 14(D)): Introduction of a Mobile Division 1934–1936 20/General/5512 (S.D.2.) marked 25A War Office to all Commands, 5 October 1936.
141 Ibid., War Office to all Commands, 12 October 1936.
142 Ibid.
143 *IV Hussars' Journal*, Vol.II, August 1928, pp.1 & 2.
144 Ibid., p.2

(D 6×4 1926–1932) made to a War Office specification with a 30 cwt. payload and
a 4 cylinder side-valve 2.5 litre engine creating 15.9 horsepower.
(Source: The Tank Museum, Bovington – 9361-A1)

extra wheels enabling these comparatively low-powered machines to negotiate boulder-strewn hillsides with amazing ease and the minimum of strain.[145]

On 12 November 1930 the 4th Hussars returned to England,[146] first to York in 1931/1932 and then to Aldershot in 1935 via Colchester where they had stayed one year. Six-wheelers remained in operation for the "Brigade Exercises" of 1931.[147]

In February 1932 the lorries went and the Machine-Gun Troop, reduced in size due to the cuts in military expenditure, was remounted on horses. The experienced men, surplus to requirements as machine-gunners, were either transferred to the "sabre-squadrons" or were redundant and placed on the Army Reserve.[148] The Signal Troop, however, learned to drive two-seater Austin cars and motor cycles; the latter certainly was much enjoyed with "ardent motor cyclists endeavouring to get "fifty... out of her" as they scorched alongside the married quarters".[149] Much applauded was the "coolness" of the MT (Motor Transport) instructors in indulging the troopers' enthusiasm for their motor vehicles.[150] The following year the Signals Troop, fully mechanized, anticipated the installation of wireless. The Signal Officer, Mr R St. Aubyn, still a

145 Ibid.
146 Scott Daniell, *4th Hussar,* p.288.
147 *IV Hussars' Journal*, Vol.III, October 1931, p.2.
148 *IV Hussars' Journal*, Vol.IV, October 1932, p.8.
149 Ibid., p.9.
150 Ibid., p.8.

subaltern although he had joined the regiment in 1925, was also the MT Officer. The previous Signals Officer was also a subaltern, Charles G G Wainman. It is interesting to note that these roles were given to relatively junior officers of the regiment, perhaps because of a younger person's enthusiasm for motor vehicles and wireless than any lack of importance of the task. Wainman resigned his commission in 1933 and St. Aubyn in February 1934. The reasons are not known, but it is reasonable to speculate that frustration in officers' career progression, pay cuts and lack of investment in the Army may have been the cause. The troop was sorry to see Wainman go, and St. Aubyn was appreciated by his troop for the interesting approach he took to their training.[151]

The 4th Queen's Own Hussars Regimental Journal, published between October and December 1936, led with the assertion that "the most important event since the last publication of the Journal has been the decision to mechanize the Regiment".[152] In Aldershot, the 4th Hussars had almost all their 250[153] horses taken away in October 1936 with "those that were fit for further service sent to other units, while the older ones went to good homes".[154] Vehicles "for driving instruction and for training purposes" were issued, although the type was not recorded as "the final decision was … pending… as to the type of vehicle that is to be issued to mechanized cavalry regiments".[155] There was some coming and going of officers, but apart from Captain J E Armstrong, a keen polo player who returned to India to serve with the 15th Lancers of the Indian Army, it appears that the mechanization of the 4th Hussars might actually have attracted officers to transfer into the regiment. Some officers retired; these were Great War veterans whose service had expired. Captain C Peel was posted in from the "motorized" 3rd Hussars, Captain J H F Collingwood from the Queen's Bays, also undergoing mechanization, and Major E G G Lillingstone was posted in from the still horsed Royal Scots Greys to become second-in-command of the 4th Hussars.[156] At the regimental "Balaclava Dinner", Lieutenant Colonel J Scott-Cockburn spoke to officers and veterans of the regiment about mechanization. He explained that all European armies were mechanizing, that the 11th Hussars and the 12th Lancers, mechanized with armoured cars:

> … six of seven years ago [had become] the best armoured car units in the whole Army. [These two regiments] had retained their spirit and their traditions despite the change… the cavalry spirit and traditions, which we ourselves have exemplified in this Regiment for 250 years, are too valuable to lose. [157]

151 *IV Hussars' Journal*, Vol.V, October 1933, p.8; Vol.VI, February 1934, p 1
132 *IV Hussars' Journal*, 1936, p.1
153 Scott Daniell, *4th Hussar,* p.289.
154 *IV Hussars' Journal*, 1936, p.1.
155 Ibid.
156 Ibid., pp.1 & 34.
157 From a speech given by Lieutenant Colonel J Scott-Cockburn at the 24th Balaclava Dinner, 24 August 1936; reported in *IV Hussars' Journal*, 1936, pp.34 & 35.

The 4th Hussars last mounted ceremony: the Mounted Party for the Coronation of King George VI, 12 May 1937. The seven Other Ranks were led by Lieutenant J de Moraville. (Source: *IV Hussars' Journal*, 1937; Lieutenant J de Moraville retired later that year to train horses; he had been well known as a cross-country rider and had joined the regiment in 1928)

4th Hussars' Camp, Lavington Park, Sussex, 1936. (Source: *IV Hussars' Journal*, 1937)

4th Hussars' Camp, Corneybury Park, Buntingford, Hertfordshire 1937. (Source: *IV Hussars' Journal*, 1937; at that time the regiment's strength was 15 officers, 120 other ranks and 60 vehicles; p.2.)

He reported that many of the 4th Hussars' horses had gone to other regiments, but that a colonel of one them said: "It is all very well getting the horses and that sort of thing, but you are really better off than we are, because it is only a matter of time before we shall be modernized too".[158]

All ranks were busy on "mechanization courses", the regiment's former Rough Riding Master was considered by the Royal Tank Corps School, Bovington, to be "one of the "spot" pupils [that illustrated] the versatile nature of the cavalry".[159]

Light tanks arrived, Mark VIBs, in November 1937, wrote Scott Daniel; these tanks had not arrived when the regiment was camped at Corneybury Park in August, there the regiment was equipped with 15 cwt trucks. The tanks being used for training (pages 170 and 171) appear to be Vickers Mark II, Mark III or Mark V, earlier models than the Vickers Mark VIB. As with other cavalry regiments undergoing mechanization, the change process was managed and facilitated by sending away a number of officers and NCOs to train as instructors. This built-up a cadre of competent staff "who in turn passed on their knowledge of mechanics to the rank and file. In this way machine-mastership took the place of horsemastership".[160] The regiment was soon fully equipped. Other than the 11th Hussars and the 12th Lancers, the 4th Hussars,

---

158 Ibid.
159 Ibid.
160 From a speech given by Lieutenant Colonel J Scott-Cockburn at the 25th Balaclava Dinner, 1937; reported in *IV Hussars' Journal*, 1937, pp.33 & 34.

The 4th Hussars undergoing tank driving instruction, 1937.
(Source: *IV Hussars' Journal*, 1937)

claimed Scott Daniel, were the first horsed cavalry regiment to be fully equipped with AFVs.[161] This might have been so, but the 4th Hussars did not keep the tanks for very long. Vickers Mark VIB tanks were in use when Tony Booth "walked into Warburg Barracks and reported to the guardroom" at the start of his army service on 4 July 1938,[162] but in October 1938, the regiment left for Tidworth with just lorries.[163] They took over the "Candahar Barracks" [sic] vacated by the 12th Lancers, but did not apparently take over their armoured cars. The 1st (King's) Dragoon Guards, the 4th Hussars and the 12th Lancers formed the 1st Light Armoured Brigade at Tidworth.[164] By the outbreak of the Second World War the 4th Hussars was fully trained and theoretically ready for action, but then this regiment lost many of its trained and key personnel and its vehicles, and much equipment, posted away to the cavalry regiments of the British Expeditionary Force (BEF). The regiments left at home were denuded of both men and tanks. On taking over Southern Command, following the evacuation of the BEF from Dunkirk and Cherbourg in May and June 1940, Alan Brooke commented in his diary that "the shortage of trained men and of equipment is appalling"; he failed to see how the country [Great Britain] could be made safe from attack.[165]

161 Scott Daniell, *4th Hussar*, p.291.
162 Booth, Tony [December 2009] "The Lost Hussar" in *The Chronicle – The Journal of The Queen's Royal Hussars Historical Society*, p.49.
163 Scott Daniell, *4th Hussar*, pp.289 and 292. The 4th Hussars were brigaded with the 3rd Hussars and the King's Dragoon Guards in the 1st Light Armoured Brigade, 1st Armoured Division; p.294.
164 Army Lists.
165 Alanbrook's diary entry, 1 July 1940; Danchev and Todman, (eds.), *War Diaries*, p.90.

The 4th Hussars undergoing tank driving instruction, 1937.
(Source: *IV Hussars' Journal*, 1937)

Captain Scott-Cockburn, horseman extraordinaire, on Carclew, India, 1924.
(Source: *IV Hussars' Journal*, 1924)

The 9th Lancers

The 9th Lancers of the Second Cavalry Brigade, like the 3rd Hussars described in the previous chapter, was originally assigned to an "experimental" role and armoured training began for them in spring 1936. The horses went: some to other regiments, others sold:

> It was a depressing business, but the new work in hand left us no time for sentiment. We were allowed to retain the officers' chargers and, until the autumn, 40 of our best troop horses, [to enable the regiment] to compete with success [at the Tidworth Show and] a final display in full-dress uniform at the Tattoo.[166]

Brigadier-General[167] D J E Beale-Browne, Colonel of the 9th Lancers, praised the leadership of the regiment's commanding officer Charles Norman, who led the regiment from March 1936 until October 1938, for enthusing the regiment during the period in which:

> He had to face the difficult task of changing over from horses to mechanization. The readiness with which the regiment then carried out its new duties and accepted this unpopular decision was largely due to the tact and personality of its commanding officer.[168]

Lieutenant Colonel Norman was equally praising of his troops:

> I want here to pay tribute to the loyalty with which all ranks took to their new role and to the enthusiasm which they displayed in learning it. For the younger soldier it was no hardship: it was an adventure; and they were at the same time equipping themselves for civilian life. But the older dog does not easily learn new tricks, and some of our senior NCOs naturally found it hard work not only to learn the new techniques but to become instructors.[169]

It would be astonishing if anything other than praise had been written in the preface to a regimental history written in 1951 following the action the regiment had seen during the Second World War. There was, however, an independent contemporary witness to the events of 1936. Robert Bright, a Royal Tank Corps officer who later

166 Bright, (ed), *The Ninth Queen's Own Royal Lancers 1936–1945*, Preface p.xx by Major General C W Norman CBE.
167 The rank of Brigadier-General in the British Army was discontinued after the Great War, but revived as just Brigadier in 1928; Beale-Browne obviously chose to continue with his old rank title.
168 Brigadier-General Dermond J E Beale-Browne in Bright, *Ninth Lancers*, Preface p.xvii.
169 Major General Norman in Bright, *Ninth Lancers*, Preface p.xx.

became a brigadier, was tasked with the role of Technical Officer to advise the 9th Lancers in training on, and maintenance of, the Carden-Loyd carriers with which they had been issued. Interviewed in 1977, Brigadier Bright said a Lancer's training in this period was identical to that of a RTC Trooper. Understandably the cavalrymen had neither the technical knowledge nor the driving ability of the Royal Tank Corps men to start with, but:

> … [the 9th Lancers] were intelligent, keen to learn and easy to teach, but they did start from scratch. [There was a] more elementary form of driving instruction – it made no difficulty – the standard of NCO was better in the cavalry than in the Tank Corps. It was traditional in the cavalry; for officers left more to the NCOs than we did in our Corps; they had more initiative than our own NCOs were expected to have.[170]

Pressed to confirm the somewhat orthodox view that cavalrymen had greatly resisted mechanization, Bright said emphatically:

> No! [not in 9th Lancers]… I should think that the senior ranks were very sad to see the horses go, but on the whole it was accepted by the junior officers and other ranks, it was regarded as inevitable and accepted as such. They were keen to learn; if they were going to do it, they were going to it as well as they could. They weren't resentful at my level, neither were they difficult to instruct.[171]

Again, officers and NCOs went on courses arranged at Bovington and locally at Perham Down. RTC officers, including Robert Bright, came to assist the regiment with local training. The regiment received "worn-out" Carden-Loyd carriers:

> Small, weapon-less armoured vehicles whose over-heating Ford engines scalded the occupants with super-heated steam from their cooling system. After every exercise the plain around Tidworth was dotted for miles with our mechanical casualties.[172]

Special arrangements were made to get food out to the stranded crews until the vehicles could be recovered by the regimental fitters and those from the Royal Army Ordnance Corps.

In 1937 the 9th Lancers had the Carden-Loyds replaced by "ancient light tanks", mainly of the earliest marks, though a small number of Vickers Mark V tanks were

---

170 Brigadier Robert H Bright, IWM Sound Collection, access number 787, recorded 1977, reel IV.
171 Ibid.
172 Bright, *Ninth Lancers*, Preface p.xx.

Cardon Loyd Mk IV. (Source: The Tank Museum, Bovington – 1839 – E1)

Vickers Light Tanks Mk.V of the 9th Lancers.
(Source: The Tank Museum, Bovington – 1609 – A1)

issued too (see page 174). These had machine-guns and wireless sets and the soldiers of the 9th Lancers began to feel "we were really getting somewhere".[173] The number of "mechanical casualties", however, remained high as these tanks had come from Egypt, and been returned to England as "unserviceable":

> Their turrets still had desert sand on the floor; the engine transmissions and the tracks in a sad state. The routine of recovery and feeding the crews after an exercise had, therefore, to be maintained; but at least they were tanks.[174]

These tanks were transferred to other regiments the following year, presumably to give these regiments some training and experience in tank driving and maintenance. The 9th Lancers continued training their soldiers using trucks "pretending to be tanks".[175] On 3 February 1939, 118 troopers from the 9th Lancers were posted to the 7th Hussars in Egypt.[176] Although these men were supposed to be already mechanically qualified, sixty of them were sent for driving and maintenance training. Perhaps the reason for their unfinished training was the lack of suitable vehicles in England; however, the situation regarding vehicles for training was no better in Egypt where the 7th Hussars had been equally challenged by a shortage of armoured vehicles.

In summary

The reports of the experience of each cavalry regiment so far ordered to mechanize would suggest their "Achilles heel" was not a resistance to change or a reluctance to give up their horses, but a lack of AVFs with which to train and equip. To reiterate an earlier point in this chapter, insufficient numbers of the general public or the political class anticipated another European war. Of those that did, few foresaw another British Expeditionary Force again having to fight in France and Belgium for which tanks would be needed, and until early 1939 this was not government policy anyway.

Chamberlain, Fisher, Strategy and the Treasury's grip on rearmament

Liddell Hart credited Neville Chamberlain, when Chancellor of the Exchequer, as "the chief promoter of the expanded rearmament plan" and the Cabinet member who more clearly than his colleagues "realised the grave extent of the [defence] deficiencies". Chamberlain realised that the priority must be to build up air and naval resources rather "than in building up great armies" and this was the government's policy.[177]

---

173 Bright, *Ninth Lancers* Preface p.xxi.
174 Ibid.
175 Ibid.
176 The 7th Hussars Unit Historical Records 1910–1939, Section 1718, 01.04.1937– 31.03.1938 Regimental Archives Warwick.
177 Smith, *British Air Strategy*, p.310.

Chamberlain "was quite sure we shall never again send to the Continent an Army on the scale of that which we put into the field in the Great War".[178] The Treasury's concern, as was Chamberlain's, was that increased expenditure on armaments would "endanger the country's economic stability".[179] What is particularly relevant to this story is the extent that the Treasury "through financial control could force ministers and defence departments to make decisions, which otherwise might have been avoided, about priorities".[180] Even when the Cabinet made decisions, it appeared the implementation of these decisions was often affected, either in timing or sometimes in content too, by the Treasury's peculiar, Byzantine-like organizational structure.[181]

Sir Warren Fisher[182] was the Permanent Secretary to the Treasury with whom it is said the Chancellor had a "particularly close" rapport developing "into something approaching adoration [until] Munich", after which there was a divergence of views. Fisher had such a relationship with Chamberlain, built up during the crucial period 1931 to 1937 that he "retained considerable influence over him".[183] Fisher, in 1933, urged the Cabinet to review Britain's defences. This was agreed and the Defence Requirements Committee (DRC) was established in November 1933.[184]

Robert Self was quite clear in his analysis that Chamberlain was determined to dominate the priorities of this committee from its inception; he "was always a pragmatic and reluctant re-armer", and saw no need to prepare an army for the Continent.[185] However, it was Fisher, according to Peden, who persuaded the Cabinet to halve the DRC's recommended expenditure for the army in favour of the Royal Air Force.[186] Neither Fisher nor Chamberlain had any military experience; they were not Great War combat veterans. Chamberlain was a professional politician with a "life-long" and "sincere" commitment to social reform "motivated by genuine humanitarian impulses".[187] With his passions, and having to govern within the predominating pacifist culture of that time, any expenditure on the army that implied perhaps a return to the trenches of the Great War was a low priority for Chamberlain. Robert Self attributed Chamberlain with being "the greatest single force in shaping British

178 Liddell Hart, *Memoirs Volume I*, pp.385/386.
179 Bialer, *The Shadow Of The Bomber*, p.138; Peden, *Arms Economics and British Strategy*, pp.346–348.
180 Peden, *British Rearmament and the Treasury*, p.14.
181 Ibid., pp.14, 203/204; Peden details the Treasury's role and organisation structure in Chapter II and Peden's Appendix I and II.
182 See Appendix C – biographies.
183 Peden, *British Rearmament and the Treasury*, p.54.
184 Ibid., p.56.
185 Self, *Neville Chamberlain A Biography*, p.236.
186 Peden, *British Rearmament and the Treasury*, p.56.
187 Self, *Neville Chamberlain*, p.105. Examination of the breakdown of government expenditure for Chamberlain's period of stewardship indicates his motivation more to social expenditure than defence – Table 4.

defence policy between 1934 and 1939".[188] Peden agreed, Chamberlain "made the most important contribution to the formation of defence policy".[189]

The General Staff intended that in the event of German belligerence the army would occupy the Low Countries. Firstly, this reduced the risk from bombing by denying the enemy their use and thereby decreasing the Luftwaffe's bomber range over England by some 80 miles.[190] Secondly, by facilitating the RAF's operation from the Low Countries' airfields it increased the British bomber threat to Germany.[191] These operationally pragmatic proposals required a British Expeditionary Force to take and defend the Low Countries and their airfields.

When Chamberlain realised that the bulk of the proposed £76.8m of the Defence Estimates of February 1934 would be directed to the formation of an expeditionary force to hold the Low Countries (and France) he was "alarmed".[192] Whilst he acknowledged Germany as a potential enemy whose possible hostility needed deterring, Chamberlain was still keener on disarmament than rearmament,[193] views that appeared very much in line with those held by a substantial number of the electorate.[194]

> But by dint of his [Chamberlain] arrogant self-assurance and overriding concern
> for financial prudence, [he] succeeded in overturning its conclusions [those of
> the Defence Requirements Committee (DRC) that included the Chiefs of Staff]
> and imposing his own strategic vision on the cabinet.[195]

Chamberlain's revised plans, driven more by financial expediency than by defence considerations, was to prioritise expenditure for the Royal Navy and the RAF; the former to protect the sea-lanes, the latter to provide the deterrent. Chamberlain "effectively established the defence agenda for the next five years". He "swept aside thought of an expensive continental commitment" and made the judgement that France would be safe behind its defences,[196] but he ignored the political necessity to support them.

Liddell Hart and Bialer subsequently argued that the value of the General Staff's strategy was diminished later by the increased range of aircraft.[197] Smith explained that the bomber of the early 1930s could not reach Germany from Britain, but by

---

188   Ibid., p.235.
189   Peden, *British Rearmament and the Treasury*, p.55.
190   WO 32/4612 09.09.1935, p.14; Bialer, *The Shadow Of The Bomber*, pp.128/129.
191   Bond, British Military Policy Between the Two World Wars, pp.201–6.
192   Self, *Neville Chamberlain*, p.237.
193   Ibid., p.237/8.
194   See Appendix F.
195   Steiner, *The Triumph of the Dark*, p.51; see also Templewood, *Nine Troubled Years*, p.37, for
        comments on Chamberlain's personality leading sometimes to mistaken decisions.
196   Self, *Neville Chamberlain*, p.238; Winton, *To Change An Army*, p.177.
197   Liddell Hart, *Memoirs Volume I*, pp.304/305; Bialer, *The Shadow Of The Bomber*, p.138;
        Group Captain Harris presented a similar argument to the War Office on 17 May 1935,
        quoted in Bialer, p.140.

1936 the range of British bombers had increased sufficiently for the RAF to no longer require a field force to take and defend the airfields of the Low Countries.[198] Harris is adamant that giving army rearmament the lowest priority set back any real development by about two years.[199]

Harold Winton summarized "the debate [that] raged back and forth" during the mid to late 1930s over the role of the army in national defence.[200] The debate was between what he called the "blue water or limited liability strategy... to use Britain's geographic isolation from the continent as the basis for a plan that took a long view of a possible European war" and, what Winton dubbed, the "continental intervention" strategy. This strategy centred on Britain being unable to "ignore [the] ensuing calls for help" from France and Belgium should Germany invade them. There had existed a tactical need to defend and to deny the enemy the use of the air bases in the Low Countries that were well within bomber range of eastern England.[201] Winton argued; "The protracted uncertainty over the army's role produced by this debate significantly influenced its deliberation over mechanized and armored [sic] warfare".[202] Chamberlain, as Prime Minister, created this uncertainty because of his policy of "hoping for the best whilst preparing for the worst".[203] But as Self correctly asserted, Chamberlain "gave mixed signals as to the appropriate balance to be struck between these two positions as circumstances and audiences varied". Chamberlain's propensity to "hope for the best" outweighed the necessity to "prepare of the worst". He stoutly resisted the mobilisation of industry for war, in case this should provoke Hitler following their so-called "peace for our time – Munich agreement" of September 1938.[204]

The Continental Commitment

A significant change in public opinion followed "Kristallnacht" in November 1938 and intelligence reports from Germany about a possible invasion of France and Holland in January 1939. Chamberlain at last accepted "the long avoided continental commitment".[205] The French Government pressured the British Government to commit more than the Royal Navy and the RAF to the defence of France. A land commitment was required from Britain, it was argued, to reassure French public

---

198 Smith, *British Air Strategy*, pp.87 & 88.
199 Harris, *Men, Ideas and Tanks*, p.253.
200 Winton and Mets, (eds.), *The Challenge of Change*, p.92.
201 Ibid., pp.91 and 92; see Howard, *The Continental Commitment*, especially pp.96–143.
202 Winton, and Mets, (eds.), *The Challenge of Change*, p.92.
203 Self, *Neville Chamberlain*, pp.332/333
204 Ibid., there is a type-setting error in the first edition of this publication, Professor Self has confirmed the above interpretation is what was intended.
205 Self, *Neville Chamberlain*, p.346; Gibbs, *History of the Second World War* Volume 1, p.491; and details pp.491–526.

opinion and stiffen their resolve to resist a German invasion.[206] The various Cabinet defence committees, the Foreign Secretary Lord Halifax and the War Minister Leslie Hore-Belisha,[207] were united in presenting to the Cabinet on 5 February 1939, the case for expanding the army with concomitant funding. Even at this hazardous stage in European affairs, the Prime Minister, supported predictably by the Chancellor of the Exchequer, Sir John Simon,[208] procrastinated on borrowing money to fund the army.

> Both argued along the same lines. The cost of defence was continually rising and there was no obvious limit to the necessary demands being made by the three Services. Since financial strength and stability were themselves an important item in national defence, then overspending might well destroy the cause it was designed to protect.[209]

A compromise was reached at a later meeting and a commitment given to the French Government.[210] The need for armouring the cavalry was now clear, unequivocal and urgent. The ability of the British armaments industry to recover quickly from the effects of a starvation of investment was causing anxiety to the Chiefs of Staff.[211] "There were very few armaments factories still functioning in the country and it took time to get them going".[212] The question was: how much time both industry and the army had left to prepare for war.

---

206 Gibbs, History of the Second World War Volume 1, p.496.
207 See Appendix C – biographies.
208 Ibid.
209 Gibbs, *History of the Second World War* Volume 1, p.510.
210 Ibid., pp.510/511 and 515.
211 Bond, *British Military Policy Between the Two World Wars*, p.95; Gibbs, *History of the Second World War* Volume 1, p.80.
212 LHCMA – MM 158/1rrr.

6

Mechanization – Finalé

The vehicle situation

The whole cavalry mechanization process when ordered to proceed was, from start to finish, from the 11th Hussars and 12th Lancers in the late 1920s to the last regular regiment in 1942, beset with challenges owing to insufficient AFVs being available with which to train and equip the regiments. The few that were available were often in poor condition and usually technically obsolete. Michael M Postan has calculated that the British Army never reached its full complement of wheeled vehicles until 1939, and by then had *only half* its complement of tracked vehicles.[1] Regarding the wheeled vehicles, John Bennett of the 15th/19th Hussars remembered that his own regiment:

> … was pretty well equipped when the balloon went up in '39. But what made me laugh was when we had a big influx of trucks. Now all these trucks were commandeered from different companies, they weren't proper army trucks. When they turned-up we had to paint them 'cause they had all the names on them, furniture trucks, coal lorries… We had to paint them khaki and paint the names out; of course you could always see the names on the side.[2]

Barney White-Spunner, who joined the Blues and Royals in 1979 and later became the Commanding Officer of the Household Cavalry Regiment (1996–1998), asserted that the regiments in 1939 were "more deficient in terms of material and training than their forebears had been twenty-five years before". Field days included non-existent anti-tank guns and machine-guns represented by football rattles. "Getting hold of the proper equipment was to be a minor war of its own".[3] This had serious implications for the cavalrymen involved with the change process from horses to AFVs

---

1   Postan, *British War Production*, p.6 – emphasis added.
2   Personal interview with Bennett (2007); by the author; Broad, *The Radical General*, p.66.
3   White-Spunner, *Horse Guards*, pp.497–502.

and featured significantly in the remembrances of veterans interviewed for this story. AFVs in appropriate numbers for the required task did not exist; they had not been manufactured, at least not for the British Army.

At Vickers

Commercially, the early 1930s had been challenging times for Vickers and other engineering companies. Vickers Armstrongs' relationship with the War Office required care and adroitness. The orders from the War Office were described by former Master General of the Ordnance (MGO), General "Curley" Birch, when he was Vickers' Managing Director, as "nothing. We shall certainly get no bulk orders this year [1930] and very likely lose money on what we do get".[4] Vickers' Directors were anxious to avoid any agreement with the War Office that would restrict the overseas sales opportunities essential for their survival. The War Office had offered Vickers what is usually known as a "cost plus contract". This form of contract allows a company an agreed profit margin, or mark-up, on its cost of production as a contribution to its overheads. Such a contractual relationship has its flaws. It is often commercially unattractive to a manufacturing company, especially one in heavy engineering. In Vickers case, 10 percent was allowed on the cost of producing a given order plus a fixed "grant" to assist with the design and development costs.[5] It is hard to be sure, but a 10 percent "profit" on production costs seems unlikely to have been sufficient cover Vickers' overhead costs, and would arguably have not been viable for them in the longer term.

The advantage to the buyer of this type of contract, when effectively negotiated, was a reduction in supply costs, and this attempt by the War Office was forced by the depression. In the long term, however, such a contract could put the continuity of supply in jeopardy, as a supplier's income would be insufficient to replace worn out plant, machinery, and, ultimately, buildings. However, a cost-plus contract can also reward inefficiencies. There is a greater incentive for the producer to allow the costs of production to increase, on which this premium can be added, than to reduce costs with speed and efficiency.

This rather unsophisticated arrangement between the War Office and Vickers was proposed to replace an agreement that, in the past, appeared fairly open-ended regarding research and development expenditure. It is not clear from the archived records whether or not Vickers accepted this arrangement for future orders, but Vickers may have done on a short-term marginal cost basis. It would not, however, have given a longer term incentive to further develop their business with the War Office, but to refuse to accept it could have resulted in orders being placed elsewhere. This was what, to some measure, took place anyway: the War Office looked "in house"

4   Vickers historical document 744; letter from Sir Noel Birch to Mr J D Siddeley CBE, Armstrong Siddeley Motors Ltd., Coventry, 1930.
5   Ibid; memorandum from Sir Noel Birch to Mr Yapp, 1930.

for the development and production of AFVs through the Royal Ordnance Factories, particularly the Royal Arsenal at Woolwich.

The MGO, Sir Hugh Ellis, insisted on Vickers being in competition for War Office AFV orders with the Royal Arsenal, later the Nuffield Organization, and the Vulcan Foundry. At the same interview with the MGO, 30 October 1936, that Vickers' Director Noel Birch, noted that the MGO had "changed his mind" about the uselessness of tanks, the MGO informed Birch of the development of the A7E3 tank at Woolwich Arsenal. Ellis somewhat naively expected these commercial competitors, Vickers and Nuffield, to share information together and with the Royal Arsenal; his was quite naturally the patriotic view of a former soldier to produce the best possible AFV for the British Army at the right price, but hardly practical in a commercial, competitive environment.[6] As it had been unclear in the past what type of tanks, if any, would be suitable for the British Army, it was reasonable therefore, that Vickers concentrated on their export market.

What type of tank to build? – The specification

In 1936 a reasonably detailed specification was produced for the War Office by the Superintendent of Design (S of D) for a fast "medium" tank. The S of D was accountable to both the Director of Artillery and the Director of Mechanization. This document signed, evidence suggests, by Campbell Clarke, the Deputy S of D, refers to the Tank Committee of the Mechanical Warfare Board, with which the S of D would have had some form of organizational relationship, if not for its full accountability.[7] This AFV, with a crew of five and armed with a 2 pounder gun, or a 3 inch howitzer, together with two .303 machine-guns, had a specification that required a speed of 25 mph on level roads, 18 mph across country and 10 mph to be maintained on an incline of 5.75 degrees. This tank was to be capable of crossing a trench 8 feet wide and a vertical obstacle 2.5 feet high and have armour plate 14 mm thick to protect the occupants.[8] The AFV was to be no more than 16 tons and be fitted with wireless sets numbers 2 and 7;[9] it was designated the A7E3 and wanted for trials in November 1936.[10]

The rationale behind the preceding debate regarding the new medium tank with which, it was envisaged, the Royal Tank Corps would be equipped from 1936, was a

6   See also Fletcher, *Mechanised Force*, p.117.
7   For a detailed narrative of the organization structure for tank design see Beale, *Death by Design*, pp.146–159.
8   TNA WO 32 3349 General and Warlike Stores: Tanks (Code 45E): Introduction of A.7.E.3. Medium Tanks and report of tests 1933–1936; Minutes 72–75, 3 November 1936–11 May 1937.
9   Ibid., marked 5A – Conference on the specification of the A7E3 Medium tank, 13 February 1934.
10   Ibid., Minutes 72–75, 3 November 1936–11 May 1937.

desire to use a single engine rather than dual engines that took up valuable space and added to the vehicle's engineering complexity and overall weight. However, "no such single engine [existed at that time] which can give the required power and torque".[11] The stumbling-block was always "price"; how much was the War Office prepared to pay? That is not to say that an infinite budget would have produced engineering perfection, but time and again price was the predominant factor. With the development of the Horstmann suspension system for light tanks, for example, the War Office needed Vickers' price halved before agreeing to order 33 sets of them.[12] The Ricardo engine, highly regarded by the War Office, was thought by Sir John Carden too expensive for Vickers to incorporate into his AFV designs.[13] The Ricardo engine in question was a diesel fuelled engine, at £400 per unit and was not installed to power production models made by Vickers; the Meadows petrol engine, however, at £110 to £200 per unit, featured in several production models.[14] A Vickers' representative, Captain A J Nannini, visited the Royal Arsenal on 31 October 1936, probably ordered there immediately by Birch to find out exactly what was going on. Nannini reported:

> [that those] responsible for the design and development of tanks... are unable to obtain concrete specification for armament, armour and performance of future medium and heavy tanks, owing to the fact that the General Staff are unable to arrive at agreement with regard to the tactical employment of tanks.[15]

The specification outlined above does seem clear enough to a non-technical reader, but for the design engineers it was apparently insufficient. The main concern was again the costs and how they might escalate. The technical development of an anti-tank gun would always be ahead of that of a tank, it was argued, because the cost of an anti-tank gun would "usually be less than one quarter the cost of a tank" to develop, and quicker to build.[16] The 40mm armoured plate that had become the requirement for a tank to withstand the latest anti-tank projectile "would be prohibitively expensive".[17]

11   Ibid., letter from the Design Department, Royal Arsenal, Woolwich to Colonel M A Studd MGO5 War Office, 15 December 1933.
12   Vickers historical document 744; memo from Charles Bridge to Mr Wonfor, 22 March 1933.
13   Ibid., memo to Sir Noel Birch from C W Craven , 3 June 1932.
14   Ibid., Vickers historical document 618 Vickers Armstrong Tanks 1934–1939.
15   Ibid., Sir Noel Birch's interview with the MGO, 30 October 1936, attached document of Captain Nannini's report. The French Army was going through the same hiatus of decision making; see Winton, Harold R. and Mets, David R. (eds.) [2003], *The Challenge of Change – Military Institutions and New Realities, 1918–1941*, (University of Nebraska Press, Lincoln and London), pp.7–24.
16   LHCMA – Broad 1–3; Lt. Gen. Charles Broad's reply to Mr R Alastair Rickard's letter, University of Ontario, May 21 1970, p.5.
17   Vickers historical document 744 Sir Noel Birch's interview with the MGO, 30 October 1936 attached document of Captain Nannini's report.

At the time the A7E3 was specified, therefore, it was already known that 14mm of armour was ineffective. There is corroborating evidence of the designer's dilemma to support Nannini's report; the MGO told Birch he favoured two new models of tanks, one with 30mm armour plate and another of 60mm armour plate, and was hoping for news of these by the end of November 1936.[18] Until then it was difficult for the design team to progress.

A two hour demonstration to Ministers of AFVs, guns and searchlights took place on Monday 2 November 1936 at Aldershot, but almost certainly the A7E3 AFV was not ready for this.[19] The demonstration was supposed to include two types of vehicles to carry mechanized cavalry, the current service medium tank, a "modern experimental" medium tank and an "infantry" tank.[20] Duff Cooper, Minister of State for War, attended the demonstrations,[21] but unfortunately his diary entry made no comment on this; "there was no certainty of war" he wrote, implying no urgency,[22] and Duff Cooper's main concern at that time, and no doubt those of the Cabinet, was King Edward VIII's impending abdication.[23] When the A7E3 was tested it was reported "the performance of this vehicle is promising, but the reliability needs improvement".[24] Failures enumerated in the report included that the suspension was barely adequate for cross country work, 12 to 15 mph was the limit of its speed and after nearly 200 miles some component parts of the suspension assemblies began to fail. There was a problem with the engine overheating in ambient temperatures above 71 degrees Fahrenheit, and some aspects of maintenance were difficult for a driver trained to the normal level of competency. This was a damning report, but the necessary modifications were possible.

What is significant to this account is that in May 1937 there was still no satisfactory fast medium tank available with which to equip either the Royal Tank Corps or horsed cavalry regiments, or both.

18 Ibid. So rapid was the later development of both armour plate for AFVs and anti-tank ordnance, that in 1933 the MGO was expecting anti-tank ordnance to penetrate 12mm – 16mm of armour plate; by 1938 trials were being conducted with the 25 pounder quick-firing field-gun against 70mm armour plate produced by the British Steel Corporation; TNA WO 32/3478 Manufacture of Warlike Stores: Shells (Code 54(E)): Provision of Anti-tank, armour piercing Shell 1927–1941.
19 Ibid; TNA WO 32/3349 General and Warlike Stores: Tanks (Code 45E): Introduction of A.7.E.3. Medium Tanks and report of tests 1933–1936; minute 72, 3 November 1936.
20 Vickers historical document 744; "Demonstration for Cabinet Ministers", Monday 2 November 1936 11 am.
21 Ibid., Sir Noel Birch's interview with the MGO, 30 October 1936.
22 Cooper, *Old Men Forget*, p.200.
23 Norwich, *Duff Cooper Diaries*, pp.229–233; Sir Samual Hoare was also present and similarly made no mention of the demonstration, but much of the King's abdication – Templewood, *Nine Troubled Years*, pp.215–224.
24 TNA WO 32/3349 General and Warlike Stores: Tanks (Code 45E): Introduction of A.7.E.3. Medium Tanks and report of tests 1933–1936; Minute 75, 11 May 1937.

In February 1938 "a great deal of thought" was given to designing a suitable vehicle for "mechanised cavalry" [sic] to enable them to carry out their "multifarious duties… under the new conditions which will exist in the movement and engagement of modern mechanised armies".[25] These multifarious duties included the traditional cavalry roles of close and distance reconnaissance, protective duties, pursuit and covering withdrawals, raids, and acting as a mobile reserve. The unsigned document appeared to be, as no other evidence exists, the draft design of the sales literature for a 30 mph, tracked machine-gun carrier, with no turret and an open two man cockpit.[26] The document is significant as it acknowledged the role of cavalry under "modern" battle conditions, and Vickers' effort to design a satisfactory vehicle.

Back at Vickers

Earlier, in June 1937, Birch had summarized Vickers' position in the world and home tank market. The production of such a machine-gun carrier for the cavalry could have been the response to his confidential memorandum.[27] Birch acknowledged the ease with which Vickers had previously dominated the market for AFVs and forecast this again would be true in "two or three years' time… when we are free to re-enter the market". This suggests the government had imposed some trading restriction upon them. He acknowledged the need to perfect a new design and the two years required to achieve it, but the untimely death of the designer Sir John Carden would hinder this. Birch complained, implying Nuffield and the Royal Arsenal, "Home competitors have learnt to manufacture at our expense".[28] Regarding foreign competitors, Birch made the telling comment, "[they] have not been hampered to the same extent as we [the British] have". Birch knew the Germans had "great numbers of anti-tank guns [and] every nation will have armour-piercing shells for field artillery". He foresaw the development of a 47mm gun. A 40mm gun could already penetrate armour at 30 degrees from 500 metres.[29] It seems likely Birch was aware of the German Krupp 88mm gun, designed for air defence, but used also as an anti-tank weapon in the Spanish Civil War the previous year. He made no mention of this weapon, however, which became the gun most avoided by British tank crews during the Second World War.[30]

25   Vickers historical document 744; "Cavalry Tank", unsigned draft, 25 February 1938.
26   Ibid.
27   Ibid., no.341/344, confidential memorandum signed by Noel Birch, 22 June 1937.
28   Ibid.
29   Ibid.
30   Personal interview with Bennett (2007); by the author; Macksey, *A History of The Royal Armoured Corps*, p.75; see also Kershaw, *Tank Men*, p.121; German 88mm Flak guns could penetrate 60–80mm of armour. Also, p.341, seventeen out of a force of nineteen tanks from the 3rd Royal Tank Regiment were knocked out by German 88mm Flak guns in Normandy 18–20 July 1944.

In a later memorandum, 11 July 1938, Birch was surely aware of the effects of anti-tank guns and the inadequacy of the Vickers Light Tank; he wrote, "The history of the Spanish War will soon receive detailed circulation and here the light tank has fallen out of favour".[31]

His comment in 1937 regarding the shortage of horses was an interesting confirmation that much of the public's opinion was that a war was not inevitable: "The cavalry will be obliged to have tanks or tracked vehicles with covered sides as the horse supply problem is getting increasingly difficult".[32] Birch was well informed and close to the government; it is surprising therefore, that he gave the reason for cavalry mechanization as the shortage of horses rather than a growing concern of a war. He urged the need for amphibious AFVs: "The cavalryman must not be less mobile than he is now, and the horse can swim rivers". Above all, the AFV must be "armour-piercing bullet proof"; bullet proof plate research was continually being developed Birch noted. Birch called on the Board of Directors to allocate at least £100,000 for AVF research.[33] Major General A E Davidson, Army Director of Mechanization, had informed Vickers six months before that the Mark VI (Light tank) "was satisfactory enough as a bullet resisting tank" and the MGO would not consider any change of model "from 18 months to two years".[34]

Clearly in 1937 Birch knew the need to press on with AFV development. He foresaw, with the development of anti-tank weapons, the obsolescence of the Vickers Mark VI Light Tank even before it had been supplied to some cavalry regiments, and until the specification of a fast medium tank was agreed, however unsatisfactory, the cavalry would have to use what was being produced. In the meantime Vickers continued to satisfy a foreign market including, up to a point, the army in India.

Mechanization and the Indian Army; a spurious argument?

It has been argued by some historians that the Cardwell system and reluctance of the Government of India to mechanize Indian Army cavalry regiments had a negative influence on the mechanization of British horse cavalry.[35] In the late 1930s, the 10th Hussars, for example, were not planned to mechanize to a motor cavalry regiment until *after* their return from India; the Queen's Bays (2nd Dragoon Guards) were brought home *early* from India in order to mechanize to a light tank cavalry

31   Vickers historical document 744; marked 385/386; "Future Research in Tanks", 11 July 1938.
32   Ibid., marked 341/344; Confidential memorandum signed by Noel Birch, 22 June 1937.
33   Ibid.
34   Ibid., memorandum to Sir Charles Craven, with a copy to Mr Yapp, 23 November 1936; almost certainly this was written by Sir Noel Birch as the majority of this file (January 1930–July 1938) contains correspondence between Birch and Yapp, either by direct memorandum or by copy.
35   Quoted in Harris, *Men, Ideas and Tanks*, p.258.

regiment.[36] The feature of the Cardwell system, relevant to this account, was training and maintaining a reserve pool of troops at home to feed the overseas garrisons. In order for this pool of troops to integrate into units abroad and perform as a team, they all had to be trained in the same way and with similar equipment.[37] It can be inferred, therefore, that as the Indian Army units, funded by the Indian Government, were not mechanized, neither could be the British Army units required to integrate with them.

Although kept separate, the British units were brigaded with Indian regiments, two Indian to one British.[38] In order that these brigades should remain operationally effective, the implication was that both Indian and British units had to have the same equipment and training; in the cavalry's case, it was either to remain horsed or to be mechanized. Even if the British Government chose to afford to mechanize the British cavalry, the Indian Government could not afford to do so, and did not think this expenditure necessary for the role that was expected from their army. The Indian Government had to fund the cost of British troops in India. This was costing a third of their total revenue; in addition, the Indian Government was later expected to fund the training of these British troops in the United Kingdom prior to their embarkation. This cost became something of a vicious spiral: the growth of Indian Nationalism meant that troop numbers had to be maintained, and the increasing burden of taxation on the Indian people to pay for these troops encouraged further the drive for self-determination.[39] As in Britain, economic pressures in the late 1920s and early 1930s caused a steady reduction in Indian Government defence expenditure.[40] This situation continued until 1933 when, in return for an Indian Division being available for Imperial Service, the UK Government contributed £1.5m to the Indian defence budget. This established the precedent that Indian troops could be considered part of a strategic reserve.[41]

In the first instance, however, it was the War Office itself that was reluctant to send AFVs to India. In 1929 George Lindsay, the Inspector of the RTC, urged the Director of Mechanization, General Peck, *not* to carry out mechanical warfare experiments in India as it was too far away to send and supervise the vehicles. Lindsay recommended Egypt.[42]

Harris clearly was correct in that "the Army at home was often considered little more than a depot for India".[43] Five British cavalry regiments were required to be stationed in India and Harris has drawn attention to the Adjutant-General Sir

36   TNA WO 32/2847 Army Organisation: Cavalry (Code 14(D)): Introduction of a Mobile Division 1934–1936 20/General/5512 (S.D.2.) 18 December 1935.
37   Bond, Brian [1980], *British Military Policy Between the Two World Wars*, p.101; quoting "one of the Army's indefatigable advocates of reform, Major B C Denning" in 1928.
38   Ibid., p.99.
39   Ibid., pp.109/110 and pp.111/112.
40   Ibid., p.111.
41   Ibid., p.112.
42   LHCMA – LH12/12/7,4; Lindsay to Peck, 27 May 1929.
43   Harris, *Men, Ideas and Tanks*, p.215.

Cecil Romer's comments in November 1934: "As cavalry regiments at home were progressively mechanized it was going to become increasingly difficult to find drafts for India".[44] In practice, this did not become an insurmountable problem as the pace of mechanization in both the British and Indian Armies was similarly restricted by the lack of appropriate equipment. In 1936 Lindsay, by then the army commander of Assam District, complained to General Wavell that "equipment and vehicles are coming along several months late... Egypt has taken most of the available stuff".[45]

When in 1937, acceleration in the pace of mechanizing British cavalry regiments was anticipated, the CIGS, Field Marshal Sir Cyril Deverell, expressed concern that "until the question of the mechanization of British cavalry regiments in India is settled... we can only mechanize six cavalry regiments at home, and two in Egypt".[46] The CIGS later reported that the Government of India had agreed "to the "progressive mechanization" of the four British cavalry regiments in India – the fifth regiment to be withdrawn "as soon as it can conveniently be released".[47]

Illustrations of light tanks in India may give an impression that these were common-place on the sub-continent. This was not so, and although ffrench Blake in 2006 was adamant that there were no tanks in India, only armoured cars that had to keep to the roads, this too seems incorrect.[48] Light tanks were tried and tested in India. Records show the failed tests of two Medium D tanks in 1922 and the two hybrid tanks based on the Mark I and II medium tanks in 1925.[49] Four light tanks, Mark 1A, were tested in India, starting in Chaklala in 1931.[50] The tests continued during 1932 and the subsequent War Office report referred to only three tanks, of slightly different specifications, although a fourth tank might have been a duplicate model of one of the others.[51] Two Carden-Loyd carriers had been in India since 1928 and Fletcher cites the one occasion these vehicles saw active service; their relative success led to the trials of these light tanks.[52] "Cooling trials" were carried out on pattern, or specification, numbers 1 and 2, and by December 1933 pattern No.1 had travelled 2,967 miles. The Director of Mechanization complained of excessive wear, but conceded, "modifications will result in a substantial increase in life".[53]

---

44   Ibid., p.258.
45   LHCMA – LH15/12/14, 8; Lindsay to Wavell who had enquired about mechanization in India, 28 March 1936.
46   TNA WO 32/4633 Army Organisation: Cavalry (Code 14(D)): Appeal against the proposed mechanisation resulting in the retention of the Royal Scots Greys and the Royal Dragoons as horsed regiments 1936–1937, Minute 9 CIGS to AG, 24 March 1937.
47   Ibid., Minute 14 to CIGS to AG, 19 October 1937.
48   Personal interview with ffrench Blake (2006); by the author.
49   See for example Fletcher, *Mechanised Force*, p.73.
50   Ibid., pp.74/75; TNA WO32/3348 General and Warlike Stores: Tanks (Code 45E): Introduction of Light (2 man) Tank Mark IV 1932–1935.
51   See Fletcher, *British Light Tanks*, pp.6/7 especially the photograph on p.7.
52   Fletcher, *Mechanised Force*, pp.74/75.
53   TNA WO 32/3348 General and Warlike Stores: Tanks (Code 45E): Introduction of

The tank designated in the War Office Report as "Mark 3" was favoured; it had a steadier gun platform, a speed of up to 20 mph, a better power to weight ratio, greater radius of action because of a bigger fuel tank, and this model cost less.[54] The problem with the other two models was stones jamming the sprockets that drove the tracks. An order was placed with Vickers for twenty-nine "Carden-Loyd, Light Tanks – Vickers Experimental".[55] These light tanks saw active service in a minor action in September 1935, but the Indian Government thought these vehicles "insufficient for the rugged conditions" with which they had to contend.[56] A new variant was designed,[57] the Mark IVA, trialled and ordered with improvements in ventilation and brakes. Fletcher speculated that no fewer than 16 were ordered[58] followed by orders for the Mark IVB (Indian Pattern). These orders were delayed and in 1938 the Royal Tank Corps was withdrawn from India and all their AFVs were transferred to newly mechanized Indian Cavalry Regiments.[59]

Interestingly, Barndollar identified that a unit of the RTC first operated light tanks in 1935. These were Mark II models and the RTC worked in combination with the Indian Army's 18th King Edward's Own Cavalry regiment. These tanks evidently proved better than armoured cars as they were more manoeuvrable and had a better cross-country capability except in wet and swampy areas.[60]

The British cavalry in India

The 17th/21st Lancers

Lieutenant Colonel R L V "Val" ffrench Blake, a Lieutenant in the 17th/21st Lancers when their mechanization programme began in India in 1938, was interviewed for this study in 2006. He recalled that he had been expecting mechanization since 1934,

---

Light (2 man) Tank Mark IV 1932–1935; minutes Report 374–13A and 18A, December 1933.
54   Ibid., minute 12 "India Pattern Tank".
55   Ibid., India Office to MGO, 14 July 1933; Vickers Historical document 895; "Tanks and Armoured cars Built by Vickers – Carden-Loyd – Vickers Light Tanks", designated A4E19 (India Pattern 1933). Fletcher, *British Light Tanks*, cites an entry in Vickers ledger that between 54 and 59 were supplied, p.11.
56   Fletcher, *Mechanised Force*, p.77.
57   Vickers Historical document 895; "Tanks and Armoured cars Built by Vickers – Carden-Loyd – Vickers Light Tanks", designated "Indian Pattern No.2" and similar in specification to the Mark IV Light Tank.
58   Fletcher, *British Light Tanks*, in this later work (2014), Fletcher states that two prototypes "were designated… but they never went to India", p.15.
59   Fletcher, *Mechanised Force*, p.78, updated in Fletcher, *British Light Tanks*, p.22.
60   Gilman Clough Barndollar, "British Use of Armoured cars 1919–1939", PhD, Cambridge University, 2010, pp.270/1. The 18th King Edward's Horse was mechanized in 1940.

and said "[horsed cavalry] was extremely dull… very, very boring".[61] He would have left the army after three years of service had his boredom not been relieved by the excitement of the polo field. Mechanization, when it came, "released the pressure". On commissioning into the 17th/21st Lancers in 1933, ffrench Blake said:

> … the first thing I asked was are we going to be mechanized … They said we are going to be mechanized sometime soon; it's long overdue and we ought to have been mechanized much earlier. The mechanization of that period [late 1920s] fizzled out in spite of everybody being in favour of it including Chetwode,[62] our chief cavalryman at the time, [who] was in favour of mechanization. Horsed cavalry was so stifling, even the training was stifling, we weren't really allowed to test our horses in any way and they were not in any way capable of great endurance. The main object was to keep them looking fat, fit and shiny, which is not really what you want. We never trained in what you might call endurance, speed and fitness.[63]

The 17th/21st Lancers began their tank driving training in Mk II light tanks in January 1938. The regiment's last mounted parade was 4 January and the horses went, but as with other cavalry regiments, the officers were allowed to keep two "chargers". ffrench Blake recalled that these "chargers" actually consisted of two polo ponies each.[64] All the horses had gone by 14 January, having left by train for Secunderabad.[65] "Mechanical training in India was brought down first of all to driving and maintenance and everyone had to learn to drive a tank. There was little confidence in the Light tank. They were a bit primitive, no wireless sets".[66]

The first mechanical vehicle, a four-seater Ford open touring car,[67] arrived on 6 February, but had to be pushed by four men from the station as a petrol ration had yet to be authorised for it; the "not yet mechanized"[68] Regimental Quartermaster-Sergeant was at the steering-wheel.[69] The Commanding Officer and the Adjutant led from the front and drove out the first Mk II tank that arrived the same month. They had to walk four miles back to the barracks after the tank had shed its tracks. The turret fell off the second Mk II tank to arrive.[70]

61   Personal interview with ffrench Blake (2006); by the author.
62   See Appendix C.
63   Personal interview with ffrench Blake (2006); by the author.
64   Ibid., p.63; *The White Lancer and The Vedette* Spring 1938, p.13.
65   *The White Lancer and The Vedette* Spring 1938, p.13.
66   Personal interview with ffrench Blake (2006); by the author.
67   ffrench Blake, *A History of The 17th/21st Lancers,* p.80; ffrench Blake, *A History of The 17th/21st Lancers 1922–1959,* p.63.
68   ffrench Blake, *A History of The 17th/21st Lancers 1922–1959,* p.80.
69   *The White Lancer and The Vedette,* April 1939, p.4.
70   Personal interview with ffrench Blake (2006); by the author.

The regiment was issued "two tanks, ten instructional lorries, two staff cars, a number of motorcycles and extra machine guns [with which to train on]. They were driven or pulled to pieces every day".[71]

Lieutenant H E (Pete) Pyman[72] and his team of four sergeants and eight other ranks from The Royal Tank Corps joined the 17th/21st Lancers to assist the regiment with their mechanization training.[73] Thomas Bishop's late brother was one of the men from a Royal Tank Regiment sent to mechanize a cavalry regiment in India, but not the 17th/21st Lancers. Bishop's brother told him the Tank Corps was all "shit and efficiency and the cavalry all bull and brass".[74] Pyman and his men joined the 17th/21st Lancers in January 1938 and that was probably what they thought too until they got the training underway:

> … and spent an immensely happy year with them for it was a very good regiment under an excellent commanding officer, Lt. Col. Pat Harris. But as good as he was, I think he was particularly lucky to have to have as his adjutant at that time Dick Hull, who later became, as a Field Marshal, Chief of Defence Staff to HM Forces.[75]

The RTC soldiers included driver/mechanics and formed a cadre on which "the Lancers had to build a system of instruction" for the new subjects that had to be assimilated. In round figures, explained Pyman, two hundred men had to be trained, equally divided between tanks and lorries, and "other wheeled vehicles". These men required three months training while another one hundred men trained to be gunners that required just six weeks.[76] Pyman described how the training was organised:

> The first six weeks of the Driving and Maintenance classes were devoted to the general principles of the internal combustion engine, and the second to the particular types of vehicles themselves. As soon as this stage was finished, the Regiment was able to take over drivers' duties from the RTC cadre. In addition, the return of the first batch of students from the Ahmednagar gunnery course greatly increased the strength of the teaching staff.

---

71   *The White Lancer and The Vedette,* spring 1938, p.13.
72   Pyman was soon promoted captain and eventually became Lieutenant General Sir Harold Pyman KCB, CBE, DSO; ffrench Blake, *The 17th/21st Lancers,* p.64.
73   ffrench Blake, *The 17th/21st Lancers,* p.64; Pyman, *Call to Arms,* p.27.
74   Personal interview with Bishop (2008); by the author.
75   Pyman, *Call to Arms,* p.27.
76   Ibid., pp.57 & 58.

Lieutenant R L V ffrench Blake 1938.
(Source: ffrench Blake, *A History of
The 17th/21st Lancers 1922–1959*)

Officer Commanding
C Squadron, the
17th/21st Lancers
signalling with flags
as there were no
wireless sets in the
Mk II tanks,
October 1938.
(Source: *The White
Lancer and
The Vedette*, April
1939, p.27)

The 17th/21st Lancers – the hazards of mechanized training, October 1938.
(Source: *The White Lancer and The Vedette*, April 1939, p.27)

Lieutenant Colonel P V (Pat) Harris led the 17th/21st Lancers during the mechanization process. (Source: *The White Lancer and The Vedette*, April 1939, p.4)

Adjutant Captain Richard "Dick" Hull, 1938. (Source: *The White Lancer and The Vedette*, April 1939, p.27)

Mk II Light Tank – (A4E13 – A4E15), circa 1931.
(Source: The Tank Museum, Bovington – 1609 – B2)

Captain Harold (Pete) Pyman (seated centre) and his team, 1938. (Source: *The White Lancer and The Vedette*, April 1939, p.22); rear rank – L/C Stein, L/C Jones, L/C Kirkpatrick, L/C Cornock, L/C Henderson, L/C Sutherland, L/C Barnard, L/C Kendall, L/C Bailey; front rank – Cpl French, L/Sgt Powell, L/Sgt Haslett, Sgt Davies, Captain H E Pyman, Sgt Wood, Sgt Ramsden, L/S Ogburn, Cpl Morris; ffrench Blake, *A History of The 17th/21st Lancers 1922–1959*.

Driver training for the 17th/21st Lancers, 1938. Captioned – "Oh dear! Oh dear!" – The adjacent text reads; "Who said 'put it in low emergency gear and reverse back?'" (Source: *The White Lancer and The Vedette* Spring 1938 p.11; clearly an "in joke", a photograph of a mishap during tank driver training in India)

In January 1938 Pyman reported that the Regimental instructors had "progressed excellently, knowledge more academic that practical", which was understandable, and he wanted to retain one RTC NCO in each squadron.[77] The Regimental journal lists the names of 16 NCOs who had passed the Driving and Maintenance Instructors course during 1938/39, another 10 NCOs the elementary course that was, presumably, what had to be passed in order to progress to the instructor's course, and 12 NCOs who had passed various armaments courses together with just two NCOs, Corporal C Evans and Lance Corporal G Tippett, who had passed the wireless instructors course at Bovington.[78] Pyman was confident the regiment would produce a "very promising technical officer" especially with the addition of a senior RTC NCO to support him.[79]

The Squadron commanders were able to take responsibility for their own vehicle maintenance by the beginning of May 1938 and by June the regiment had forty-eight

77 LHCMA – Pyman 1/1–28, 1/6 "Royal Tank Corps Cadre 17/21 Lancers".
78 *The White Lancer And The Vedette*, April 1939, p.49.
79 LHCMA – Pyman 1/1–28, 1/2 and 1/7.

trained drivers.[80] Not everything had gone to plan, however, as Pyman had reported to Harris on 20 June 1938.[81] A "shortage of vehicles, instructional turrets and other kit [that included guns for the Mk IV]" had restricted progress, the five lorries promised were still to arrive, also the instructional vehicles were beginning to suffer from over-use and insufficient time to clean and maintain them. There were inevitably "duller" students, but Pyman was clearly encouraged by the number of "bright boys appearing who will work up to Driver Mechanic standard".[82] Some instructors who had returned from Ahmednagar were singled-out for special mention; Sergeant Beeby was "outstanding", Corporals Sheean, Smith and Wylie, were "well up to standard" and Sergeants Fowler and Davies soon would be. Pyman had selected Lieutenant M E L Heathcote as "exactly the sort of person" wanted as the Technical Officer. Heathcote did become the regiment's first Technical Adjutant and later became an expert on Matilda tanks.[83]

ffrench Blake explained the army pay structure:

> Everyone had to learn to drive and maintain their vehicle because their pay depended on being a driver [see Appendix H for some of the tasks that had to learnt]. Gunnery got no extra pay because there was no status for a tank gunner. They [the men] could be a tradesman driver, they could be a tradesman signaller, but you couldn't be a tradesman gunner. You either had to learn to drive to get your pay or you had to learn Morse code to be a signaller.[84]

Pyman also reported that "gunnery has not the same vocational value as D and M [driving and maintenance]".[85] ffrench Blake recalled the determination of Lieutenant Colonel P V Harris, his regiment's "non-mechanized" commanding officer:

> [He] looked after his soldiers first, and to see that they got their extra pay by becoming drivers. We were rather starved in material and men in the gunnery department, which was myself, a Corporal [Tizzard], and a Private [Moss].[86]

80 Pyman, *Call to Arms*, p.28.
81 LHCMA – Pyman 1/1–28, 1/7; Pyman to Harris, "Progress Report", 20 June 1938.
82 Ibid.
83 Ibid; Lieutentant Heathcote is referred to in three different ways in the regimental archives: M.L.E. Heathcote, M.L.E. Edwards-Heathcote and Michael L. Edwards-Heathcote, and Pyman refers to him as Edward Heathcote Amory. He was commissioned into the 17th/21st Lancers in 1934 and joined them in India. He was Acting Captain 22.11.1939 to 3.4.1940 and from 12.9.1940. After organising various training establishments and tank replacement groups, he returned to the regiment in Greece in 1945. Subsequently he organised hunter trials, race meetings, musical rides and riding schools. He was at the Royal Military College of Science and rose to the rank of Lieutenant Colonel. He retired from the Army in 1962 and died 20.9.1998.
84 Personal interview with ffrench Blake (2006); by the author.
85 LHCMA – Pyman 1/1–28, 1/7; Pyman to Harris, "Progress Report", 20 June 1938.
86 Personal interview with ffrench Blake (2006); by the author.

In India, as in England, the light tanks first issued to the cavalry regiments had no guns fitted on which to practise. "They were supposed to have .303 machine guns and .5s [Boys anti-tank rifle]".[87] ffrench Blake wondered if the .5 had ever existed, as he had never seen one. The Bren machine gun, by then his regiment's standard machine gun, would not fit into the light tank.[88]

Later the 17th/21st Lancers received four Medium tanks of 1922 vintage in which to practise, but there was no ammunition for the main armament. ffrench Blake, was in charge of the gunnery department:

> The only gun we had was a 2 pounder without any mountings, so it just lay on the bench and we could open the breech and that was it. All that could be done to train the gunners was to take the gun apart and put it back together again. We only had machine guns, we knew about these already.[89]

Pyman and his men were engaged in further training classes in early 1939. Pyman did not record when his cadre returned to their RTC regiment or to another cavalry regiment, but he went to the Quetta Staff College as a student in January 1939.

The 17th/21st Lancers returned to England in May 1939, first to Colchester, armed with just rifles and revolvers and without transport. The regiment was brought up to strength with returning reservists who were "without mechanical training".[90] Later the regiment moved to Newmarket, Suffolk, to be part of the newly created motor machine-gun brigade of the 6th Armoured Division. They were equipped with .303 Vickers machine guns transported in an assortment of "Austin pick-up trucks… [and] four old medium tanks".[91] "Then the Matilda tank arrived which had thick armour and hardly moved at all. It only had one machine-gun; it did not have a 2 pounder gun".[92] Valentine tanks arrived later and more extensive exercises began. ffrench Blake remembered:

> There were a great many of the Valentines, which we had got by then, had broken down and shed their tracks miles from home. The crews were sometimes stranded and unable to get hot food.

Colonel ffrench Blake said that this was the catalyst for issuing "tank cookers" to each crew, and the tank cooker brought with it a huge social change:

87   Ibid.
88   Ibid.
89   Personal interview with ffrench Blake (2006); by the author.
90   ffrench Blake, *The 17th/21st Lancers*, p.83.
91   Ibid.
92   Personal interview with ffrench Blake (2006); by the author.

This was part of the great social breakdown between officer and man because you no longer had the officers retiring to the officer's mess and the sergeants to the sergeant's mess; everybody cooked in their tanks or their lorry or whatever it was while you were in the field, so you not only travelled in it, but you cooked in it and you slept under it in row – one, two, three, four – however many it was. He [the officer] would "bivi down" with his men, a sort of tarpaulin-like lean-to would be attached to the side of the tank and we would all have some form of sleeping-bag… not provided by the army… we lay in a row there. We became what you might call a social group. That was a very good change and a really good one for esprit des corps, and the relationship between officers and soldiers was far, far closer than ever before. It changed when we got the cooker that was the big change really.[93]

ffrench Blake confirmed that although "training facilities were not very good" in India, and most of the tanks had no guns, "the regiment devised its own tactical roles, adapting the old cavalry tasks of reconnaissance, protection, and the rapid occupation and holding of ground".[94] The only difference was the method of conveyance, an armoured vehicle instead of a horse.[95] In his history of the regiment ffrench Blake wrote: "The men of the 17th/ 21st Lancers soon showed that they could master the tank as well as they had mastered their horses: the pity was that they had not been set to the task ten years earlier".[96]

The 17th/21st Lancers in 1940 moved to Marlborough to join their new 6th Armoured Division, which was forming under Major-General J T Crocker. With them in the 26th Armoured Brigade, along with the 2nd Lothians and Border Horse, was the 16th/5th Lancers.[97]

The 16th/5th The Queen's Royal Lancers

The 16th/5th The Queen's Royal Lancers had been on the North-West Frontier of India and had been patrolling on their horses when the outbreak of war was announced. A war in Europe was something of a surprise to them because keeping up with news from home had been difficult for the ordinary trooper. There were no radios to listen to and letters from home took three months to arrive. George "Yorkie" Husband, a trooper then and interviewed for this account in 2010 recalled:

93   Ibid.
94   ffrench Blake, *The 17th/21st Lancers*, p.80.
95   Scott Daniell, *4th Hussar*, p.290.
96   ffrench Blake, *The 17th/21st Lancers*, p.82.
97   Ibid., p.83.

The war in Europe had no effect on us; we should have been in India for another year. The officers told us that war was declared and we had to come home. There was a full mounted parade on 9 November [1939], they told us [the] day after, on the 10th, but "bush telegraph" had let out news. We knew we would not fight on horseback as there was no [horsed] cavalry left in England. [The 16th/5th Lancers had relieved the 13th/18th Hussars on the N.W. Frontier and it was troopers from the Hussars who had told the Lancers about mechanization in England]. We were all annoyed horses were going to be destroyed, horses were all we had, and .303 machine-guns [on the N.W. Frontier], horses came first and last.[98]

The day after the parade all four hundred and thirty horses were shot and only one was spared, a grey show-jumper, later to represent England in a leading equestrian event.[99]

Thomas Parnell of the 16th/5th Lancers, recorded in an interview for the Second World War Experience Centre in October 2000, explained that a few of the regiment had attended "conversion" courses, but these courses were stopped when war was declared. After leaving India the regiment first moved to Port Said where those who had attended the conversion courses were separated from the rest of the regiment and sent to the Royal Armoured Corps Depot at Cairo.[100] The remainder of the regiment proceeded to England. Once in England "three hundred odd men [from the regiment] went to form 2nd Tanks, to be [a] nucleus, those who didn't have a special job. I was regimental baker", said Husband. Husband therefore stayed with the regiment with one hundred and twenty others, those he said, with perhaps a suggestion of nepotism, "who either knew something or somebody".

The Army Lists for this period recorded no transfer of officers from 16th/5th Lancers to the 2nd Royal Tank Regiment, or to any other regiment, and the records of individual troopers are not yet available to other than their next of kin.[101] Neither the archives of the Queen's Royal Lancers Museum nor those of the Royal Tank Regiment can confirm these transfers either. Major Colin Hepburn, the Regimental Secretary of the Royal Tank Regiment, however, believes transfers from the 16th/5th Lancers to the 2nd RTR could have taken place, but were not recorded because "it may not have been regarded as significant, or even too embarrassing to mention".[102] Equally interesting were the regimental records of the transfers of returning RTR reservists who were then posted to the 5th Royal Inniskilling Dragoon Guards; "all who resented being called trooper and [being] made to wear a side cap at first [instead

---

98   Personal interview with Husband (2010); by the author.
99   Ibid.
100 Interview with Thomas Parnell by Dr Peter Liddle, October 2000; Tape 623, The Second World War Experience Centre, Yorkshire.
101 The Army Lists.
102 Personal correspondence with Major Colin Hepburn (2012); by the author.

Shooting the horses of the 16th/5th Queen's Royal Lancers N W Frontier India, 1939.
(Source: George Husband's personal collection and reproduced with his kind permission)

Shooting the horses of the 16th/5th Queen's Royal Lancers N W Frontier India, 1939.
(Source: George Husband's personal collection and reproduced with his kind permission)

The 16th/5th Queen's Royal Lancers N W Frontier India, 1939. Trooper George Husband is second from the left. (Source: George Husband's personal collection and reproduced with his kind permission)

Mr George Husband aged 93, 2010. (Source: Author's collection)

of the RTR black beret], but they got over it and became "Skins" [5th Inniskilling Dragoon Guards] in the end".[103]

Conscripts who had all been trained at the Royal Armoured Corps centre at Bovington replaced those men transferred out of the 16th/5th Lancers. None, as far as Husband could remember, were former horsed cavalrymen. The men from Bovington, NCO instructors among them, trained the remaining one hundred and twenty Lancers to operate in tanks. The 16th/5th Lancers soon had more men who had trained directly in armoured vehicles than those who had previously served as horsemen. If Husband's recollections were correct, the 2nd Royal Tank Regiment had a greater number of former horsemen within its ranks than it had original tank men, and certainly the 5th Royal Inniskilling Dragoon Guards had among its ranks of former horse cavalry troopers a high proportion of men from the Royal Tank Regiments.

Matilda and Churchill tanks did not reach the 16th/5th Lancers until late 1941; until then the regiment was equipped similarly to the 17th/21st Lancers with only .303 Vickers machine-guns and some Austin cars.[104]

Cavalry resistance to mechanization

But what of the remainder, the cavalry regiments stationed in England in the late 1930s? They got on with the job of mechanization equally quickly and efficiently, except for two of them. The exceptions were the Royal Scots Greys and The 1st (Royal) Dragoons, usually known as The Royals. In these two regiments mechanization was resisted by two senior officers. It is likely therefore, that the myth regarding the cavalry's reluctance to mechanize originated from these much publicised, but relatively minor, events.

The Royal Scots Greys' Commanding Officer created quite a commotion when in 1937 he expected that the Greys might lose their horses, a prospect to which he strongly objected. Lieutenant Colonel Cyril Gaisford St. Lawrence lobbied Members of Parliament and stimulated a press campaign that resulted in questions being asked in parliament.[105] The public and some historians might have inferred from this press campaign that all cavalry regiments were resistant to mechanization. This was not the case, and neither were The Royals nor the Greys. The issue with the Greys appeared on examination to be about Scottish nationalism not mechanization. The evidence is not clear as to how the rumour began that the Greys might lose their horses, not even

103 Ibid. A "side cap" in the British Army it was usually worn towards one side of the head. The Royal Tank Corps (and the Westminster Dragoons) wore black berets – these fitted much more securely on the head and the colour masked oil stains and were more practical for entering and exiting AFVs.
104 Personal interview with Husband (2010); by the author and confirmed in the interview by Dr Peter Liddle with Colonel G R Simpson DSO, in May 2004, Tape 2480; The Second World War Experience Centre, Yorkshire.
105 Wood, *In The Finest Tradition*, p.130.

to Buckingham Palace.[106] On file is an early reference to the controversy in a personal letter dated 22 October 1936. This letter was from retired Lieutenant Colonel G F A Pigot-Moodie MC, to a War Office official whose identity and signature, other than that of "Victor", has not been established. Pigot-Moodie, who signed himself "Doodie", asked if his friend knew "if they proposed to put my old Regiment into motor cars".[107] Pigot-Moodie believed, correctly as it turned out, that one cavalry brigade was to remain horsed whist all the other Regular cavalry regiments were, or would soon be, mechanized. Significant to this account is Pigot-Moodie's comment on the attitude of the troopers:

> Scotland will not like to lose the grey horses. Serving soldiers will not make [illegible] move in that direction because they have been told to do their best to make mechanisation [sic] a success and they are obedient people.[108]

On 24 October an acknowledgement was sent to Piggot-Moodie with a promise to "scout around [for] any proposal to mechanise the Greys".[109] A reply on 5 November accurately informed him:

> No definite decision has been taken as to which Cavalry Regiments are to be mechanized in the future, but I fear that we cannot rule out the possibility that the Greys will be one of the Regiments which will lose their horses.[110]

This information was supported by correspondence between the Department of Agriculture and Fisheries, apparently on behalf of Walter E Elliot, Secretary of State for Scotland, and G D Roseway of the War Office. In reply to Elliot's enquiry on 1 December 1936, Roseway stated:

> The position is that further mechanization of the Cavalry is in contemplation in certain circumstances, but no definite decision has yet been taken to which Cavalry regiments are to be selected if this further mechanization proceeds.[111]

---

106 TNA WO 32/4633 Army Organisation: Cavalry (Code 14(D)): Appeal against the proposed mechanisation resulting in the retention of the Royal Scots Greys and the Royal Dragoons as horsed regiments 1936–1937; 24A letter from Alexander Hardinge, Buckingham Palace, to the Secretary of State for War, 30 October 1937, wondering "what was the origin of the rumours about the Greys which have caused such a stir".
107 Ibid., 1A. In 1934 "Doodie" Pigot-Moodie, then the regiment's Commanding Officer, toured Scotland with 270 officers and other ranks and 250 horses to publicize the regiment and increase recruiting. He was successful, recruitment increased by around 30 percent the following year; Wood, *In The Finest Tradition*, p.129.
108 Ibid., F.M. B.M. No 3104 1A.
109 Ibid., F.M. B.M.No 3104 1B.
110 Ibid., F.M. B.M.No 3104 4A.
111 Ibid.

On 11 March 1937, Elliot received a letter signed by the Lord Provosts of Scotland's five major cities. Not wishing "to express an opinion on a question of military organisation", the Lord Provosts made clear to the minister the "considerable concern in Scotland" at the prospect of mechanizing the Royal Scots Greys and the "strong feeling in Scotland that Scotland's only cavalry regiment should be retained as a mounted regiment".[112] On 15 March 1937 Elliot wrote personally to A Duff Cooper, the Secretary of State for War. He expressed sympathy for the views of the Lord Provosts, enclosed their letter with his own and asked that further consideration be given to mechanizing the Greys.[113] Duff Cooper was clearly cognisant of public opinion and "the mind of the British people that was unprepared for war... In a democracy such as ours the Government was bound, in forming policy, to take public opinion into account".[114] Duff Cooper had mouthed platitudes before. On 10 March 1936, when the mechanization of the 3rd Hussars and the 9th Lancers was ordered, he said that those who were sorry to see the end of horsed cavalry likened horsemen to virtuoso musicians forced now just to play recordings.[115] Lobbyists for the Greys thought they were pushing at an open door, as proved to be so for them.

Representation from Scottish organizations continued to be made to Duff Cooper's successor, Leslie Hore-Belisha.[116] Lieutenant Colonel St. Lawrence apparently started his lobbying campaign on 14 October 1937 with letters to a number of Scottish Members of Parliament.[117] This invoked correspondence from them and Scottish organizations, such as the Saint Andrew's Society,[118] that streamed into the War Office. The Duke of Atholl, the "President of so many Caledonian Societies", pointed out, "rightly or wrongly the political reaction [in Scotland] will be intense, [whether or not mechanizing] the Greys [was] a good thing or not from a military point of view". Atholl forecast a "real emeut [if mechanizing] the Greys happened, not on account of objections from the Regiment", he stressed, but from what he called "the national conscience".[119]

---

112 Ibid., 20/Cav/887 1D.
113 Ibid., 7A.
114 Cooper, *Old Men Forget*, p.196/197.
115 Ellis, *Cavalry*, pp.181.182; Liddell Hart, *Memoirs Volume I*, p.277; for the context see Minney, *The Private Papers of Hore-Belisha*, pp.92–98.
116 TNA WO 32/4633 Army Organisation: Cavalry (Code 14(D)): Appeal against the proposed mechanisation resulting in the retention of the Royal Scots Greys and the Royal Dragoons as horsed regiments 1936–1937: 20/Cav/887 1A The Association of Lowland Scots 13 October 1937 citing an article of 15 September in *The Scotsman*.
117 Ibid., 20/Cav/887 16A – C, E, G & E, 17 D, F, H, L & M & 18A with cutting from *The Cork Examiner*, 18 October 1937.
118 Ibid., 16J.
119 Ibid., 17B; letter from Atholl to Sir Herbert Creedy, copied to the Secretary of State for War, 16 October 1937; "emeut" is from the French "Que m'émeut", that which moves, stirs or upsets me.

Elements of the Army were concerned too. It was demonstrated earlier in this account that attracting recruits to the Army was challenging. Brigadier (later General) Charles Willoughby Moke Norrie, the Commander of 1st Cavalry Brigade, was concerned that since the press campaign recruits to the Royal Scots Greys of his 1st Cavalry Brigade[120] had ceased. Previously, "continuous" recruitment to the regiment had been maintained which contrasted to the poor performance for other regiments. The Royal Scots Greys was a glamorous regiment and "catch the eye… mounted on grey horses… [and] is connected to Scottish national traditions".[121] The General Officer Commanding the Aldershot Command forwarded Norrie's concerns, in which, regarding recruitment, he was "in full sympathy", to the Under-Secretary of State at the War Office.[122] Norrie,[123] somewhat incongruously, because he was an experienced cavalry officer, must have actually contemplated the possibility of taking these horses to war. Absurdly he stated, agreeing with St. Lawrence in his letters to Members of Parliament,[124] that the horses could be dyed with permanganate of potash to make them less conspicuous, as they had been in the Great War.[125] Norrie acknowledged most of the cavalry "will have to become mechanized at a very early date", but if a few regiments remained horsed, the Royal Scots Greys had "a very special claim" for consideration. He asked for a decision as soon as possible so that recruitment could continue.[126]

Brigadier-General Sir Ernest Makins, Member of Parliament for Knutsford, and the Colonel of The Royals since 1931, mounted an equally notorious campaign to keep his own regiment horsed; he even lobbied the King. Makin's argument was based around St. Lawrence's somewhat spurious claim that the Greys were the "Household Cavalry of Scotland" (the epithet coined earlier by Churchill). If this was the case,

120 1st Cavalry Brigade (1937); the 2nd Dragoon Guards (The Queen's Bays), the 2nd Dragoons (Royal Scots Greys) and the 4th (Queen's Own) Hussars.
121 TNA WO 32/4633 Army Organisation: Cavalry (Code 14(D)): Appeal against the proposed mechanisation resulting in the retention of the Royal Scots Greys and the Royal Dragoons as horsed regiments 1936–1937, 14 October 1937, 20/Cav/887 1A.
122 Ibid., 17P. The signature of the Lieutenant General is not clear although it appears to be that of Sir Maurice Grove Taylor "i/c Admin. Aldershot Comd. 1/4/34 to 14/12/37". October 1937 was the hand-over point in the commands of Sir John Gathorne-Hardy and Sir John Dill, both of whom were infantrymen and Taylor was a Royal Engineer; the signature cannot be identified to either of these officers. The appointment of GOC Aldershot Command dates from 12 October 1937 and this letter was sent on 19 October. If it was sent with Dill's approval, he had not been many days in post. Source: The Army List.
123 See Appendix C – biographies.
124 TNA WO 32/4633 Army Organisation: Cavalry (Code 14(D)): Appeal against the proposed mechanisation resulting in the retention of the Royal Scots Greys and the Royal Dragoons as horsed regiments 1936–1937, 14 October 1937, 20/Cav/887 17M.
125 Ibid., Permanganate of potash had also been used in the South African War (1899–1902); Wood, *In The Finest Tradition*, p.112.
126 Ibid., 17M 1A.

and The Greys were allowed to keep their horses, argued Makins, The Royals, "as the senior English regiment", should keep their horses too.

In October 1937 the Army Council knew there were insufficient vehicles to mechanize all cavalry regiments and to supply the growing Royal Tank Corps, and horse-mounted soldiers remained useful for imperial policing.[127] With pressure from the press and politicians, perhaps the Army Council took the obvious line of least resistance. The "Informal Army Council Précis (No.3)" of October 1937 made no reference to the press campaign, but of course the members were aware of it. The catalyst for mechanizing more horsed regiments, it was said, was the agreement by the Government of India to accept them. The distribution of cavalry regiments would be:

> At Home: – Mechanized regiments (including one armoured car regiment) –
> 11 Horsed regiments – 1
> Egypt: – Mechanized regiments (including one armoured car regiment) – 3
> India: – Mechanized regiments – 4
> Palestine: – Horsed regiment – 1[128] being the most suitable conveyance at the time for the imperial policing role.

The précis stated "in the not far distant future, all Cavalry Regiments of the Line will be mechanised [sic] except two which will remain horsed".[129] The Household Cavalry regiments were not "Cavalry of the Line" and not included in that list. The seniority of each regiment was appended to the précis together with details of those "affected by amalgamation or mechanisation [sic] since 1921". The previous selection criteria for amalgamation and mechanization had been "juniority". This principle had been adhered to up until now, with the exception of the mechanization of the 3rd Hussars (see Chapter Four). Had this principle been applied in October 1937, the order for mechanization should have been the Royal Scots Greys and The Royal Dragoons thus "leaving the 3rd Carabiniers (the old 3rd Dragoon Guards and 6th Carabiniers) and the 4th/7th Dragoon Guards, the two oldest *amalgamated* cavalry regiments horsed".[130] The principle of "juniority" had been the Army's policy. When further mechanization was mooted, therefore, the mechanization of the Royal Scots Greys and the Royal Dragoons would have been expected, so stimulating the campaign to keep these regiments horsed. Leslie Hore-Belisha, the new Minister of War, had perhaps been unaware of the principle of "juniority". He remained unclear as to what

127 LHCMA – Broad 1–3; Lt. Gen. Charles Broad's reply to Mr R Alastair Rickard's letter, University of Ontario, May 21 1970, p.5.
128 TNA WO 32/4633 Army Organisation: Cavalry (Code 14(D)): Appeal against the proposed mechanisation resulting in the retention of the Royal Scots Greys and the Royal Dragoons as horsed regiments 1936–1937, 14 October 1937, 20/Cav/887 21A.
129 Ibid.
130 Ibid., emphasis added.

had led to the assumption that the Royal Scots Greys and the 1st The Royal Dragoons were to be mechanized. He told Hardinge:

> It must have been obvious to every Cavalry soldier that owing to the accepted necessity for further mechanization of the Cavalry that the Greys might have to be mechanized and certain people have jumped to the conclusion that the Army Council had already decided to mechanize the Regiment.[131]

Hore-Belisha thought "undoubtedly one prime cause" was the letters from St. Lawrence to the Scottish Members of Parliament, but the question of which regiments were to remain horsed was not put before the Army Council until 28 October 1937.

It was the last time such a decision was necessary and the two oldest regiments, the Greys and Royal Dragoons (although unaffected by amalgamation) were allowed to remain horsed.[132] Gaisford St. Lawrence and Makins had won their argument, but Makins certainly went on to rue his success.[133]

This incident was not the first time Makins had pressed for the cavalry to remain unaffected by the obvious need to modernise. Makins did so during the House of Commons debate on the 1933/1934 Army Estimates, and is cited by Liddell Hart as an example of "the predominant outlook of that period".[134] Some other cavalry officers had been something of a *bête noire* for Liddell Hart too: Field Marshal Chetwode and General Seely were two of his so-called pro-cavalry "people in the House [of Commons] and in the counties,"[135] Chetwode in December 1920 had spoken, as Fuller described it, "for the cavalry" in a debate with J F C Fuller (with Winston Churchill in the chair) at the Senior Officer's School. ffrench Blake asserted:

> Sir Philip Chetwode in fact held some views in favour of mechanization, which he must have been forced to conceal in this debate. The discussion was indecisive and no positive action seems to have come from it.[136]

Chetwode's opinion, as Liddell Hart must have known, as it was in his own files, was that mass mounted combat was "plainly not worth the money"; motor transport was faster over roads, but horses still surpassed motor vehicles off-road, as Chetwode stated,

131 Ibid., 24B letter to Lord Hardinge, Buckingham Palace, from the Secretary of State for War, 3 November 1937.
132 Ibid., 27 October 1937, 20/Cav/887 21A.
133 White-Spunner, *Horse Guards*, pp.495/496; Liddell Hart, *Memoirs Volume I*, pp.239/240; see Appendix C re Makins biography.
134 Liddell Hart, *Memoirs Volume I*, p.239.
135 Ibid., p.242; a further reference to BLH's frustration with Chetwode, this time over the use of aircraft, see p.329.
136 ffrench Blake, *A History of The 17th/21st Lancers 1922–1959*, p.60.

"with all that means". Horse mounted soldiers were still required in 1920, particularly for reconnaissance.[137] In 1926 Chetwode, at a cavalry exercise, was concerned that "under the pressure of modern weapons and modern methods of movement, if we [the cavalry] are to take our full share of work in war, we must increase our speed, increase our radius of action and increase our hitting power".[138] Chetwode's exercise was intended to suggest "what weapons and mechanical devices are most likely to help [for the future]", and recommended, among other things, a regiment of light tanks, two companies of armoured-cars and mechanizing first-line transport.[139]

Chetwode, in 1937, described St. Lawrence as "an idiot, [but was] overjoyed, and only wished there were going to be more [horsed regiments] left".[140] This gives some credence to Liddell Hart's comments on Chetwode's attitude to mechanization, but this does appear incongruous when set against Chetwode's comments, his earlier efforts to mechanize the Indian Army, and ffrench Blake's opinion of Chetwode's overall enthusiasm for cavalry mechanization. Liddell Hart insisted that Chetwode, "a bluff and breezy cavalryman of imposing personality [had] dismayed [him] by his continuing belief in the value of horsed cavalry... and by his inclination to discount the value of tanks".[141] Liddell Hart failed to date this comment, but he again cites Chetwode's "gleeful" comment of 1932. This was on the development of the Halger-Ultra bullet[142] "that sounded the death knell" to Liddell Hart's armoured forces theories.[143] ffrench Blake disagreed, "Sir Philip Chetwode... the most influential cavalryman serving at that time... declared himself on paper in the War Office to be in favour of mechanizing the cavalry".[144]

The reader might like to consider that, perhaps, Chetwode did not care too much for Liddell Hart; his pretensions, opinions and his influence, that for a time, far exceeded his status as a newspaper correspondent and that Chetwode, in modern parlance, liked to "wind him up".

137 LHCMA – LH15/12/5, 85–87.
138 Ibid., Cavalry Staff Exercise by Lt. Gen. Sir Philip Chetwode, 19–22 April 1926.
139 Ibid.
140 TNA WO 32/4633 Army Organisation: Cavalry (Code 14(D)): Appeal against the proposed mechanisation resulting in the retention of the Royal Scots Greys and the Royal Dragoons as horsed regiments 1936–1937; Chetwode to General Sir Harry Knox, Adjutant General, 2 November 1937.
141 Liddell Hart, *Memoirs Volume I*, p.70.
142 The Halger-ultra bullet was developed by Dr H Gerlich, of Kiel, Germany and "at short distances can penetrate armor plate more than one and a half inches in thickness" (40mm) and was very accurate – Major J K Boles "The new Halger-Ultra Bullet" [1932] in *Field Artillery Journal* No.4 July 1932, p.445; Team Civil Air Patrol Digital Publications Library; URL: <http://www.scribd.com/doc/111453828/Field-Artillery-Journal-Jul-1932>accessed 07.11.2012.
143 Liddell Hart, *Memoirs Volume I*, p.242.
144 ffrench Blake, *A History of The 17th/21st Lancers 1922–1959*, p.62.

The facts are that the Royal Dragoons and the Royal Scots Greys remained horsed cavalry regiments, the remainder were mechanized. Makins and Prince Arthur of Connaught, Colonel of the Greys were informed of the decision on 1 November 1937 prior to the announcement in the House of Commons on 2 November 1937.[145] The Colonels of the regiments to be mechanized were also informed of the decision.[146] White-Spunner was sure that not all the men of the Royal Dragoons were as keen to keep the horses, fond of them as no doubt most of them were, as Makins assumed. There were still men serving, he noted, who had suffered the "frustration" of long periods of inactivity, or serving as infantry during their time in The Great War. It seemed to some that another war was likely and this time they wanted to play a full role. There were similar feelings among the officers of the Royal Scots Greys; Major General (Charles) Clement Armitage, General Officer Commanding the 1st Infantry Division (later General Sir Clement), told Liddell Hart that St. Lawrence's officers "by no means shared his objections [to mechanization]".[147] Later the officers of the Greys were disappointed to be left out of the start of the Second World War.[148] White-Spunner recalled Humphrey Wyndham's frustration that if Winston Churchill's advice had been taken in 1918, The Life Guards and The Blues "would have led the way in the mechanization of the cavalry, instead of being made to follow it".[149] Before two years had passed General Makins was again lobbying the King, but this time *for* AFVs for his regiment.[150]

The Household Cavalry

In September 1939 The Royals were in the Middle East, The Blues were in Windsor and The Life Guards were in London. The Blues and The Life Guards formed a composite regiment for deployment. Two other regiments were formed, one as a reserve that also continued what ceremonial duties there were in London. The third regiment was for training new men. The composite regiment – to be named 1st Household Cavalry Regiment (1HCR) – soon joined The Royals in Palestine as part

145   TNA WO 32/4633 Army Organisation: Cavalry (Code 14(D)): Appeal against the proposed mechanisation resulting in the retention of the Royal Scots Greys and the Royal Dragoons as horsed regiments 1936–1937; Knox to Makins and to Lieutenant Colonel T Thornton, Equerry to His Royal Highness Prince Arthur of Connaught, 1 November 1937.
146   Ibid., examples include letters from Knox to General Sir George A Weir, the 3rd Carabiniers and General Sir Herbert A Lawrence, the 17th/21st Lancers.
147   LHCMA – LH11/1937/82, "Talk with Major General C C Armitage", 1 November 1937.
148   Personal interview with Sprot (2007); by the author.
149   White-Spunner, *Horse Guards*, pp.496/497; see Appendix C – biographies regarding Colonel The Hon. Humphrey Wyndham.
150   Ibid., pp.504 & 505.

Marmon-Herrington armoured car. (Source: The Tank Museum, Bovington – 0559 – C3)

of the First British Cavalry Division. Like some officers in the Greys, some 1HCR officers "experienced an uncomfortable feeling of being irrelevant".[151]

After Makins lobbied for his regiment to be mechanized, The Royals were, unusually, given a choice between being equipped with tanks or with armoured cars. Armoured cars were chosen and the horses went in December 1940.[152] Six South African modified Mark III Marmon-Herrington armoured cars arrived from the Royal Army Ordnance Corps in February.

By 22 February 1941 A and B Squadrons had completed their wireless and driving and maintenance courses at the Royal Armoured Corps School, Abbassia. There had also been a "technical course" for certain personnel. It is significant that no reluctance was shown by the officers and other ranks to mechanize the regiment, but the

---

151 White-Spunner, pp.502/503.
152 *War Diary*; The Royal Dragoons, January 1941; Household Cavalry archives, Windsor. War Diaries 1st Royal Dragoons 1939/46 Box 22; "Consequent on the receipt of G.H.Q., Middle East letter No. CRME/4011/A.G.1 dated 4 Jan 41 the unit was reorganised as an Armoured Car Regiment, Royal Armoured Corps on War Establishment I/1931/5F/1".

same problem persisted of a lack of equipment with which to train. "Throughout the regiment great enthusiasm is being shown by all ranks in the various branches of mechanical training… [but further training within the squadrons] was considerably hampered by a lack of equipment".[153]

Training continued by using the existing horsed cavalry motor transport, but no additional signals equipment was made available.[154] C and Head-Quarters Squadrons commenced their mechanical training at Abbassia on 24 February 1941.[155] The squadrons carried-out tactical and firing exercises under the 11th Hussars Commanding Officer Lieutenant Colonel J Leatham.[156] By 29 March 1941, The Royals were equipped with twenty-nine Marmon Herrington and four Rolls Royce armoured cars, also eleven No.9 wireless-sets; the regiment was, however, short of lorries for the B echelon (supply).[157] Twenty more armoured cars were collected in April. All the available equipment was diverted to A Squadron, after which A Squadron deployed for action with the 7th Armoured Brigade, 7th Armoured Division.[158] B Squadron proceeded to action on 31 May 1941 under the command of the Australian Division, and C and HQ Squadrons received orders to move to "the Western Desert on or after 15 June 1941", to join the 11th Hussars.[159]

1HCR continued on horseback until February 1941 when the regiment was issued with 15 cwt. trucks as a forerunner to armoured cars. This enabled the personnel to train on driving and maintenance. An emergency occurred in Iraq whose oil was vital to the British war effort. The pro-British Iraqi ruler was ousted by a pro-German and Italian ruler, who then besieged the mostly RAF servicemen at the Habbaniya air base. The 1HCR was deployed in its training trucks as part of the force assembled to rescue those besieged.[160] In March 1942, after the Iraqi surrender, 1HCR moved to Cyprus where sixty-three 15 cwt. trucks and forty-eight "carriers" together with some other vehicles were taken over from Skinner's Horse.[161] During April and May 1942

---

153 *War Diary*; The Royal Dragoons, February 1941.
154 Ibid., "Wireless training was carried out with five No.11 sets and three No.1 sets held on our old establishment".
155 Ibid.
156 Ibid.
157 Ibid., March 1941; the officers were conducted through various schemes and "TEWTs" (tactical exercises without troops). The 11th Hussars, to which some officers from The Royals were attached, had been an armoured car regiment since 1930; amongst 7th Armoured Division in Egypt the regiment was considered very experienced; personal interview with Davidson (2009); by the author.
158 Ibid., April and May 1941.
159 Ibid., June 1941.
160 White-Spunner, *Horse Guards*, pp.506–519.
161 *War Diary*; Household Cavalry Regiment Volume No.31 March 1942 (no box number, filed under 1HCR War Diary 1942). Household Cavalry archives Windsor. Skinner's Horse, 1st Duke of York's Own Skinner's Horse, an Indian Army Regular cavalry regiment of some renown. The regiment was raised on 23 February 1803 by Captain James Skinner and was still horsed in September 1939, but was converted to a mechanized

sixty-seven armoured cars arrived by ship enabling the regiment to organise as an armoured car regiment.[162] In September 1942 1HCR joined the 8th Army.[163]

The remainder of the horsed cavalry regiments in England

The 10th Hussars

The remainder of the horsed cavalry regiments in England had rushed to mechanize, as much as the dearth of vehicles had allowed. Manoeuvres on Dartmoor for the 10th Hussars were in their "motor wagons representing light tanks".[164] During 1938 "some eighteen year old obsolete Mark IV light tanks and a number of Bren carriers" arrived at the regiment. It was certainly after April 1938, as the Gazette Volume XVII of April 1938 states, "We have not up to the present received any tanks"[165] At the outbreak of war in September 1939, most of the 10th Hussars, and the other regiments with which they were brigaded, were still using the obsolete Mark IV tanks armed only with machine guns.[166] Just one squadron per cavalry regiment in the 2nd Armoured Brigade had the new cruiser tanks.[167] At some time, a number of Mark VI tanks arrived and were issued to half of each squadron. It was the Mk VI tank in which most of the regiment fought in France.[168] On 21 May 1940 the regiment embarked from Southampton for France with tanks yet to be fitted with guns. "The 2 pounder guns [for the cruiser tanks] were still in crates and lashed to the sides of the tanks". They were fitted when the tanks disembarked in France,[169] only then could training the gunners on this type of weapon begin.

The 15th/19th and the 13th/18th Hussars

In England, at Fulford Barracks, York, also in 1938, the 15th/19th Hussars began their driving instruction in 15 cwt. trucks as no tanks were available.[170] The parade ground was turned into an obstacle course. Four men with an instructor in a vehicle

reconnaissance unit soon after. URL: <http://www.skinnershorse.co.uk/historic.htm> accessed 03.06.2010.

162 *War Diary*, 1HCR, May 1942; some armoured cars were given up leaving the regiment with 45 vehicles, June 1942.

163 Ibid., September 1942.

164 *X Royal Hussars Gazette* Volume XVII, October 1937 No.1, pp.6/7.

165 Brander, *The 10th Royal Hussars*, p.105; Gazette Volume XVII April 1938 No.3, p.93.

166 2nd Armoured Brigade, 1st Armoured Division at that time included the 10th Royal Hussars (Prince of Wales's Own), the 2nd Dragoon Guards (The Queen's Bays) and the 9th Queen's Royal Lancers.

167 Brander, *The 10th Royal Hussars*, p.106.

168 Ibid., p.108.

169 Ibid., p.107.

170 Personal interviews with Jeffcut (2007); and Bennett (2007); by the author.

"A few training prototypes [tanks] arriving within the 15th/19th Hussars at York", 1938.
(Source: HHQ The Light Dragoons)

learnt to steer, change gear and reverse the trucks. This was practiced all day for five or six days, after which road driving was undertaken eventually leading to some sort of qualifying test. By the summer of 1938, the 15th/19th Hussars had some "obsolete" Carden-Loyd tracked vehicles in which to train. Driving skills were then practiced on the old horse training area as the tracks of the Carden-Loyds tore up the tarmac of the parade ground. The Mk VI tanks arrived in mid-1939, the majority of which were in a poor condition.[171]

John Bennett reflected:

> There was a bit of a scramble for those, but there were a few boys from the farms who could drive tractors, they were the ones who could get on well driving the tanks. I did a week or two on the Mk VI Vickers at various times. There was a bit of a difficulty driving the tanks, handling the tracks you know, turning and that, you had to slow the tank down on the corner, you went too fast you went straight through a wall the other side of the road.[172]

---

171 Mallinson, *Light Dragoons*, p.221; personal interview with Bennett (2007); by the author. Personal correspondence with Eric Clayton (09.05.2008); by the author. Clayton complained that learning Morse code and flag waving was thought to be a waste of time.
172 Personal interview with Bennett (2007); by the author.

Eric Clayton's experience was similar:

> Sometimes there was a problem leaving the tank testing ground, ninety-degree turn right, down the hill which by reaching the bottom the steering had used up the air pressure, and then there was nothing left for the right hand turn onto the main road, which meant continuing across the road and knocking down a stone wall before stopping in the front garden of the house on the corner.[173]

When mechanization eventually came about some of the men were sorry to see the horses go. "Nobody wanted to give up their horses" explained 13th/18th Hussar Charles Need, although he knew the days of horsed cavalry were over.[174] Basil Jeffcut, of the 15th/19th Hussars, agreed that the horses were greatly loved, and when they were led down to York railway yard to be despatched to an unknown destination the men "said good-bye to them with lumps in their throats".[175] Jeffcut also recalled, as did Bennett,[176] that the feelings regarding the horses' departure was not helped by disturbing rumours regarding their ultimate fate.

In England as in India, gunnery could not be practised much by the cavalry undergoing mechanization. "Everyone had to have a go on the Bren", remembered Bennett, but not in the tanks: the tank guns, .303 machine-guns and .55s Boys Anti-Tank rifles, did not arrive for the 15th/19th Hussars until after war was declared and the regiment had arrived in France.[177] Asked how the gunners were able to train, Sergeant Lucas retorted: "they didn't".[178] In a later interview, however, Lucas said that training took place in France after the regiment was equipped. Therefore the gunners should have been competent in the use of their guns by the time the regiment was engaged in battle.[179]

The 13th/18th Hussars had done "some familiarization training [on vehicles] with the Royal Tank Corps in Peshawar", India, before they returned to Shorncliffe Barracks, England, in November 1938.[180] Shorncliffe Barracks had not been equipped or prepared for a mechanized cavalry regiment, but the War Office made a grant of the extraordinarily meagre sum of £10 "to equip a driving and maintenance school with engines and parts to be bought for instructional purposes".[181] The Mk VI tanks arrived for the 13th/18th Hussars at Shorncliffe Barracks in the summer of 1939, about the same time as the 15th/19th received their tanks:

173 Personal correspondence with Clayton (2008); by the author.
174 Personal interview with Need (2007); by the author.
175 Personal correspondence with Jeffcut (2007); by the author.
176 Personal interview with Bennett (2007); by the author.
177 Ibid.
178 Personal interview with Lucas (2007); by the author.
179 Ibid.
180 Courtesy of The Light Dragoons archives, Newcastle upon Tyne.
181 Ibid.

August 1938, the 15th/19th Hussars first "mechanized" camp at Binnington near Scarborough attended by John Bennett "for about three weeks… we didn't know what we was doing". Note – the Vickers Light tank on the left had shed a track. (Source: HHQ The Light Dragoons; Personal interview with Bennett (2007); by the author)

Most were well worn. The majority of them failed to make it to the barracks from the railway sidings. It could have done little to inspire confidence amongst the onlookers in Shorncliffe, but for the 13th/18th it was thoroughly disheartening.[182]

Charles Need was a recalled reservist to the 13th/18th Hussars, his service with the Colours having expired when the regiment returned from India in 1938 and before the regiment was mechanized. When Charles Need reported back to his regiment, by then stationed at Tidworth, he was put into the tank-training unit, but there were no tanks with which to train. Some Royal Tank Regiment reservists had been drafted into the 13th/18th Hussars presumably, as with the other cavalry regiments, to help with training and to provide the nucleus of a skills base on which the regiment might build its mechanical knowledge. Need's former troop sergeant told him to say that he could ride a motorcycle, but he could not and did not wish to lie. There were some arbitrary decisions taken; the 13th/18th Hussars' regimental band was disbanded to

182 Mallinson, Alan [2006], *Light Dragoons*, p.222.

form a motor cycle despatch troop using 500cc Nortons.[183] What transferable skills were utilised when this was done is open to speculation, but bandsmen, being musicians, were some of the best-educated and intelligent men in a regiment, and this might have been the reason. Mallinson recorded: "When the 13th/18th's motorbikes arrived there were still no instructors. The bandsmen were simply given the handbook, told to teach themselves driving and maintenance, and generally get on with it".[184]

Some of the former horsemen who had previously "passed riding school" were posted to Palestine where British cavalry regiments were still horsed. A comrade of Need's was one who was posted to Palestine. Need remembered his friend had already been on a course to train as a "fitter", but was posted to join:

> ... a composite squadron of the Life Guards and the Blues and Royals, or just The Blues as they were then, and he went there and I suppose that suited him up to a point. But eventually he went from the Blues and Royals squadron to the Ordinance Corps, something to do with the job he was doing, and I don't know what happened to him then.[185]

But Need was "unlucky" and was posted to the Dock Labour Corps and later moved to the prisoner of war camp staff. Here he joined other men from all different regiments, "but they were all cavalrymen, we were put together as though we were all the same regiment".[186] All these men had been horsed cavalrymen and had not so far undergone mechanical training for whatever reason. During the BEF's retreat to Dunkirk, Need found himself at Bergues, part of the Dunkirk defence perimeter. Here his group of cavalrymen fought a rear guard action, in true cavalry tradition, for about a week in infantry-vacated foxholes while, as what seemed to them, the rest of the British Army passed through the village. Armed with Lee Enfield rifles and a light machine-gun none of them had been trained to use, they fought on through dive bomber attacks until eventually relieved by French soldiers.[187] These cavalrymen had performed a role for which they had been trained, a rear-guard action, but with neither horses nor tanks for transport.

Back in the regiments, "they [the 13th/18th and the 15th/19th Hussars] managed somehow", said Mallinson. By the "eve of war [both regiments] had been officially mechanized... there were however grave deficiencies in equipment".[188]

---

183 Personal correspondence with Cruddace (2007); by the author.
184 Mallinson, Alan [2006], *Light Dragoons*, p.221.
185 Personal interview Need (2007); by the author.
186 Ibid.
187 Ibid.
188 Mallinson, *Light Dragoons*, p.222.

A Sergeant of the 13th/18th Hussars learning to "get-on" with a 500cc motorcycle. (Source: HHQ Light Dragoons)

Queen Mary inspecting her regiment, the 13th/18th Hussars, at Shorncliffe, summer 1939. In the photograph can be seen an example of the regiment's transport: the Vickers Mark VI Light Tank, and a Bren-gun carrier, behind which is a 15 cwt. open-back truck. (Source: HHQ Light Dragoons)

The Royal Scots Greys

The Royals,[189] as has been said, were sent to Palestine in the autumn of 1938 as part of a counter-insurgency operation. The Royals joined the Royal Scots Greys and, other than the Household Cavalry in London, were the last remaining Regular horsed cavalry regiments.[190] Lieutenant Colonel Sprot praised the work of Captain "Teacher" Davidson and his six sergeant instructors from the 42nd Royal Tank Regiment who joined the Greys to get their training underway:

> It's quite interesting because when you think back to then, that only about, not more than 50 soldiers, knew how to drive a car, nobody had cars in those days and the 50 who could were usually officers' batmen, and the very few members of MT [Motor Transport] troop – nobody else could even drive a car let alone a tank.[191]

Although every cavalryman was supposed to be trained as a driver, James Randall, quite exceptionally, managed to avoid learning to drive then, and for the rest of his life.[192] In Palestine the Greys started their driver training in a truck. Colonel Sprot remembered:

> We used to go off in a three-tonner we had, probably ten to twelve people in the back, and I had to teach them how to drive, and it was great fun in Palestine. We used to take our sandwiches and pick up an orange (when we stopped to eat them).[193]

The Greys in Palestine were:

> ... thrilled [to receive two Mk IV tanks] although they were always breaking down... The bulk of the troop horses went away in June [1941] to the remount depot, and we were allowed to keep 20 chargers for recreation and were to remain in Jenin in August 1941. We got these two Mk IV tanks – they were British tanks. These tanks had no means of wireless internal communications so you

---

189 The Royal Dragoons, always called The Royals, were founded in 1661 as Tangier Horse and became the Royal Dragoons in 1684. The Regiment amalgamated with The Royal Horse Guards, always called The Blues, (also founded 1661), in 1969 to form The Blues and Royals; White-Spunner, *Horse Guards*, p.xii Author's Note.
190 Ibid., p.495. Some Yeomanry Regiments remained horsed. The Cheshire Yeomanry claims the distinction of "the last British regiment to fight on horses". The Regiment finally parted with its horses in March 1942; Verdin, *The Cheshire (Earl of Chester's) Yeomanry*.
191 Personal interview with Sprot (2007); by the author.
192 Personal interview with Randall (2007); by the author.
193 Personal interview with Sprot (2007); by the author.

couldn't talk to your driver, so we tied strings round the two arms and steered them like a horse – with reins – so I suppose that was a throwback to cavalry otherwise you would have to shout down to the bottom of the tank. We had a very amusing time. I remember my very fiery Squadron Leader, Roland Findlay, and we had, after the MK IVs, we very shortly then got two General Stuart tanks, the light American tank [the M3 Light Tank known as a "Honey"]. In front of them you had a driver and if you wanted, a co-driver and they both had a flap that went up in front and they were very useful to sit on if you wanted some fresh air as you were going along. And the idea was that the teacher would sit on the flap of the co-driver telling the driver what to do as he was being taught, and the very fiery Roland Findlay was going hell for leather across the Plain of Eacha El Arane in Palestine, and the sergeant was trying to slow him down doing this and he just said, "Take your fucking hand away"! and went even faster. So we had a lot of fun doing all this, but we did learn, and I think, very remarkable that we learned so much. Eacha El Arane – a wonderful place – an enormous expanse from Nazareth to Haifa – the hills of Nazareth. A wonderful training ground – no one thought of all the damage that we were doing to people's property. So that's what we did and then suddenly we up-sticks and were sent down to Egypt to the desert.[194]

Mechanization – "It was a different world …"

The cavalryman, both officers and other ranks, had to adapt to other changes in his life-style, not just to a change in his form of transportation. Communications changed: no longer would the men move as a body of horsemen, directed by the call of a trumpet. "[A trumpet] was the only way, with 700 horses, [but] you never knew the trumpet calls and had to have a trumpeter handy by you to ask".[195] In an AFV the required formation was eventually directed in battle, but not always in training, by wireless communication.[196] The cavalrymen's individual role changed too when he became part of a tank crew. As a horseman he was still part of a team, but he was an individual soldier with a dual role, equipped and trained to fight with sword and rifle mounted or on foot.[197] In an AFV he became part of a crew, with just a revolver for personal protection.[198] His weapons platform changed from his personal conveyance, unprotected by armour, but alive, free and fleet of foot, to a mechanical confinement with noise, heat and odour that had to be shared with other men.[199] As

194 Personal interview with Sprot (2007); by the author.
195 Personal interview with ffrench Blake (2006); by the author.
196 Ibid.
197 Ibid.
198 Personal interview with Randall (2006); by the author.
199 Interview with Parnell by Dr Peter Liddle (2000); Tape 623, The Second World War Experience Centre.

George Husband explained, it was a different world for all of them and it "takes a bit of getting used to, one horse and you together and then you finish up [in a tank] with five of you".[200]

Anticipated or not, this was a huge cultural change for cavalry regiments. As horsemen they had a personal responsibility firstly to take care of their animal, then their kit and then themselves. They were all trained in a similar way as riders, swordsmen and riflemen. Some, a minority with in a regiment, had additional training and specialist roles, such as machine-gunners, signallers, saddlers, farriers and bandsmen. In an AFV all the men had specialist roles and had to weld together to form an effective fighting team; driver, signaller/gun-loader, gunner, commander, and there were vehicle maintenance duties to be shared too. The supplies echelon of the regiment, in soft-skinned trucks, had different jobs to do, but evidence from research suggests all were similarly trained as tank crewmen to replace battle casualties. This new close team-work between all ranks changed the nature of leadership within a cavalry regiment too.

"The man who commanded my tank, he was an officer", recalled Sergeant James Randall of the Royal Scots Greys, later a tank commander himself:

> Now, back in [horsed] cavalry days officers had a completely different life to troopers, they had two servants, one to look after the horse, one to look after the kit. We didn't get close contact with them, but in a tank of course you are living cheek by jowl… you all had to muck in and share everything.

James spoke with affection of his first tank commander; they shared books together that had been sent out from England. James was sad to recall that this officer was later killed fighting in Italy. George Husband's tank commander was a lieutenant (16th/5th Lancers); everyone was on first-name or "nick-name" terms, he recalled, "there was no rank in a tank", but in horsed days in India if an officer was addressed in such a manner, "your feet would never have touched the ground, rank meant rank until the tanks", explained Husband.[201] "Yorkie" Husband added that the men had been reluctant to take promotion if it would mean a move to a different tank crew.

"The great beauty about the Armoured Corps [was] being part of a tank crew, a troop of tanks, it was complete and utter team work", reflected Thomas Parnell.[202] This was later stressed in the "Operator's Guide" for the Royal Tank Regiment; "The whole secret of this tank business lies in team work, and in particular in the team work of the tank crews".[203]

200 Personal interview with Husband (2010); by the author.
201 Personal interview with Husband (2010); by the author.
202 Interview with Thomas Parnell by Dr Peter Liddle (2000); Tape 623 The Second World War Experience Centre.
203 Personal correspondence and telephone conversations with Hodgeson (2008); by the author; Operator's Guide 110th REGT RAC (The Border Regt.) 1942; copy kindly supplied by Hodgeson.

Technical training and support

Every cavalry regiment, as far as evidence can confirm, was trained using the original programme laid down by the War Office in 1928 when the conversion to armoured cars of the 11th Hussars and the 12th Lancers was ordered.[204] The ratio of 1 NCO to 6 or 7 troopers, was most effective for leadership and close instruction; it is doubtful that any trooper struggling with the change would have gone un-noticed or unsupported. Specialist trainers were developed, led by regimental officers trained in that particular function; for example, the signals officer took charge of signals training, the Technical Adjutant commanded the gunnery and maintenance training. But other specialists were seconded to the regiment too; a Royal Electrical and Mechanical Engineers (REME) detachment became part of every mechanized cavalry regiment. Although this must have happened after the REME was established in 1942, ffrench Blake recalled:

> Quite early in mechanization it was quite obvious that we had to have these. They [the REME soldiers] trained the fitters and so you got regimental fitters as well as REME fitters. Initially they were under the Royal Tank Regiment officer.[205]

Before 1942 these engineers would have come from the RAOC. The 15th/19th Hussars in York had fitters drafted to them in 1938 or 1939, although Lucas could not recall from which corps or regiment; these fitters would probably have come from the RAOC too. When he returned to his regiment from his mechanical engineering course he felt rather superior, but "I soon got taken down a peg [by these fitters, and his own regimental fitters] from the old motor transport section, because these guys had been doing it for a long time".[206] The Royal Scots Greys had their own regimental fitters too, until the REME was formed in 1942, when more fitters were posted in and some of the regimental fitters transferred to the REME.[207] There was also a detachment of men from the Royal Corps of Signals who dealt with technical problems and radio set breakdowns and they may have helped with training.[208] John Bennett confirmed that men of the Royal Signals joined the 15th/19th Hussars too, "towards

---

204 TNA WO 32/2844 Army Organisation: Cavalry (Code 14(D)): Armoured Car Regiment: Organisation 1927–1928 20/Cavalry/619 War Office letter to all Commands, 4 April 1928; See Chapter One.
205 Personal interview with Bennett (2007); by the author.
206 Personal interview with Lucas (2007); by the author.
207 Personal interview with Sprot (2007); by the author; The Corps of Royal Electrical and Mechanical Engineers was formed 1 October 1942 from the Royal Army Ordnance Corps Engineering Branch and trades and technical elements of the Royal Army Service Corps and Royal Engineers. Source; The British Army website, accessed 30.01.2013.
208 Personal interviews with Sprot (2007); and Randall (2007); by the author.

the end of '39, just before the war broke out". The arrival of these signalmen came as something of a surprise to Bennett, but, "they manned some of the tanks as wireless operators which we was [sic] short of, we had a certain amount of wireless operators, but not enough to man all the tanks and the Bren carriers".[209] Sprot recalled:

> We had classrooms; quite a lot of it had to be done on a board, how an engine worked, how a gun fired and how a wireless set worked and ah… we had that awful Morse code we had to learn. I remember sitting around the officers' mess billiard table – di di di da di and things.[210]

ffrench Blake commented:

> As far as signals were concerned in India, we were still using what my father had used [in the Great War]… flags, lamps even a helio and that was all … they [the men] had to get their trade. The signaller, or radio operator, had to double-up as the tank gun-loader when in action.[211]

In the three-man crew of a Stuart (Honey) tank, the commander had to double-up as the gun loader. Each trade or crew role was trained separately in the beginning. Recollected Sprot:

> But in the end the object was to get everyone doing everything. It was quite a complicated thing for someone who had never driven a motorcar to then suddenly start driving a tank. And for someone who had never played with a wireless before, nobody had wirelesses in those days. It was remarkable, I think, that within those few months we went from a completely horsed regiment to a completely mechanized one.[212]

The trainers drafted in from the "technical Corps", the RAOC, REME and Royal Signals, and from the RTC, were soon supplemented and later superseded by regimental instructors. Whilst the basic regimental training was taking place on driving and maintenance, a number of cavalry officers and NCOs were sent away for training. These men become specialist instructors themselves, and returned to their regiments qualified to teach driving and maintenance, signalling or gunnery.[213] Ronald Lucas, a lance corporal by mid-1938, was chosen to leave his barracks in York and go to Aldershot to train as a mechanical engineer. The training was an intense nine-month

209 Personal interview with Bennett (2007); by the author.
210 Personal interview with Sprot (2007); by the author.
211 Personal interview with ffrench Blake (2006); by the author.
212 Personal interview with Sprot (2007); by the author.
213 Ibid.

course. The trainers were civilian instructors. There were a hundred men from all different regiments on the course that included a period of time spent at the Meadows tank engine manufacturing plant, and six weeks at the Royal Tank Corps Head Quarters at Bovington. Lucas returned to his regiment as a Sergeant Instructor tasked with training the men on motor vehicles especially back axles and gearboxes. The former horse stables had been converted to workshops where gearboxes were stripped down.[214] Basil Jeffcut also became a NCO instructor and Aiden Sprot qualified as a gunnery instructor.[215] In Egypt many officers, including Sprot, and many NCOs, went to the Royal Armoured Corps School at Abbassia to train as instructors in gunnery, driving and maintenance, and wireless. There was not, however, a tank commander's course. Sprot recalled: "I don't think that there was a commander's course; that is the sort of thing that you naturally pick up". When there were enough instructors trained from within the regiment, men like "Teacher" Davidson and "Pete" Pyman and their NCOs from the Royal Tank Regiment, went elsewhere.

To reiterate, no evidence has been found that any form of aptitude or intelligence tests were used within horsed cavalry regiments to determine which of the men would be most suitable to train for the different roles. Nor has evidence been found that any form of psychometric test was employed to successfully balance the personalities of the crew members to ensure cohesion.[216] In that regard, however, strong leadership that inculcated a clear sense of common purpose together with tight deadlines to achieve the task almost certainly overcame any personality clashes. Sprot speculated that selecting men for particular jobs had been down to choosing those who were clearly more intelligent or better educated, and directing them towards the more specialist trades such as signalling. It was quite often the signallers who later became tank commanders [217] as was the experience of James Randall, a former school teacher. His boyhood experience in Scouting, and his knowledge of Morse code and semaphore, helped him to be "pushed into" a wireless operator/loader role.[218] Randall went to Abbassia on a wireless instructor's course; he remembered:

> We did two or three months training on the edge of the desert between Cairo and Alexandria. We would go out on schemes practicing mock battles and map reading and you got used to receiving messages over the wireless, and I spent all my time with a pair of earphones on.[219]

214 Personal interview with Lucas (2007 & 2012); by the author.
215 Personal correspondence with Jeffcut (2007); personal interview with Sprot (2007); by the author.
216 See Broad, *The Radical General*, Chapter 8, p.89.
217 Personal interview with Sprot (2007); by the author.
218 Personal interview with Randall (2006); by the author.
219 Ibid.

ffrench Blake considered it was more difficult to train a horsed cavalry trooper than an armoured cavalry trooper. The main difference was learning to ride a horse "which was more difficult than to teach a chap to drive a motor car, but you still had to be a "marksman" to get your pay, and that continued until we got the Valentines [tanks] and abandoned the rifle as a weapon".[220] Sprot still mused on the "remarkable" success of their training. Before mechanization so few men in the Royal Scots Greys had driven a motor vehicle, or had had any experience of wireless-sets, and after ten months of hard work and intensive training the regiment was fit to do battle with Rommel's Panzers in the North African desert.[221] Almost every man in the regiment had previously been a horseman.[222] Many of the men of the Greys had been posted out to Palestine from the Army Reserve in England. They had not all been Greys originally, but had previously served, for at least six years, as horsemen in a cavalry regiment. "A complete mixture", said Randall, "all talking about the regiment they had served with in India before the war".[223] There were, however, also some men who had previously served in a mechanized cavalry regiment such as the 4th Hussars.[224]

When a cavalry regiment was mechanized, not every cavalryman was trained or succeeded in their training in armoured warfare. Any details of why certain men were not trained and what happened to them might only be determined if and when records become generally available. John Bennett recalled that the older soldiers and NCOs, a good 70 percent in the 15th/19th Hussars, started to "disappear" soon after the horses left. Many could have been time-served men and were discharged only to be recalled later, like Charles Need, and perhaps sent out to the Royals or the Greys as horsemen. Some of these men were unhappy at being recalled to The Colours.[225] Some horsemen, it was thought by Bennett, were sent to re-mount depots to serve with what remained of the army's horses.[226]

Tactics and Doctrine

The tactical training provided to the officers during or after the mechanization process seemed sparse. To reiterate, Sprot was quite sure there was no training for a tank commander; that had to be learnt "on the job".[227] Raymond Bullock confirmed this to some extent. Although he attended a tank commander's course during his training for the Guard's Armoured Division at Pirbright in 1942/1943, he recollected, "even

220 Personal interview with ffrench Blake (2006); by the author.
221 Personal interview with Sprot (2007); by the author.
222 Royal Scots Greys historical records G219 Case GB51, p.4.
223 Personal interview with Randall (2006); by the author.
224 Ibid.
225 Personal interviews with Bennett (2007); and Lucas (2007); by the author.
226 Personal interviews with Bennett (2007); by the author.
227 Personal interview with Sprot (2007); by the author.

with a tank commander's course we didn't get into tactics".[228] What little evidence was found regarding tactical training came from Colonel G R Simpson. In his interview for The Second World War Experience Centre in May 2004 he commented that "senior officers" attended a tactics course.[229] The veterans interviewed for this account were either subalterns or "other rank" soldiers during the mechanization period and perhaps were not senior enough to attend such a course.

Harrison Place wrote that:

> Ultimately, doctrine was disseminated by word and deed… officers and NCOs instructed their men by demonstration, explanation and practice. It is likely that that much of what those officers and NCOs taught their men they had themselves learned in much the same way.[230]

ffrench Blake, the longest serving horsed cavalry veteran interviewed, was adamant that the doctrine was the same anyway for armoured cavalry as for horsed cavalry:

> It was our doctrine, as it were, and it was easy to adapt that to light tanks that could go across country; they should go for longer distances, they could shoot when they get there because they had their weapon with them and the only thing you didn't have to do was to tie them up at night.[231]

The use of light tanks in a cavalry role did depend, ffrench Blake explained:

> Entirely on the cross-country ability of your vehicle and that depends on the sort of ground you are on. A horse will go through practically anything, even quite deep mud, but of course, it is extremely vulnerable while it is doing it. On [Operation] Torch, the tanks were all right, but the Bren-gun carriers couldn't get through the mud.[232]

Sprot agreed, and so did Lucas; although they had not had to fight on horseback, horse cavalry tactics were transferable to armoured warfare, and the previously mounted troopers had been indoctrinated in tactics of mutual support.[233]

---

228 Personal correspondence with Bullock (2008); by the author.
229 Interview with Simpson by Dr Peter Liddle (2004); Tape 2480, The Second World War Experience Centre.
230 Harrison Place, *Military Training*, p.8.
231 Personal interview with ffrench Blake (2006); by the author.
232 Operation Torch; the opening of the Anglo-American campaign in North Africa with the landing in French North Africa, November 1942, and the later advance and link up with British forces in Tunisia; Holmes, *The Oxford Companion to Military History*, pp.655/656.
233 Personal interviews with Sprot and Lucas (2007); by the author.

John Buckley cites examples of historians who have argued the weaknesses of the British armoured battle doctrine during the Second World War.[234] Both Buckley and David French were critical of British armoured cavalry tactics, charging their tanks against German and Italian anti-tank gun positions unsupported by artillery and infantry, but asserted that this was not due to old horsed cavalry tactics, but because "official doctrine" had failed to demand "all arms" cooperation.[235] The interviewees remembered two instances of tanks charging head-on against German anti-tank positions. One incident failed and resulted in the death of the crew,[236] the other succeeded and a Military Medal was awarded to the tank commander.[237]

Buckley acknowledged that British armoured units did encounter tactical problems even in the Normandy campaign of 1944, but this was not the result of "antediluvian thinking".[238] That which has attracted most attention, argued Buckley was the "dynamic aspect of armoured warfare... fast moving armour that would pass through a breach". The armoured tactics described, developed in Britain in training and still taught in 1943, were similar to those of an orthodox cavalry "mounted attack", but with different equipment; "static firing at squadron level with massed 2-pounder [tank] guns, followed by a frantic charge by the other two squadrons".[239] Plate XLI in *Cavalry Training (Horsed) 1937*, diagrammatically illustrates a similar principle using machine-guns or horse artillery as supressing fire on one half-flank of an enemy position followed by a mounted charge from the other.[240]

American tanks, after 1941, had enabled greater flexibility in tactics with more suitable armaments, notably the 75mm gun with high explosive ordnance;[241] ffrench Blake confirmed the 75mm gun "totally altered the tactical aspects of the attack".[242] In 1943 Major General G P D "Pip" Roberts, who, as a subaltern, had helped mechanize the 12th Lancers in 1929, trained the armoured troops in Great Britain in the fire and movement tactics that had been developed earlier in the North African desert campaign. These tactics, however, were later found inappropriate in the close confines of the battle for Normandy.[243] Buckley asserts that it was in infantry-armour cooperation doctrine where the main challenges of battle were experienced. It is interesting to note that none of the horsed cavalrymen interviewed for this account mentioned combined training with infantry during the inter-war period.

234 Buckley, John [2010] "Tackling the Tiger: The development of British Armoured Doctrine for Normandy 1944" in Vandervort, Bruce (ed.) *The Journal of Military History* Volume 74, No 4 October 2012, pp.1162–1164.
235 Ibid p.1167; French, D., *Raising Churchill's Army*, p.221.
236 Ibid.
237 Personal interview with Randall (2006); by the author.
238 Buckley "Tackling the Tiger", p.1164.
239 Ibid., p.1167.
240 *Cavalry Training (Horsed) 1937*.
241 Buckley, "Tackling the Tiger", p.1166.
242 Personal interview with ffrench Blake (2006); by the author.
243 Buckely, "Tackling the Tiger", p.1168.

Elizabeth Kier's comments were, in the main, correct that "tactical training received little attention [in the 1930s],"[244] although it was certainly taught later in the war at Sandhurst, at the 11th Armoured Division in 1943 by Roberts, and by ffrench Blake and others at the Royal Armoured Tactical School in Oxford.[245] The Royal Tank Corps had supposedly been developing tactical doctrine between the wars, but views had diverged on how, in a future war, armour should be deployed. Paddy Griffith was right when he pointed out that there was little or no difference in tactics between The Royal Tank regiments and the armoured cavalry regiments.[246] David French was also correct that a doctrine of mechanized "all arms" operations did lack a common understanding and with it an effective training, and command and control system.[247] Griffith and Buckley agreed in essence, that in terms of tactics, training manuals were found wanting of advice, and armour commanders were forced to improvise and formulate their own styles.[248]

Sprot, from his experience in battle, confirmed that flexibility and learning from each situation was how a commander developed tactics.[249] Major William Davidson, whilst at an Officer Cadet Training Unit (OCTU) in 1940, did receive "tactical training without tanks" at Brookwood and Bovington, and later with tanks, at a Royal Armoured Corps Training Regiment near Salisbury. Tactical training continued when Davidson joined the 2nd Royal Tank Regiment. Davidson recalled, however:

> No matter how much training you have before going into battle, the real thing, for the first time, is an experience that you will never forget. You learnt fast, paid attention to those who had done it before.[250]

Davidson commented on his time as Brigade Major of the 7th Armoured Brigade:

> As far as I am aware, all cavalry regiments were organised in the same way as the RTR; they certainly did everything the same way as we did in battle, and I

---

244 Kier, *Imagining War*, p.126.
245 Personal telephone interview with Hodgeson (2008); by the author. Hodgeson spent part of his army career assisting RAC OCTU cadets training at Sandhurst: "We drove the cadets around so that they could concentrate on tactics". Also Personal interview with ffrench Blake (2006); by the author; after convalescence in England from a wound sustained in the Western Desert, ffrench Blake was posted to the Armoured Corps Tactical School where battle experiences were passed on "particularly to the Americans who had not been to the war". Buckley, "Tackling the Tiger", p.1168.
246 Griffith, P. G. "British Armoured Warfare in the Western Desert" in Harris, J. & Tose, F. N. (eds.) [1990] *Armoured Warfare*, (B.T. Batsford, London), p.73.
247 French, D., *Raising Churchill's Army*, pp.173/174.
248 Griffith, P. G. "British Armoured Warfare in the Western Desert" in Harris, J. & Tose, F. N. (eds.) [1990] *Armoured Warfare*, (B.T. Batsford, London), p.72; Buckley, p.1162.
249 Personal interview with Sprot (2007); by the author.
250 Personal interviews and correspondence with Davidson (2008 & 2009); by the author.

cannot recall any problems with any cavalry regiment with which we might have made contact. When I was Brigade Major of the 7th Armoured Brigade, I was in direct contact with the 7th Hussars, just as I was with the 2nd Royal Tanks and the 6th Royal Tanks, and I dealt with each regiment in exactly the same way. We remained with the 7th Hussars for the remainder of the war. We got on very well with each other, and the 7th Hussars were just as much a part of the Brigade as we were, with exactly the same organisation, and of course, on the same Brigade wavelength. The only apparent difference between us was that when we wore our black berets with the RTR badge, the Hussars wore flat caps.[251]

Reflections on the effectiveness of mechanization training

It is not within the scope of this account to examine critically or in detail the role or success of British armour in the Second World War. It is relevant, however, to comment on the veterans' own reflections on the effectiveness or otherwise of their mechanization training. In contrast to Liddell Hart's assertion that the early tank battles of the Second World War were lost in the Cavalry Club in London, there were successes to celebrate. Davidson recounted when the 11th Hussars was the reconnaissance battalion in armoured cars and part of his 7th Armoured Division:

> They [the 11th Hussars) well deserved the tribute of being the finest reconnaissance group in the British Army. They knew the Western Desert very well indeed, had been in Egypt for a long time, and we worked with them day in and day out, getting to know them well, greatly admiring them for the way they went about things. They were known as the "Cherry Pickers" as their officers all wore pink trousers.[252]

Liddell Hart acknowledged the "brilliant" performance of the regiment in North Africa that "amply fulfilled expectations".[253]

Of the veterans interviewed who fought against the German Army in France and Belgium in 1940 in British tanks, the majority agreed that their training had been effective, but all asserted that the armour and armament deployed was woefully inadequate.[254] John Bennett said:

---

251 Ibid.
252 Personal interviews and correspondence with Davidson (2008 & 2009); by the author. The 7th Armoured Brigade was for a time, part of the 7th Armoured Division, known as "The Desert Rats" that was made up of the 2nd and the 6th Royal Tank Regiments and the 7th Hussars. In January 1942 the 7th Armoured Brigade left the 7th Armoured Division to go to Burma, but without the 6th RTR, and became an independent brigade. The Brigade reformed with 6th RTR, and with the 8th Army later in Italy.
253 Liddell Hart, *Memoirs Volume I,* p.132.
254 Personal interviews with Lucas (2007); Bennett (2007); and Jeffcut (2007); by the author.

The Vickers Mk VI tank had a .303 machine gun and a .5, what they called the "long rifle", would fire a bullet through armour plate. Well, the .5 was ideal against German armoured cars; knock 'em to bits, but no good against German tanks. We had nothing to touch them, we just turned and scoot you know.[255]

John Bennett was correct; it was very difficult to wreck a German tank with a .55 inch Boys "Anti-tank" rifle mainly because this weapon was not designed for that purpose. It was none the less much criticised for its poor performance by the men returning from Dunkirk in May 1940.[256] The Boys Anti-tank rifle was intended for use against lightly armoured AFVs, such as an armoured car and soft-skinned vehicles, and "was never intended to stop modern tanks".[257] At a range of 100 yards and with a direct hit, a .55 round from the Boys rifle could penetrate just 23.2 mm of armour: at an angle or at a greater range, its penetrating power was reduced. The weapon was "extremely accurate" up to 300 yards, but at that range could penetrate only 20.9 mm of armour.[258] This would have been inadequate in most cases as the depth of the armour of German tanks in 1940 ranged between 7mm to 15mm in the Panzer Mk I, but of a greater thickness in Mk IIs and Mk IIIs and up to 70mm in the Panzer Mk IVs.[259]

The Royal Scots Greys' veterans, who fought in the North African desert, Italy and Normandy in American tanks, agreed that their training must have been effective because they never suffered "a reverse".[260] Asked if his training in tanks had been adequate, former 16th/5th Lancer 94-year-old George "Yorkie" Husband retorted: "well I'm still here"! ffrench Blake of the 17th/21st Lancers, 6th Armoured Division, said by Operation Torch, the Allied landings in Morocco and Algeria in 1942, they were the best trained armoured division anywhere, but lacked experience: "Everything went like clockwork, except for the fact that our tanks were about as good as clocks for fighting in".[261]

In summary

Historians and veterans agreed that the army was short of all mechanical vehicles in 1939. Regarding AFVs, Vickers had been given little support and commercial encouragement to produce them, partly because Sir Hugh Ellis, the General responsible for procurement, had had doubts whether or not tanks were still useful and if so, what

255 Personal interview with Bennett (2007); by the author; confirmed by Lucas in a further interview (2011); by the author.
256 *Boys Anti-Tank Rifle Mark I*, p.7.
257 Ibid.
258 Ibid., p.8.
259 Burns, *Tanks of World War II*, Mk I, 7–15mm, p.103; Mk II, 14.4mm, p.112; Mk III, 10–70mm, p.113; Mk IV, 8–50mm, p.122.
260 Personal interviews with Sprot (2007); and Randall (2006); by the author.
261 Personal interview with ffrench Blake (2006); by the author.

type of tank and at what price. The government's defence priority was air deterrent, air defence and keeping the sea-lanes open. Rearming the army was sacrificed partly to maintain a strong economy and partly because, until January 1939, there was no government intention to fight a ground war on Continental Europe.

It has been argued that a reluctance to mechanize the cavalry in India had been a contributory factor to the delay in mechanizing the British Regular cavalry, but the cavalry in India was also short of vehicles suitable for the policing role and the terrain in which they had to operate. When, in India, the 17th/21st Lancers were ordered to mechanize it was greeted with some relief; the commanding officer, supported by officers and NCOs from the RTC, organized and managed a swift conversion from horses to AFVs. The AFVs issued for training the regiment were two obsolete, unreliable, Vickers Mk II tanks in which they had little confidence, and an assortment of a few other petrol driven vehicles. The 16th/5th Lancers were still horsed-mounted and patrolling the North West Frontier when ordered back to England to mechanize in 1939, but modern AFVs were not issued to them until 1941.

In England in 1936/37, two officers of regiments each considered unique, successfully resisted mechanization until 1941/42. This much publicised, but contextually insignificant event, was probably the influence on later historians' opinions of the cavalry's resistance to change. The remainder of the regiments stationed in England got on with the job of mechanization as quickly as they could and coped with huge cultural and operational changes, but they were inadequately equipped to fight the Germans in France.

7

Conclusion

The effectiveness and the efficacy of deploying horsed cavalry in a so-called "modern war" had been a contentious issue for military theorists, planners, and soldiers alike for some time prior to the Great War of 1914–1919.[1] But before, during, and for some time after the Great War, equines remained the only reliable cross-country conveyance on which to mount troops, tow guns and transport equipment. The invention of the tank with its slow, all-terrain, caterpillar-like tracks and the development of the speedier armoured car during the Great War illuminated a way forward for the possibility of cross-country vehicles for reconnaissance, wide troop movement protection, advance, rear and flank guarding and for transportation. This was especially relevant to the cavalry, whose role in war was reconnaissance, fire and movement, to be in the vanguard and on the flanks to protect a moving troop column, and in retreat to act as its rear-guard. This role demanded a versatile cross-country vehicle. It is quite clear from the War Office files that after the Great War the Army Council had every intention to mechanize horsed cavalry regiments as soon as suitable all-terrain armoured vehicles were available. Successive Secretaries of State for War expected this too. They anticipated that the developments in engineering would soon enable the production of the necessary AFVs.

Most serving professional soldiers viewed the end of the Great War as an opportunity to return to "the type of soldiering… which had been its wont before 1914".[2] In the main that was policing the Empire and in that regard horsed cavalry troopers were most useful as mounted policemen. For the everyday job of the British Army in peacetime, therefore, horse mounted cavalry was perfectly adequate. Soldiers posted to operational duties had no urgent need for a change from horses to AFVs.

The Secretary of State for War, Sir Lamming Worthington-Evans, in 1921 acknowledged that the lessons of war had shown the cavalry vulnerable to machine-guns and air attack, but the mobility of the army had to be maintained. He planned to *replace*

1   Badsey, *Doctrine and Reform,* pp.101–103.
2   Harris, *Men, ideas and tanks,* p.195.

four cavalry regiments with tanks and armed motor-cars.[3] In 1921 the Army General Staff hoped horsed cavalrymen would be transferred to an expanded Tank Corps by 1922.[4] The General Staff envisaged that the cavalry regiments would transfer intact to the Tank Corps so that they could retain their regimental traditions and maintain the morale of their officers and men.[5] This was what, in effect, did happen, but not until 1939, with the formation of the Royal Armoured Corps from the Royal Tank Regiments and the mechanized cavalry regiments. What actually took place by 1925 was a reduction in the Tank Corps and a move away from tank battalions to armoured car companies; there were seven tank battalions in 1920 and four in 1925 (plus a Depot battalion). In 1920 there were nine armoured car companies and in 1925 this had risen to eleven including eight in India and three in Egypt.[6]

On 23 November 1926 the committee for the Reconstruction of the Corps of Cavalry envisaged that a further two-year period was necessary to develop a "reliable cross-country armoured car". The committee was, however, still keen to mechanize as much of the cavalry as possible.[7] This was what Prime Minister Stanley Baldwin expected in 1927 and he took Worthington-Evans to task for not fulfilling the Cabinet's expectations on this matter. It was pointed out to Baldwin "that an efficient mechanical substitute for the horse does not at present exist".[8] Vehicles were currently on trial and Worthington-Evans thought these showed promise for future deployment as cavalry AFVs. Baldwin was not concerned how the army managed mechanizing the cavalry; he just expected horsed cavalry to be abolished with concomitant savings in the Army Estimates.[9] The CIGS, Field Marshal G F Milne, had told Worthington-Evans that the cavalry *must* be mechanized. Milne's dilemma was not if, but when could or would mechanization be affordable: it could be five to ten years away, he assessed. This estimate of November 1927 proved to be essentially correct.[10]

3   Emphasis added. *The Times*, 12.04.1921, p.15; see Phillips, Gervase, "Who Shall Say That the Days of Cavalry Are Over? The Revival of the Mounted Arm in Europe", 1853–1914 in *War in History*, URL: <http://wih.sagepub.com/content/18/1/5> accessed 01.12.2011, for similar assertions made in the mid nineteenth century that "the days of cavalry were passed" due to the development of new weapons.
4   TNA WO 32/5959 Army Organisation: Cavalry (Code 14(D)): Scheme for reduction of Cavalry Regiments; hand written note, p.3, 24 February 1921.
5   Ibid.1921.
6   URL: <www.army.mod.uk/documents/general/RAC_History_Royal_Tank_Regiment> accessed 15.02.2013.
7   TNA WO 32/3059 Army Organisation: Cavalry (Code 14(D)): Reconstruction of the Corps of Cavalry; Précis For Army Council No. 1279, Cavalry Establishments and Organization (Interim Report of the Cavalry Committee), marked 6A, February 1927, pp.5 & 7. The Interim Report is dated 23 November 1926.
8   WO 32/2846 Reduction of Expenditure on Cavalry: Memorandum on the reorganization of The Cavalry, War Office Marked Secret, 30 June 1927.
9   Ibid., Baldwin to Sir Laming Worthington-Evans, 20 July 1927.
10   WO 32/2846 Register 16/General/5558, minute 14; Milne to Sir Lamming Worthington-Evans, 3 November 1927.

A substantial number of cavalry horsemen were successfully retrained

The evidence from archived records, supported by oral testaments, confirmed without doubt that cavalry regiments, when eventually mechanized, did re-train and re-equip a substantial number of their horsemen to enable them to fight in AFVs. The recorded experiences of the veteran cavalrymen who have contributed to this account bear witness to that. The Royal Scots Greys' statement that there was hardly a man who had not previously served as a mounted cavalryman added strong evidence too, and this was most likely the situation within the Household cavalry regiments and the 16th/5th Lancers, which were similarly late to mechanize. These regiments were still mounted on horses after the Second World War had begun in 1939. A corresponding conclusion regarding the proportion of horsemen successfully trained in AFVs can be reached in respect of the regiments mechanized early on: the 11th Hussars and 12th Lancers in the late 1920s followed by the 3rd Hussars and the 9th Lancers in the mid-1930s. Had their officers and men transferred or been posted to other Regular horsed regiments, they would, had their service commitment not expired, eventually have undergone the change process to mechanization.

Research has been unable to confirm two interesting areas regarding personnel. Firstly, what proportion of the horsemen was unable to "fathom mechanics" and what happened to them, particularly in the regiments that were mechanized in the mid to late 1930s? Veterans confirmed that some existing soldiers were not able to cope with the complexities of mechanization and were transferred out of the regiment to other postings.

Secondly, what proportion of the other rank soldiers in previously horsed regiments had passed out of riding school *before* they underwent training as driver/mechanics, gunners and radio operators? Some of the regiments were mechanized soon after they had returned from an overseas posting, such as the 13th/18th Hussars and the 2nd Dragoon Guards. Time-expired men, like Charles Need, an experienced horseman, left the regiment, probably with many others like him, and would have been replaced by whatever new recruits could be mustered. It was discussed earlier in this account that during some of the inter-war years recruitment was difficult, and the army was sometimes understrength. Cavalry regiments had no permanent depots in the way that infantry regiments did, and no central training establishment either, such as the RTC had at Bovington. Cavalry recruits were trained by their own regiment and it follows, therefore, that if horses had never been taken over by the regiment returning from abroad, the recruits could not have been taught to ride them. These recruits would straightaway have been trained in whatever motor vehicles became available.

Without the availability of the muster-rolls, so useful in researching military units of earlier periods, it has been impossible to determine the numbers of cavalrymen who had never been horsemen in the first place, or those who had been, but because they could not cope with mechanized training, were posted out to other units. Officers' careers can of course be traced through the Army Lists. As has already been stated, most officers stayed with their regiments, horsed or mechanized, and when considering the veterans' testimonies, an inference can be drawn that the same applied to the majority of the other rank soldiers too.

Mechanization: a blessing to some, a curse to others

Almost all of the interviewees chose to join a cavalry regiment because they were interested in horses and wanted to ride them. James Randall, Basil Jeffcut and Ronald Lucas are particular examples. Jeffcut had followed his father and two brothers into the cavalry. Others, such as John Bennett, joined the cavalry because they were influenced by their pals who had enlisted earlier. Lieutenant Colonels ffrench Blake and Sprot, although they were horse-lovers, or became so later, followed a family tradition into their respective cavalry regiments and would have joined them regardless of horse or armour. Some of the interviewees have testified that not all the cavalrymen with whom they had served loved horses and these soldiers preferred their new mechanized life and duties. Randall and Jeffcut "hated" mechanization; Randall tried to get a transfer to the Jordanian Frontier Force which was to remain mounted, but his sergeant-major forbade this. Lucas saw mechanization as an opportunity and made the best of it. All three later distinguished themselves in battle fighting in tanks. The number of interviewees who have contributed to this account is acknowledged as too few in number to constitute a truly representative sample; it is most likely, however, that their stories varied little from those of their comrades whose experiences have gone unrecorded, be they officers or other ranks. These cavalrymen, in the main, were not keen to give up their horses, but neither were they keen to take their horses to war.

Clearly there was a concern in Parliament about the cavalry's attitude to part with horses. The Secretary of State for War, Duff Cooper, perhaps was influenced by some "silly questions", when on 10 March 1936 he thought that mechanization was an unwelcome imposition on the cavalry, and a great sacrifice for the cavalryman.[11] Whilst this might have been so for some, it was not the case for the majority, and Duff Cooper should have known that because the men of the 12th Lancers in 1928, for example, had been "bent on mechanization" and were "very, very keen";[12] this continued to be so. Both Colonels ffrench Blake of the 17th/21st Lancers and Sprot of the Royal Scots Greys were also keen to see their respective regiments mechanized.

11 Ellis, *Cavalry*, pp.181/182; Liddell Hart, *Memoirs Volume I*, p.277; for the context see Minney, *The Private Papers of Hore-Belisha*, pp.92–98.
12 IWM Sound Collection; Horsburgh-Porter, reel 1.

For some the change to armour should have happened ten years earlier.[13] Both officers and other ranks knew there was no place for the horse in a modern war. With horses the regiment would "just sit in a backwater, doing nothing… with no more battle honours or Military Crosses which was no good for the regiment of which one was proud".[14] Lieutenant Colonel Aiden Sprot acknowledged: "we must have realised that the horse could not cope in [a modern] war". In quiet retrospection, Sprot mused that he was pleased not to have had to look after a horse in war; it had been hard enough taking care of himself. The thought of all that shrapnel that had hit his tank lacerating a horse horrified him.[15] The 3rd Hussars' regimental journal told of how those who had fought in the Great War no longer wished to see their "long-nosed pal" suffer again in battle. David French was correct, as these veterans have testified, that "the significance of the oft-cited reluctance of cavalry officers to give up their horses in favour of tanks and armoured cars can be exaggerated".[16] David French also confirmed that many troopers welcomed the change to tanks, as the mechanical skills taught them by the army would be useful later in civilian life.[17]

Caring for horses was hard work and riding to the cavalry standard took some time to learn; a skill like that once, and sometimes painfully, acquired would be unwillingly forsaken. Charles Need of the 13th/18th Hussars, when he volunteered in 1933, remembered that for the first six months in the cavalry "you never saw a horse's back, but from day one you were grooming horses or mucking out… [later] riding training took twelve months". Ronald Lucas of the 15th/19th Hussars agreed: "We went straight in, mixing with horses, which suited me, because that's what I joined for".[18] Need had not ridden a horse before riding training began. The lessons were hard; horses reared, cantered off, and men were strewn all over the ground. Need "did several summersaults" that he never forgot. Need thought that the cavalry was a "dead end… more or less finished… Talk of mechanization was always there… a couple of regiments were already mechanized".[19] Need also remembered the first time he saw anti-tank guns: "That's when it struck me, those sorts of things we are going to see; we [horsed cavalry] were out of date". Sergeant James Randall of the Royal Scots Greys had a contrary view:

> Mechanization broke my heart… I wasn't a sort of "death or glory" boy wanting to get into battle or anything like that, I wanted to ride horses…The regiment made a glorious sight, three hundred horsemen in half-sections [riding in pairs]

13 ffrench Blake, *The 17th/21st Lancers*, p.82.
14 Personal interviews with ffrench Blake (2006); and Sprot (2007); by the author.
15 Personal interview with Sprot (2007); by the author.
16 French, D., *Raising Churchill's Army*, p.61.
17 French, D., *Military Identities*, p.263.
18 Personal interview with Lucas (2007); by the author.
19 The 11th Hussars and the 12th Lancers.

with bare brown hills on the right and the lush vegetation of the Jordan on the left.[20]

Randall asserted he did everything he could in 1942 to get out of having to train in a tank. He tried unsuccessfully to transfer to the Trans Jordan Police Force that remained horsed; he did not want to be in a tank at all. Asked if any of his comrades successfully transferred to the Transjordan Police Force, he admitted:

> Not many of them wanted to. Some had already served in mechanized units already, they didn't enjoy horses. Most of them were probably pushed into the job in the first place and didn't want it, but they were all keen to drive and to use vehicles rather than horses. No, lots of them had no time for horses, bloody "goras" they were called.[21]

John Bennett explained that some of the older men, "old Indian soldiers [were] a bit peeved and cut–up" at losing the horses, but the younger men, like him, accepted it and knew it was the end of horsed cavalry. Many of the men wanted to learn to drive.[22] Randall agreed this to be so[23] and it was so for Ronald Lucas and John Bennett who, after 1945, had careers in motor vehicle engineering.[24] The horses had to be cared for twenty-four hours a day. Tanks and armoured cars did not need round-the-clock attention.[25] Some of the men had "not the slightest interest in riding", and welcomed the opportunity to learn new skills.[26] Learning to drive a tank was fun and the men enjoyed it "up to a point".[27] "Quite a lot of the chaps were keen to be gunners. Macho wasn't it" mused Randall[28] who did not learn to drive a motor vehicle then or since. Regarding mechanization he exclaimed: "Well what could you do about it? There was nothing, you had to accept that was how things were".[29] Randall nonetheless became a gallant tank commander serving with Sprot in the Reconnaissance Troop of the Royal Scots Greys and was awarded a Mention in Despatches at the end of the Second World War.[30]

20 Personal correspondence with Randall (2009); by the author.
21 Ibid., "Gora" comes from an Indian expression, a mildly derogatory term referring to white people or those with a pale skin – the Greys were mounted on grey horses; URL: <http://www.urbandictionary.com/define.php?term=gora> accessed 12.12. 2011.
22 Personal interview with Bennett (2007); by the author.
23 Personal interview with Randall (2006); by the author.
24 Personal interview with Lucas (2007); by the author.
25 French, D., *Military Identities*,p.263; Personal interview with Lucas (2007); by the author.
26 Personal interview with Randall (2006); by the author.
27 Personal correspondence with Jeffcut (2007); by the author.
28 Personal interview with Randall (2006); by the author.
29 Ibid.
30 A Mention in Despatches is a fourth level gallantry award and is denoted by a bronze oak leaf displayed diagonally across the war or campaign medal for which it was awarded.

In the Household Cavalry:

> When the horses finally went it tended to be only the sentimentalists who regretted their passing; the majority of troopers found armoured cars much less work and they did not miss the endless rounds of stables and kit cleaning.[31]

Many soldiers must have taken the same view as Ronald Lucas; the horses were gone and in a disciplined service life orders had to be obeyed. Learning to drive was welcomed by many, and according to Lucas, "no one left because they didn't like it".[32] It was probably just men of the 16th/5th Lancers who had to endure the distress of actually seeing their horses destroyed, although the 15th/19th Hussars at York were unhappy at not knowing the planned destination for their mounts when they took them to the railway yard in York.

Bearing down on the task to maintain morale

As far as it was possible with the equipment and vehicles provided, speed was of the essence for each of the regiments to change; to "get on with it [mechanization] quickly"[33] with an "utter determination to make a success of it".[34] Morale had to be maintained because mechanization was a big change for cavalry regiments and any change from the familiar can be stressful and cause a loss of confidence. These changes were considerable, in equipment, modus operandi and dispersion (five horsemen could occupy more ground than a crew of five in a Rolls Royce armoured car or three in a Light tank). Perhaps even more significant were the changes in the culture, relationships and leadership style within the regiment when the officers and men, as AFV crews, formed close-knit teams or "social groups". Both officers and men of other ranks might have found this difficult to cope with at first, although none of the interviewees said so. A regiment undergoing mechanization could be considered "non-operational" and out of the action, something quite unacceptable within the can-do ethos of the British Army. The quicker a regiment was re-equipped and properly trained the sooner it could return to the order of battle and "feel" useful.

The change process from horses to vehicles had to be managed well and the key element was speed, keeping the momentum going. No evidence has been found that morale within any cavalry regiment was affected by the loss of the horses. However, under circumstances when the men's morale might have been questionable, pressure

31   White-Spunner, *Horse Guards*, p.496.
32   Personal interview with Lucas (2007); by the author.
33   IWM Sound Collection, Horsburgh-Porter, reel 1; Lieutenant Colonel H V S Charrington MC had taken command of the 12th Lancers in September 1927. Lieutenant Colonel J W Hornby MC took over command 6 September 1931; *Army Lists* 1928–1931.
34   IWM Sound Collection, Allenby, reel 1.

was put on them to achieve the task: this was appropriate leadership. The Cavalry Corps was a combat arm and the men needed to feel competent and effective for battle again as soon as this could be achieved. The commanding officers were right to set demanding time scales that at the time some officers and men thought quite a challenge, but achieving these targets would ensure morale was maintained and the objective achieved. This was leadership of the highest quality; the reputation of their regiment was at stake and the veterans have asserted that it mattered so much to them to have pride in their unit whatever the circumstances.

The War Office had prescribed the method by which the cavalry regiments should manage their change from horses to AFVs. So well-constructed and practical was this method that its principles were used by all the cavalry regiments, with varying degrees of pace, throughout the gradual process of mechanization. As a comparison, the 11th Hussars took one year to convert from horses to AFVs from 1928, as did the 17th/21st Lancers from 1938; the 12th Lancers took three years from 1928 and the Royal Scots Greys took just eight months during 1942. The pace of change was much dependent on having the vehicles on which to train. The horses, with the exception of two for each officer (later reduced to one), were sent away very quickly after the order to mechanize was announced. All the saddle equipment was withdrawn. It was essential that the men understood there was no going back; the horses were gone for ever, in spite of the spurious promise made to the 3rd Hussars in 1934.[35] A team of officers and NCO instructors and technicians was seconded from the Royal Tank Corps to the cavalry regiments to get their mechanical and driving training underway. The regiments began to train their own nucleus of driving, mechanical and gunnery instructors by sending a number of officers and NCOs away to the Royal Tank Corps Schools at or around Bovington in Dorset. Second and subsequent tranches of officers and NCOs were sent later. Almost all cavalrymen learnt to drive a motor vehicle, but not all of them went on to drive AFVs. As the regimental instructors returned from their courses at Bovington, and became competent, they gradually replaced the RTC team. Regimental fitters, as they too became more competent, supplemented or replaced the fitters and mechanics provided by the Royal Army Ordnance Corps to maintain the AFVs.[36]

Utilising transferable skills and experience

Evidence has suggested a pragmatic approach was taken in deciding which element of the regiment to train first and which officers and NCOs to send for training. As far as has been established, no intelligence or aptitude tests were applied until after 1939;

---

35   TNA WO 32/2847 Army Organisation: Cavalry (Code 14(D)): Introduction of a Mobile Division 1934–1936 20/Cav/831; 1C; War Office letter to various military commands, schools and overseas establishments, 8 December 1934.
36   IWM Sound Collection, Wiggin, reel 2.

research has been unable to explain, therefore, precisely why certain men were chosen over others to undertake the various tasks. Each regiment had had a motor transport section for some time. Some motor vehicle knowledge and experience was already contained within a small group of the regiment that had included the Signals Troop in Austin Seven cars, and these men could have become instructors. Ronald Lucas realised how experienced these soldiers were "in the old motor-transport section" who had been doing the job for a long time when he returned to the 15th/19th Hussars in 1939 from nine months of intensive motor engineering training.[37] Lucas had served part of an engineering apprenticeship before enlisting in 1935 and his regiment must have been aware of this as he was chosen to train as an instructor.[38] Other NCOs were chosen because they could already instruct well in another subject.[39] James Randall of the Royal Scots Greys, previously a school teacher and Boy Scout, was trained as a signals instructor.[40]

Training the men in driving and maintenance might not have been quite the challenging prospect that was envisaged. The men were used to instruction and most had been trained to ride, a skill that ffrench Blake assessed was far harder to learn than tank driving.[41] But for the majority of men it was their first introduction to a motor vehicle and that must have been daunting for them. Sprot of the Royal Scots Greys estimated that in 1942 only about 50 men out of around 400 could drive a motor vehicle.[42] The 12th Lancers, in order to get the conversion off to a solid start, chose to train B Squadron first as B Squadron had included the more intelligent men of the machine-gun section.[43] In the 13th/18th Hussars, their former bandsmen, also intelligent men were "motorized" as despatch-riders on 500cc motor-cycles and left to get on with it with just an instruction book.[44] Training the brighter men first will have formed a new skill-base as an example and inspiration to less able or less confident troopers.

The RTR and the Cavalry

The officers drafted in from the RTC to train the cavalrymen found no resistance to the change to AFVs and were made welcome by their new cavalry colleagues. Inter-unit rivalry within the Army was encouraged by competitions, sports tournaments and military exercises; every unit wanted to be best, better than the rest. This culture, when kept within sensible boundaries, was constructive and conducive to the

37   Personal interview with Lucas (2007); by the author.
38   Ibid.
39   Personal interview with Sprot (2007); by the author.
40   Personal interview with Randall (2006); by the author.
41   Personal interview with ffrench Blake (2006); by the author.
42   Personal interview with Sprot (2007); by the author.
43   IWM Sound Collection, Horsburgh-Porter, reel 1.
44   Mallinson, *Light Dragoons*, pp.178/179.

development of a team spirit within the service. Almost certainly there were arguments over scarce resources among senior level army officers, but any animosity that might have existed between the cavalry and the Royal Tank Corps at regimental level seems to have been overstated, portrayed as destructive, and has itself become a myth. No evidence has been found to support any antipathy between these two service arms. Any bad feeling that might once have existed had long since disappeared by 1928, as 11th Hussar officer Peter Wiggin recounted from his own experience.[45] The officers, Uniacke, Roberts, Prendaghast and Dow, and the NCOs of the 3rd Armoured Car Company RTC were welcomed as "nice, helpful people" into the 12th Lancers.[46] Harold Pyman and his RTC men "spent an immensely happy year" mechanizing the 17th/21st Lancers, where the cavalrymen taught his family to ride horses.[47] "Teacher" Davidson and his men from the 42nd RTR were much appreciated by the Royal Scots Greys in 1942.[48]

The RTR detachments found that the cavalrymen "were intelligent, keen to learn and easy to teach".[49] The cavalry NCOs were of a better quality than their own, having developed through an organizational culture that encompassed a greater delegation of tasks by officers to NCOs compared to that of the RTR.[50] The relatively small ratio of NCOs to men in the cavalry would have supported this ethos and would have helped to develop the NCOs into competent instructors and junior leaders.[51] Later, with Second World War battle experience, 2nd RTR officer and 7th Armoured Brigade-Major William Davidson could not "recall any problems" between the cavalry and the tank regiments; they were organized and operated in exactly the same way as each other. Davidson was particularly impressed with the performance of both the 7th and 11th Hussars.[52]

Manpower turnover – a drain on skill building

The constant posting of men in and out of a regiment being converted to AFVs in order to maintain a full establishment of regiments serving overseas would have hindered building-up the required skills base. This must have been particularly so

45   IWM Sound Collection, Wiggin, reel 2.
46   Ibid., Savill, reel 1; Harding –Newman, reel 1; Kidston-Montgomerie, reel 1 & Horsburgh-Porter, reel 1.
47   Pyman, *Call to Arms,* p.27.
48   Personal interview with Sprot (2007); by the author.
49   Brigadier Robert H Bright, IWM Sound Collection, access number 787, recorded 1977, reel IV.
50   Ibid.
51   French, D., *Military Identities*, p.148.
52   Personal interviews and correspondence with Davidson (2008 & 2009); by the author.

while existing horsed regiments still needed men who had "passed riding school,"[53] especially when these men were being trained in vehicle driving and maintenance. In 1936 thirty-two men went from the 3rd Hussars in England to the 10th Hussars in India, just as the 3rd Hussars was commencing the conversion process. A further draft of thirty-four men went later to the 13th/18th Hussars, also in India. The 4th Hussars lost many of their trained men under different circumstances; these men were required to make up the establishment for the mechanized cavalry regiments sent to France in 1939. It is a credit to the consistency and continuity of the army's training system that men could move usefully from regiment to regiment. The out-going draft of trained men was then replaced by untrained new recruits and the training process was repeated again and again.

Frustrated by the lack of appropriate equipment

The process, well planned and organized as it was, was frustrated, not from resistance to change or any lack of determination, but from a lack of suitable and sufficient equipment. Such was the chronically slow development and production of AFVs between the two World Wars, that some of the well-used armoured cars transferred to the 12th Lancers in 1928 were driven by them in battle during the Second World War. Trying to get enough of the right equipment was quite a battle in itself, as White-Spunner had assessed.[54] Beset with the constant need to use "token" equipment (15 cwt. box vans were used instead of AFVs), the exasperation of the officers and other ranks of the 3rd Hussars was expressed in their Regimental Journal in 1938 by wanting to ban "token" from the English language.

What research has made clear and irrefutable is that, with the exceptions of the Royals and the Royal Scots Greys, the delay in the mechanization of British Regular and Household cavalry regiments was not due to an insular regimental culture, a reluctance to change or to give up its horses. Cavalry mechanization was, nevertheless, retarded, especially when reflected against such an early intention for this to happen following the experiences of the Great War. What retarded this process was a reason or reasons other than those commonly attributed in popular military history. Winton encapsulates the reasons: the "modernization [of the army] was impeded by an indifferent Cabinet, a parsimonious Treasury, and a pacifist electorate".[55] However, as has been demonstrated, there were good reasons for these attitudes that, without the benefit of hindsight, prevailed during much of the inter-war period.

53 See, for an example: The 3rd The King's Own Hussars Historical Records 01.04.1934–31.03.1935, p.2 File 1716; "From Cairo to Berlin With The Desert Rats"; the memoirs of 555950 S.Q.M.S. C F A Newman in *The Chronicle – The Journal of The Queen's Royal Hussars Historical Society*, p.26 Volume 1 Number 3, November 2002.
54 White-Spunner, *Horse Guards*, p.497–502.
55 Winton, *To Change An Army*, p.1.

There were reasons

The future role of the army in war was seen at times at best confused, at worst redundant, having been superseded by the bombers of the RAF. Historians have often described the British Army of this inter-war period as the "Cinderella service,"[56] denuded of investment, sufficient modern equipment and often of men too. Recruitment into the army was difficult. Some units were so under-strength that to attract more men to join up the standard of physique was lowered; but not for the cavalry.[57] Relatively few British people foresaw the Second World War; of those that did, most, including the Prime Minister Neville Chamberlain in 1938, hoped for the best that it could be averted.[58] Many people knew from their personal experience of the consequences of war – the Great War, a war to end wars. Much of the population had been involved in bereavement or the disablement of mind and body of themselves, a relative or someone in the neighbourhood.[59] They were not prepared to countenance another war.[60]

If Prime Minister Baldwin, reassessing the security risks in 1932, was keen to re-arm,[61] Chamberlain certainly was not; he considered this a provocative act certainly in regard to rearming the British Army.[62] Whether elected politicians should lead or follow public opinion has been often debated; it is beyond the scope of this account. What is pertinent was the significant role played by public opinion, or the politician's perception of it, during the inter-war period. This all turned on the extension of the franchise in 1918 and then again in 1928, after which everyone over age 21 was given the vote.[63] The electorate grew significantly and included all adult men and women; the political class could no longer appeal only to the patronage of a privileged few as it had done previously. Prime Minister David Lloyd George had promised in 1918 to build for the people "homes fit for heroes to live in" and voters' expectations were raised by his political rhetoric. There were concerns then regarding public disorder, perhaps even revolution, and under such circumstances the government could take

---

56 For example, Anglesey, *A History of the British Cavalry* Volume 8, p.313; Feiling, Keith [1946], *Life of Neville Chamberlain*, (Macmillan, London) quoted in Minney, *The Private Papers of Hore-Belisha*, p.36.

57 Evans, Gary, "The British Cavalry 1920–1940", PhD, University of Kent Canterbury, 2011, p.165.

58 Britain by Mass Observation papers; 1937 – Ilford – 1/A; Britain by Mass Observation papers; 1939, The Oxford By-Election; Harrison, & Madge, *Britain by Mass Observation*, p.101.

59 Personal interview with Chapman (2008); by the author.

60 Hobsbawm, *The Age of Extremes*, p.26.

61 Barnett, Corelli "The Illogical Promise" in Panichas, George A. (ed.) [1968] *The Promise of Greatness: The War of 1914–1918*, (Cassell, London) p.571.

62 Self, *Neville Chamberlain*, pp.237/8 & pp.332/333; Liddell Hart, *Memoirs Volume I*, pp.385/386.

63 There were and still are exceptions, such as convicted people in prison.

some risks with defence but none with social and economic affairs.[64] In 1919 the military was told to assume that another war would not occur for the next ten years; this became a policy and was not revoked until 1932. It proved to be the appropriate decision, there was no major war for Great Britain until 1939, and there was no revolution either. The dogma of the "ten year rule", however, dominated the allocation of government defence expenditure and the Defence Estimates fell continuously from 1919 until 1932 and the Army Estimates until 1933.[65] Social expenditure increased considerably; health care from £25m in 1920 to £46m in 1930, education form £110m to £154m and welfare from £156m to £251m over the same period. Defence spending fell steadily from £694 to £119m in the period 1920 to 1930, and then fell further to £103m before rising again in 1933; deflation affected the purchasing power of this money, but not that much. Within the falling budget the armed services had to defend and police an Empire that had grown following the Great War. The responsibility for mandated and former enemy territories and the occupation of Germany soaked-up resources. Later in the decade these responsibilities lessened, but so too did the Army Estimates.

There were logical reasons why the British Government had not invested more and sooner in AFV development. It was the advent of the Second World War, unforeseen for much of the period, which has raised questions. Between 1929 and 1933 there was an expectation that national armies might not even exist in the future, replaced by a "police-force" under the auspices of the League of Nations. Certainly tanks, heavy-guns and bombers would be banned; this had been headlined in *The Times*![66] The League of Nations meeting regularly in Geneva had, by 1930, successfully undertaken much work in conflict reduction. Significant inter and intra-national treaties had been agreed and member nations were committed to settle disputes without recourse to military action.[67] An agreed restriction on the number and size of battleships had taken place from 1922 that included, principally, the United States, Great Britain, France, Italy and Japan.[68] A similar agreement was renegotiated by Japan, the United States and Great Britain in 1927,[69] and again in London in 1935/1936 that also included an agreement with Germany.[70] When the Geneva Disarmament Conference opened in 1932, therefore, it was a reasonable expectation that an agreement on general disarmament would be reached. The wider public's opinion on disarmament, and other political matters of the period, is impossible to know for certain as no surveys existed

---

64   Middlemass, *Thomas Jones – Whitehall Dairies Volume I*, Thomas Jones to the Prime Minister, 8 February 1919, pp.73–74; Gibbs, *History of the Second World War* Volume 1, p.5.
65   Bond, *British Military Policy*, p.39; see also, Peden, *British Rearmament and the Treasury*.
66   *The Times*, 12.04.1932; *The Daily Mail*, 21.04.1932, p.3.
67   Gibbs, *History of the Second World War* Volume 1, pp.39/42.
68   The Washington Naval Conference.
69   The Geneva Naval Conference.
70   The London Naval Conference and the Anglo-German Naval Agreement.

at that time.[71] Given the time and events that have passed, the historian can only deduce what was public opinion from a number of sources. These sources include: how an indicative number of the population behaved, what they wrote, read, and took as entertainment, and the agenda of newspapers that were found by later surveys to have shaped opinions.[72] Interviews of veterans have helped to illuminate some of these socio-political issues and have been reported in this account.

There was considerable support for the popular peace movement as a whole, whether active or passive, whether by religious faith or pragmatism, whether absolute pacifists or pacificists (those that would only countenance war as sometimes necessary although an irrational and inhumane way to solve disputes).[73] The Peace Ballot result on its own, supported as it was by 11,000,000 participants, was sufficiently large to have considerably influenced government thinking.[74] Newspapers, cinema news-reels and "next-war" literature stoked up fears of bombing and poison gas within public and politicians alike. Sir David Banks, the Permanent Secretary at the Air Ministry, was "seriously concerned with the tonnage of bombs which could now be dropped on England; there could be 1,000,000 casualties.[75] The war in Spain catalysed these fears from a possibility to a probability. The political left, whose growing popularity was manifest in the ballot box,[76] particularly in by-election results, was pacifist in ethos until it coalesced more around anti-fascism than anti-war. With this split in the peace movement's thinking the absolute pacifists, Sheppard, Lansbury, Brittain et al, stood alone with a much reduced influence that lowered the barriers to an accelerated rearmament programme.

Too little and too late

In terms of re-equipping the army, however, and the cavalry and the RTC in particular, the damage had been already been done. There had been insufficient investment in the development and production of AFVs between 1918 and 1939 for the engineering industry to catch up in time. Re-armament for the army had concentrated on air-defence, the principal concern of the man and woman on the so-called Clapham omnibus. The government's naivety regarding a military commitment to their French allies had further exacerbated the situation. It was not until early 1939, under political pressure, that the government accepted their obligation to send again a British Expeditionary Force (BEF) to fight alongside the French Army. A field force would need tanks, appropriately armed and armoured, to combat the German Panzers.

71   Winton, *To Change An Army*, p.228 agreed the public mood was difficult to gauge.
72   Harrison, & Madge, *Britain by Mass Observation*, p.30.
73   Ceadel, *Pacifism in Britain*.
74   See Appendix F.
75   LHCMA – LH 11/1937/34, "Lunch with Sir D Banks", 6 May 1937.
76   See Appendix D.

Vickers Armstrong, the United Kingdom's only commercial tank manufacturer for much of the inter-war period, had received little incentive to produce tanks for the British Army of a quality and quantity superior to that of the German Army, the likely enemy. They were on the road to success when the Vickers "Sixteen-Tonner" medium tank was prototyped in 1929/1930, but economic worries superseded those of defence and the "Sixteen-Tonner" development programme was axed. Vickers, always under pressure from the War Office to minimise the price, concentrated on the production of a light tank, variants of which were attractive to foreign markets. For a time there was in the War Office the strong influence of the Tank Corps pioneer Sir Hugh Ellis, who had considered that tanks had become useless. His judgment had been influenced by the more rapid development of anti-tank guns and armour piecing ordnance than in armour plating engineering for tanks.

Neither could Vickers have been encouraged by the "tank-banning" proposals at Geneva in 1932, nor by the Royal Commission on the Private Manufacture of and Trade in Arms of February 1935. The Commission was required to consider, among other matters, "a prohibition of private manufacture of and trade in arms and the munitions of war".[77] The Commission was presented information on Vickers' overseas investments and the form of any government subsidies.[78] It was argued that Vickers had, by the nature of their overseas sales and investments, contributed to an increasing demand for armaments both abroad and in the United Kingdom.[79] The Union for Democratic Control (UDC), presenting evidence to the Commission, argued that Vickers' true profits were deliberately hard to determine. This was because of inter-linking trusts and internal trading and transfers among subsidiary companies within the Vickers group that included the English Steel Corporation.[80] It was, almost certainly, a legitimate accusation. It is significant to this account that in presenting their case, the UDC hardly mentioned tanks; such was their insignificance in terms of Vickers' overall arms manufacture. The Commission's investigations, however, came to nothing, but it was a hesitant time to be in the arms industry; heavy engineering required long-term decisions to commit investment in jigs, tools and machinery, and in manpower planning.[81] The tank situation was dire.

In 1932 there were still no tanks available to mechanize the cavalry. The CIGS, George Milne, in a minute to his Army Council colleagues, reported that five tank battalions would be needed for an Expeditionary Force, but only four battalions

77 URL: <www.fredsakademiet.dk? Udc.pdf >"Verbatim Summary of the Evidence presented by The Union of Democratic Control July 17 and 18 1935", accessed 23 January 2013.
78 Templewood, *Nine Troubled Years*, confirmed The Government "set aside [£4,000,000] for grants to firms for plant and equipment" after rearmament had commenced, p.207.
79 URL: <www.fredsakademiet.dk? Udc.pdf> "Verbatim Summary of the Evidence presented by The Union of Democratic Control July 17 and 18 1935', accessed 23 January 2013.
80 Ibid.
81 See also LHCMA – LH15/12/12, 43 & 44; Peck to Pope, for Peck's assessment of the process of tank development from 1933, 20 December 1941.

existed and with only enough medium tanks to equip two battalions. The Army Council was always more aware of a need for a continental expeditionary force than were the politicians at that time. With irony Milne exclaimed: "This situation cannot be regarded as satisfactory".[82] The earlier tank pioneers were concerned too: George M Lindsay, a previous Inspector of the RTC (1925–1929) and in 1934, as commander of the 7th Infantry Brigade, had written the notes for the CIGS' Research Committee suggesting a programme of development to bring up-to-date the obsolescent machines of the Tank Brigade battalions.[83] Lindsay was, by 13 February 1935, the GOC Assam District in India, when he received a reply to his letter from the previous assistant Director of Mechanization (1928–1932), Fredrick "Tim" Pile, who was, until 1936, commanding the Canal Brigade. Pile wrote that "[we] have a host of obsolete machines... this niggardliness must cease... or we will not have enough machines on which to train our crews, let alone fighting machines".[84]

On 17 June 1936, a secret report on the RTC at home recorded "At the present moment we have only training tanks, none of which are fit to go to war" and for which there were no spare parts to keep them running.[85] On 17 October 1936 the Secretary of State for War Duff Cooper produced a report entitled "The Tank Situation".[86] He outlined the previous thinking regarding the role of the Light tank:

> ... reconnaissance, protection and inter-communication. These tanks were required to be speedy, with a good cross-country performance and with sufficient armour to afford protection against the smaller type of anti-tank weapons; and only the lighter types of armament were considered necessary.[87]

The Medium tank, of which there were 166, was considered the main battle tank. 164 of these had been built between 1923 and 1930; the other two were the prototype models of the "Sixteen-Tonner" project axed earlier to save money.

In 1936, 209 Light tanks of different marks were in operation and Duff Cooper considered these "barely sufficient for the peace training requirements of existing

---

82   TNA WO 32/2852 "General Situation of Tanks Units at Home and in Egypt"; Register 20/Tanks/304, 15.08.1932.
83   LHCMA – LH15/12/1–2, 30; paragraph 7.
84   Ibid., A2b13; Pile to Lindsay 13.02.1935.
85   LHCMA – LH 15/11/4–3, "Unpreparedness for War, Royal Tank Corps – Secret", from Brigadier P C S Hobart Commander 1st Tank Brigade to HQ Southern Command 17 June 1936; LHCMA, LH 15/12/21, 27 from Lindsay's Private file 12 July 1936, "Martel has replaced Studd in MGO 5 and is faced with many problems. No spares for old tanks which hinder training".
86   TNA WO 32/4441; 57/Tanks/2180 1A SECRET, 17.10.1936; see also Beale, *Death by Design*, p.114; LHCMA – LH 15/11/6, extract from Duff Cooper's statement and in response [to questions] of November 1936, "medium tanks are completely obsolete and have been so for some years".
87   Ibid.

units". There were no war reserves and none for the formation of any new units. A final decision had yet to be taken to equip all the cavalry with these vehicles, but as around 140 of the 209 were the two-man model with armour that would barely keep out "modern armour-piercing rifle bullets", they were anyway effectively obsolete.[88] The remainder of the light tanks had been manufactured that year – 1936. These tanks were reckoned to be "superior" to those of other nations and a further 680 had been ordered for delivery by April 1938.[89] Fulfilling this order on time would have made available approximately 750 light tanks by May 1938. In theory, that was just enough light AFVs to equip the cavalry regiments, assuming 40 tanks per regiment with no spares or reserves. The cavalry regiments were in fact equipped later, partly with Bren-gun carriers as well as tanks; Lucas remembered the 15th/19th Hussars in France in 1940 had one troop in each squadron operating in Bren-gun carriers, the rest in Mark VIB Light tanks.[90] It is clear from these figures that it would have been arithmetically impossible to have fully equipped all cavalry regiments until the spring of 1938 at the earliest, regardless of the cavalry's attitude to change.

In that spring of 1938, however, General Edmund Ironside, then the GOC-in-C of Eastern Command recorded:

Mechanized division; cavalry regiments are not yet equipped or trained with tanks... Tanks; obsolete medium tanks, no cruiser tanks, no infantry tanks, obsolete armoured cars, no light tanks (we have one unit now in Egypt).[91]

This was so, but the light tanks in Egypt were unreliable according to Colonel (later Brigadier) J A L Caunter, the commanding officer of the 1st Battalion (Light) RTC in Egypt.[92] In discussion with Liddell Hart at the Tank Corps dinner in November 1936 he detailed the difficulties. It seems that 50 out of the 76 light tanks were Mark II models with suspension systems insufficiently robust to cope with the rough ground. Spindles, eight of which made up part of the suspension system, fractured about every six miles. The main problem, however, if that one was not enough with which to cope, was that there were a total of only 12 spare spindles in Egypt. Gradually Caunter's tank force had been reduced as one by one his tanks were cannibalized of spindles in order to the keep the others mobile.[93] Brigadier Giffard le Quesne Martel, the Deputy Director of Mechanization at the War Office, told Liddell Hart on 28 November

88   LHCMA – LH15/12/9, 9; concern had been expressed in the House of Commons that bullet development was progressing faster than bullet-resisting armour plate; 15 March 1934, Orders of The Day Supply: Army Estimates.
89   Ibid.
90   Personal interview with Lucas (2011); by the author.
91   Ironside's diary entry, 29 March 1938, cited in Beale, *Death by Design*, p.116.
92   LHCMA – GB99 KCLMA, Caunter.
93   LHCMA, LH 11/1936/109, 23 November 1936.

1938 that tanks were "now coming through at 2 or 3 a day... by next August [1939] we should have about 1000 delivered... mostly light tanks".[94]

Beale, citing a government paper of July 1942, reported that on 3 September 1939 "834 light tanks of the Mk VI series... [were] available for operations or training".[95] Therefore, sometime between the spring and autumn of 1939 enough tanks were reported to have become available. From the experiences of some regiments, however, recounted earlier in this account, an insufficiency of AFVs still existed when the cavalry regiments of the BEF were embarked for France in September 1939. The Cavalry Brigade in Palestine remained horsed, therefore not requiring AFVs until later.

The delay – No AFVs, not the cavalry's reluctance to give up their horses

It matters little how the figures are calculated, and whether or not the reports are absolutely accurate. There is an overwhelming weight of evidence from these statistics, the cavalry regimental records, and the recorded testimonies of veteran soldiers that conclusively demonstrates that an earlier mechanization of the British cavalry could not have been possible. The reason for this was a lack of AFVs, whether suitable or not, with which to equip them. The delay in mechanizing the cavalry was certainly *not* due to a misplaced love of horses and the reluctance of cavalrymen to part with them.

Duff Cooper reported to parliament that the main reasons for the lack of operational AFVs prior to 1936 were: financial stringency from 1927 to 1936 in which the allotment of funds for tank experiments each year varied from £22,500 to £93,750; the limitation of armaments which Cooper said was 16 tons for tanks, but 20 tons was the proposed limit at the Geneva Disarmament Conference. However, this was never ratified or implemented. It was probably true that the public's concern over the arms trade had limited the work at Vickers creating a dearth of ideas; it certainly would not have encouraged Vickers to accelerate tank development. Cooper also listed a lead time of two-and-a-half years to develop a model, and that British tanks had to operate in many parts of the world (that complicated any specification). These were somewhat spurious arguments considering the age of the existing tanks. Given the political will and the money to do so, there had been plenty of time to develop a satisfactory model, even since the "Sixteen-Tonner"; the Soviets had done so. The widespread development of anti-tank weapons, Cooper assessed, had had a great effect on tank designs. This argument had some merit; anti-tank guns had developed more quickly than tanks and were cheaper to produce. This had caused some hesitation in the minds of Sir Hugh Ellis and the Army Council on the specifications of future AFVs and their value on the battlefield altogether.[96]

94   Ibid.,/1938/122, "Talk with Brigadier G le Q Martel", 28 November 1938.
95   Beale, *Death by Design*, pp.116/117.
96   LHCMA – LH 15/11/6, "The tank Situation October 1936", p.11.

Lieutenant Colonel Aden M Sprot MC 09.11.2014; courtesy of *The Southern Reporter*.

What was quite amazing was that the morale and efficiency of regiments could be maintained under such poor circumstances. The lack of support from the electorate, manifested in the low numbers of recruits, the lack of interest in public school and university cadet forces that would have supplied officers; a confused role in war, or perhaps for a time, no role at all, could have affected morale. The equipment, with which to train and modernize, was minimal and often obsolete, and could have affected efficiency. The feeling the officers and men had had towards their animals mattered not at all when it was time for the horses to go, as Randall with resignation remembered, "Well – what could you do about it, there was nothing, you had to accept that was how things were,"[97] and Lucas explained that because soldiering was a disciplined life "you just got on with it".[98] Given these circumstances, it is a testament to the efficacy of the management of change process, the consistency of a rigorous and appropriate training programme, the organization and quality of the instruction, and the clear and determined leadership to get the job done quickly that British Regular and Household Cavalry regiments were all mechanized by 1942. "Everything worked like clockwork…".[99]

97   Personal interview with Randall (2006); by the author.
98   Personal interview with Lucas (2007); by the author.
99   Personal interview with ffrench Blake (2006); by the author.

Appendix I

British Household and Regular Cavalry – Order of Battle

1918–1922

1st Life Guards
2nd Life Guards
Royal Horse Guards [The Blues]
The 1st (King's) Dragoon Guards
The 2nd (Queen's Bays) Dragoon Guards
The 3rd (Prince of Wales's) Dragoon Guards
The 4th (Royal Irish) Dragoon Guards
The 5th (Princess Charlotte of Wales's) Dragoon Guards
The 6th (Carabiniers) Dragoon Guards
The 7th (Princess Royal's) Dragoon Guards
The 1st (Royal) Dragoons [The Royals]
The 2nd (Royal Scots Greys) Dragoons
The 6th (Inniskilling) Dragoons
The 3rd (King's Own) Hussars
The 4th (Queen's Own) Hussars
The 7th Queen's Own Hussars
The 8th (King's Royal Irish) Hussars
The 9th (Queen's Royal) Lancers
The 10th (Prince of Wales's Own) Hussars
The 11th (Prince Albert's Own) Hussars
The 12th (Prince of Wales's Royal) Lancers
The 13th Hussars
The 14th (King's) Hussars
The 15th (The King's) Hussars
The 16th (The Queen's) Lancers
The 17th (Duke of Cambridge's Own) Lancers
The 18th (Queen Mary's Own) Royal Hussars
The 19th (Queen Alexandra's Own Royal) Hussars

20th Hussars
21st (Empress of India's) Lancers

The 1922 Amalgamations

Army Order 133 1922
By taking two squadrons from the senior regiment and one from the junior regiment, amalgamations of regiments of the Cavalry of the Line became:

The 3rd/6th Dragoon Guards
The 4th/7th Dragoon Guards
The 5th/6th Dragoons
The 13th/18th Hussars
The 14th/20th Hussars
The 15th/19th Hussars
The 16th/5th Lancers
The 17th/20th Lancers

And in 1927 – 1st and 2nd Life Guards formed The Life Guards (1st and 2nd)[1]

There were changes to some regimental titles: the 3rd/6th Dragoon Guards became The 3rd Carabiniers Dragoon Guards, and the 5th/6th Dragoon Guards became the 5th Inniskilling Dragoon Guards;[2] and there was consolidation of regimental badges during the inter-war period in order to maintain traditions and other historical links,[3] but no changes as such occurred to the entity of each regiment until motorization and mechanization. The following regiments, therefore, underwent the process of mechanization. Eventually the regiments were equipped with tanks or armoured cars, carriers and scout-cars either before or during the course of the Second World War:

1st and 2nd Household Cavalry Regiments
The 1st (King's) Dragoon Guards
The 2nd (Queen's Bays) Dragoon Guards
The 3rd Carabiniers (Prince of Wales's Dragoon Guards)

1   White-Spunner, Barney [2006], *Horse Guards* pp.489/490. TNA WO 32/2843 Army Organisation: Cavalry (Code 14(D)): Regiment of Household Cavalry: Reorganisation 1927, 20/Cav/599 minutes 1–31 March – July 1927and 13B; In the interests of economy there was a further consolidation of the Household Cavalry Regiments in 1927–1928.
2   TNA WO 32/3271 Regimental Dress and Badges: Cavalry (Code 43(D)): Dress of the amalgamated Cavalry Regiments 1927 and TNA WO 32/3272 Regimental Dress and Badges: Cavalry (Code 43(D)): Change of titles of amalgamated Cavalry Regiments 1927–1929; minute 64.
3   Ibid., minute 6.

The 4th/7th Dragoon Guards
The 5th Royal Inniskilling Dragoon Guards
The Royal Dragoons (1st Dragoons)
The Royal Scots Greys (2nd Dragoons)
The 3rd (King's Own) Hussars
The 4th (Queen's Own) Hussars
The 7th Queen's Own Hussars
The 8th (King's Royal Irish) Hussars
The 9th (Queen's Royal) Lancers
The 10th (Prince of Wales's Own) Hussars
The 11th (Prince Albert's Own) Hussars
The 12th (Prince of Wales's Royal) Lancers
The 13th/18th Royal Hussars (Queen Mary's Own)
14th/20th King's Hussars
15th/19th The King's Royal Hussars
16th/5th The Queen's Royal Lancers
17th/21st Lancers

Appendix II

British Household and Regular Cavalry – Role, function and organization between the two World Wars

---

The dispositions of units of the British Army, and many of its officers, during the inter-war period reflected the Government's responsibilities to its allies, and when and where the authorities "required the use of troops for the maintenance of law and order".[1] Examples were: the occupation of Turkey and Germany, the security of Great Britain and the British Empire, Dominions and Colonies, and the administration and protection of the mandated states, such as Palestine. In 1919 the Master General of the Ordnance, Lieutenant General Sir W T Furse, wrote that it was already difficult for the army to "keep abreast [of the needs in] almost every corner of the globe".[2] Across the two decades, January 1921, April 1929 and September 1939 are detailed below as significant examples of the size and deployment of army units. January 1921 was the first post-Great War *Army List* detailing the deployment of individual units. The total strength of all British armed services was 438,500,[3] and the army was recorded as 370,000 in late 1920,[4] reduced to 231,062 in 1922.[5] In April 1929, the total strength of all British armed services was 325,600, but the Army was reduced still further to 207,537 in 1931,[6] in response to some reduction in the Army's overseas commitments such as Turkey and Ireland. The occupation of Germany ceased in 1929, and except for the growth of self-determination, principally in India, reflected the more peaceful and stable world political environment. September 1939 was the last

---

1   Oatts, *I Serve – Regimental History of 3rd Carabiniers (Prince of Wales's Dragoon Guards)* p.244.
2   TNA WO 32/5685 Army Organisation: Tanks (Code 14 (G)): Proposals concerning formation of tank expeditionary force and use of tanks in Russia – 1919; minute 14.
3   URL: <http://www.guardian.co.uk/news/datablog/2011/sep/01/military-service-personnel-total> 09.05.2016.
4   Bond, Brian in Chandler, David (ed.) [1994], *The Oxford Illustrated History Of The British Army* p.263.
5   Bond, *British Military Policy Between the Two World Wars*, p.91.
6   Ibid.

Army List detailing the deployment of most units before the Second World War. By then the total strength of all British armed services had grown to 1,068,800[7] with the expectation of and the preparation for war.[8]

United Kingdom Commands

Aldershot Command

January 1921–
General Officer Commanding (GOC) Lieutenant General F R Earl of Cavan with a full complement of staff.

1st Cavalry Brigade – The 3rd, 4th and the 13th Hussars with details of the 17th Lancers and one signal troop of the Royal Engineers. Attached; a brigade of the Royal Horse Artillery (RHA), a Field Squadron of Royal Engineers and an Air Defence brigade of three batteries.

1st Division – three brigades of infantry of between two and four battalions each, Divisional troops included eight batteries of field artillery and a signals company of Royal Engineers.

2nd Division – two infantry brigades of between two and five battalions each together with three brigades of field artillery, a signals company of Royal Engineers, two brigades of garrison artillery and three field companies of Royal Engineers.

April 1929–
GOC – Lieutenant General Sir David Campbell.

The make-up of the Command was similar; 1st Cavalry Brigade consisted of The King's Dragoon Guards, the 11th and the 14th/20th Hussars and a brigade of the RHA of three batteries (A, B and O batteries).

2nd Division had an extra brigade of infantry.

Other Regular troops in the command included the 2nd Battalion Royal Tank Corps, field artillery, the Mechanical Warfare Establishment, Farnborough and "detached War Office" corps troops from the Royal Army Service Corps (RASC), Royal Army

7   URL: <http://www.guardian.co.uk/news/datablog/2011/sep/01/military-service-personnel-total> 09.05.2016.
8   Bond, *British Military Policy Between the Two World Wars*, pp.118 &119.

Medical Corps (RAMC), Royal Army Ordnance Corps (RAOC), Royal Army Veterinary Corps (RAVC) and the Royal Army Pay Corps (RAPC).

September 1939–
GOC Lieutenant General Sir John Dill.

The changes in establishment reflected the preparation for a possible European war with the inclusion of the Army Tank Brigade of three battalions (4th, 7th and 8th) Royal Tank Corps. Divisional troops included a company of Royal Military Police (RMP), eight batteries of anti-tank guns, and a Royal Armoured Corps (RAC) brigade consisting of the King's Dragoon Guards, the 12th Lancers and the 3rd battalion RTR. Also as 1st Division troops, the 13th/18th Hussars and as 2nd Division troops, the 4th/7th Dragoon Guards.

There was in 1939 a vast recruiting organization that came under various commands throughout the United Kingdom.

Eastern Command

January 1921–
GOC General H S Lord Horne.

As well as a full staff, the command included eleven companies RASC, mostly horse transport companies, four companies each of the RAMC and RAOC, three sections of the RAVC and a veterinary hospital at Luton.

Field Troops –
4th Cavalry Brigade – The Royals at Hounslow and the 10th Hussars at Canterbury.
4th Division of two infantry brigades (the 11th and 12th) each of three battalions.

Other troops included four batteries of the Royal Garrison Artillery (RGA), a field company of Royal Engineers and a number of Territorial Divisions and Brigades that included regular officers and men.

London District included three companies each from the RASC (motor transport) and the RAMC. Field troops included the Life Guards, the Royal Horse Guards and N battery RHA, also Territorial Divisions and Brigades.

April 1929–
GOC – General Sir Robert Wigham.

The command included the counties of Essex, Norfolk and Sussex with coastal defences, also London District. London District included depots at Caterham,

Warley, Pirbright, Windsor and Woolwich and the Rainham rifle range, the 4th (Guards) Infantry Brigade, the Life Guards and the Royal Horse Guards, M Battery RHA at St. John's Wood, also various Territorial Divisions and Brigades including the 26th and 27th (London) Air Defence Brigades. Divisional troops included those from the RAOC, the Royal Signals and the Royal Engineers.

The 4th Division had an additional infantry brigade (the 10th) and other regular troops included the 7th Hussars at Colchester, 13th/18th Hussars at Shorncliffe and the 17th/21st Lancers at Hounslow.

September 1939–
GOC Lieutenant General Sir Guy Williams.

The make-up of the command looks generally similar. Divisional troops included the 5th Inniskilling dragoon Guards at Colchester, six batteries of Royal Artillery, three companies Royal Engineers and two companies RASC, also the officer commanding signals.

Other Regular troops in the command were; the 13th/18th Hussars (under Aldershot) but based in Shorncliffe and the 17th/21st Lancers at Colchester and two battalions of infantry.

The Royal Artillery "Fixed Defences" on the south east coast such as Shoeburyness and Brighton came under Eastern Command, also the RASC units including the driving school at Feltham, eleven companies, workshops and depots, a unit of RMP and numbers 44 and 54 Territorial Divisions.

London District was made up of an infantry brigade of three Guards' battalions and other Regular troops; the Household Cavalry, a Guards' battalion, K Battery RHA, three companies of the RASC and one of the RMP, also the Territorial London Division.

Ireland

January 1921–
GOC General Right Honourable Sir C F N Macready.

The command had headquarters in Dublin, The Curragh, Cork, Belfast, Ballincollig and Carrickfergus.

Field troops –
3rd Cavalry Brigade – The Royals at Ballinasloe, the 10th Hussars at Ennis and the 17th Lancers at Galway; the brigade included IV Brigade RHA with two batteries.

1st Division – the 15th Brigade of four battalions and the Londonderry Infantry Brigade on four battalions.

5th Division – three brigades each of two infantry battalions – the Galway, 13th Infantry Brigade at Athlone and 14th Infantry brigade at The Curragh, three brigades of field artillery each of four batteries.

6th Division – of three Infantry Brigades; the 16th (four battalions) at Fermoy, Buttevant, Tipperary and Waterford; the 17th (five battalions) at Cork, Kinsole, Ballincollig and Queenstown, and the 18th (five battalions) at Ennis, Rathkeal, Limmerick and Templemare.

Dublin District –
Two Provisional brigades of infantry each of five battalions, a mobile searchlight group, one battalion of field artillery and the 5th Armoured Car Company.

Numbers 11 and 12 Districts included cavalry and infantry regimental depots and such staff as was needed.

April 1929–
Northern Ireland District of eight infantry battalions was under Northern Command.

September 1939–
Northern Ireland, under Northern Command, included four battalions of infantry, coastal defences and companies and detachments from the following Corps – RASC, RAMC, RAOC and RAPC.

Northern Command

January 1921–
GOC Lieutenant General Sir F I Maxe.

Field troops –
Part of the 4th Division – the 10th Infantry brigade of three battalions.

Other troops included the 6th Inniskilling Dragoons, a Fortress company of the Royal Engineers and number of infantry and cavalry depots and their staff and Territorial Divisions and Brigades.

April 1929–
GOC Sir Cameron D Shute.

Field troops –
The 13th Infantry Brigade, 5th Inniskilling Dragoon Guards (York), a coastal defence division and Territorial Divisions and Brigades.

September 1939–
GOC General Sir William Bartholomew.
Companies, sections and detachments from the following corps; RAMC, RAOC, RAPC AND RAVC.

Field troops –
5th Division of two brigades of infantry and divisional troops from the Royal Engineers, Royal Signals and RASC.

Other troops included the 15th/19th Hussars at York, 7th battalion Royal Tank Corps, four anti-aircraft battalions, two field artillery batteries and the Royal Artillery's fixed defences at northern ports. Also included in the command were 49th (West Riding) and 50th (Northumbria) Territorial Divisions.

Scottish Command

January 1921–
GOC Lieutenant General Sir F J Davies.
A motor transport troop of the RASC, one company from the RAMC and one section from the RAOC.

Field Troops –
The King's Dragoon Guards, three battalions of infantry and two companies of Royal Engineers. In the Highland Area were Royal Artillery depots and in Lowland Area were depots for six cavalry and five infantry regiments. Also in the command were Territorial Divisions and Brigades.

April 1929–
GOC General sir William E Peyton.

Field troops – The Royal Scots Greys.
In both the Highland and Lowland Areas were five infantry battalion depots, Territorial Divisions and Brigades.

September 1939–
GOC General Sir Charles Grant.

The command was made up from; a company from the RAMC, a section from the RAOC, three detachments from the RAPC and one from the RAVC; one battery of field artillery, Royal Artillery fixed defences in Scottish ports, three battalions of infantry together with Territorial Divisions and Brigades including the 51st (Highland) and 52nd (Lowland) Divisions.

Southern Command – this included the vast army training area of Salisbury Plain.

January 1921–
GOC Lieutenant General Sir G M Harper.

Troops from Corps included nine companies, both motor and horse from the RASC, six companies from the RAMC and four section of the RAOC.

Field troops –
2nd Cavalry Brigade – made up of the 4th Dragoon Guards, the 9th Lancers (temporarily serving in Ireland), the King's Dragoon Guards and a signal troop of Royal Engineers.

3rd Division made up of the 7th Infantry Brigade, just details of one battalion and 8th Infantry Brigade, two infantry battalions and details from another.

Divisional troops were three brigades of field artillery of four batteries each and three field companies of Royal Engineers. Other troops were three brigades of various units of the Royal Artillery.

Southern Command also included the Tank Corps Centre; numbers 7, 8, 9 and 10 Armoured Car Companies at Wareham, but bound for India; Number 1 Depot Battalion and a cadre of the 4th Battalion were also at Wareham; 2nd Battalion, a cadre of the 3rd Battalion and the 5th Battalion, less one company were stationed at Wool. Also at Wool were the Head Quarters of the Tank Corps, the workshop and the training battalion.

The command also included Territorial Divisions and Brigades.

April 1929–
GOC Lieutenant General Sir Montgomery Massingberd.

Field troops –
2nd Cavalry Brigade made up of The Bays, the 3rd Dragoon Guards and the 16th/5th Lancers. 3rd Division contained the 7th, 8th and 9th Infantry brigades and divisional troops.

The command included Territorial Divisions and Brigades.

September 1939–
GOC Lieutenant General A F Brooke.
This very much reflected the change in the security situation in Europe.

Field troops –
The Armoured Division:-
1st Light Armoured Brigade (Tidworth) – the King's Dragoon Guards and the 3rd and 4th Hussars.

2nd Light Armoured Brigade (Tidworth) – The Bays, the 9th Lancers and the 10th Hussars.

1st Heavy Armoured Brigade – the 2nd, 3rd and 5th Royal Tank Regiments.

The divisional troops included men from the Royal Signals, six companies from the RASC and one company of RMP.

3rd Division made up of the 8th and 9th Infantry Brigades with divisional troops that included six batteries of Royal Artillery, divisional signals and three companies each from the RASC and the Royal Engineers.

The command also included the Territorial Divisions – 43 (Wessex) and 48 (South Midland) together with their divisional troops.

Western Command

January 1921–
GOC Lieutenant General Sir H de B De Lisle.

Field troops – one battalion of infantry.

Welsh Area – four cavalry and four infantry regiment depots and a company of Royal Engineers.

West Lancashire Area – three infantry battalion depots

East Lancashire Area – Reserve Brigade Royal Field Artillery and six infantry depots.

The command included Territorial Divisions and Brigades.

The Channel Islands:
Guernsey – a company of Royal Engineers, a detail from an infantry battalion and a section of RAOC.

Jersey – one infantry battalion and one section of RAOC

April 1929–
RHA F and J Batteries and one battalion of infantry.
Welsh Area – four infantry regiment depots.
West Lancashire Area – three infantry regiment depots.
East Lancashire Area – six infantry regiment depots.
Also Territorial Divisions and Brigades.
The Channel Islands: an officer commanding – no troops listed

September 1939–
GOC Lieutenant General Sir R H Haining.
Two companies of the RASC
One company of the RAMC
One section of the RAOC
Three detachments of the RAPC
2nd Anti-Aircraft Brigade
One battery of field artillery and the coastal defences of northwest and Welsh ports.

Territorial Divisons:-
38rd (South Welsh) Division
42nd (East Lancs) Division
53rd (Welsh) Division
55th (Welsh) Division
The Channel Islands:
A small staff, no troops.
Anti-Aircraft Command

September 1939
GOC Lieutenant General Sir Fredrick Pile
Five anti-aircraft divisions based at:-
Uxbridge
Hucknall (Nottinghamshire)
Chester
Reading

The Army of The Black Sea (Constantinople and Turkish Police Control)

January 1921–
GOC Lieutenant General Sir C H Harington.

The 28th Division of three infantry brigades.
Divisional troops included the 20th Hussars (bound for Egypt),

A brigade of field artillery of four batteries
Two companies of the Royal Engineers
Two battalions of infantry and a company of the Machine-Gun Corps
Two companies of the RAOC and a detachment of the RAPC.

France and Flanders

January 1921–
Administrative and technical staff dealing with matter such as railways, police and labour.

The Army of The Rhine

January 1921–
GOC Lieutenant General Sir T L N Morland (with a full staff).
British troops in Command –
The 14th Hussars
One brigade of field artillery of four batteries and one brigade of garrison artillery of one battery
A field company of the Royal Engineers
Seven battalions of infantry and a machine-gun company
B Company of the Tank Corps
Three motor transport companies of the RASC
Four companies of the RAOC and a detachment of the RAPC; there was also staffing for the Military Inter-Allied Commissions of Control in Berlin and Austria.

April 1929–
GOC Lieutenant General Sir William Thwaites; also the Office of the Judge Advocate-General.
The 8th Hussars
One section of the 12th Armoured Car Company
1st and 2nd Rhine Brigades each of three infantry battalions

East Indies Command

The Army in India

January 1921–
GOC General H S Lord Rawlinson (with a full staff including branches of the Adjutant General and Quartermaster General, medical, ordnance and military works).
British troops in Command –
Northern Command – no British troops, but British officers are listed.
Lahore District – a battery each of the RHA and the Royal Field Artillery.

Western Command

Sid-Rajputana District – one infantry battalion, a brigade of three batteries of field artillery and one company of garrison artillery.
Southern Command
Bombay District – one infantry battalion and two companies of garrison artillery.
Madras District – two battalions of infantry and a company of garrison artillery.

April 1929–
GOC Field Marshal Sir William Birdwood.
Northern Command
Peshawar District
The 15th/19th Hussars
Number 1 Armoured Car Company, Royal Tank Corps (RTC)
Units of the Royal Artillery and three infantry battalions.
Kohat District
Kohat Brigade – 12th Light Battalion, Royal Artillery.
Rawalpindi District
XXII field Brigade, Royal Artillery, and three infantry battalions.
Lahore District
The 4th/7th Dragoon Guards
N Battery, the RHA
XII Battery, the Royal Field Artillery
Number 7 Armoured Car Company, RTC, and six infantry battalions.
Waziristan District
Two light batteries of artillery and an infantry battalion.

Western Command

Baluchistan District – in two Independent Brigade areas;
Zhob Area in Loralai
Number 10 Armoured Car Company, RTC, I Royal Artillery Brigade of four light batteries, and two infantry battalions.
Sind Area in Karachi
A detachment I Brigade, Royal Artillery, a battery of heavy artillery and a battalion of infantry.

Eastern Command

Meerut District
The 4th Hussars
I Field Brigade, Royal Artillery of three batteries,

XXVII Field Brigade, Royal Artillery of three batteries, and four battalions of infantry.
Lucknow District
The 3rd Hussars
Number 9 Armoured Car Company, RTC
Four batteries of artillery and five infantry battalions.
Delhi Independent Brigade Area
Number 11 Armoured Car Company, RTC
Three batteries of medium artillery and two infantry battalions.
Presidency and Assam District
Three infantry battalions.

Southern Command
Mhow District
Four batteries of artillery and two infantry battalions.
Deccan District
Four batteries of artillery, five infantry battalions and a company of the Royal Corps of Signals
The 9th Lancers
Poona Independent Brigade Area
Number 8 Armoured Car Company, RTC
One battery of artillery and two infantry battalions.
Bombay District
Two batteries of artillery an infantry battalion, and Number 31 Company, RAMC.
Madras District
Southern Brigade Area
Number 6 Armoured Car Company, RTC
Three batteries of artillery and three infantry battalions.

Burma – Independent District
Rangoon Area
A Royal artillery headquarters and two infantry battalions.

September 1939
GOC General Sir Robert Cassels

Northern Command
Peshawar District
The 16th/5th Lancers,
Numbers 1, 7 and 11 Light Tank Companies of the RTC,
Three artillery and one anti-aircraft batteries, and two infantry battalions.
Rawalpindi District
Three artillery batteries and two infantry battalions.

Lahore District
The 3rd Dragoon Guards,
Three artillery batteries, six infantry battalions and a company of the Royal Engineers.
Waziristan
An infantry battalion.

Eastern Command
Meerut District
Six artillery batteries and two infantry battalions.
Lucknow District
Four artillery batteries and five infantry battalions
Delhi District
Two artillery batteries and two infantry battalions.
The Presidency and Assam District
Three infantry battalions.

Southern Command
Deccan District
The 14th/20th Hussars,
One signals company, two artillery batteries and two infantry battalions.
Poona District
One artillery battery and two infantry battalions.

Bombay

Seven artillery batteries, eight battalions of infantry and one company of the RAMC.
Madras (Bangalore)
Three infantry battalions
Western District (Quetta)
One artillery battery and two infantry battalions.

Burma

One artillery battery and two infantry battalions.

Dominions, Colonies and Protectorates

January 1921
West Africa – British troops in Sierra Leone.
One company of garrison artillery, a company of the Royal Engineers.

April 1929
One company of garrison artillery, a company of the Royal Engineers. And detachments from the RAOC and RAPC.

September 1939
One artillery battery, a company of the Royal engineers and detachment from the RAMC, the RASC and the RAPC.

Bermuda

January 1921
A company of both the Royal Engineers and the RAMC and a detachment of infantry.

April 1929
Detacments from the Royal Engineers, infantry, RAPC a signals section and Number 25 Company RAMC.

September 1939
A battalion of infantry, a company of the RAMC and detachments from the Royal Engineers, the RASC, the RAOC and the RAPC.

Ceylon

January 1921
A company of the Royal Engineers.

April 1929
Two batteries of artillery, a company of Royal engineers, a signals section and detachments from the RASC, the RAMC, the RAPC and the RAOC.

China – Hong Kong

January 1921
A company of the Royal Engineers, two companies of the RAMC and an infantry battalion.

April 1929
South China – Hong Kong
Seven artillery batteries, a company of Royal engineers, three battalions of infantry, a signals section Number 27 Company RAMC and detachments from the RASC, the RAPC and the RAOC.

September 1939
Six artillery batteries for coastal defence and anti-aircraft and four artillery mountain and field batteries. Two companies of Royal Engineers and one company from each of the Royal Corps of Signals, the RASC, RMP and the RAMC; one section from the RAPC and a detachment of the RAVC.

North China – Shanghai –

January 1921
Two battalions of infantry, Number 12 (Motor Company) and supply depot RASC. Number 7 General Hospital and Number 12 Field Ambulance (less one company) RAMC.
RAOC Advance Depot and Mobile Workshop, a signals section and detachments from the Royal Engineers, the Army Postal Service, the RAPC and the RMP.
Tientsin Area –
Two infantry battalions, a signals section and detachments of the Royal Engineers, the RASC, the RAMC and the RAPC.

September 1939
Shanghai Area
Two infantry battalions, sections of the RMP and the Royal Corps of Signals and detachments for each of the RASC, the RAMC, the RAOC and the RAPC.
Tientsin Area
A battalion of infantry, a signal section and detachments form each of the Royal Engineers, the RASC, the RAMC, the RAOC and the RAPC.

Cyprus

April 1929
One infantry Company.

September 1939
One infantry Company.

Aden

April 1929
Two batteries of artillery and units of the Royal Engineers and Royal Corps of Signals.

Egypt and Palestine

January 1921
GOC Lieutenant General Sir W N Congreve VC with a full staff.

British troops in Command –
The 4th Cavalry Division – the 5th Dragoon Guards and the Royal Scots Greys.
The 3rd (Lahore) Division – three battalions of infantry and a brigade of four batteries of field artillery.
The 10th (Irish) Division) – the 11th Hussars, a brigade of the RHA and two battalions of infantry.
Cairo Brigade – three battalions of infantry.
Khartoum – one battalion of infantry.

April 1929
GOC Lieutenant General Sir E Peter Strickland
The Cavalry Brigade – The Royals, the 10th Hussars and the 12th Lancers.
The Canal Brigade – three infantry battalions
The Cairo Brigade – three infantry battalions
Other British troops –
Three batteries of the RHA and three batteries of the Light Royal Artillery,
Two field companies each of the Royal Engineers and Royal Corps of Signals, four Motor Transport Companies and one Supply Company of the RASC. A company each from the RAMC and the RAOC, Number 20 Veterinary Hospital RAVC and detachment of the RAPC.
From the RTC, one Section of the 3rd Battalion, Numbers 3 and 5 Armoured Car Companies.

September 1939
GOC Lieutenant General H M Wilson.
The Armoured Division
The Light Armoured Brigade
The 7th, 8th and the 11th Hussars.
The Canal Brigade – three infantry battalions
The Cairo Brigade – three infantry battalions
The (Armednagar) Infantry Brigade
One British infantry battalion and two Indian infantry battalions.
18th Infantry Brigade of three infantry battalions.

Other British troops in the Command:-
Numbers 1 and 6 Battalions the RTC, six artillery batteries, five companies of the Royal Engineers, "Egypt" signals, ten companies RASC, Number 11 General Hospital, three field ambulances and two hygiene sections of the RAMC, a section and a workshop of the RAOC, three companies of RMP and a detachment from each of the RAPC and the RAVC.

Palestine and Trans Jordan

September 1939
GOC Lieutenant General M G H Barker – with a full staff of British and Indian Army officers.
The 7th Division
British troops included the 19th Infantry Brigade of two battalions.
Divisional troops included – The Greys
One company of the Royal Engineers and two companies of the RASC.
The 8th Division
British troops included the 14th Infantry Brigade of three battalions and the 16th Infantry Brigade of four battalions.
Divisional troops included – The Royals
One company of the Royal Engineers, two companies of the RASC and an artillery detachment.
Other British troops in the Command –
An artillery battery, a company from each of the Royal Engineers and the Royal Corps of Signals and the RMP, three infantry battalions, a RAMC Base General Hospital and a Field Ambulance, and a mobile section of the RAVC.

Sudan

April 1921
Two infantry battalions.

September 1939
Two infantry battalions and detachments of the RAPC, the RAMC and the RASC.
Two infantry battalions

Falkland Islands

January 1921
A battalion of infantry, two companies of the Royal Engineers and a company of the RAMC.

Jamaica

January 1921
A battalion of infantry, one company each of the Royal Engineers and RAMC.

April 1921
A cadre of heavy artillery, a company from each of the Royal Engineers and the RAMC, an infantry battalion, a signals section and a detachment from the RAPC.

Malta

January 1921
Two battalions of infantry, two companies of the Royal Engineers and a company of the RAMC.

April 1921
Two batteries of artillery, a company each of the Royal Engineers, the RASC and the RAMC, a signals section and a detachment of the RAPC.

September 1939
The Malta Infantry Brigade of four battalions.
Other troops –
An anti-aircraft regiment, three companies of the Royal Engineers, the RASC, and the RAMC and detachments from each of the RMP and the RAOC.

Mauritius

January 1921
One company of the Royal Engineers.

April 1921
One company of the Royal Engineers, an artillery battery, a signals section and a detachment of the RAPC.

September 1939
An artillery battery, one company of the Royal Engineers, a signals section and detachments of the RAPC, the RAMC and the RASC.

Gibraltar

April 1921
Three artillery batteries, a battalion of infantry, a company from each of the Royal Engineers, the RASC, and the RAMC, a signal company and a detachment of the RAPC.

September 1939
Coastal and anti-aircraft batteries, three infantry battalions, three companies of the Royal Engineers, a company form each of the RASC, the RAMC and the RAOC, sections from each of the Royal Corps of Signals and RMP and detachments from the RAPC and the RAVC.

Iraq

April 1921
A signals section.

Jamaica

September 1939
An artillery battery, infantry battalion, a company of each of the Royal Engineers and the RAMC, a signals section and detachments of the RASC, the RAOC and the RAPC.

Malaya

September 1939
GOC Major General L V Bond
Changi – Five artillery batteries.
Singapore – Eight batteries of anti-aircraft and coastal defence, six companies of the Royal Engineers and one company from each of the Royal Corps of Signals and the RAMC together with one section from each of the RAOC, the RMP and the RAPC. The Malay Infantry Brigade of three British battalions plus another in Taiping, and The 12th (Secunderabad) Infantry Brigade of one British battalion and three Indian Army Battalions.

January 1921
British officers were listed as serving in: New Zealand, Saint Helena, The Seychelles and with the Egyptian Army.

April 1921
British officers were listed as serving in: The Leeward Island, Iraq, Canada, Australia, The Union of South Africa, Newfoundland, New Zealand, Malaya and Brunei

The locations, or stations, of cavalry regiments from 1920–1939 Location and Station of British Household and Regular cavalry regiments 1920–1922

	1920	1921	1922
The 1st Life Guards	H London	H London	H London
The 2nd Life Guards	H Windsor	H Pirbright	H London
The Royal Horse Guards [The Blues]	H London	H Windsor	H Windsor
The 1st (King's) Dragoon Guards	Mesopotamia	H Edinburgh	H Edinburgh
The 2nd (Queen's Bays) Dragoon Guards	Palestine	I Bangalore	I Bangalore
The 4th (Royal Irish) Dragoon Guards	H Tidworth	H Tidworth	I Secunderabad
The 5th (Princess Charlotte of Wales's) Dragoon Guards	H Colchester	Palestine	Palestine
The 6th (Carabiniers) Dragoon Guards	Ireland Curragh	Ireland Curragh	H Aldershot
The 7th (Princess Royal's) Dragoon Guards	Mesopotamia	Egypt	H Aldershot
The 1st (Royal) Dragoons [The Royals]	H Hounslow	Ireland Ballinasloe (temporary)	H Hounslow
The 2nd (Royal Scots Greys) Dragoons	H Edinburgh	Palestine	Palestine
The 3rd (King's Own) Hussars	H Aldershot	H Aldershot	Constantinople
The 4th (Queen's Own) Hussars	H Aldershot	H Aldershot	I Muttra
The 5th (Royal Irish) Lancers	I Risalpur	I Risalpur	Disbanded
The 6th (Inniskilling) Dragoons		H York	H York
The 7th Queen's Own Hussars	H York	I Mhow	I Mhow
The 8th (King's Royal Irish) Hussars	I Lucknow	Mesopotamia	Egypt
The 9th (Queen's Royal) Lancers	H Tidworth	H Longford (temporary)	Egypt
The 10th (Prince of Wales's Own) Hussars	H Canterbury	Ireland Hare park – Curragh	H Canterbury
The 11th (Prince Albert's Own) Hussars	Egypt	Egypt	India Meerut
The 12th (Prince of Wales's Royal) Lancers	Ireland Curragh	Ireland Curragh Ccmp	H Tidworth

	1920	1921	1922
The 13th Hussars	H Aldershot	H Aldershot	H Aldeshot
The 14th (King's) Hussars	H Tidworth	Rhine	Rhine
The 15th (The King's) Hussars	Ireland Kilkenny for Dublin	Ireland Dublin	H Tidworth
The 18th (Queen Mary's Own) Royal Hussars	I Secunderabad	I Secunderabad	I Risalpur
The 19th (Queen Alexandra's Own Royal) Hussars	I Muttra	I Muttra	Disbanded
The 20th Hussars	Palestine	The Black Sea	Disbanded
The 21st (Empress of India's) Lancers	I Meerut	I Meerut	Disbanded

Location and Station of British Household and Regular cavalry regiments 1923–1928

	1923	1924	1925	1926	1927	1928
1st and 2nd Life Guards [Amalgamated 1927]	H London & Windsor	H London & Windsor	H London	H London	H Windsor	H Windsor for London
The Royal Horse Guards [The Blues]	H Windsor for London	H London	H Windsor	H Windsor	H London	H London & Windsor
The 1st (King's) Dragoon Guards	H Edinburgh	Rhine	Rhine	Rhine	H Aldershot	H Aldershot
The 2nd (Queen's Bays) Dragoon Guards	I Bangalore	I Sialkot	I Sialkot	I Sialkot	H Colchester	H Colchester
3rd/6th later 3rd Carabiniers Dragoon Guards	I Sialkot	H Colchester	H Colchester	H Colchester	H Tidworth	H Tidworth
The 4th/7th Dragoon Guards	I Secund-erabad	I Secund-erabad	I Secund-erabad	I Secund-erabad	I Sialkot	I Sialkot
The 1st (Royal) Dragoons [The Royals]	H Aldershot	H Aldershot	H Aldershot	H Aldershot	H Hounslow for Egypt	Egypt
The 2nd (Royal Scots Greys) Dragoons	I Risalpur	I Risalpur	I Meerut	I Meerut	I Meerut for Edinburgh	H Edinburgh
The 3rd (King's Own) Hussars	Constan-tinople	Egypt	Egypt	Egypt	Egypt for Lucknow	I Lucknow
The 4th (Queen's Own) Hussars	I Muttra	I Lucknow	I Lucknow	I Lucknow	I Lucknow for Meerut	I Meerut

	1923	1924	1925	1926	1927	1928
The 5th/6th later The 5th Inniskilling Dragoon Guards	Egypt	I Bangalore	I Bangalore	I Risalpur	I Risalpur	I Risalpur
The 7th Queen's Own Hussars	I Mhow	H Edinburgh	H Edinburgh for Tidworth	H Tidworth	H Tidworth	H Tidworth
The 8th (King's Royal Irish) Hussars	Egypt	H York	H York	H York	Rhine	Rhine
The 9th (Queen's Royal) Lancers	Egypt	Palestine	Palestine for Egypt	Egypt	I Secund-erabad	I Bolarum for Wellington
The 10th (Prince of Wales's Own) Hussars	H Aldershot	H Aldershot	H Aldershot	H Aldershot	H Aldershot for Hounslow	H Hounslow
The 11th (Prince Albert's Own) Hussars	I Meerut	I Meerut	I Meerut	I Risalpur for Shorncliffe	H Shorn-cliffe for Aldershot	H Aldershot
The 12th (Prince of Wales's Royal) Lancers	H Tidworth	H Tidworth	H Tidworth for Egypt	H Hounslow	Egypt	Egypt
The 13th/18th later (Queen Mary's Own) Hussars	H Aldershot	H Aldershot	H Aldershot for Edinburgh	H Edinburgh	H Edin-burgh for Shorncliffe	H Shorncliffe
The 14th/20th later (King's) Hussars	Rhine	H Tidworth	H Tidworth	H Tidworth	H York	H York
The 15th/19th later (The King's) Hussars	H Tidworth	Egypt	Egypt for Palestine	Egypt	Egypt	Egypt
The 16th/5th Lancers	I Lucknow	Egypt	Egypt for Tidworth	H Tidworth	H Tidworth	H Tidworth
The 17th/21st Lancers	H Tidworth	H Tidworth	H Tidworth for Aldershot	H Aldershot	H Aldershot	H Aldershot

Location and Station of British Household and Regular cavalry regiments 1929–1935

	1929	1930	1931	1932	1933	1934	1935
1st and 2nd Life Guards	H London	H London	H Windsor	H Windsor	H London for Windsor	H Windsor	H London for Windsor
The Royal Horse Guards [The Blues]	H Windsor	H Windsor	H London	H London	H Windsor for London	H London	H Windsor for London
The 1st (King's) Dragoon Guards	H Tidworth	H Tidworth	H Tidworth	H Hounslow	Egypt	Egypt	Egypt For Secund-erabad
The 2nd (Queen's Bays) Dragoon Guards	H Tidworth	H Tidworth	H Tidworth	H Shorncliffe	H Shorn-cliffe for Aldershot	H Aldershot	H Aldershot
3rd/6th later 3rd Carabiniers Dragoon Guards	H Canterbury	H Canter-bury	H Colchester	H Colchester	H Aldershot	H Aldershot	H Aldershot for Hounslow
The 4th/7th Dragoon Guards	I Sialkot for Shorncliffe	H Shorncliffe	H Shorncliffe	H Tidworth	H Tidworth	H Tidworth	H Tidworth for Edinburgh
The 1st (Royal) Dragoons [The Royals]	Egypt For Secund-erabad	I Bolarum	I Bolarum	I Bolarum	I Meerut	I Meerut	I Meerut for Shorncliffe
The 2nd (Royal Scots Greys) Dragoons	H Edinburgh for Tidworth	H Tidworth	H Tidworth	H Tidworth	H Tidworth for Edinburgh	H Edinburgh	H Edinburgh for Aldershot
The 3rd (King's Own) Hussars	I Lucknow	I Lucknow	I Lucknow	I Lucknow	H York	H York for Tidworth	H Tidworth
The 4th (Queen's Own) Hussars	I Meerut	I Meerut	H York	H York	H Colchester	H Colchester for Aldershot	H Aldershot
The 5th/6th later The 5th Inniskilling Dragoon Guards	H York	H York	H Aldershot	H Aldershot	H Aldershot	H Aldershot For Colchester	H Colchester

	1929	1930	1931	1932	1933	1934	1935
The 7th Queen's Own Hussars	H Colchester	H Colchester	H Aldershot	H Aldershot	H Aldershot for Hounslow	H Hounslow	1935 Hounslow for Egypt
The 8th (King's Royal Irish) Hussars	Rhine for Aldershot	H Aldershot	H Aldershot	H Aldershot	H Hounslow for Egypt	Egypt	Egypt
The 9th (Queen's Royal) Lancers	I Bolarum for Sialkot	I Sialkot	I Sialkot	H Edinburgh	H Edinburgh for Tidworth	H Tidworth	H Tidworth
The 10th (Prince of Wales's Own) Hussars	Egypt	Egypt	I Meerut	I Meerut	I Lucknow	I Lucknow	I Lucknow
The 11th (Prince Albert's Own) Hussars	H Aldershot	H Aldershot	H Tidworth	H Tidworth	H Tidworth	H Tidworth for Edinburgh	H Edinburgh
The 12th (Prince of Wales's Royal) Lancers	Egypt	Egypt	Egypt	Egypt	Egypt	Egypt for Tidworth	H Tidworth
The 13th/18th later (Queen Mary's Own) Hussars	En-route to Egypt	Egypt	Egypt	I Sialkot	I Sialkot	I Sialkot	I Sialkot
The 14th/20th later (King's) Hussars	H Aldershot	H Aldershot	H Hounslow	Egypt	Egypt For Risalpur	I Risalpur	I Risalpur
The 15th/19th later (The King's) Hussars	I Risalpur	I Risalpur	I Risalpur	I Risalpur	I Risalpur for Shorncliffe	H Shorncliffe	H Shorncliffe for Tidworth
The 16th/5th Lancers	H Tidworth for Edinburgh	H Edinburgh	H Edinburgh	H Tidworth	H Tidworth	H Tidworth for York	H York
The 17th/21st Lancers	H Hounslow	H Hounslow	Egypt	Egypt	I Bolarum	I Bolarum	I Bolarum for Meerut

Location and Station of British Household and Regular cavalry regiments 1936–1939

	1936	1937	1938	1939
1st and 2nd Life Guards	H Windsor	H London	H Windsor	H London
The Royal Horse Guards [The Blues]	H London	H Windsor	H London	H Windsor
The 1st (King's) Dragoon Guards	I Secunderabad	I Secunderabad	H Aldershot	H Tidworth 1st Light Armoured Brigade
The 2nd (Queen's Bays) Dragoon Guards	H Aldershot	H Aldershot	H Tidworth	H Tidworth 1st Light Armoured Brigade
3rd/6th later 3rd Carabiniers Dragoon Guards	H Hounslow	I Sialkot	I Sialkot	H Aldershot
The 4th/7th Dragoon Guards	H Edinburgh	H Edinburgh	H Edinburgh	France
The 1st (Royal) Dragoons [The Royals]	Egypt	H Shorncliffe	H Shorncliffe	Palestine
The 2nd (Royal Scots Greys) Dragoons	H Aldershot	H Aldershot	H Hounslow	Palestine
The 3rd (King's Own) Hussars	H Tidworth	H Tidworth	H Aldershot	H Tidworth – 1st Light Armoured Brigade
The 4th (Queen's Own) Hussars	H Aldershot	H Aldershot	H Aldershot	H Tidworth 1st Light Armoured Brigade
The 5th/6th later The 5th Inniskilling Dragoon Guards	H Colchester	H Colchester	H Colchester	H Colchester
The 7th Queen's Own Hussars	Egypt	Egypt	Egypt	Egypt
The 8th (King's Royal Irish) Hussars	Egypt	Egypt	Egypt	Egypt
The 9th (Queen's Royal) Lancers	H Tidworth	H Tidworth	H Tidworth	H Tidworth 1st Light Armoured Brigade
The 10th (Prince of Wales's Own) Hussars	I Lucknow	H Tidworth	H Tidworth	H Tidworth 2nd Light Armoured Brigade
The 11th (Prince Albert's Own) Hussars	Egypt	Egypt	Egypt	Egypt

	1936	1937	1938	1939
The 12th (Prince of Wales's Royal) Lancers	H Tidworth	H Tidworth	H Tidworth	H Tidworth 2nd Light Armoured Brigade
The 13th/18th later (Queen Mary's Own) Hussars	I Sialkot	I Risalpur	I Risalpur	H Shorncliffe
The 14th/20th later (King's) Hussars	I Risalpur	I Lucknow	I Lucknow	I Bolarum
The 15th/19th later (The King's) Hussars	H Tidworth	H York	H York	H York
The 16th/5th Lancers	H York	H Hounslow	I Secunderabad	I Peshawar
The 17th/21st Lancers	I Meerut	I Meerut	I Meerut	H Colchester

Source – *The Army List* – As a state of war existed before 1920 and after 1939, detailed locations were not published.

Appendix III

Biographies[1]

Atlee, Clement Richard, first Earl Atlee (1883–1967) was educated at Haileybury College and University College Oxford. Lawyer, lecturer and politician. He was Manager of Haileybury House Boys' Club in Stepney for 14 years, where his east London experience converted him to socialism and he became secretary for the Stepney Independent Labour Party. He served in the Great War in Gallipoli and Mesopotamia where he was wounded. By 1917 he was a Major in the Tank Corps. Atlee became Mayor of Stepney in 1919, Member of Parliament in 1922, and became Principal Parliamentary Secretary for Ramsay MacDonald and Undersecretary for War in the first Labour Government. In 1930 he was Chancellor of Duchy of Lancaster and in 1931 Postmaster General; he did not serve in the National Government. Atlee became deputy leader of the Labour Party under Lansbury, and the leader in 1935. He served in the War Cabinet from 1940 and as Churchill's deputy from 1942. He was Prime Minister from 1945–1951.

Baldwin, Stanley, First Earl of Bewdley (1867–1947) was educated at Harrow and Trinity College Cambridge. He joined the family iron and steel business, becoming Managing Director in 1902, and remained in post until resigning to take up ministerial office in 1917. He was elected to the Commons unopposed in his late father's seat in 1908. He was Financial Secretary in 1919, Board of Trade 1921, Chancellor of The Exchequer 1922, Prime Minister 1923–1924 and 1924–1929; Leader of The Opposition 1929–1931, Lord President of The Council 1931–1935, Prime Minister again 1935–1937, when he resigned and accepted a peerage.

Belisha, Isaac Leslie Hore (1893–1957) was educated at Clifton College, Heidelberg, the Sorbonne, and St John's College Oxford. He was commissioned into the Army Service Corps and saw action during the Great War in France, Salonika, Cyprus and

---

1   Summarized from various sources, but principally from the Oxford Dictionary of National Biography; URL: <http:// www. Oxforddnb.com> 02.12.2012.

Egypt. He attained the rank of Major, but was invalided home in 1918. Admitted to the Inner Temple in 1922, he was elected Member of Parliament in 1923 and served at the Board of Trade, Financial Secretary to the Treasury, 1932, Minister of Transport, 1934, Cabinet, 1936 and Secretary of State for War in 1937.

Birch, General Sir James Fredrick Noel (Curly), (1865–1939) was educated at Giggleswick School, Marlborough College and the Royal Military Academy, Woolwich. He was commissioned into the Royal Horse Artillery in 1885. He served with the Ashanti Expedition, and later in the Boer War. From 1905–1907 he commanded the Riding Establishment at Woolwich, and published two books on horse riding. Birch served in France throughout the Great War and became Haig's artillery advisor. He was promoted Lieutenant General in 1919 and later served as Director of Remounts at the War Office, and Director General of the Territorial Army. He was promoted General in 1926 and was Master General of the Ordnance until 1927 when he retired from the army to become a director of Vickers. Birch was married to Florence Hyacynth Chetwode, sister of Philip Chetwode – later Field Marshal Sir Philip Chetwode, 7th Baronet.

Broad, Charles Noel Frank (1882–1976) was educated at Wellington College, Berkshire, and Pembroke College, Cambridge. He served as a Private in the militia during the South African War, and was commissioned into the Royal Artillery in 1905. After passing Staff College, Broad served as a Brigade Major in France from the summer of 1915, the year he married Lillian Mary Mackintosh. He was awarded the DSO in 1917. After the war he became an artillery instructor at the Staff College and transferred to the Royal Tank Corps in 1923 where he continued to instruct gunnery, becoming a chief instructor at the Tank Corps Central School in 1925. Board was the author of the "purple primer" – *Mechanized and Armoured Formations* – in 1929 and later, as a brigadier, commanded the experimental mechanized force (later the armoured force) in the Salisbury Plain exercises.

In 1939, Broad first led the Aldershot Command and later, as a Lieutenant General, commanded the Eastern Army in India. He was appointed CB in 1938 and KCB in 1941; he retired in 1942, but continued as colonel-commandant of the RTC until 1948.

Chetwode, Sir Philip Walhouse, 1st Baron Chetwode, 7th Baronet, GCB, OM, GCSI, KCMG, DSO (1869–1950) was educated at Eton and commissioned into the 3rd Battalion the Oxfordshire Light Infantry Militia. He entered the Regular Army November 1889 as a Second Lieutenant in the 19th Hussars. Chetwode became a protégé of his commanding officer Lieutenant Colonel, later Field Marshal Sir J P D French; he served in India and saw action in South Africa where he was twice Mentioned in Despatches and awarded a DSO. Later he spent time on the Staff at Aldershot and then became Commanding Officer of the 19th Hussars from 1908 until 1911 when he was transferred, as Colonel, to a newly formed mounted Territorial Unit. He commanded the 5th Cavalry Brigade in August 1914, and saw action on the Western Front until November 1916 when he was given command of the Desert Mounted Corps in Palestine, and played a major role under Sir Edmund Allenby. He was wounded, and eight times mentioned in Despatches. Chetwode became a Lieutenant General 1919, served at the War Office, as GOC Aldershot, Commander-in-Chief India, and was appointed Field Marshal 1933. He married in 1899 into the Stapleton-Cotton family – a famous cavalry family – later his daughter married the poet John (later Sir John) Betjeman.

Churchill, Sir Winston Leonard Spencer (1874–1965) was educated at Harrow and Sandhurst, being commissioned 20.02.1894 into the 4th Queen's Own Hussars. He served in India, Sudan and South Africa and was also a journalist and author. Elected Member of Parliament October 1900, he served at the Board of Trade 1908 and as First Lord of the Admiralty 1911. He left office and served with the British Army in France November 1915 to May 1916, leaving to return to government as Minister of Munitions in 1917, and Chancellor of Exchequer 1924. Out of office for a time, he returned to The Admiralty in the autumn of 1939 and was Prime Minister 1940–1945 and 1951–1955.

Fisher, Sir Norman Fenwick Warren (1879–1948) was educated at Winchester College and Hertford College, Oxford. He became a civil servant. Fisher served on the Board of Inland Revenue in 1903 where he worked his way up to become Chairman in 1918. He became Permanent Secretary to the Treasury 1919, and the first ever Head of the Civil Service.

Fuller, John Frederick Charles (1878–1966) was educated at Malvern College and the Royal Military Academy, Sandhurst. He was commissioned in 1899 into the Oxfordshire Light Infantry and served in the South African War (1899–1902). He served as a Staff Officer in the Great War. After a regimental administrative post, he was Chief Instructor at the Camberley Staff College (1923–1926) and then Military Assistant to the CIGS. Fuller retired in 1933 and devoted his time to writing and speaking on military matters. He is popularly considered a military theorist, historian and pioneer, certainly an advocate, of armoured warfare in which he collaborated with Basil Liddell Hart.

Haig, Douglas, first Earl Haig (1861–1928) was educated at Clifton College, Brasenose College, Oxford, and Sandhurst, and was Commissioned in 1885 into the 7th Hussars. He served in India, and was allowed to attend Staff College by nomination 1896. Haig served in Sudan and as a Staff Officer in South Africa. He was Corps Commander in 1914, Army Commander 1915, and Commander in Chief BEF from late 1915 until November 1918.

Hankey, Maurice Pascal Alers, 1st Baron Hankey (1877–1963) was educated privately and then at Rugby School and Trinity College, Cambridge. He passed out "first" from the Royal Naval College being awarded the Sword of Honour and was commissioned into the Royal Marine Artillery in 1897. He served on HMS Ramillies doing intelligence work and came to the notice of Admiral Sir John Fisher. Hankey joined the Whitehall staff in 1902 where he remained for his entire career except for another brief spell at sea in 1907, again as an intelligence officer. He joined the Admiralty Committee of Imperial Defence and, in various roles and positions, remained part of the committee for over thirty years. Hankey was Secretary to the Committee of Imperial Defence from 1912–1938 during which time his administrative duties expanded to include the War Cabinet and the Privy Council. He was created a peer in 1939 and returned from retirement to serve in Chamberlain's War Cabinet and chaired the Scientific Committee. He retired in 1952. He was awarded many honours including KCB, GMCG and GCVO.

Henderson, Arthur (1862–1935) was an Iron-moulder, trade unionist and politician. He was a committed Christian and had first been a Liberal supporter, moving to Labour with his trades union. He was elected Member of Parliament 1903 and served as Labour Party Treasurer and Chairman. He was a member of the Union of Democratic Control and became a Cabinet member and Chief Whip in 1915. His son was killed on the Somme in 1916. Henderson chaired many boards and advisory committees. Henderson was vehemently opposed to communism, and, with Lord Robert Cecil, a great supporter of the League of Nations. He became Home Secretary in the first Labour Government in 1924, and Foreign Secretary in 1929. He was elected Labour Leader in 1931 after MacDonald's departure; he lost his seat, but continued as Leader (with George Lansbury) for a short time. Henderson was passionately interested in world peace and was nominated to open the Geneva Disarmament Conference in 1932; he presided over it until 1935 and died shortly afterwards. He had been awarded the Nobel Peace Prize in 1934.

Hobart, Percy Cleghorn Stanley (1885–1957) was educated at Clifton College and the Royal Military Academy, Woolwich; he was commissioned into the Royal Engineers in 1907, and was posted to an Indian Army engineer regiment. Hobart enjoyed equestrian sport and was a great lover of poetry. He served in France from 1915 and was awarded the MC. From 1916 he served as a staff officer in aerial reconnaissance in Mesopotamia, was wounded and was awarded the DSO. After recovering he served with the Egyptian Expeditionary Force. He was appointed OBE in 1919, and the same year he passed through Staff College. Hobart joined the RTC in 1923. He served in various appointments including as an instructor at the staff college at Quetta. His "prickly" personality and impropriety in his personal life did not endear him to some of his superiors, he was, however, supported by CIGS Montgomery-Massingberd. He became deputy director of staff duties (AFVs) in 1937 and, later, as Major General, the director of military training. In 1938 Hobart was appointed to command the Mobile Division in Egypt, but after disagreements, both professional and personal, with his superiors he was sacked.

Hobart served as a corporal in the Home Guard, but was then appointed to command the 11th and then 79th Armoured Divisions to develop special armoured equipment for D Day, which he did with great success. He was appointed CB in 1939 and KBE in 1943, retiring in 1946, but continued as Colonel Commandant of the RTR until 1951. His sister, Elizabeth (Betty), married Field Marshal Lord Montgomery.

Hogg, Douglas McGarel 1st Viscount Hailsham, (1872–1950) was educated at Eton College and vocationally in the West Indies. He served in the Boer War and was called to the bar in 1902. He became a Conservative politician and served in government as Attorney General, Minister of War (from 5 November 1931 until 7 June 1935), when he became Leader of the House of Lords and Lord Chancellor.

Jones, Dr Thomas, CH (1870–1955) was born in Rhymney, Monmouthshire, and until aged 13, when he started work, he attended the local grammar school. After saving money and with encouragement from family and management, he later reached the University of Wales in 1895, followed by the University of Glasgow. Until 1917 Jones was the Secretary to the Welsh National Health Insurance Commission and was an influential academic. He was said to have been one of the architects of Lloyd George's "bid for supreme power" in 1916. Jones joined the War Cabinet Secretariat and later, as secretary to Sir Maurice Hankey, became the secretary of the Committee of Imperial Defence. Jones was an assistant secretary and then Deputy Secretary to the Cabinet and for the next fourteen years served four Prime Ministers.

Lansbury, George (1859–1940) Leader of the Labour Party, was born in Suffolk and brought up in east London. He had an elementary education and originally worked as a labourer, but later took over his father-in-law's timber business. Originally he was a liberal, but later he converted to socialism and became a local councillor; he was elected Member of Parliament in 1910. He founded the *Daily Herald* in 1912 and was its editor until 1922. Lansbury was appointed Commissioner of Works in the MacDonald Government of 1929 and was the only cabinet minister to survive the 1931 General Election, after which he became Labour Party leader. Already in conflict with trades unionists over his pacifist views, he resigned in 1935. Later he became President of the Peace Pledge Union.

Liddell Hart, Sir Basil Henry (1895–1970) was educated at St Paul's School and Corpus Christi, Cambridge, and became a military historian and strategist. He was commissioned into the King's Own Yorkshire Light Infantry; he became a casualty of the Somme in 1916. He left the army aged 28, after 10 years' service. Later, he became a Military Correspondent for the *Daily Telegraph* 1925–1935 and *The Times* 1935–1939.

He published over 30 books and for a short time was an "unofficial advisor" to the War Minister Leslie Hore-Belisha. He was knighted in 1966.

MacDonald, James Ramsay (1866–1937) Labour politician and Prime Minister 1924 and 1929–1935; previously Leader of the Opposition 1922–1924. MacDonald served as Lord President of the Council until just before his death in 1937. He was educated in the Parish School and became a teacher in Lossiemouth, later assistant to a clergyman in Bristol. His interests in socialist ideas grew. He later took classes at Birkbeck Institute and gained experience as a private secretary to a Liberal politician. MacDonald joined Keir Hardy's Independent Labour Party (ILP) in 1894 and was elected Member of Parliament in 1906 for the Labour Party, which had absorbed the ILP. He became party leader in 1911, but resigned in opposition to the war in 1914, being replaced by Arthur Henderson. Despite his opposition to the war, he visited the Western Front with an ambulance unit. He lost his seat in 1918, was returned again in 1922 and was re-elected as party leader.

Makins, Major General Sir Ernest (1869–1959) was educated at Winchester and Christ Church College, Cambridge. He served in South Africa 1899–1902, was Mentioned in Despatches, and in The Great War as Temporary Brigadier-General of a Cavalry Brigade, where he again was Mentioned in Despatches. He was later appointed KBE, CB and DSO. Makins was elected Member of Parliament for Knutsford and served from 1922.

Norrie, Lieutenant General Charles Willoughby Moke 1st Baron Norrie, a former 11th Hussar and distinguished Great War veteran, he commanded the 1st Armoured Division in England in 1940 and later in the Middle East. He commanded XXX Corps during "Operation Crusader" and later became Commander, Royal Armoured Corps.

Simon, John Allsebrook, first Viscount Simon (1873–1954) was educated at kinder-garten in Manchester, King Edward's School, Bath, Fettes College, Edinburgh and Wadham College, Oxford. He was called to the Bar in 1898 and his legal career "prospered". Simon was elected Liberal MP for Walthamstow in 1906. At aged 37 he was the youngest ever solicitor-general and later became attorney-general and member of the Cabinet. Simon was Home Secretary in 1915, but resigned in 1916 over the introduction of conscription. He joined the Royal Flying Corps and served with distinction. He lost his seat in 1918, but was re-elected in 1922 and became deputy leader of the Liberal Party. In the hiatus of the late 1920s and early 1930s, Simon formed the Liberal national group and served as Foreign Secretary in the MacDonald Government. He moved to the Home Office 1935–1937, having been accused as being the worst Foreign Secretary since "Ethelred the Unready". Simon became Chancellor of the Exchequer when Chamberlain became Prime Minister. After Churchill took control, Simon served as Lord Chancellor. He left political office in 1945, but remained active in the House of Lords.

Snowden, Philip (1864–1937) First Labour Chancellor of the Exchequer 1924, again in 1929, and in the National Government of 1931. A Methodist and originally a Liberal, he became convinced of socialist ideology and joined the Independent Labour Party. Originally an insurance clerk in Burnley, he later joined the Inland Revenue in the North and West Country. He was elected Member of Parliament 1906. Snowden maintained his pacifist beliefs during the Great War and supported conscientious objectors. He lost his seat in 1918, was re-elected 1922 and created Viscount Snowden; he served as Lord Privy Seal 1931–1932. He resigned over a trade protection issue.

Thomas, George Holt (1869–1929) made his "name and fortune" by founding the newspapers *The Bystander* – in which appeared the comic character "Old Bill" and *Empire Illustrated.* He formed the Aircraft Manufacturing Company Limited in 1912 and later, to Geoffrey de Havilland's design, made a significant number of fighters and bombers used by the British and Americans during the Great War. He later became an advocate for civil aviation.

Weir, William Douglas, first Viscount Weir (1877–1959) was educated at Glasgow High School, an engineer, industrialist and public servant. By 1913 two thirds of his companies' work was on warships. He served on the central advisory committee on munitions during the Great War. He was knighted in 1917. He was involved with the formation of the RAF and was created Baron Weir in 1918. Baron Weir was a supporter of Basil Liddell Hart's theories on the pre-eminence of tanks.

Wyndham, Colonel The Hon. Everard Humphrey (1888–1970) commanded a machine-gun squadron in France during The Great War, and The Life Guards for four years. He is the author of *The Household Cavalry at War: The First Household Cavalry Regiment* (Gale and Poldon, Aldershot, 1952) and *War Diary of the 1st Life Guards. First Year, 1914–1915.*

Appendix IV

Growth in the support for Labour, 1900–1929

Election	Number of votes for the Labour Party	Share of votes	Seats	Outcome of the election
1900	62,698	1.8%	2	Conservative victory
1906	321,663	5.7%	29	Liberal victory
1910 January	505,657	7.6%	40	Liberal minority government
1910 December	371,802	7.1%	42	Liberal minority government
1918	2,245,777	21.5%	57	Coalition victory
1922	4,076,665	29.7%	142	Conservative victory
1923	4,267,831	30.7%	191	Labour minority government
1924	5,281,626	33.3%	151	Conservative victory
1929	8,048,968	37.1%	287	Labour minority government

Growth in the support for Labour, 1931–1935

Election	Total votes for the Labour Party including Independent Labour but NOT including National Labour	Approximate share of the votes	Total number of all Labour seats	Outcome of the election
1931	6,339,306	30.6%	52	Labour (MacDonald) led National Govt.
1935	8,121,196	38.7%	158	Conservative (Baldwin) led National Govt.

Appendix V

President Woodrow Wilson's Fourteen Points

---

1. Open covenants of peace, openly arrived at, after which there shall be no private international understandings of any kind but diplomacy shall proceed always frankly and in the public view.

2. Absolute freedom of navigation upon the seas, outside territorial waters, alike in peace and war, except as the seas may be closed in whole or in part by international action for the enforcement of international covenants.

3. The removal, so far as is possible, of all economic barriers and the establishment of an equality of trade conditions among all the nations consenting to peace and associating themselves for its maintenance.

4. Adequate guarantees given and taken that national armaments will be reduced to the lowest point consistent with domestic safety.

5. A free, open minded and absolutely impartial adjustment of all colonial claims, based on a strict observance of the principle that in determining all such questions of sovereignty the interests of the populations concerned must have equal weight with the equitable claims of government whose title is to be determined.

6. The evacuation of all Russian territory and such a settlement of all questions affecting Russia as will secure the best and freest cooperation of the other nations of the world in obtaining for her an unhampered and unembarrassed opportunity for the independent determination of her own political development and national policy and assure her of a sincere welcome into the society of free nations under institutions of her own choosing; and, more than a welcome, assistance of every kind that she may need and may herself desire. The treatment accorded to Russia by her sister nations in the months to come will be the acid test of their good will, of her comprehension of her needs as distinguished from their own interests, and of their intelligent and unselfish sympathy.

7. Belgium, the whole world will agree, must be evacuated and restored, without any attempt to limit the sovereignty she now enjoys in common with all other free nations. No other single act will serve as will to restore confidence among the nations in the laws which they have themselves set and determined for the government of their relations with one another. Without this healing act the whole structure and validity of international law is forever impaired.

8. All French territory should be freed and the invaded portions restored, and the wrong done to France by Prussia in 1871 in the matter of Alsase-Lorraine, which has unsettled the peace of the world for nearly fifty years, should be righted, in order that peace may once more be made secure in the interests of all.

9. A readjustment of the frontiers of Italy should be effected along clearly recognised lines of nationality.

10. The peoples of Austria-Hungary, whose place among the nations we wish to see safeguarded and assured, should be accorded the freest opportunity of autonomous development.

11. Roumania [sic] Serbia, and Montenegro should be evacuated: occupied territories restored; Serbia accorded free and secure access to the sea: and the relations of several Balkan states to one another determined by friendly counsel along historically established lines of allegiance and nationality; and international guarantees of political and economic independence and territorial integrity of the several Balkan states should be entered into.

12. The Turkish portions of the present Ottoman Empire should be assured a secure sovereignty, but the other nationalities which are now under Turkish rule should be assured an undoubted security of life and an absolutely unmolested opportunity of autonomous development, and the Dardanelles should be permanently opened as a free passage to the ships and commerce of all nations under international guarantees.

13. An independent Polish state should be erected which should include the territories inhabited by indisputably Polish populations, which should be assured a free and secure access to the sea, and whose political and economic independence and territorial integrity should be guaranteed by international covenant.

14. A general association of nations must be formed under specific covenants for the purpose of affording mutual guarantees of political independence and territorial integrity of great and small states alike.[1]

---

1   Cecil and Liddle, (eds) *At The Eleventh Hour*, pp.xxviii & xxix.

Appendix VI

The analysis of the Peace Ballot announced by Viscount Cecil at the Royal Albert Hall, June 27 1935[1]

Question 1. Should Great Britain remain a member of the League of Nations?

yes	no	doubtful	abstentions
11,090,387	355,888	10,470	102,425

Question 2. Are you in favour of an all-round reduction in armaments by international agreement?

yes	no	doubtful	abstentions
10,470,489	862,775	12,062	213,839

Question 3. Are you in favour of an all-round abolition of national military and naval aircraft by international agreement?

yes	no	doubtful	abstentions
9,533,558	1,689,786	16,976	318,845

Question 4. Should the manufacture and sale of armaments for private profit be prohibited by international agreement?

yes	no	doubtful	abstentions
10,417,329	775,415	15,076	351,834

1   Templewood, *Nine Troubled Years,* p.128.

Question 5. Do you consider that, if a nation insists on attacking another, the other nation should combine to compel it to stop by

a)   economic and non-military measures?

yes	no	doubtful	abstentions
10,027,608	635,074	27,255	855,107

b)   if necessary, military measures?

yes	no	doubtful	abstentions
6,784,368	2,351,981	40,893	2,364,441

Total votes – 11,599,165 i.e. 27.9 percent of the total number of voters in Great Britain and Northern Ireland.

Appendix VII

Provision of Army Estimates for the purchase and maintenance of animals and vehicles, 1927–1938[1]

Year	Total Army Estimate £000	Wheeled Combat Vehicles £000	Tracked Vehicles £000	% Spend on Vehicles	% Spend on Animals
1927	41,565	190.25	520	2.48	1.75
1928	41,050	171	555	2.65	1.78
1929	40,545	254	540	3.04	1.70
1930	40,500	178	319	2.35	1.65
1931	39,930	221	357	2.36	1.47
1932	36,488	226	309	2.24	1.32
1933	37,950	158	348	2.34	1.26
1934	39,600	193	501	2.64	1.15
1935	44,900	407	772	3.95	1.05
1936	55,881	1,729	842	6.29	.7
1937	82,174	2,747	3,625	9.24	.25
1938	106,500			10.35	.16

1   Winton, *To Change An Army*, Appendix 4.

Appendix VIII

Part of the list of maintenance and repair tasks for AFVs needed to be learned and undertaken by cavalrymen as suggested by Lieutenant Harold "Pete" Pyman for the 17th/21st Lancers, 20 June 1938[1]

A. Armoured Fighting Vehicles
1. In peace of when tactical situation is favourable.
   a) <u>Suspensions</u>
       Fitting and replacement of:
       Fulcrum bushes
       Bogie wheels
       Bogie wheel bearings and glands
       Spring and Spindles
       Ball End Liners
       Idler Wheel, Idler Wheel bearings, Glands and Pawl Spring
       Top Roller, Top Roller bearings and Glands
       Condemnation and Fitting of:
       Tracks
       Sprocket Ring
       Replacement of all small parts

   b) <u>Engine</u>
       Replacement of:
       Exhaust and Inlet Packings
       Water Joints and Packings
       Overhaul of water Pumps
       Re-fitting of Fan Bearings, Pullies and Belts

---

1   LHCMH, Pyman 1/1–28, 7, 1938.

Replacement of:
Gasket for Rocker Box
Parts of Rocker Gear
All small parts

c)   <u>Transmission</u>
Adjustment of Wilson Gear Box (senior Mechanist only)
Replacement of all small parts

d)   <u>Cooling</u>
Replacement of Rubber Washer for Relief valve
Replacement and fitting of Drain Plugs, and other small parts

Appendix IX

An example of the standard required for the classification for a Diver eligible for Tradesmen's Rates as a Driver Operator[1]

Class III.

a) Must be a good driver on forward and reverse gears on the wheeled and tracked internal combustion engine vehicles with which his unit is equipped.
    Must be able to change gears proficiently, turn a vehicle and negotiate traffic in narrow streets. Drive at night and in column. Drive across running boards, when applicable. Must have through knowledge of traffic signals, rules of the road, road signs, and action to be taken in case of collision or accidents on public highways. Must be able to tow a vehicle.

b) Must have an elementary knowledge of the function sof the various parts of the engine, carburettor, petrol feed and lighting systems, accumulators, ignition set, transmission, lubrication and cooling systems. Must understand anti – frost precautions and duties in case of fire. Must have a knowledge of the aids to apply in starting on a cold day.

c) (i) Must be able to detect and rectify such minor defects as can be delt with by means of the tools with which the vehicle is equipped.
    (ii) Must be able to prepare the vehicles of his unit for running and keep them in a general state of cleanliness. Must have good knowledge of care of tyres and be able to remove and replace outer covers, where applicable.

1   LHCMH, Pyman 1/1–28,7, 1938.

Class II – As for Class III, and in addition:-

a) Must be thoroughly proficient driver on the wheeled and tracked vehicles with which his unit is equipped under all conditions laid down in Class III (a).

b) Must have a good knowledge of the functions of various parts of the engine, carburettor, petrol systems, ignition starting and lighting sets, accumulators, transmission, suspension, lubrication and cooling systems, in order to enable him to detect faults, make adjustments and maintain the vehicle in good mechanical condition.

Appendix X

Breakdown of the interviewees by Unit

Service and Unit	Number of Interviewees
Royal Tank Corps	
First Light Battalion	2
Second Battalion	4
Fifth Battalion	2
Sixth Battalion	3
3rd Armoured Car Company	1
4th Armoured Car Company	1
Regular Cavalry/Royal Armoured Corps	
1st Dragoon Guards	2
2nd Dragoon Guards	1
3rd Dragoon Guards	1 attached
Royal Scots Greys	3
7th Hussars	1
9th Lancers	1 attached
11th Hussars	3
12th Lancers	3
13th/18th Hussars	2
15th/19th Hussars	4
16th/5th Lancers	2
17th/21st Lancers	1
110 Regiment Royal Armoured Corps	1
Armoured Infantry	
Guards Armoured Division	1
Yeomanry Cavalry Regiments	
Westminster Dragoons	1
Northamptonshire	1

Service and Unit	Number of Interviewees
Fife and Forfar	1
Cheshire	1
British Empire	
15th Northern Rivers Lancers – Australian Light Horse	1
Others	6
Total	50

Bibliography

PRIMARY SOURCES

Author's Interviews and Correspondence

Ash, Mrs Kay Emily, Auxiliary Territorial Service (ATS). Personal Interview by the author, 2008. Kay Ash was born in Southend-on-Sea, Essex, on 2 April 1920, where she was educated, and later worked on the secretarial staff of the agent for the local Member of Parliament, "Chips" Channon. She served in the Women's Royal Army Corps during the Second World War at the Ministry of Defence in Whitehall, and later married Corporal Kenneth Ash of the Sherwood Foresters, 14th Army, a "Chindit"; he later served during the "Cold War" as Civil Defence Officer for a large area of Essex. Kay Ash died in 2013.

Bate, William, the Home Guard and the Royal Air Force. Personal discussions and correspondence by the author, 2008–2011. William Bate was born in 1925 in a mining village in the South Staffordshire coalfield. In 1939 he began an apprenticeship as a toolmaker in Birmingham, and during the Second World War served in the Home Guard until his conscription into the Royal Air Force Medical Service in 1945, where he served as a radiographer. After demobilization William Bate retrained as a teacher and taught in army schools in many parts of the world. He died in 2011.

Bennett, John, Trooper, the 15th/19th Hussars. Personal interview by the author, 2007. John Bennett was born in Kent on 5 June 1921, the son of a Royal Engineer. Giving a false age, Bennett enlisted in the 15th/19th Hussars at Woolwich in 1937 and joined the regiment at Fulford Barracks, York. After training he passed out to 1st Troop, A Squadron, in March 1938. Very soon after this the horses went and driving training began with 15 cwt. trucks. Carden-Lloyd carriers arrived in early 1939. When war was declared the regiment sailed from Clifton docks to Saint Nazaire, and fought under the command of Major General Bernard Montgomery in the 3rd British Division. The regiment returned from Dunkirk having lost two-thirds of its strength as casualties. John Bennett, with Ronald Lucas (see below), was evacuated from Dunkirk on HMS *Malcolm*. He died in February 2008.

Bishop, Thomas, the 3rd, 8th and 11th Battalions, The Royal Tank Regiment. Personal telephone interview by the author, 2008. Thomas Bishop was born in Tadley in 1919, and followed his elder brother into the Tank Corps in 1936. He was trained at Bovington and later served in India and Egypt.

Bullock, Raymond, Sergeant, the Brigade of Guards (Armour), email correspondence with the author, 2009. "Ray" Bullock, from Stoke-on-Trent, Staffordshire, was born in Norwich, Norfolk on 12 June 1924. He volunteered for air crew in November 1942, but colour-blindness prevented his selection. He trained as an infantryman at Caterham. After taking a test it was established that he "apparently had an aptitude for mechanics". He was transferred to Pirbright for fifteen months' tank training, then on to join the 4th Battalion Grenadier Guards in France; he finished the war at Kiel on the Baltic. During the fighting Ray Bullock, by then a NCO, was wounded and lost two turret crews and two tank commanders.

Chapman, Stanley, the Royal Navy. Personal interview by the author 2008. "Stan" Chapman was born in 1922 and grew up in north-west rural Essex; his working career was in retail grocery management. He served in the Royal Navy on minesweepers and fast anti-submarine sloops during the Second World War and was awarded the Atlantic Star medal. Chapman is a committed Anglican and has been much involved in his church continuously from boyhood. He is widely read and much travelled in pursuit of his interests in politics and current affairs.

Cross, William, Sergeant, the 2nd Dragoons (Royal Scots Greys). Personal interview by the author at the Royal Hospital Chelsea, 2010. "Bill" Cross was born in Scunthorpe on 21 November 1917, the son a Sergeant Major of the Coldstream Guards of Scottish descent. He attended Gordon School as an army band-boy and was posted to the Royal Scots Greys. Eventually he became fond of horses. He played trombone in the mounted band and later joined the Signal Troop in Austin Cars. Sergeant Cross served with the horsed regiment in Palestine with James Randall (see below) and trained as a mechanics instructor in Cairo during the mechanization period. He saw action in the desert where he lost the sight in one eye. He later fought again at Salerno and Monte Casino. On D-Day Cross landed on Sword Beach at Ouistreham. After the war, Cross became a State Trumpeter with The Life Guards.

Cruddace, Robert, Trooper, 13th/18th Hussars. Personal Correspondence with the author, 2007. Mr Robert "Bob" Cruddace was born in 1914 and joined the 13th/18th Hussars regimental band at Shorncliffe Barracks August 1929. The following month the regiment sailed for Egypt, and after two years in Egypt went to India for seven years, serving two years of that time on the North West Frontier. On return to England, driving training began. The regimental band became despatch riders on 500cc Norton motorcycles. On the outbreak of war the regiment formed part of the British Expeditionary Force and fought on "Dyle line" in Belgium in May 1940 covering the British 1st Division under the command of Major General Harold Alexander. Eventually the regiment was pushed back to Dunkirk and evacuated on 30 May. On D-Day, 6 June 1944, Cruddace landed with the regiment on the Normandy beaches in amphibious "Duplex-drive" Sherman tanks known as "Hobart's Funnies". He was demobilised in Hanover, Germany, in 1945 and returned to Folkstone where he still resides. Robert Cruddace and Charles Need (see below) had served together as horsed cavalrymen.

Davidson, William, Major, the Royal Armoured Corps / 2nd Royal Tank Regiment. Several discussions and personal correspondence with the author, 2009. "Bill" Davidson was born in Liverpool 15 July 1921. His father was an active TA Officer in the 6th Rifle Battalion The King's (Liverpool) Regiment and was wounded in France in 1918. His father died in 1928, and Davidson joined the same regiment in memory of him as soon as he was 17 years old. In December 1939 he was selected for officer training in the Royal Armoured Corps at Brookwood and then at Bovington. Davidson joined the 2nd Royal Tank Regiment in Egypt in January 1941, the regiment he remained with apart from a time as Brigade Major of the 7th Armoured Brigade. Major Davidson served in the Western Desert, Burma and Italy, and was awarded the MBE (Military Division). He died in 2011.

ffrench Blake, R.L.Valentine, Lieutenant Colonel, the 17th/21st Lancers. Personal interview and subsequent correspondence with by the author, 2006 to 2009. "Val" ffrench Blake, was born 3 March 1913 in Rawalpindi. He was educated at Eton and the Royal Military Collage, Sandhurst, and joined the 17th/21st Lancers in India in 1933. Later he fought in North Africa, and was wounded. On recovering, he returned to command the regiment in Italy. He was awarded the DSO. He was part of the team to re-start the Royal Military Academy, Sandhurst, after the Second World War had ended. Colonel ffrench Blake died in 2011. His memorial service was held in September in the chapel at Sandhurst.

Hodgson, Joseph Edward Gillet, Lance Corporal, the Royal Armoured Corps. Personal correspondence with the author, 2008. "Joe" Hodgson was born on 4 August 1921 in Preston, Lancashire. He enlisted under the "Young soldier Scheme" on 4 June 1940, and was posted to the 6th (Home Defence) Battalion, The East Lancashire Regiment, and later to the 70th (Young Soldiers) Battalion, The Border Regiment. He later volunteered for The Royal Armoured Corps hoping to see action in the Desert. Hodgson spent the Second World War in various training establishments, including Sandhurst, and he later worked on different fuel systems at the Petroleum Warfare Research Station near Horsham, Surrey. He was demobilised 25 March 1946. Joseph Hodgeson died on Sunday 21 August 2011, aged 90. His funeral cortege was flanked by eight military standards.

Husband, George, Corporal, the 16th/5th The Queen's Royal Lancers. Personal interview and subsequent correspondence by the author, 2010. George "Yorkie" Husband was born in the farming village of Howden, Yorkshire, in 1916 and grew up with horses. He enlisted aged 18 into the 16th/5th the Queen's Royal Lancers in York and served on the North West Frontier of India. The 16th/5th Lancers were mechanized in Colchester with Matilda and Churchill tanks in late 1941 and saw action in North Africa and Italy, where the regiment was equipped with Sherman tanks.

Jeffcut, Basil, Corporal, the 15th/19th Hussars. Personal correspondence with the author, 2007. "Jeff" Jeffcut was born 21 February 1921 into a "cavalry family"; his father a Squadron Sergeant Major with the 3rd Dragoon Guards and two brothers in other cavalry regiments. Jeffcut enlisted April 1921 aged 15 using his brother's birth certificate. Jeffcut was a colleague of John Bennett (see above) and Ronald Lucas (see below). Jeffcut survived Dunkirk and returned to fight in France in August 1944 mounted, first in a Cromwell tank, and later the 17-pounder variant Challenger tank as part of the 11th Armoured Division. At some stage during the battles for north-west Europe Jeffcut's tank was knocked out and he and his crew were wounded. He was invalided out of the army. Later he returned to riding and became a British Horse Society riding instructor and continued teaching until 2004, aged 83.

Lucas, Ronald, Sergeant, the 15th/19th Hussars. Personal interviews with by the author, 2007–2012. "Ron" Lucas was born in 1917 in Sheperton, Middlesex. He served part of an engineering apprenticeship and joined the 15th/19th Hussars in November 1935. He qualified as an instructor during the mechanization of the regiment in 1938 and in 1940 commanded a tank in France. He is a Dunkirk veteran, and later served as an instructor to Canadian troops in London.

Need, Charles W, Lance Corporal, the 13th/18th Hussars. Personal interview and subsequent correspondence by the author, 2007. Charles Need was born in Birmingham on 4 August 1914. He left school at age 14 and worked for a company making motor bodies. On 28 June 1933 he joined the Cavalry of The Line and was sent to the 4th/7th Dragoon Guards for initial training. He was posted to the 13th/18th Hussars in India in February 1935, and served for a period on the North West Frontier. Need became a signaller. On returning to England in 1938 Need attended a vocational course in woodwork and was placed on the Army Reserve. Need was re-called to The Colours on the outbreak of war, to his now mechanized regiment. Being untrained in driving and mechanics, Need was posted to the prisoner of war staff with no prisoners to guard. Posted then to France, Need fought a rear-guard action with a mixed force of former cavalry soldiers at Berues on the outskirts of Dunkirk. Eventually he was evacuated on the coaster SS *Hythe*. Later, Need escorted prisoners of war to Canada and on return was posted to the Royal Corps of Signals. Need served with the Head-Quarters, 14th Army Signals, in India and Burma under General William Slim. Following the defeat of the Japanese and suffering from malnutrition and worms, Need left Rangoon via India for recuperation, and arrived for demobilisation in Hereford in December 1945. He died in 2010.

Randall, James, Sergeant, the 2nd Dragoons (Royal Scots Greys). Personal interviews and subsequent correspondence by the author, 2006. "Jim" Randall was born in 1916 and, answering an advert, volunteered for the Cavalry of The Line in 1939. After riding school and basic army training in Colchester he embarked for Palestine, where British horsed cavalry, the 1st Cavalry Division, was engaged on peacekeeping operations under the British Mandate. Randall was posted to the Royal Scots Greys and spent a year as a horsed cavalry trooper until the regiment was mechanized with Sherman and Stuart tanks in 1941. Randall served in the Western Desert, Italy, Normandy, France, Holland, Germany and the Baltic coast. As a sergeant of the reconnaissance troop he led his regiment across hundreds of miles of enemy held territory and was "Mentioned in Despatches" at the end of hostilities.

Sprot, Aiden M., Lieutenant Colonel, the 2nd Dragoons (Royal Scots Greys). Personal interview and subsequent correspondence by the author, 2007. Aidan M Sprot was born in 1919 and brought up in the Borders and educated at Stowe. In 1940 he left The City and after basic training and riding school joined his father's old Regiment, the Royal Scots Greys, still a horsed-mounted regiment. He commanded the reconnaissance troop, James Randall was his sergeant (see above), and fought in the Western Desert, Italy and the battles of North West Europe. He was awarded the MC. Lieutenant Colonel Sprot commanded the regiment from 1959–1962. After retirement he became Lord-Lieutenant of Tweedale.

Stead, Miss Margorie, the Civil Defence Corps. Personal interview by the author, 2008. Margorie "Nan" Stead was born in 1914 in Hackney, east London where she was educated, lived and worked. She was, and still is, a practising Christian and was keen member of the Methodist Church. She served in the ARP during the Second World War and in particular the London "blitz" of 1940 and 1941.

Imperial War Museum (IWM) Department of Sound Records

Allenby, Viscount Dudley Jaffray Hynman, Captain, the 11th Hussars. IWM Sound Collection, access number 878, recorded 1977. Viscount Allenby was born in 1903 and served in the 11th Hussars from 1923 until 1936, when he became the Adjutant (Driving and Maintenance) at Bovington until 1940.

Bright, Robert, Brigadier, the Royal Tank Corps. IWM Sound Collection, access number 787, recorded 1977. Robert Bright was born in 1912, educated at Wellington and The Royal Military Academy, Woolwich; he served in the Royal Tank Corps and the Royal Armoured Corps from 1932 until 1943.

Forster, Douglas, Lieutenant Colonel, the 11th Hussars and the Northamptonshire Yeomanry. IWM Sound Collection, access number 919, recorded 1977. Forster was commissioned into the 11th Hussars in 1922 and served for ten years before transferring to the Northampton Yeomanry as the Adjutant. In 1942, serving in Tunisia, Forster took command of the Northampton Yeomanry. He was awarded the DSO and "Mentioned in Despatches".

Harding-Newman, Rupert Norton, Brigadier, the Royal Tank Corps. IWM Sound Collection, access number 834, recorded 1977. Rupert Harding-Newman was educated at St. Edward's School, Oxford, and at the Royal Military College, Sandhurst. He served with the Royal Tank Corps, later the Royal Armoured Corps 1928–1958. He was awarded the MC.

Horsburgh-Porter, Sir Andrew Marshall, Colonel, the 12th Lancers. IWM Sound Collection, access number 905, recorded 1977. Sir Andrew Horsburgh-Porter was born in 1907 and served with the 12th Lancers from 1927 in Egypt, Germany and England. During the Second World War he commanded D Squadron in France in 1940 and later served in Italy. He was wounded in battle, and was twice awarded the DSO, and "Mentioned in Despatches" and

Kidston-Montgomerie, George, Colonel, the 12th Lancers and the 3rd County of London Yeomanry. IWM Sound Collection, access number 892, recorded 1977. George Kidston–Montgomerie was born in 1907. He served in the 12th Lancers 1926–1937, the 3rd County of London Yeomanry 1937–1940, and commanded the 4th Queen's Own Hussars 1947–1949. He was awarded the DSO and the MC.

Savill, Kenneth Edward, Colonel, the 12th Lancers and the 1st King's Dragoon Guards. IWM Sound Collection, access number 933, recorded 1977. Kenneth Savill was born in 1906, was educated in Winchester and the Royal Military College Sandhurst. Commissioned into the 12th Lancers in 1926, he served with the regiment until 1936, and with the 1st King's Dragoon Guards from 1937 until 1939.

Wiggin, Peter Milner, Colonel, the 11th Hussars and the Northampton Yeomanry. IWM Sound Collection, access number 918, recorded 1977. Peter Wiggin was born in 1907; he served with the 11th Hussars from 1927 until 1936 when he succeeded Douglas Forster (see above) as Adjutant of the Northampton Yeomanry until 1942.

Younger, Ralph, Major General, the 7th Hussars. IWM Sound Collection, access number 913, recorded 1977. Ralph Younger was born in 1904; he served with the 7th Hussars from 1926 until he took command of the 3rd Carabiniers, and later the 255 Indian Tank Brigade in the Burma campaign during the Second World War. He was awarded the CB, CBE, DSO and MC.

The Second World War Experience Centre

Parnell, Thomas, the Lancashire Yeomanry, the Royal Dragoons, the 16th/5th Lancers and the 10th Hussars. Born in Lancashire in 1918, Parnell left school at 14 to go into the cotton mills. The pay was bad for hard and dirty work, and always having an interest in horses, he joined the Lancashire Yeomanry aged 16, and the Regular Army in 1936, enlisting in The Royal Dragoons. The regiment had just returned from India and the 16th/5th Lancers wanted volunteers to go to India and so he volunteered for the Lancers, later serving on the North West

Frontier. After mechanization Parnell served with the 10th Hussars in North Africa in Sherman Tanks.

Simpson, Colonel, Territorial Army Officer, The Lothian and Border Horse. Prior to 1939 the Lothian and Border Horse, a Yeomanry Regiment, was mobilized to a motor machine-gun brigade. The regiment was brigaded with the 16th/5th Lancers and the 17th/21st Lancers equipped with machine-guns, anti-tank rifles and Austin vans. He later served with the 6th Armoured Division.

DOCUMENTS

Regimental Archives

The Household Cavalry Archives, The Household Cavalry Museum, Combermere Barracks, Windsor.

The Royal Scots Greys and Carabiniers archived document T70, TB12, G219, G269 Regimental Archives, Edinburgh Castle.

The 3rd The King's Own Hussars Historical Records 01.04.1932–31.03.1938 File 1716, Regimental Archives, The Queen's Hussars Museum, Lord Leycester Hospital, Warwick.

The 4th Queen's Own Hussars and the 8th King's Royal Irish Hussars Archives, The Queen's Royal Hussars, Home Head Quarters, Regent Park Barracks, Albany Street, London, NW1 4AL.

The 7th Hussars, Unit Historical Records 1910–1939, Section 1718, 01.04.1932 31.03.1939, Regimental Archives, The Queen's Hussars Museum, Lord Leycester Hospital, Warwick.

The 9th/12th Lancers Archives, The 9th/12th Lancers and Derby Yeomanry Museum, Derby Museum and Art Gallery, Derby.

The Queen's Royal Lancers, Regimental Archives, The Queen's Royal Lancers Museum, Lancer House, Prince William of Gloucester Barracks, Grantham, Lincolnshire.

The 15th/19th Hussars Archives, The Light Dragoons (15th/19th King's Royal Hussars) Museum Collection "A Soldier's Lif", Discovery Museum, Blandford Sq., Newcastle-upon-Tyne.

The National Archives of Great Britain, Kew (TNA)

TNA WO 32 various files – 2826–16407.
TNA WO 95/1466 4th Division War Diaries – 19th Hussars – 1914–1915.

The Tank Museum Archives Bovington

355.6 Mechanization E2005 .622

The Liddell Hart Centre for Military Archives (LHCMA), King's College London

The Papers of:
Lieutenant General Sir Charles Broad.
Brigadier H V S Charrington.
Major General Sir Percy Hobart.
Liddell Hart, selected papers 1928–1939.
Major General George Lindsay.
Field Marshal Montgomery-Massingberd.
Major General Sir Harold Pyman.

The Britain by Mass Observation Papers, Brighton (The University of Sussex)

Chepstow Left Book Club, 1939. Topic Collection; the Oxford By-Election.
Conscientious Objectors, Report on, COs and Pacifism, 1940.
Fulham 1938; File G2/C.
Ilford 1937, in By-Elections 1937–1947; File E 1E.
Left Leaflets, 1936–1938; File TC25/9/P.
Newspaper reading 1937–1961. Topic Collection.
Political Attitudes and Behaviour (Fulham 21st February 1939). Special Collections.
Westminster 1939; File 2F.

Cambridge University Library, Cambridge

The Vickers Papers.

Official Manuals

Manual of Horsemastership, Equitation and Driving 1929, [1929] (The War Office, London).
Cavalry Training (Horsed) 1937, [1937], (The War Office, London).
Boys Anti-Tank Rifle Mark I, [undated], (The Naval and Military Press, Uckfield from an original from Gale & Polden Ltd., Aldershot).

Newspapers and Journals

The Daily Mail.
The Manchester Guardian.
The Times.
3rd The King's Own Hussars Magazine.
3rd The King's Own Hussars Journal.

IV Hussars' Journal.
The Journal of The VIII King's Royal Irish Hussars.
XI Hussar Journal Vol. XII.
XII Lancers Journal.
The White Lancer and The Vedette – The Journal of The 17th/ 21st Lancers.
The 110th Royal Armoured Corps (Borders) *Newsletter.*
Mars & Clio; the Newsletter of the British Commission for Military History ; Barnett, Corelli "The Desert Generals Revisited" British Commission for Military History [2005], (notes of the address at the Annual General Meeting 5 February 2005) <URL: http:// ww.bcmh.org.uk> accessed 29.06.06.
The Chronicle – The Journal of The Queen's Royal Hussars Historical Society.
Stand To! – The Journal of The Western Front Association.
Strachey, John "The Peace Alliance" in Gollancz, Victor (ed.) *The Left News*, [1938], (Special Collections, University of Sussex, Brighton).

PUBLISHED SOURCES

The Army Lists [1928–1937], (London: HMSO, 1928–1937).
Modern Formations [1931], (London: HMSO).

Regimental Histories

Anon [1949], *Short History of the 4th Royal Irish Dragoon Guard 7th (Princess Royals) Dragoon Guards 4th/7th Royal Dragoon Guards.* (Gale & Polden Limited, Aldershot).
Bastin, Jeremy [1981], *The History of The 15th/19th The King's Royal Hussars 1945–1980,* (Keats House Limited, Chichester).
Blacker, General Sir Cecil and Woods, Major General H G [1978], *Change And Challenge. The Story of the 5th Royal Inniskilling Dragoon Guards,* (privately published).
Bolitho, Hector, [1963], *The Galloping Third: The Story of The 3rd The King's Own Hussars* (John Murray, London).
Brander, Michael [1969], *The 10th Royal Hussars,* (Leo Cooper London).
Brereton J M [1982], *A History of the 4th/7th Royal Dragoon Guards and their predecessors 1685–1980,* (The Regiment).
Bright, Joan (ed.) [1951], *The Ninth Queen's Own Royal Lancers 1936–1945,* (Gale & Polden Ltd, Aldershot).
Carnock, Lord [1932], *The History of the 15th The King's Hussars 1914–1922* (originally privately published, now The Navy and Military Press Ltd., Uckfield).
Chadwick, K [1968], *Seconds Out, A History of the 2nd Royal Tank Regiment* Volume One, (unpublished).
Evans, Roger [1951], *The Story of The Fifth Royal Inniskilling Dragoon Guards,* (Gale & Polden, Aldershot).

ffrench Blake, R L V [1962], *A History of The 17th/21st Lancers 1922–1959*, (Macmillan & Co Ltd., London).

ffrench Blake, R L V [1993], *The 17th/21st Lancers 1759–1993*, (Leo Cooper, London).

Fitzroy, Olivia [1961], *Men of Valour – The Third Volume of the History of The VIII King's Royal Irish Hussars 1927–1958*, (Liverpool).

Liddell Hart, Sir Basil [1959], *The Tanks: The History of the Royal Tank Regiment and its Predecessors, Heavy Branch MGC, Tank Corps and Royal Tank Corps, 1914–1939*, (Cassell, London).

Macksey, Kenneth [1983], *A History of The Royal Armoured Corps 1914–1975*, (Newtown Publications, Beaminster).

Mallinson, Alan [2006], *Light Dragoons*, (Pen & Sword, Barnsley).

Mileham, Patrick [1984], *The Yeomanry Regiments*, (Canongate Academic, Edinburgh).

Oatts, L B [1966], *I Serve – Regimental History of 3rd Carabiniers (Prince of Wales's Dragoon Guards)*, (Jarrold & Sons, Norwich).

Scott Daniell, David [1959], *4th Hussar – The Story of The 4th Queen's Own Hussars 1685–1958*, (Gale and Polden, Aldershot).

Strawson, J M, Pierson, H T and Rhoderick-Jones, R J [1986], *Irish Hussar* (The Queen's Royal Irish Hussars Association, London).

Stirling, J D P [1946], *The First and The Last, The Story of The 4th/7th Royal Dragoon Guards 1939–1945*, (Arts & Educational Publishers Ltd., London & Glasgow).

Thompson, Ralph [1989], *The 15th/19th The King's Royal Hussars – A Pictorial History*, (Quoin Publishing Limited, Huddersfield).

Verdin, Sir Richard [1971], *The Cheshire [Earl of Chester's] Yeomanry 1898–1967*, (Willmer Brothers Limited, Birkenhead).

White-Spunner, Barney [2006], *Horse Guards*, (Macmillan, London).

Wood, Stephen [1988], *In The Finest Tradition*, (Mainstream Publishing Company, Edinburgh).

Memoirs

Brittain, Vera [1957], *Testament of Experience*, (Victor Gollancz, London).

Churchill, Winston S [1971], *The Second World War: The Gathering Storm*, (Cassell, London).

Cooper, Duff [1954], *Old Men Forget*, (Rupert Hart Davis, London).

Danchev, Alex and Todman, Daniel (eds.) [2001], *War Diaries 1939–1945 – Field Marshal Lord Alanbrooke*, (Weidenfeld & Nicolson, London).

"Friends" [1938], *Dick Sheppard By His Friends*, (Hodder and Stoughton, London).

Katherine, Duchess of Atholl [1958], *Working Partnership*, (Arthur Baker Limited, London).

Kennedy, Sir John [1957], *The Business of War – The war narrative of Major-General Sir John Kennedy*, (Hutchinson, London).

Liddell Hart, Sir Basil [1965], *Memoirs Volume I*, (Cassell, London).

Liddell Hart, Sir Basil [1965], *Memoirs Volume II*, (Cassell, London).

Lloyd George, David [1936], *War Memoirs of David Lloyd George Volume II*, (Odhams Press Limited, London).

Martel, Gifford le Quense [1935], *In The Wake of the Tank*, (Sifton, Pread & Co., London).

Middlemass, Keith (ed.) [1969], *Thomas Jones – Whitehall Dairies Volume I 1916–1925*, (Oxford University Press, London).

Minney, R J [1991], *The Private Papers of Hore-Belisha*, (Gregg Revivals, Aldershot).

Norwich, John Julius [2005], *The Duff Cooper Diaries*, (Weidenfeld and Nicolson, London).

Orwell, George [1975], *The Road to Wigan Pier*, (Penguin Books Ltd., Harmondsworth).

Plowman, Max [1936], *A Faith Called Pacifism*, (Dent & Sons Ltd., London).

Pyman, General Sir Harold [1971], *Call to Arms – The Memoirs of General Sir Harold Pyman GBE KCB DSO MA*, (Leo Cooper, London).

Sprot, Aiden [1998], *Swifter Than Eagles*, (The Pentland Press, Edinburgh).

Templewood, Viscount, Samuel John Gurney Hoare [1954], *Nine Troubled Years*, (Collins, London).

SECONDARY SOURCES

Allen, Walter "A Literary Aftermath" in Panichas, George A (ed.) [1968], *The Promise of Greatness: The War of 1914–1918*, (Cassell, London).

Aldcroft, Derek H [1986], *The British Economy – Volume 1 – The years of Turmoil 1920–1951*, (Wheatsheaf Books Ltd., The Harvester Press Publishing Group, Brighton).

Andrew, Christopher [2009], *The Defence of the Realm – The Authorized History of MI5*, (Allen Lane, London).

Anglesey, The Marquess of [1997], *A History of the British cavalry 1816–1919, Volume 8, The Western Front 1915–1918 Epilogue, 1919–1939*, (Leo Cooper, London).

Badsey, Stephen "Cavalry and the Development of Breakthrough Doctrine" in Griffith, Paddy. [1996], *British Fighting Methods in the Great War*, (Frank Cass, London).

Badsey, Stephen [2008], *Doctrine and Reform in the British Cavalry 1880–1918*, (Ashgate Publishing Limited, Aldershot).

Bialer, Uri [1980], *The Shadow Of The Bomber – The Fear of An Air Attack and British Politics 1932–1939*, (London Historical Society, London).

Barnett, Corelli "The Illogical Promise" in Panichas, George A (ed.) [1968], *The Promise of Greatness: The War of 1914–1918*, (Cassell, London).

Barnett, Corelli [2007], *The Desert Generals –The Men who led Britain's Armies in the Epic Desert Warfare of 1940–43*, (Orion Books, London).

Bartley, Paula [1998], *Votes for Women 1860–1928*, (Hodder and Stoughton, London).

Beale, Peter [1998], *Death by Design, The Fate of British Tank Crews in The Second World War*, (Sutton Publishing, Stroud).

Beevor, Antony [2006], *The Battle For Spain – The Spanish Civil War 1936–1939*, (Phoenix, London).

Bidwell, Shelford & Graham, Domonic [2004], *Fire Power: The British Army - Weapons and Theories of War, 1904-1945*, (Pen & Sword, Barnsley).

Bond, Brian [1980], *British Military Policy Between the Two World Wars*, (Oxford University Press, Oxford).

Bond, Ralph "Cinema in the Thirties: Documentary Film and the Labour Movement" in Clark, J Heinemann, Margot, Margolies, David and Snee, Carole (eds.) [1979], *Culture and Crisis in Britain in the Thirties*, (Lawrence and Wishart, London).

Broad, Roger [2013], *The Radical General*, (Spellmount, Stroud).

Brewerton, Paul & Millward, Lyn [2001], *Organizational Research Methods*, (Sage, London).

Brown, Malcolm [1999], *1918 Year of Victory*, (Pan Macmillan, London).

Briggs, Asa [1983], *A Social History of England*, (George Weidenfeld and Nicolson Limited, London).

Buckley, John "Tackling the Tiger: The development of British Armoured Doctrine for Normandy 1944" in *The Journal of Military History* Volume 74, No 4 October 2012, (The Society for Military History).

Burns, Chris [1981], *Tanks of World War II*, (Octopus Books, London).

Carr, E H [1975], *What is History?*, *(*Penguin Books Ltd., Harmondsworth).

Ceadel, Martin [1980], *Pacifism in Britain 1914–1945*, (Clarendon Press, Oxford).

Ceadel, Martin "The Peace Movement between the wars: problems of definition" in Naylor, Richard & Young, Nigel (eds.) [1987], *Campaigns for Peace, The British Peace Movement in the Twentieth Century* (Manchester University Press, Manchester).

Cecil, Hugh and Liddle, Peter H (eds.) [1998], *At The Eleventh Hour – Reflections, Hopes and Anxieties at the Closing of the Great War, 1918*, (Leo Cooper, Barnsley).

Chamberlain, Peter and Ellis, Chris [1969], *British and American Tanks of World War II*, (Arco Publishing Company Inc., New York, N.Y.).

Chappell, Mike [1991], *British Cavalry Equipment 1800–1941*, (Osprey Publishing Ltd., London).

Clarke, Ignatius Frederick [1970], *Voices Prophesying War 1763–1984*, (Panther Books, London).

Cohen, L & Manion, L [1996], *Research Methods in Education*, (Routledge, London).

Cohen, Robert, [1997], *When the Old Left Was Young: Student Radicals and America's First Mass Student Movement, 1929–1941*, (Oxford University Press, USA).

Coombes, Benjamin [2013], *British Tank Production and the War Economy, 1934–1945*, (Bloomsbury, London).

Coombes, H [2001], *Researching Using IT*, (Palgrave, Basingstoke).

Corrigan, Gordon [2006], *Blood, Sweat and Arrogance and the Myths of Churchill's War*, (Weidenfeld & Nicolson, London).

Crow, Duncan [1972], *British and Commonwealth Armoured Formations (1919–1946)*, (Profile Publications, Windsor).

Devine, Fiona "Qualitative Methods" in Marsh, David and Stoker, Gerry (eds.) [2002], *Theory and Methods in Political Science second edition*, (Palgrave Macmillan, Basingstoke).

Dixon, Norman [1976], *On The Psychology of Military Incompetence*, (Pimlico, London).

Edgerton, David [2008], *Warfare State – Britain, 1920–1970*, (Cambridge University Press, Cambridge).

Ellis, John [2004], *Cavalry – The History of Mounted Warfare*, (Pen and Sword Books Ltd., Barnsley).

Evans, Alan [1994], *On The Breadline*, (B T Batsford Ltd., London).

Fletcher, David [1991], *Mechanised Force – British tanks between the wars*, (HMSO, London).

Fletcher, David "Tanks" in Holmes. R (ed.) [2001], *The Oxford Companion To Military History*, (Oxford University Press, Oxford).

Fletcher, David [2014], *British Light Tanks 1927–45*, (Osprey Publishing, Oxford).

Flick, U [1998], *An Introduction to Qualitative Research*. (Routledge, London).

Foss, Christopher and McKenzie, Peter [1988], *The Vickers Tanks*, (Patrick Stephens Limited, Wellingborough).

French, David [2001], *Raising Churchill's Army*, (Oxford University Press, Oxford).

French, David "The Mechanization of the British Cavalry between the World Wars" in *War in History*, July 2003 10, pp.296–320.

French, David [2005], *Military Identities – The Regimental System, the British Army & the British People c.1870–2000*, (Oxford University Press, Oxford).

French, E G The Hon. [1951], *Goodbye To Boot And Saddle, or The Tragic Passing of British Cavalry*, (Hutchinson & Co., London).

Gander, Terry & Chamberlain, Peter [1976], *British Tanks of World War II*, (Patrick Stephens, Cambridge).

Gat, Azar [2000], *British Army Theory and the Rise of the Panzer Arm – Revising the Revisionists*, (Macmillan, Oxford).

Gibbs, N H [1976], *History of the Second World War Grand Strategy* Volume 1 *Rearmament Policy,* (HMSO, London).

Gilbert, Martin [2000], *Churchill A Life*, (Pimlico, London).

Graves, Robert & Hodge, Alan [1995], *The Long Weekend, A Social History of Great Britain 1918–1939*, (Abacus, Ilford).

Griffith, P G "British Armoured Warfare in the Western Desert" in Harris, J & Tose, F N (eds.) [1990], *Armoured Warfare*, (B.T. Batsford, London).

Gwynn, Major General Sir Charles W [1939], *Imperial Policing – Second Edition*, (Macmillan & Co Limited, London).

Gyseghem, Andre van [1979], "British Theatre in the Thirties: An Auto Biographical Record" in Clark, J Heinemann, Margot, Margolies, David and Snee, Carole (eds.) [1979], *Culture and Crisis in Britain in the Thirties*, (Lawrence and Wishart, London).

Harris, J P [1995], *Men, Ideas and Tanks, British Military Thought and Armoured Forces 1903–1939*, (Manchester University Press, Manchester).

Harrison, Tom & Madge, Charles [1986], *Britain by Mass Observation*, (The Cresset Library, London).

Harrison Place, Timothy [2000], *Military Training in the British Army 1940–1944 – From Dunkirk to D-Day*, (Frank Cass, London).

Hinton, James [1989], *Protests and Visions – Peace Politics in 20th Century Britain*, (Hutchinson Radius, London).

Hobsbawm, Eric [1969], *Industry and Empire*, (Penguin Books Ltd, Harmondsworth).

Hobsbawm, Eric [1995], *The Age of Extremes 1914–1991*, (Abacus, London).

Holden Reid, Brian [1998], *Studies in British Military Thought – Debates with Fuller and Liddell Hart*, (University of Nebraska, Nebraska).

Holmes, Richard [2003], *The Oxford Companion to Military History*, (Oxford University Press, Oxford).

Howard, K & Sharp, J [1996], *The Management of a Student Research Project* (2nd Edition), (Gower, London).

Howard, Michael [1972], *The Continental Commitment – The dilemma of British defence policy in the era of the two world wars. The Ford Lectures in the University of Oxford*, (Maurice Temple Smith Ltd., London).

Howson, Susan [1975], *Domestic Money Management In Britain 1919–38*, (Cambridge University Press, Cambridge).

Hudson, Miles [2004], *Intervention in Russia 1918–1920 A Cautionary Tale*, (Leo Cooper, Barnsley).

James, Lawrence [2002], *Warrior Race – A History of The British at War*, (Abacus, London).

Jeffery, Keith [2010], *MI6: The History of the Secret Intelligence Service, 1909–1949*, (Bloomsbury, London).

Jenkins, Roy [2001], *Churchill*, (Pan Macmillan Ltd., London).

Jones, Gareth Stedman [1983], *Languages of Class – Studies in Working Class History 1832–1982*, (Cambridge University Press, Cambridge).

Joslin E C, Litherland, A R, Simpkin, B T [1988] *British Battles and Medals*, (Spink and Son Ltd., London).

Kershaw, Robert [2009], *Tank Men – The Human Story of Tanks at War*, (Hodder and Stoughton, London).

Kennedy, Paul [1989], *The Rise and Fall of The Great Powers*, (Fontana, London).

Kenyon, David [2011], *Horseman in No Man's Land*, (Pen and Sword Military, Barnsley).

Kier, Elizabeth [1999], *Imagining War, French and British Doctrine Between The Wars*, (Princeton University, Princeton, New Jersey).

Klugmann, James "A View from the Left" in Clark, J Heinemann, Margot, Margolies, David and Snee, Carole (eds.) [1979], *Culture and Crisis in Britain in the Thirties*, (Lawrence and Wishart, London).

Knightley, Phillip [2000], *The First Casualty*, (Prion Books Ltd., London).

Lannon, Frances [2002], *The Spanish Civil War 1936–1939*, (Osprey Publishing, Oxford).

Larson, Robert H [1984], *The British Army and the Theory of Armored Warfare 1918–1940*, (University of Delaware Press, Newark).

Leavis, F R "The Scrutiny Movement and the Crisis" in Clark, J Heinemann, Margot, Margolies, David and Snee, Carole (eds.) [1979], *Culture and Crisis in Britain in the Thirties*, (Lawrence and Wishart, London).

Lewin, Ronald [1976], *Man of Armour, A Study of Lieutenant General Vyvyan Pope CBE DSO MC, and the development of armoured warfare*, (Leo Cooper, London).

Lewis, W Arthur [1970], *Economic Survey 1919–1939*, (George Allen and Unwin Ltd., London).

Lynch, Cecelia [1999], *Beyond Appeasement – Interpreting Interwar Peace Movements in World Politics*, (Cornell University Press, Ithaca and London).

Maiolo, Joseph [2010], *Cry Havoc, How the Arms Race drove the World to War*, (advance uncorrected proof, Basic Books, New York).

Marks, Sally [1976], *The Illusion of Peace – International Relations in Europe 1918–1933*, (The Macmillan Press, London and Basingstoke).

Marwick, Arthur [1989], *The Nature of History – Third Edition*, (Macmillan Education Ltd., Basingstoke).

Mearsheimer, John J [1998], *Liddell Hart and the Weight of History*, (Brassey's Defence Publishers, London).

Montgomery Hyde, Harford [1973], *Baldwin The Unexpected Prime Minister*, (Granada Publishing, London).

Mowat, Charles Loch [1962], *Britain between the Wars 1918–1940*, (Methuen & Co Ltd., London).

Neveh, Shimon [2004], *In Pursuit of Military Excellence The Evolution of Operational Theory*, (Frank Cass, London).

Norman, E R [1976], *Church And Society In England 1770–1970 A Historical Study*, (Clarendon Press, London).

Nowell, R "Questionnaires" in Gilbert, N (ed). [1993], *Researching Social Life*, (Sage, London).

Overy, Richard, with Wheatcroft, Andrew [1999], *The Road To War*, (Penguin, London).

Overy, Richard [2009], *The Morbid Age – Britain Between the Wars*, (Allen Lane – Penguin Books, London).

Peden, G C [1979], *British Rearmament and the Treasury*, (Scottish Academic Press, Edinburgh).

Peden, G C [2007], *Arms, Economics and British Strategy – From Dreadnoughts to Hydrogen Bombs*, (Cambridge University Press, Cambridge).

Phillips, Gervase "The Obsolescence of the Arme Blanche and Technological Determinism in British History" in [2002], *War in History* Volume 9 No. 1, (Arnold, London).

Phillips, Gervase "Scapegoat Arm: Twentieth-Century Cavalry in Anglophone Historiography" in Vandervort, Bruce (ed.) [2007], *The Journal of Military History* Volume 71, No. 1, (Society for Military History, Lexington, Virginia).

Phillips, Gervase "Who Shall Say That the Days of Cavalry Are Over? The Revival of the Mounted Arm in Europe, 1853–1914" in *War in History* URL:http://wih.sagepub.com/content/18/1/5 accessed 01.12.2011.

Piekalkiewicz, Janusz [1979], *The Cavalry Of World War II*, (Orbis Publishing Limited, London).

Postan, Michael M [1952], *British War Production*, (HMSO, London).

Pugh, Martin [1985], *The Tories and the People, 1880–1935*, (Basil Blackwell Ltd., Oxford).

Pugh, Martin [1993], *The Making of Modern British Politics 1867–1939*, (Blackwell Publishers, Oxford).

Reid, Betty "The Left Book Club in the Thirties" in *Culture and Crisis in Britain in the Thirties* in Clark, J Heinemann, Margot, Margolies, David and Snee, Carole (eds.) [1979], *Culture and Crisis in Britain in the Thirties*, (Lawrence and Wishart, London).

Reynolds, David [2004], *In Command of History – Churchill and Writing The Second World War*, (Allen Lane, London).

Richardson, Dick [1989], *The Evolution of British Disarmament Policy in the 1920s*, (Printer Publishers, London).

Richardson, Julie [1980], *Riding*, (Ward Lock Limited, London).

Robinson, Brian [1996], *Swords of the British Army*, (National Army Museum, London).

Roynon, Gavin (ed.) [2006], *Home Fires Burning*, (Sutton Publishing Limited, Stroud).

Ruskin, John [1886], "The Crown of Wild Olive" in lecture IV: *The Future of England*, section 151 (University of Birmingham Library).

Sampson, Peter, "Qualitative Research and Motivational Research" in Worcester, Robert M and Downham, John (eds.) [1978], *Consumer Market Research Handbook – Second Edition* (Van Nostrand Reinhold Company, Wokingham).

Seldon, Anthony [1988], Contempory *History Practice and Method*, (Basil Blackwell, Oxford).

Scott, Carolyn [1977], *Dick Sheppard*, (Hodder and Stoughton, London).

Self, Robert [2006], *Britain, America and the War Debt Controversy – The economic diplomacy of an unspecial relationship, 1917–1941*, (Routledge, London and New York).

Self, Robert [2006], *Neville Chamberlain A Biography*, (Ashgate, Aldershot).

Self, Robert "The Perception and Posture in Anglo-American Relations: The War Debt Controversy in the 'Official Mind' 1919–1940". in Ingham, Edward (ed.) [2007], *The International History Review* XXIX (No2), (Routledge, London).

Shay, Robert Paul Jnr. [1977], *British Rearmament in the Thirties*, (Princeton University Press, Princeton, New Jersey).

Smith, Malcolm, [1984], *British Air Strategy Between The Wars*, (Clarendon Press, Oxford).

Stanton, Doug [2009], *Horse Soldiers*, (Simon & Schuster, London).

Steiner, Zara [2007], *The Lights That Failed, European International History 1919–1933*, (Oxford University Press, Oxford).

Steiner, Zara [2011], *The Triumph of the Dark, European International History 1933–1939*, (Oxford University Press, Oxford).

Stevenson, David [2004], *Cataclysm, The First World War as Political Tragedy*, (Basic Books, Cambridge, MA.).

Stevenson, John, Cook, Chris [1979], *The Slump – Society and Politics During the Depression*, (Quartet Books Limited, London).

Thorpe, Andrew [2001], *A History of The Labour Party – Second Edition*, (Palgrave, Basingstoke).

Traynor, John [1991], *Europe 1890–1990*, (Macmillan Education Limited, Basingstoke).

Tylden, Major G [1980], Horses and Saddlery, (J A Allen & Company, London).

Ure, John [1999], *The Cossacks*, (Constable and Company Limited, London).

Wasserstein, Bernard [2007], *Barbarism and Civilization: A History of Europe in our Time*, (Oxford University Press, Oxford).

Wavell, General Sir Archibald [1941], *Allenby – A Study In Greatness*, (George G Harrap & Co. Ltd. London).

Way, Olwen [1994], *The Poetry of Horses*, (J A Allen & Company Limited, London).

Winch, Donald [1972], *Economics and Policy – A Historical Survey*, (Collins/Fontana, London).

Winter, J M [1986], *The Great War And The British People*, (Macmillan, London).

Winton, Harold R [1988], *To Change An Army – General Sir John Burnett-Stuart and British Armoured Doctrine 1927–1938*, (Brassey's Defence Publishers, London).

Winton, Harold R and Mets, David R (eds.) [2003], *The Challenge of Change – Military Institutions and New Realities, 1918–1941*, (University of Nebraska Press, Lincoln and London).

Theses

Badsey, Stephen, [1984] "Fire and the Sword: The British Cavalry and the Arme Blanche Controversy 1871–1921", (Cambridge University).

Barndollar, Gilman Clough, [2010] "British Use of Armoured cars 1919–1939", (Cambridge University).

Evans, Gary, [2011] "The British Cavalry 1920–1940", (University of Kent Canterbury).

Hacker, Barton C, [1968] "The Military Machine. An Analysis of the Controversy over the Mechanization of the British Army 1919–1939", (University of Chicago).

Kenyon, David, [2007] "British Cavalry on The Western Front 1916–1918", (Cranfield University Defence College of Management and Technology Department of Defence Management and Security Analysis).

Kyba, John Patric, [1967] "British Attitudes Toward Disarmament and Rearmament 1932–1935", (University of London – Faculty of Economics).

Index

INDEX OF PEOPLE

INDEX OF PLACES

Abbassia ix, 37-38, 90, 155-156, 160, 162, 210-211, 223

Abyssinia 107, 113, 140, 142, 144

Africa iv, xxiv, 37, 40, 103, 125, 136, 225, 228, 265, 271, 280-281, 284, 300-301, 304, 317

Ahmednagar 191, 196

Aldershot xx, 37, 66, 94-97, 100, 113, 133, 146, 148, 160, 162, 166-167, 184, 205, 222, 254, 256, 272-277, 280-281, 285, 305-308, 313

Alexandria 37, 223

Australia 117, 125, 271

Austria 51, 104, 262, 288

Ballinasloe 256, 272

Beersheba 61, 156

Belgium 164, 175, 178, 228, 288, 299

Berlin x, 156-157, 159, 163, 241, 262

Bermuda 103, 266

Birmingham xvii, 105, 111, 298, 301, 313

Bombay 37, 263-265

Bovington ix-xii, xvii, 68-69, 75, 91, 93, 96, 99-100, 128, 136, 156, 165-166, 169, 173-174, 194-195, 202, 210, 223, 227, 233, 238, 299-300, 302, 304

Brighton xvii, 256, 305-306, 308

Brookwood 227, 300

Cairo x, 37, 131, 153, 156-157, 159, 161, 163, 199, 223, 241, 268, 299

Canada 125, 271, 301

Caterham 255, 299

Ceylon 103, 266

China 44, 106, 109, 266-267

Colchester 37, 166, 197, 256, 272-273, 275-278, 301-302

Constantinople 37, 261, 272-273

Cyprus 103, 211, 267, 279

Delhi 37, 42, 165, 264-265

Dublin 256-257, 273

Dunkirk x, 132, 165, 170, 216, 229, 298, 300-301, 311

Edinburgh xvii, 37, 272-277, 284, 304, 307-308, 312

Egypt vii, x, 37, 43-44, 87-88, 90-92, 97, 103, 117-118, 129-130, 140, 145, 153, 156, 159-162, 175, 187-188, 206, 211, 219, 223, 228, 232, 246-247, 261, 267-268, 272-277, 280, 283, 299-300, 303

Essex v, xvii, 255, 298-299

Feltham 124, 149, 256

France xxxii, 51, 62, 65, 93, 112, 175, 177-178, 212, 214, 228, 230, 241, 243, 247-248, 262, 277, 279-282, 285, 288, 299-303

Fulham 141, 305

Germany 51, 53, 59, 104, 107, 112-113, 138, 146, 148, 177-178, 208, 243, 253, 300, 302-303, 317

Greece 109, 196

Helmieh ix, 37-38, 153, 158

Hertfordshire xi, 169

Holland 178, 302

Hong Kong 103, 266

Hounslow x, 37, 153-154, 160, 255-256, 272-278

India xi-xii, 37, 39-40, 42-45, 63, 79, 83, 87-88, 97, 103, 107, 109, 114, 117-118, 123-124, 129-130, 132, 150, 153, 165, 167, 171, 186-191, 195-201, 206, 214-215, 220, 222, 224, 230, 232, 241, 246, 251, 253, 259, 262, 272-273, 280-281, 299-301, 303, 317

Iraq 43, 211, 271

Ireland 40-41, 43-45, 51, 62, 103, 253, 256-257, 259, 272-273, 290

Italy 107, 113, 136, 138, 144-145, 220, 228-229, 243, 288, 300-303, 317

Japan 106-107, 113, 138, 243

INDEX OF MILITARY FORMATIONS & UNITS

Wolverhampton Military Studies

www.helion.co.uk/wolverhamptonmilitarystudies

Submissions

The publishers would be pleased to receive submissions for this series. Please contact us via email (info@helion.co.uk), or in writing to Helion & Company Limited, 26 Willow Road, Solihull, West Midlands, B91 1UE.

Titles

No.1 *Stemming the Tide. Officers and Leadership in the British Expeditionary Force 1914* Edited by Spencer Jones (ISBN 978-1-909384-45-3)

No.2 *'Theirs Not To Reason Why'. Horsing the British Army 1875–1925* Graham Winton (ISBN 978-1-909384-48-4)

No.3 *A Military Transformed? Adaptation and Innovation in the British Military, 1792–1945* Edited by Michael LoCicero, Ross Mahoney and Stuart Mitchell (ISBN 978-1-909384-46-0)